Augustan Worlds

Augustan Worlds

EDITED BY J. C. HILSON, M. M. B. JONES AND J. R. WATSON

LEICESTER UNIVERSITY PRESS 1978

First published in 1978 by Leicester University Press
Published in North America by Harper and Row
Publishers, Inc.,
Barnes & Noble Import Division

Designed by Douglas Martin
Set in Intertype Baskerville
Printed in Great Britain by
Western Printing Services Ltd, Bristol
Bound by Redwood Burn Ltd, London and Esher

British Library Cataloguing in Publication Data

Augustan Worlds
1. English literature – History and
criticism – addresses, essays, lectures
I. Humphreys, Arthur Raleigh II. Hilson, J C
III. Jones, M M B IV. Watson, J R
820' .9 PR403

ISBN 0–7185–1159–X

Contents

Editors' Preface

In 1976, Arthur Humphreys retired from the Chair of English at the University of Leicester which he had held since 1947. During the years of his tenure he was probably best known among scholars for his editions of Shakespeare's Histories, and for his survey of eighteenth-century England, *The Augustan World*. The subtitle of the latter is 'Life and Letters in Eighteenth-Century England', and it is characteristic of the author that he should have related the literature of the period to the life which surrounded it; for him the appreciation of good literature has always involved an understanding of the values which it included, and an awareness of the relationships or aspirations which were found in its period and which gave the period its flavour. He has never ignored the formal beauties of a literary work, but he delighted in relating it to its age, and in the complex interaction of forces within that age. On page 3 of *The Augustan World* he wrote:

> To say that the Augustan age progressed in social sympathy, and that this progress encouraged the human interests of literature, is not to deny its limitations. Its social conscience was superficial; it put up with much injustice (partly from ignorance of how to remedy it), and it relieved only the barest fringe of misery. The crowds who sotted on gin (as Hogarth drew and Fielding described them) were not seeking merely the zest of a spree. The debtors who decayed in prison, the mobs who rioted when harvests failed, the wretches press-ganged to a sea-life, which Johnson called a degree worse than gaol – these and their like could not congratulate themselves on their time. Poets, journalists and novelists drew grim pictures of suffering: Augustan excellences were erected on much misery and despair. Yet with all its evils the age strove to become less brutal, and gave to many the sense of strong humanity bearing good fruit in art, letters, philosophy and social life.

A balanced understanding of this complex period was one of Arthur Humphreys's achievements in *The Augustan World*; and when we were looking for a topic on which this *Festschrift* could focus, it seemed natural to turn to the eighteenth century, and to invite contributions which would supplement the continuing critical debate on the meanings of terms such as

'Augustan' and 'Augustanism'. The title, *Augustan Worlds,* in addition to echoing Arthur Humphreys's own title, has a two-fold reference, to the many 'worlds' which exist in the individuality of each author and the uniqueness of artistic creation, and to the 'Augustan' cultural matrix to which they belong.

There are other appropriate features of this volume. It is a happy accident that it begins with William Myers's essay on 'Dryden's Shakespeare', which may serve as a reminder of Arthur Humphreys's love of Shakespeare and his scholarly editing. Another fortunate characteristic is the notable and generous part played in this tribute by distinguished American scholars, especially in view of Arthur Humphreys's great affection for America, which dates from his time at Harvard and which was largely responsible for the creation of a Department of American Studies in Leicester. Finally, it is a collection which has both local and world-wide sources. Several of the essays are written by members of the English department at Leicester, which was shaped by Arthur Humphreys in its formative years; others are from former colleagues, such as T. W. Craik and Colin Horne; others represent the international world of literary scholarship on both sides of the Atlantic.

We wish to thank all the contributors for their generosity and patience, and the Secretary of the Leicester University Press and his staff for their continual encouragement and help. In accordance with the Press practice, in the notes to papers, places of publication are given only for books published outside the United Kingdom.

J. C. Hilson
M. M. B. Jones
J. R. Watson

Arthur Humphreys: an Appreciation

RICHARD HOGGART

The outstanding quality of the Leicester English department, and I ascribe it almost wholly to Arthur Humphreys's influence, is its general evenness of temper. Of course, there are snide glances between colleagues from time to time; but in general the department conducts itself with a very decent respect for persons. The fact that Arthur was there in the centre and for so long, wholly without rancour or malice, held the department remarkably steady. I never knew of his making secret deals or using sly devices. He did not play the ends against the middle or use selective flattery. He kept on being fair; so that, whatever undercurrents and tensions there might be in the department's internal relationships, he was not caught up in them or *parti pris*; and by his example and his presence he helped to keep them in manageable limits.

That was one main quality: loyalty to his department and to his role as the head of it. It was part of a larger loyalty: that to the demands of his profession as an academic. He is, I don't have to underline and the essays which follow bear out well, a distinguished critic and editor; and it is perhaps worth pausing here to recall, as we honour his fine work in eighteenth-century studies, from the early book on Shenstone to *The Augustan World* and beyond, that Arthur Humphreys is respected as a world authority on Shakespeare, and particularly on the Histories, which in their celebration of courage, loyalty and integrity embody values which are very much Arthur's own. But for my purposes, the inwardness of his professional life is more exactly caught in recalling all he did through almost 30 years to create a large and distinguished department, in weighing all this must have meant cumulatively in thinking and planning, in meetings, examining, teaching. There are few Heads of Department (and their hesitation is understandable and justifiable) who give themselves roughly as much week-by-week teaching as their junior colleagues. Few Heads of Department have given such sustained, patient, deliberately unspectacular attention to the detail of getting things right year by year. He says himself, and I am sure it is the simple truth: 'My working programme, for long spells, was a minimum of a 70-hour week, not counting coffee- or meal-breaks or other respites, and all of it called for alert attention.'

It seems ironic now that Arthur Humphreys's own appointment in 1947 – a bold choice of a young and relatively inexperienced man by a small university college – was at first strongly resisted by the students. They favoured the candidature of the existing non-professorial Head of Department, whose devotion to the work and concern for them they greatly respected. The affair disturbed Arthur deeply, but, sooner than most people thought possible, he had won from the students an equal respect and had become friends with his former rival.

I was once given a lift by a man who proved to have been a student of Arthur's, years before I went to Leicester. He had been a refugee from Hitler. He told me that Arthur Humphreys's whole style of running a department had made him feel able to trust people again; and that, as soon as he had made a reasonable amount of money, he had established a prize in the department. If Arthur had so willed, if he had *prima donna*'d, or simply given himself a lighter load, or refused to give his best at committees (so that he was asked to serve on fewer of them) then we might well have had several *Augustan Worlds*. There is always a price to be paid. That there are not several such books does not lower Arthur Humphreys's stature; it reduces our visible legacy, that is all; the rest – the less visible legacy – is all around us, in the department's strength, in staff and students all over Britain and the world who have been affected for good by the care he gave them and the example he set them.

The circles widen. More than one Leicester Vice-Chancellor has had very good cause to be grateful for Arthur Humphreys's solid loyalty to the tenacious British university idea, to the idea that we should run ourselves, served by good administrative officers, rather than being managed by a superior 'Administration'. Sometimes the mind quails at the thought of what all that means in slog for those who are willing to face the implications, all those unhistrionic orderings and efforts at just judgment whilst some of their colleagues think only of their own departments or of their own histrionically 'scholarly' personae. In Arthur Humphreys's case one could extend the record of responsibility assumed to include the city of Leicester itself. He served for many years on the Council of the Literary and Philosophical Society, and the Board of the Leicester Theatre Trust; and in many other ways the city's intellectual and cultural life was enriched because a professor up the hill there was willing to sit down and help to sort out problems and map futures.

Those are three kinds of loyalty: to the idea of a department, of a university and of civic duty. A fourth is the most important of all, because all-embracing: to the demands of our common humanity, as individuals. It is here that one remembers Arthur and Jean's enormous and unexpectedly wide circle of friends; not just academics or other professionals but all sorts of people met in various situations and kept as friends. That is the difference. We have all met people in unusual circumstances but have not all had the patience or charity to sustain links with them. So this list includes very old people, and very unusual people; and it runs back for decades. One example will have to do for many. Not long ago Arthur was run over in crossing the road from home to the University. So much is incontrovertibly true; the rest may not be accurate in every detail but is, in its general spirit and essence, true. In hospital, he was of course cross-questioned by the police. He insisted from the start that he did not wish to lay charges, that it was really his fault for being insufficiently attentive. So the policeman became a friend too, and there was great mutual pleasure when his promotion came through some time later.

A passage in Arthur's own lecture on the English department from 1947 to the present sums up the prescription he wrote for himself. He speaks of 'those things one ought to do – teach with zest [a favourite word], write productively, know and entertain colleagues and students, administer soundly, take part in the outside world, and yet keep up life with family and friends and personal interests'. It is dauntingly comprehensive, but he has pretty well fulfilled the lot.

One is always tempted, seeing decent unpushy men, to think that, though undeniably nice, they may be perhaps a bit lacking in bite or even in risk-taking. I have to be personal here. Back in 1957 I applied for a lecturer's post in the Leicester department. I didn't get it, and don't know if I was even near to getting it. I was a tutor in extra-mural work at Hull and not greatly used to internal teaching, let alone examining. The post went to George Fraser and that was a very good choice indeed. I think Arthur felt that the department could do with a practising man of letters, a writer and poet of very catholic tastes: and he stood out for such a person against the predictable queries of some of his Senatorial colleagues who felt that scholarship should be all. About a year later the department advertised yet another vacancy, this time for a senior lecturer. It seemed on the face of things silly for me to put in; but after consulting Philip Collins I applied. Arthur was due to go to the United States one term after his new (and only) senior lecturer would have arrived, so there were even stronger reasons than usual against appointing someone new to the complications of departmental life. My experience suggests that most Heads of Department would not have appointed such an unknown quantity. Arthur walked round the park – this was an additional nice touch – with George Fraser, speculating on whether it was fair to the department to take such a risk; and then decided he was justified in doing so. I have told the story partly because it illustrates his concern for building a varied department, whatever the more rigid among his peers might say, and also because it shows that there is a very determined gambler in Arthur Humphreys. In fact, there is, one soon discovers in emergencies or when difficult and unpalatable decisions have to be taken, quite remarkable firmness there. You realise then that that firm and strongly-boned chin, which seems in moments of crisis to lift and jut upwards, is an accurate indicator of character. There is great force underneath; and one senses that considerable restraint is often being exercised, way past the point at which most people would have exploded in the face of tiresome behaviour in their colleagues and staff. Still, a line has been drawn and should not be crossed. I don't ever remember Arthur evading a difficult, even a painful, decision. But he was never to my knowledge punitive or lacking in charity; so that, when he did utter a judgment, it came with all the more force for the sense of disinterested objectivity behind it; it had enormous moral authority. He never wrung his hands or vacillated and, if one was tempted to mistake him for someone who was 'too nice to be firm', you had only to hear him say with total finality, apropos an apparent high-flyer who had put in for a post: 'Yes, he was an attractive candidate in several ways. But in the end – well – we didn't think he really measured up to the job'.

Set against that, or complementary to it, is his capacity to 'bring out the best in people'. That apparently silly and soft old phrase took on a fresh meaning when you worked with Arthur. What it meant then, I think, was that he did see the best that was in you; and he did trust you to bring it out for your common ends. It wasn't at all that he was taken in. But he had drawn a very large cheque on the bank of your potentialities, and he trusted you to rise above your weaknesses so as to honour it. That's why, I see now, he was and is loved by so many and such different people, people who are not all of them very nice, at first glance, and who certainly do not all love one another. But we all behaved better – in his company – towards each other and to some extent lived up to his gamble on us; and so we *were* indeed that bit better. It wasn't that he would have said of or to Iago that to understand all is to forgive all; but he would have seen what was biting at Iago, have been anxious to help him out of it, and have convinced him that he had at least one dispassionate well-wisher.

Overall, the chief impression one takes away is of a shining readiness before life. One remembers his favourite words and expressions such as 'splendid', 'enthusiastic', 'generous', 'alert', spoken with a pleased lift to the voice; or 'quite captivating', said with a slight laugh, or 'keen anticipation', about something he and Jean are looking forward to, spoken with a boyish stress on the adjective. Most of his favourite words are warm and positive; dry, oblique, allusive tones are almost wholly alien to him. It is all of a piece: his quick, firm stride across the park to the University; or the sudden erupting laugh when something has touched his funny bone; or the giggle which makes him look as he must have looked back in Liverpool when he was about eighteen. Then he would turn to his work again; he didn't try to cap someone else's joke.

To adapt a line by an author I particularly admire – Auden – about an author he particularly admires – Melville:

Goodness is unspectacular and always human.

Arthur has not been one who consciously sought the spectacular or the stylish; but because of his inner character and qualities a remarkable personal style has emerged over the years. He is, even at the moment of retirement, a very fine figure of a man whose straightness shines out of him, the bearer of immense innate dignity. Leicester has been very lucky indeed to have such a pair as him and Jean.

1 Dryden's Shakespeare

WILLIAM MYERS

F. R. Leavis, in *The Living Principle*, reprints the devastating attack on the verse of *All for Love* which he first published in *Scrutiny* in 1936. Its re-publication transforms the task of defending Dryden's work on Shakespeare. Leavis's book is so of a piece that to dissent from any one of its judgments is to raise fundamental issues of principle, which need at least to be stated if only briefly and tentatively. At the heart of his argument is the conviction that 'good thinking' and 'an intimate acquaintance with a subtle language in its fullest use' are inseparable;[1] that 'major creative writers are concerned with a necessary kind of thought',[2] and that 'tentativeness, incompleteness and compromise' are marks of such thought.

> Born into Dryden's age [Leavis argues], when 'logic' and 'clarity' had triumphed, Shakespeare couldn't have been Shakespeare . . . you can't, without basic reservations, subscribe to the assumptions implicit in 'clear' and 'logical' criteria without cutting yourself off from most important capacities and potentialities of thought.[3]

Clearly Dryden must have been so cut off, since he undoubtedly came to attach a special value to 'logic' and 'clarity' especially in the 1670s. In addition, as L. C. Knights has argued, Dryden's deficiencies as a critic of Shakespeare deserve noting. Dryden complains of Shakespeare's 'superfluity and wast of wit',[4] his solecisms,[5] the 'meanly written' *Winter's Tale*, *Love's Labour's Lost* and *Measure for Measure*,[6] the 'bombast speeches' in *Macbeth*[7] and the tameness of Mercutio.[8] Most of these misjudgments are in fact intended to illustrate the point that faults can be condemned and genius recognized simultaneously, but he persists in condemning Shakespeare's style as 'pompous . . . and obscured by figures'[9] and pairs him too undiscriminatingly with Fletcher. Perhaps his oddest criticism is that Shakespeare's sense of 'the Justness of the Occasion' is weak and unequal to the passions his thoughts and words evoke.[10] Thus even without an analysis of Dryden's 'Shakespearean' verse, there is a strong *prima facie* case against him.

Leavis's main complaint against Dryden's dramatic verse is that it exhibits 'eloquence' not 'life',[11] it is not 'the product of a realizing emotion working from within a deeply and minutely felt theme'.[12] The metaphors rely on 'simple, illustrative, point by point correspondence . . .; there is never any complexity, confusion or ambiguity'.[13] *The Tempest* and *Troilus and Cressida* provide as much support for this point of view as *All for Love*. In *The Tempest* for example Dryden damages the scene in which Ariel lures Ferdinand to Miranda with only the most minor alterations to the original. In the interest – presumably – of decorum, Naples becomes a Dukedom, and 'sitting on a bank weeping the Duke/My Father's wrath'[14] is sadly unresonant. Again for

> This Musick crept by me upon the waters,
> Allaying both their fury, and my passion
> With its sweet ayre[15]

Dryden has

> This musick hover'd o're me
> On the waters, allaying both their fury and my passion
> With charming Airs
> (II. ii. 14–16)

The flight from allegedly obscure figures which Leavis objects to is clearly illustrated by the rejection of 'crept by me' for the rhythmically slacker 'hover'd o're me'. A preference for obvious rhythms also explains the change from 'sweet' to 'charming'. This verbal insensitivity has structural consequences. Dryden moves the opening lines of Shakespeare's fifth act to the middle of Act III, scene i. Again he slackens the rhythm: 'My charmes cracke not: my Spirits obey' becomes 'My spirits are obedient to my charms' (l. 145). But more serious is what happens to Ariel's 'Mine would, Sir, were I humane' (l. 171) which depends for its considerable effect on the approaching end of his relationship with Prospero and the recent exposure of Prospero's full humanity – in his meditation on the ending of all revels, in his efforts to still his beating mind, and in his brutality to Trinculo, Stephano and Caliban. Dryden thus reveals ironically a weaker sense of 'occasion' than Shakespeare. This, and the cutting of, for example, the 'Ye Elves of hils' soliloquy, suggest a disturbing capacity to ignore the explosive fusions of meaning and passion in Shakespeare's verse. The case of *Troilus and Cressida* is similar. False criteria of correctness, clarity and decorum soften the verse. Real improvements may be effected in terms of continuity and order, but the tonal and ethical disjointedness of the original is lost. Dryden's Agamemnon is more kingly, his Nestor less senile, his Achilles less corrupt, his Ulysses less unscrupulous; Troilus's heart is no longer an open ulcer; and notoriously Cressida is faithful. There is admittedly the fine scene between Troilus and Hector but it is insufficient to justify the notions of correctness which apparently dictate Dryden's modification of the play's structure and tone. Both Dryden and neoclassicism clearly have a lot to answer for.

One can begin Dryden's defence by pointing to the lively and organic sense of form which makes his reconstruction of the first Act of *The Tempest* so intelligently professional. In the first scene he presents Stephano and Trinculo as master and bosun (presumably because Shakespeare's Antonio called the latter drunkards). This makes for a more manageable distribution of the parties throughout the island in later scenes. Next he skilfully edits Prospero's long explanatory speech in the second scene with only a slight loss of grandeur. He then organizes the remainder of the Act into a model *Protasis*, giving 'light onely to the Characters of the persons, and [proceeding] very little into any part of the action'.[16] All the characters are fluently introduced, except Caliban's sister Sycorax, and Hippolito, the man who has never seen a woman. He is being held neatly in reserve – like Sir Fopling Flutter – for 'the *Epitasis*, or working up of the Plot'. And in addition to this mechanical good order, the first Act reveals an interesting tonal development. From horror and remorse, it moves through Prospero's progressively less solemn dialogues with Miranda, Ariel and Caliban, to a neatly erotic exchange between Miranda and Dorinda. However disconcerting this last development, it is certainly adroit. Dryden leads his audience through scenes of cleverly varied fantasy only to confront them abruptly with a snatch of totally unexpected fashionable dialogue. It is a beautifully managed first Act.

The final note it strikes, of course, is what most critics find unpleasant, and they are unlikely to be mollified by the California editor's comparison of the double-entendres in the play to modern 'nightclub entertainment'.[17] They also imply that Dryden's purposes are largely formal, 'to separate ... disparate elements and to simplify what had been ambiguous ... along the lines of class and decorum.'[18] The structurally significant point at which Dryden first sounds the note of contemporary eroticism, however, suggests another possibility, that Dryden has thematic as well as formal purposes in his re-shaping of Shakespeare's text. What these may be is perhaps implicit in Robert Hume's suggestion that Dryden's belief in 'the uniformity of human nature'[19] forces him into a neoclassical stance. A 'natural man' like Hippolito must inevitably develop into a recognizable type; he and all the other characters in the play will necessarily speak and act, in the end, like their Restoration counterparts. If human beings are as predictable as this, however, their moral freedom becomes questionable, and if they are not free, not responsible, that is, for what they become, the systematic generalizations about the laws of nature, society and literature which the Restoration world purported to believe in, and which justify Hippolito's characterization in the first place, are rendered meaningless. It is explicitly with such possibilities in mind that Dryden organizes a complete breakdown of order in the fourth Act. On Prospero's island – a comic paradigm of Charles II's – the claims of kings and playwrights to the sanction of Natural law are gaily, yet also seriously, put at risk, in a confusion of hudibrastic civil war, masculine sexual pride, feminine sexual jealousy and Prospero's lawful but tyrannical power. The situation is resolved by what the California editors call 'the hocus pocus of weapon salves and off-color buffoonery',[20] This may well reflect, not a failure on Dryden's part to appreciate Shakespeare's 'expansive symbolic meanings', but a recognition that, in the Restoration atmosphere of the revised text, a reliance on them would be facile. 'Shakespeare's Magick' is not to be deployed in a complacent reassertion of official notions of decorum and order in literature or life. Dryden's increasingly radical 'tampering' with the original may thus indicate a proper sense on his part of the distance between his world and Shakespeare's. His *Tempest* may be sceptical but it is honest. The purity of Miranda's delight in her brave new world full of royal rogues and ruffians has a redemptive force in Shakespeare. Dryden, however, gives her most famous lines to the saucy Dorinda and libidinous Hippolito, and the relish with which they greet their brave new world decisively reverses Shakespeare's effect. The truly cynical conclusion, however, would surely have been to have given his 1667 audience the delicate hope which Shakespeare's Miranda offers.

By the standards Rymer was soon to impose on dramatists, Dryden's version of *The Tempest* was flagrantly incorrect. Rymer, Hume notes, regarded absolute fidelity to factual probability as supremely important. In the 1660s, Dryden approached the rules more light-heartedly, but he did not ignore them. On the contrary he expected his audience to relish the calculated incorrectness of *The Tempest*, and in this he was being truly Shakespearean. As Earl Miner has recently pointed out, Shakespeare was familiar with the conventions. Like Rymer, he knew a soldier must not 'deliver more or less than the truth' but he understood, as Rymer confronted by Iago did not, 'that decorum could be used, varied and even countered'.[21] This is exactly how Dryden approaches *The Tempest*. Just as he measures the distance between his world and Shakespeare's, so he consciously keeps his distance from a tame conformity to convention, probability and decorum. In no sense then is he presuming to 'correct' Shakespeare. On the contrary he is *translating* his text, bringing it, that is, into an intelligent witty and original relationship with the professed values and accepted conventions of his own time. He may, thereby, have turned *The Tempest* into a minor work but he has emphatically not turned it into a corrupt one.

It has often been assumed that when, in the late 1670s, Dryden became more conservative about the rules, he became in consequence more out of tune with Shakespeare. How far this change was due to Rymer's influence and its effect on *All for Love* have also been disputed. L. A. Beaurline believes that only the play's preface reflects a conservatively neoclassical outlook, and that the play itself 'makes little' of the unlawfulness of Antony and Cleopatra's passion. 'Our sympathy and pity', he writes, '... outweigh any sense of poetic justice.'[22] The preface, however, refers to the moral of the original story only to explain why it has attracted the attention of 'the greatest Wits of our Nation, after *Shakespeare*.'[23] Dryden himself, however, has an additional interest in the forbidden nature of the play's central relationship. It has prevented him, he says, from working 'up the pity to a greater heighth'. This is significant because Dryden was coming to distrust tragedy based, in the French manner, on pity alone. Admittedly in the 'Heads of an Answer' to Rymer he explores the possibility of defending English drama on the grounds that the function of tragedy is to encourage virtue and that the sight of 'goodness depressed' would achieve this end by arousing feelings of indignation in an audience. Thus pity and terror may not after all be 'the Prime, or at least the Only Ends of Tragedy'.[24] Significantly, however, in the 'Grounds of Criticism of Tragedy', he re-affirms the central importance of terror, which, he argues, Shakespeare evokes with special success. In thus resisting plays that 'run all on the *Tendre*',[25] he is being, of course, conservative and Aristotelian. Significantly, he feels this brings him closer to Shakespeare. The same is true of his rejection of that other experimental form the heroic play, again an example of middle-aged literary conservatism. When, in the Prologue to *Aureng-Zebe,* he evokes 'Shakespeare's sacred name' and the principles of decorum and verisimilitude in his famous repudiation of rhyme, Shakespeare, if anything, confirms rather than qualifies Dryden's belief in neoclassical order. The result is a notable strengthening of the neoclassical position. Rymer's devotion to probability, Hume notes, was based on a broad identification of 'Homer, nature, reason, and the rules'.[26] Dryden added Shakespeare – the English Homer, 'that nature' which others paint and draw – to this confining equation, and thereby brilliantly enlarged it. It is in the context of Dryden's growing sense that Shakespeare was normative for the classical dramatist that *All for Love* needs to be examined.

I have argued elsewhere that the principles of poetic justice are applied enigmatically in *All for Love*. They may require Antony's death, but hardly the triumph of a man fit only 'to buy, not conquer Kingdoms' (III. 125).[27] Caesar is a brutally neutral figure in the play, a Roman Alexas, and it is worth recalling that in all Dryden's later writings he is presented as a usurper.[28] But Leavis's attack on the play deserves an answer based on less schematic, more verbally detailed ambiguities and confusions than that.

His position is evidently consistent with L. C. Knights's contention that 'the Shakespearean idiom' was 'out of the reach of criticism' in Dryden's lifetime, that Dryden was incapable of what Knights argues is 'the only profitable approach to Shakespeare... a consideration of his plays as dramatic poems, of his use of language to obtain a total complex emotional response.'[29] Against this one can set the fact that (like Knights) Dryden came to believe that plays were more profitably studied in the closet than on the stage. His later neoclassical vigour led him also to the view that the mechanical beauties of a play's design should be thoroughly integrated with what he called its Moral, its Thoughts and Words, into a complex and consistent whole. But the central task remains to be done. What will 'an exact and sensitive study' of the verse of *All for Love*, 'of the rhythm and imagery of the controlled association of the words and their emotional force', yield to a defender of Dryden's achievement in the theatre?

An immediate and just response to the verse of *All for Love* is that these are shallow linguistic waters indeed. In the fifth Act, for instance, Antony meditates on the problem of justice and fate. 'Innocence and Death!' he exclaims,

> This shows not well above. Then what am I,
> The Murderer of this Truth, this Innocence!
> Thoughts cannot form themselves in words so horrid
> As can express my guilt!
> (ll. 240–4)

Such formulaic abstraction might be thought to illustrate nothing but the poetic consequences of believing in the uniformity of human nature. Words and thoughts like these could (symptomatically) occur to virtually any character, on any 'occasion', in any play, of the period. Such easily available diction clearly calls in question the seriousness of the play's smoothly organized debates (in which Antony twice changes his mind in the first three Acts), the schematic frustration of Roman and Egyptian plotting in the fourth, and the final eloquent catastrophe in which 'Love' and 'Friendship', 'Egyptian' and 'Roman' are reconciled in 'Death', but driven from the 'World' in the fifth. This effect of shallowness, however, is, I believe, intended and deceptive. The verse of *All for Love* can sustain a surprisingly complex analysis.

A key to the play's complexity is the apparently inert and facile word 'Death'. At the end of the first Act Antony likens Ventidius and himself to 'Time and Death marching before our Troops' and beginning 'the noble Harvest' of the battlefield (ll. 450–3). In the second Act Cleopatra uses the word several times in the sense of sexual climax. She says that she deserves to die with Antony, adding perversely

> Go; leave me, Soldier;
> (For you're no more a Lover:) leave me dying:
> Push me all pale and panting from your bosome
> (ll. 410–12).

Finally, kissing him, she promises to 'die apace' and end his trouble (ll. 422–3). As at the end of the first Act, Antony takes up this much-worked metaphor in his closing speech. He longs, he says, for night

> That both the sweets of mutual love may try,
> And once Triumph o're *Caesar* e're we dye
> (ll. 460–1)

The very obviousness of the word, however, makes it theatrically useful: the audience can at once see the irony of the parallel Act endings. Both Ventidius and Cleopatra, Roman Honour and Egyptian Love, are going to involve Antony in 'Death' and so may not be as exactly polarized as might have been thought. 'Death', itself is notably ambiguous, being at once the punishment and the vindication of Love, the just destiny of Hero, Queen, and Friend alike. It is also frighteningly irrational to Egyptian eunuch and Roman politician, and even Cleopatra is terrified when she finds the world dancing and swimming before her 'in the maze of death' (III. 471). But by the end of the fifth Act she escapes from order and reason and freely enters the Abyss. Ventidius has said of those who die well that their 'Deaths will speak themselves, And need no living witness' (V. 304–5). Cleopatra now gives those words a sense Ventidius had not intended, leaving Caesar, who insisted that he had 'more wayes than one to dye' (II. 122), and Alexas, who searched desperately for something to say to save himself from death, to make what they can of Reason and Life. And yet the play does not in any simple way sanction the Deaths of its principal characters. Death remains Life's enemy: the 'two long Lovers, Soul and Body dread Their final separation' (V. 136–7); Antony recognizes that the gratuitous death of the Innocent 'Will Make us think that Chance rules all above'; and Cleopatra explicitly deceives herself and us, in applying the Aspick to her arm, with an image that softens the reality of Death by making it look like Sleep. Serapion's last speech (V. 508–19) is not therefore as triumphant as it appears. The lovers only *seem* to be 'giving Laws to half Mankind'; on Cleopatra's face there is only 'Th'impression of a smile'; and though the lovers 'Sleep Secure from humane Chance', we already know from Cleopatra's own lips that the identification of Sleep and Death is a deceit. In effect the simple illustrative point-by-point correspondence which characterizes the style and structure of *All for Love* has revealed some very real complexities, confusions and ambiguities at the heart of order itself.

All for Love was 'Written in Shakespeare's Stile'. It is in fact a dramatic poem in Knights's sense exactly. In Shakespeare, of course, the abundance of images and the play between them is infinitely more complex, but Dryden's approach is nevertheless exactly what he said it was, an imitation of Shakespeare's methods in the formally obvious, but elaborate and consciously ironic manner of the baroque. The very conventionality of Restoration vocabulary and psychology relieved Dryden of the need to give his attention to the specious irrelevancies of a biographical approach to his characters. Questions about Lady Macbeth's children did not interest him either. *All for Love* shows clearly his realization that plays, and Shakespeare's plays especially, are poetic structures of word, image, event and idea, and in this respect he has anticipated a crucially important development in the criticism of Knights's generation. 'Thoughts and words', Hume notes, '. . . to these [he returns] again and again, for they are the center of a literary outlook which is more rhetorical than generic.'[30] It is true that 'Thought' for Dryden and his age was by definition logical, systematic and so unShakespearean. There is thus no question but that his work is less than Shakespeare's. Yet he did have the ability to use Shakespeare and his 'Stile' as a testing ground for some characteristic Restoration assumptions about language, art and life. The results, in *All for Love*, work steadily and significantly against the systematic and the logical. Dryden realized, also, that his thoroughly neoclassical definition of wit as a propriety of Thoughts and Words, could take us to the very heart of Shakespeare, that *Antony and Cleopatra* is a notably thoughtful play. This is not a trivial achievement in a period when 'the Shakespearian idiom was' – according to Knights – 'out of the reach of criticism'.

Dryden's last Shakespearean play, *Troilus and Cressida*, has proved, with its Preface, the most damaging to his reputation. Saintsbury simply wished it undone. The Preface has been read as a cowardly submission to Rymer, the play as a crass consequence of such a submission. Once again the assumption is that Shakespeare and neoclassicism created a conflict in Dryden's mind. In fact the Preface celebrates Shakespeare's exemplary correctness, notably in his characters' 'Manners'. Equally overlooked has been the discrepancy between the principles outlined in the Preface and the play itself. This goes beyond the failures Dryden admits to, imperfect liaison-des-scènes and unity of place.

> The third property of manners [he notes in 'The Grounds of Criticism in Tragedy'], is resemblance; and this is founded upon the particular characters of men, as we have them delivered to us by relation or history . . . Thus, it is not a poet's choice to make Ulysses choleric, or Achilles patient, because Homer has described them quite otherwise.[31]

But Dryden makes his Cressida faithful none the less. Scott blames this on a neoclassical predilection for virtuous heroines but observance of one rule does not excuse breach of another. Shakespeare, rather than the rules, however, provides an explanation. One of the principal effects of the original play, after all, is the way it confirms the traditional standing of some characters – Hector, Cressida and Pandarus – while it mocks or reverses the reputations of others – Ajax, Nestor, Agamemnon and above all Achilles. As a result Hector's heroic faith in honour and renown after death is seen to be naive: time will not discriminate between the chivalrous hero and cowardly bully; reputation in the long term will be as unrelated to merit as according to Ulysses it is in the short term. Shakespeare concentrates in the texture of his verse an extraordinarily dense and tonally complex disillusionment which Dryden cannot match. Nevertheless Dryden was the first critic to grasp this central conception in Shakespeare's play and he made it the key factor in his own original contribution to the Troilus legend. He only did to Shakespeare's *Troilus*, after all, what Shakespeare had done to Chapman's Homer; and he did so to make a telling and difficult point to his own audience about their own times.

Dryden in the middle of his career had become particularly attached to the authentically Aristotelian belief that there ought to be an unbreakable unity between the structural unity of a work and its ethical centre. The Moral of *Troilus and Cressida*, however, might be considered rather too obvious. 'Now peaceful order has resumed the reins,' declares Ulysses at the end of the play,

> Old Time looks young, and nature seems renewed.
> Then, since from home-bred factions ruin springs,
> Let subjects learn obedience to their kings
> (p. 390)

This surely is too neat and, for a Tory poet at the height of the Exclusion crisis, too slickly convenient a conclusion. There is no question but that the Popish Plot hysteria is in Dryden's mind. Agamemnon represents Charles II, Ulysses, possibly, Halifax. The king's crafty patience is almost explicitly described in one of Ulysses' earlier speeches:

> Oppose not rage, while rage is in its force,
> But give it way a while, and let it waste.
> The rising deluge is not stopped with dams;
> Those it o'erbears, and drowns the hope of harvest:
> But, wisely managed, its divided strength,
> Is sluiced in channels, and securely drained
> (p. 379)

There are a number of possible objections to such topicality. Dryden has apparently made his Greeks more decorous than Shakespeare's, not just from neoclassical principle but out of deference to his Stuart paymaster. He has also, it seems, fused neoclassical ethical prescriptiveness with brutally insensitive Tory policy. On the other hand he can be given a little credit for recognizing the specifically political element in Shakespeare's play in spite of his certain ignorance of its possible connections with the Essex conspiracy. He has also – and far more importantly – made Cressida youthful and Ajax wise. The latter's reaction to Achilles' boast that he has avenged Patroclus and Diomedes, in fact has as much bearing on the Moral of the play as Ulysses' complacent conclusion which follows it. 'Revenged it basely', Ajax mutters,

> For Troilus fell by multitudes oppressed,
> And so fell Hector; but 'tis vain to talk
> (p. 390)

Dryden's point here is by no means easy, consistent or complacent. He is explicitly allowing political order to triumph at the expense of poetic justice, an effect which can only be strongly felt in an overtly neoclassical play. So too with Cressida. Her violent, undeserved death on stage grossly offends against many proprieties, but it is a necessary means to Agamemnon's triumph. Troilus's fury at her supposed infidelity is what drives Hector into battle and so brings home-bred factions among the Greeks to an end. Thus even Achilles' cynical assertion that 'Revenge is honour, the securest way' (p. 383) proves to be over-optimistic, since Troilus's vengeful response to the gratuitous taunting of Dryden's notably unpleasant Diomedes serves only to secure Cressida's perpetual dishonour. It is true that, unlike Shakespeare, Dryden is a party man. But he reckons the cost of seeing his party triumph with remarkable rigour and realism. In admittedly limited, but intelligent and (for his age) pressingly relevant terms, Dryden in consequence finds himself stating, but not gratuitously resolving, the problem of evil itself.

My case for Dryden as a Shakespearean rests on three main assertions. Firstly, his critical approach is remarkably consistent with modern critical method. He recognized that detailed verbal ambiguity is centrally important in Shakespeare's work, and that the plays are not just enacted stories but aesthetic structures in which theme, image and thought are supremely important. Secondly, he accommodated neoclassicism to Shakespeare and not the other way round. In making Shakespeare Homer's equivalent and equal, he gave strength and substance to neoclassicism which it notably lacks in Rymer. In particular Shakespeare's example is used in 'The

Grounds of Criticism' to give specificity and weight to the neoclassical concept of manners. Shakespeare's Homeric status also enables Dryden to resist the degenerate fashion for pathetic tragedy and to reaffirm the traditional centrality of terror. My third contention attempts to meet the proposition that even if the first two are valid, neither in his criticism nor in his reworking of Shakespeare is Dryden *sufficiently* tentative, incomplete, and compromised. But the controlling, co-ordinating preoccupation of all Dryden's work on Shakespeare (and on Jonson, for that matter), is, it seems to me, based precisely on a recognition of the inadequacy of the social, cultural and linguistic resources which the Restoration world makes available to him. In his case, at least, neoclassicism, trapped in undoubted limitations of idiom, sensibility and thought, repeatedly, wittily and movingly, criticizes itself, precisely on the lines advanced by Leavis, thus at once confirming his judgments and making them incomplete. The question of Dryden's own royalist and neoclassical order does not, of course, provoke him into reductive repudiations. He belongs to, and flourishes in, conditions which also appal him. His situation has thus an inherent complexity with which, as a critic and a poet, he was superbly equipped to cope. As evidence for this claim one can offer the magnificent series of poems which he addressed to his fellow poets from 1677 onwards. The cumulative impression of the addresses to Lee, Oldham, Roscommon, Kneller, Congreve, Motteux and Granville is of a poet so absolutely master of the idiom of his age, its 'pauses cadence and well-vowell'd Words', that he could not repudiate it without dishonourable self-mutilation; but it is clear also that Dryden knows how his age has trapped him: the lines to Congreve generously anticipate the defeat of his own standards; the comparison of Kneller with the Italian masters states why such a defeat is necessary:

> That yet thou hast not reach'd their high Degree
> Seems only wanting to this Age, not thee:
> Thy Genius bounded by the Times like mine,
> Drudges on petty Draughts, nor dare design
> A more Exalted Work, and more Divine.

As in the noble *Aureng-Zebe* prologue, Dryden, in the poem to Kneller, places himself as a 'son' and a subordinate of Shakespeare with courage, pride and humility all equally proper.

Hence my wish to modify some of the criteria advanced in *The Living Principle*. Leavis has not, it seems to me, taken the capacity of 'logic' and 'clarity' to see and suffer from their own limitations sufficiently into account. 'Good thinking' is possible, I believe, even when writers find themselves denied 'intimate acquaintance with a subtle language in its fullest use'. The 'nature of livingness in human life' can be manifest even within the idiomatic constraints associated with 'Cartesian-Newtonian dualism' provided the writer, like Dryden, achieves precisely that poise of mind which Leavis so impressively recommends to the modern teacher of English – 'opportunism combined with a firm conception'. In Dryden's case the opportunities were found 'snatched on the margins and in the interstices'[32] of a linguistic and literary culture which, especially in the theatre, was perilously close to decay. If Dryden's work on Shakespeare is placed beside the other triumphant assimilations, in the closing years of his life, of Homer, Virgil, Ovid, Boccaccio and Chaucer, the scope, flexibility and intelligence of his opportunism become finally apparent. He belongs (in a way that I find Pope does not) to a tradition of English literary humanism which includes Jonson and Milton as well as Shakespeare, though his contribution to it is still awaiting the ample and weighty explication which it deserves. Such a revaluation will certainly require a fuller account of Dryden's Shakespeare than I have been able to give.

NOTES

1. *The Living Principle* (1975), 13.
2. *Ibid.*, 20.
3. *Ibid.*, 97.
4. 'Preface to *An Evening's Love*', *The Works of John Dryden*, X, ed. Maximillian E. Novak and George Guffey (Berkeley, Los Angeles and London, 1970), 206.
5. 'Defence of an Epilogue', *John Dryden's Works*, ed. Sir Walter Scott and George Saintsbury (1883), IV, 228.
6. *Ibid.*, 229.
7. *Ibid.*, 231.
8. *Ibid.*, 239.
9. 'Preface to *Troilus and Cressida*', *ibid.*, 254.
10. 'Heads of an Answer', *The Works of John Dryden*, XVII, ed. Samuel Holt Monk (1971), 190.
11. *The Living Principle*, 145.
12. *Ibid.*, 151.
13. *Ibid.*, 152.
14. *The Tempest* quotations from *The Works of John Dryden*, X, ed. Novak and Guffey.
15. Shakespearean quotations are from *A New Variorum Edition of Shakespeare*, IX, ed. Horace Howard Furness (Philadelphia, 1892).
16. *Of Dramatick Poesy*, *The Works of John Dryden*, XVII, ed. Monk, 23.
17. *The Works of John Dryden*, X, ed. Novak and Guffey, 333.
18. *Ibid.*, 328–9.
19. *Dryden's Criticism* (Ithaca and London, 1970), 113.
20. *The Works of John Dryden*, X, ed. Novak and Guffey, 340.
21. 'Mr. Dryden and Mr. Rymer', *Philological Quarterly*, LIV (1975), 147.
22. John Dryden, *Four Tragedies*, ed. L. A. Beaurline and Fredson Bowers (Chicago and London, 1967), 193.
23. *Ibid.*, 196.
24. *The Works of John Dryden*, XVII, ed. Monk, 191.
25. *Ibid.*, 190.

26. *Dryden's Criticism*, 182.
27. *All for Love* quotations are from *Four Tragedies*, ed. Beaurline and Bowers.
28. *Dryden* (1973), 43–5.
29. *Explorations* (Peregrine Books edn, 1964), 18.
30. *Dryden's Criticism*, 59.
31. *John Dryden's Works*, ed. Scott and Saintsbury, VI, 268.
32. *The Living Principle*, 17.

2

A Reading of *A Modest Proposal*

C. J. RAWSON

The title is famous, but still bears examination: *A Modest Proposal for Preventing the Children of Poor People from Being a Burthen to their Parents, or the Country, and for Making them Beneficial to the Publick.*[1] The form of title is that of many 'modest proposals' and 'humble petitions' which appeared in the seventeenth and eighteenth centuries, 'dealing with economic problems, particularly with problems concerning population, labor, unemployment, and poverty'.[2] It captures accurately the conventional postures: concern for the public good, profitability, the air of planned or scientific management of human material. It is hard for the modern reader, more familiar with the gruesome irony of Swift's *Modest Proposal* than with conventional formulas of pamphleteering, to realize that the title would be taken quite straight and give no hint of shocks to follow. At the same time, it would be wrong to infer, when the shocks do come, that what is at work in any important sense is 'a burlesque on projects concerning the poor' or 'on the titles of certain types of economic tracts'.[3] If there is a poker-faced mimicry of these things, it is only a seasoning, not the main point. And to suggest that Swift was radically attacking the notion of economic planning of human affairs, or even that his attitude on certain central questions (poverty, beggars, the care of children) was 'humane' or 'liberal' in a sense which a modern reader would understand or assent to, is misleading.

A crucial part of the title speaks of preventing the children of the poor 'from Being a Burthen to their Parents, or the Country'. Swift himself used this sort of phrase unironically and (some readers might feel) quite callously when, for example, he noted that society ought to be protected from strolling beggars, and proposed schemes for reducing the 'burden' to the community (IX, 191, 209; XIII, 132, 137).[4] Wittkowsky has shown that behind such a phrase, in the social thinking of the day, lay a hard-headed distinction between the 'able' and the 'impotent', or unproductive, poor.[5] The latter (including the sick, beggars, vagrants etc.), unable to work for their keep, are, in the words of Charles Davenant in 1699, 'nourish'd at the Cost of Others; and are a Yearly Burthen to the Publick'. The seventeenth-century economist, Sir William Petty, commenting on losses from the plague, regretted that the plague made no distinction between 'the bees and the drones', but killed 'promiscuously'.[6]

More recently, an Irish law of George I's reign 'classified unemployable children as impotent poor', declaring that there were many children who had to beg and who thus risked becoming '"*not only unprofitable but dangerous to their country*"'. The Act empowered 'the ministers to bind out these children to tradesmen, provision being made to prevent cruel treatment'. Wittkowsky also cites a work of 1695–6, *A Modest Proposal for the More Certain and yet More Easie Provision for the Poor. And Likewise for the Better Suppression of Thieves . . . Tending Much to the Advancement of Trade, Especially in the most Profitable Part of it.*[7] This plan advocates the setting up of workhouse-hospitals and workhouse-prisons, answers the objection 'that the plan will be a needless burden on the public, "in loading it with the Charge of so many children"' by saying that '"it is a fault not to encourage the increase of Lawful Children, especially when they are likely to be train'd up in all Frugality and Industry"'. This training will be inexpensive, and '"a mighty Advantage to the Public"'.

It is tempting to think of Swift's *Modest Proposal* as a parody of this kind of thing. But there is no reason to suppose that his own attitude was radically different, or to attribute to him a Dickensian protest about child-labour. He was no exception to Dorothy Marshall's statement that 'Despite the growth of the Charity School movement, charity to children in the seventeenth and eighteenth centuries meant enabling them to earn their own living at the earliest possible moment, no matter how laborious their life might be'.[8] In his sermon on the 'Causes of the Wretched Condition of Ireland' he gave qualified support to charity schools, agreeing, as Louis Landa has pointed out, with those criticisms of the schools which said that they had failed in their purpose of supplying cheap labour, and had over-educated their pupils, making them unfit for menial work (IX, 130, 202ff.).[9] He argued in particular that the schools ought to instil in their pupils a 'teachable Disposition' (a phrase, as it happens, which calls to mind the Houyhnhnm master's patronizing praise of the Yahoo Gulliver, IV, iii; XI, 234), in order to make of them good household servants, since the common run of servants were, in Swift's view, an idle and vicious lot (IX, 204–5, 203ff.). He made it clear that pupils must 'be severely punished for every Neglect' in study, religion, cleanliness, honesty, industry and thrift. After this training, they should be 'bound Apprentices in the Families of Gentlemen and Citizens, (for which a late Law giveth great Encouragement)' – the late law being the one cited by Wittkowsky, presumably as an instance of what Swift would be inclined to deplore.[10] They would thus be learning useful things whilst being at the same time 'very useful in a Family, as far as their Age and Strength would allow' (IX, 205). In such a passage, Swift gets close to the flat economic utilitarianism which the *Modest Proposal* is alleged to be attacking.

Swift's comments on charity schools in the sermon have yet more light to throw on the *Proposal*. He argued that the children admitted to these schools should be those of 'honest Parents' struck by misfortune, rather than

> the Brood of wicked Strolers; for it is by no means reasonable, that the Charity of well-inclined People should be applied to encourage the Lewdness of those profligate, abandoned Women, who croud our Streets with their borrowed or spurious Issue.
>
> (IX, 202)

(Cf. Swift's distinction in the *Modest Proposal* between 'Beggars by Profession' and those worthy persons who have become 'Beggars in Effect' because of the wretched condition of Ireland, XII, 117). It was also wrong, except in the bigger well-endowed schools, to train poor children to anything but 'the very meanest Trades':

> otherwise the poor honest Citizen who is just able to bring up his Child, and pay a small Sum of Money with him to a good Master, is wholely defeated, and the Bastard Issue, perhaps, of some Beggar, preferred before him. And hence we come to be so over-stocked with 'Prentices and Journeymen, more than our discouraged Country can employ; and, I fear, the greatest Part of our Thieves, Pickpockets, and other Vagabonds are of this Number.
>
> (IX, 203)

Against the background of such passages, the opening paragraphs of the *Modest Proposal* acquire an irony a good deal less simple than is normally thought:

> It is a melancholly Object to those, who walk through this great Town, or travel in the Country; when they see the *Streets*, the *Roads*, and *Cabbin-doors* crowded with *Beggars* of the Female Sex, followed by three, four, or six Children, *all in Rags*, and importuning every Passenger for an Alms. These *Mothers*, instead of being able to work for their honest Livelyhood, are forced to employ all their Time in stroling to beg Sustenance for their *helpless Infants*; who, as they grow up, either turn *Thieves* for want of Work; or leave their *dear Native Country, to fight for the Pretender in* Spain, or sell themselves to the *Barbadoes*.
>
> I think it is agreed by all Parties, that this prodigious Number of Children in the Arms, or on the Backs, or at the *Heels* of their *Mothers*,

> and frequently of their *Fathers*, is *in the present deplorable State of the Kingdom*, a very great additional Grievance; and therefore, whoever could find out a fair, cheap, and easy Method of making these Children sound and useful Members of the Commonwealth, would deserve so well of the Publick, as to have his Statue set up for a Preserver of the Nation.
> (XII, 109)

If there is compassion in this passage, it is no straightforward feeling. Swift was intensely hostile to beggars. 'There is not a more undeserving vicious Race of human Kind than the Bulk of those who are reduced to Beggary, even in this beggarly Country', he wrote in 1737, in a serious sociological tract, the *Proposal for Giving Badges to the Beggars* (XIII, 135). This explosive irritation recalls the King of Brobdingnag's 'little odious Vermin' speech (*Gulliver*, II. vi; XI, 132). But Swift went further, in the same late tract, making his own Modest Proposer seem modest indeed by comparison, when he added that the strolling beggars from the country were 'fitter to be rooted out off the Face of the Earth, than suffered to levy a vast annual Tax upon the City' (XIII, 139): the Gulliverian analogy here is with the Houyhnhnms who debate 'Whether the *Yahoos* should be exterminated from the Face of the Earth' (*Gulliver*, IV. ix; XI, 271). This is, no doubt, a rhetoric of exasperation and not an advocacy of massacre. But we should recognize squarely that this exasperation is present also in the *Modest Proposal*, and that ridding society of its beggarly 'burdens' was not a notion which Swift identified exclusively with the cant of the profiteering and the inhumane. If Yeats was right that Swift 'understood that wisdom comes of beggary' ('The Seven Sages'), Swift would not have understood what Yeats meant.

The beggars were usually poor through their own fault.[11] The notion runs through the whole pamphlet, and had been strongly expressed in the sermon on the 'Wretched Condition of Ireland': 'there is hardly one in twenty of those miserable Objects who do not owe their present Poverty to their own Faults; to their present Sloth and Negligence; to their indiscreet Marriage without the least Prospect of supporting a Family, to their foolish Expensiveness, to their Drunkenness, and other Vices' (IX, 206).[12] Family relations among the Irish poor are part of the whole 'anti-nature' of the state of Ireland:

> In all other Nations, that are not absolutely barbarous, Parents think themselves bound by the Law of Nature and Reason to make some Provision for their Children; but the Reason offered by the Inhabitants of *Ireland* for marrying, is, that they may have Children to maintain them when they grow old and unable to work.
> (XIII, 136)

Thus the *Proposal for Giving Badges to the Beggars*, in non-ironic analysis. It gives an edge to the Modest Proposer's sixth argument in support of his cannibal scheme:

> This would be a great Inducement to Marriage, which all wise Nations have either encouraged by Rewards, or enforced by Laws and Penalties. It would encrease the Care and Tenderness of Mothers towards their Children, when they were sure of a Settlement for Life, to the poor Babes, provided in some Sort by the Publick, to their annual Profit instead of Expence. We should soon see an honest Emulation among the married Women, *which of them could bring the fattest Child to the Market*. Men would become as *fond* of their Wives, during the Time of their Pregnancy, as they are now of their *Mares* in Foal, their *Cows* in Calf, or *Sows* when they are ready to farrow; nor offer to beat or kick them, (as it is too *frequent* a Practice) for fear of a Miscarriage.
> (XII, 115)

There is about this a fierce, angry compassion. But it is hardly a flattering glimpse of the domestic mores of the Irish poor.[18] The Proposer is, of course, writing *de haut en bas*, as a Protestant member of the ruling class (as, in his own different way, is Swift). When he coolly protests his own disinterestedness, and his absence of family-inducements to profit, he begins squarely as a solid, patriotic and profit-minded economist:

> I profess, in the Sincerity of my Heart, that I have not the least personal Interest, in endeavouring to promote this necessary Work; having no other Motive than the *publick Good of my Country, by advancing our Trade, providing for Infants, relieving the Poor, and giving some Pleasure to the Rich.*
> (XII, 118)

But he comes in his next (and final) sentence to be queerly identified with the values of the Papist poor: 'I have no Children, by which I can propose to get a single Penny; the youngest being nine Years old, and my Wife past Child-bearing.' It is all much more decorous, of course, than the glimpse of Papist family life. Conveniently, the Proposer has not the same temptations. But this convenience was set up by Swift, and is very double-edged. For it confirms our strong instinctive tendency to separate the cool Proposer from the messy and intimate sub-humanities of the Papist poor, while at the same time establishing a profound link. The mindless brute with his base family life, and the soundly calculating Whig planner, unite in their commercial priorities, with Swift wishing a plague on both their houses.

This charged, quizzical note is very important. Swift chose to end the tract with it. The Papists' profit-motive was largely the result of conditions brought about by the Whig planner and his like (the governing Anglo-Irish, and the English), as Swift knew. But his emphasis in the *Modest Proposal* is not 'judicial', and his intense exasperation lurches throughout the tract from one side to the other. The jibe in the opening paragraph about the Irish catholics who 'leave their *dear Native Country, to fight for the Pretender in* Spain' (XII, 109) contains protest at real Irish 'disloyalty', as well as at the cruelties of economic circumstance which force them into the armies of Catholic princes.[14] There may also be anger at the apparent tolerance of this situation by the government, and the following year, in the 'Answer to the Craftsman' (1730 but published posthumously; XII, 171ff.), Swift found himself using his Modest Proposer's voice to satirize an arrangement between George II and the French to allow French recruiting officers in Ireland. And running in a sense against both these feelings was a third, in which Swift complains of exaggerated anti-Papist fears, and a Whiggish cant always ready, at the drop of a hat, to accuse anyone (Swift was not excepted) of Jacobitism. It is this kind of scaremongering which is parodied in the Modest Proposer's 'first' argument:

> [the cannibal scheme] would greatly lessen the *Number of Papists*, with whom we are yearly over-run; being the principal Breeders of the Nation, as well as our most dangerous Enemies; and who stay at home on Purpose, with a Design to *deliver the Kingdom to the Pretender*; hoping to take their Advantage by the Absence *of so many good Protestants*, who have chosen rather to leave their Country, than stay at home, and pay Tithes against their Conscience, to an idolatrous *Episcopal Curate*. (XII, 114)[15]

Here, moreover, the Papist pauper comes into yet another surprising proximity, this time with Protestant Dissenters who emigrated to America, and who, like Catholic defectors to foreign armies, betray Ireland by going away. (Swift hated these most of all: the sarcasm about clergymen's tithes is a sure additional sign of angry Swiftian grievance.) Both groups of underprivileged defectors might, in an essential respect, be likened to that other, by no means underprivileged category, the Anglo-Irish landlords whose economically ruinous absenteeism from Ireland is complained of in the *Proposal* and elsewhere (XII, 116, 126 etc.).

These comparisons do not raise the Papist poor in estimation. The compassion Swift feels for them is real. But at some of the places where a modern reader senses this compassion (in the opening paragraphs about the beggars and vagrants, and in the many exposures of family cruelty)

Swift is partly exposing to derision his modest proposer's sentimental show of tenderness where it is not due. When the proposer says of 'that horrid Practice of *Women murdering their Bastard Children*' that it 'would move Tears and Pity in the most Savage and inhuman Breast' (XII, 110); or when he protests that cruelty 'hath always been with me the strongest Objection against any Project, how well soever intended' (XII, 113), Swift is only partly exposing the hypocrisy of profiteering do-gooders. He is also, and importantly, guying a lazy-minded (and mainly Whiggish) benevolism, given to indiscriminate tolerance, misguided charities and that whole sentimental euphoria which drives moderns to write books like those projected long ago by Swift's first mad 'author': *A Panegyrick upon the World*, and, better still, *A Modest Defence of the Proceedings of the Rabble in all Ages* (*Tale of a Tub*, Preface; I, 32).

The complicated interplay of compassion and contempt is not to be taken as a finely-textured, sensitively judicial blend, a mellowly-pondered product of the liberal imagination. It is an explosive mixture, and Swift's feelings oscillate starkly among extreme positions. When he discloses that it is not only the English but also (and at times especially) the Irish and, among the Irish, not only the ruling classes but the ruled, who are to blame for the state of Ireland, fierce convergences of anger take place which make the rational lucidities of the most subtle and comprehensive political analysis seem irrelevant. These convergences gain a particular edge from the fact that Swift was always insisting to himself and to others on the *differences* between the English and the Irish, and between the Anglo-Irish and the Catholic natives; and that it was frequently important to him to identify himself now with the English, now with the Anglo-Irish Protestant establishment, even at moments when his most heartfelt compassion was directed towards the Papist poor whom he despised. To some extent, these complexities were due to factors inherent in the Irish situation itself.[16] But Swift's intensely individual charge of feeling was very strong. He wrote in 1734 in 'A Letter on the Fishery':

> As to my Native Country, (as you call it) I happened indeed by a perfect Accident to be born here . . . thus I am a *Teague*, or an *Irishman*, or what People please, although the best Part of my Life was in *England*. What I did for this Country was from perfect Hatred of Tyranny and Oppression . . . I have done some small Services to this Kingdom, but I can do no more . . .
>
> (XIII, 111–2)

There is here something of the self-righteous hauteur that we find in the *Verses on the Death*, and the presumably unconscious echo of Othello's 'I have done the state some service' (V.ii.341) is not without an element of valedictory self-indulgence. But Swift understood the risks and temptations of such luxurious postures, and usually shied from them to assert more low-pitched and untidy motives. He said to Pope on 1 June 1728: 'I do profess without affectation, that your kind opinion of me as a Patriot . . . is what I do not deserve; because what I do is owing to perfect rage and resentment, and the mortifying sight of slavery, folly, and baseness about me, among which I am forced to live' (*Correspondence*, III, 289). If the denial of 'affectation' has itself a touch of affectation, and if the denial of higher motives is hardly altogether fair to himself, the passage conveys well the enforced emotional raggedness, the self-conscious impossibility for Swift of any clear self-ennobling stand. English tyranny was vicious, but the 'Letter on the Fishery' is quick to say that 'corrupt as *England* is, it is an Habitation of Saints in Comparison of *Ireland*. We are all Slaves, and Knaves, and Fools, and all but Bishops and People in Employments, Beggars' (XIII, 112).[17] The last word thrusts the Anglo-Irish (Members of Parliament and others), into the familiar sarcastic identification with 'the vulgar Folks of *Ireland*', 'so lazy and so knavish' that any economic scheme is doomed to founder among them. But 'Oppressed Beggars are always Knaves' (XIII, 113), and the 'Letter on the Fishery' comes quickly to all the giddy circularities of guilt which make it so hard and so absurd to apportion blame clearly, or to hope for a remedy. It is not surprising that the targets of Swift's Irish satires cannot always, and are not always meant to, be clearly distinguished from one another, nor that Swift's allegiances as between the English, the Anglo-Irish and the natives are blurred and irrationally fluctuating things, whose very confusions provide the essential energies of his style.

Thus the sarcasms of the 'Answer to the Craftsman' aim at England, and simultaneously at the Anglo-Irish and Ireland's original native rulers:

> For, as to *England*, they have a just Claim to the Balance of Trade on their Side with the whole World; and therefore our Ancestors and we, who conquered this Kingdom for them, ought, in Duty and Gratitude, to let them have the whole Benefit of that Conquest to themselves; especially, when the Conquest was amicably made, without Bloodshed, by a Stipulation between the *Irish* Princes and *Henry* II. by which they paid him, indeed, not equal Homage with what the Electors of *Germany* do to the Emperor, but very near the same that he did to the King of *France* for his *French* Dominions.
>
> (XII, 177)

Behind this are various further ironies. The speaker is ostensibly expressing that Anglo-Irish point of view with which, among the three alternatives, Swift himself was most closely identified. The speaker here, however, is the

Modest Proposer himself, Swift's Whiggish opposite, selling Ireland out to England as (it would seem to be implied) the native Irish rulers had before. But what Molyneux had called the 'Intire and Voluntary Submission' of the Irish to Henry II was one of the bases of that constitutional doctrine of Ireland's status as a kingdom rather than a conquered or colonial territory which Swift himself accepted.[18] That submission Swift recognized to have been somewhat qualified. In *The Story of the Injured Lady*, Ireland is made to say that she was won 'half by Force, and half by Consent' (IX, 5). When the speaker of the 'Answer to the Craftsman' says it is 'our Ancestors and we' who 'conquered' Ireland, he is speaking not only of conquests as distinct from free compacts, but of more *recent* conquests, including those of William III, which fell within Swift's lifetime and to which Swift himself felt loyal, though not without ambiguity. And since the Irish have continuously needed subduing in spite of their 'Intire and Voluntary Submission', there may even be some kind of exasperated hint that that submission was not only less than 'Voluntary' but also less than 'Intire', and therefore also unreliable and insincere.[19] To make things seem still more confused, Swift was mocking a Whiggish supporter of the English government for defending a scheme by the present King of England which was clearly to England's disadvantage, since it encouraged disaffected Irish Catholics to enlist in the armies of a potential enemy. And it seems clear at the same time that the Irish mercenaries who did so enlist are (as in the opening of the *Modest Proposal*) viewed by Swift as traitors. The follies are viciously intermerged, and so are the turpitudes.

This is notably true in the cannibal theme, and in other elaborations of the *mythe animal*. England '*would be glad to eat up our whole Nation*' (without salt!; XII, 117), but the Whig proposer expects his scheme to commend itself to his own profit-minded Irish fellow-Protestants, while (as we have seen) the Papist poor are assumed to be likely not only to embrace it heartily, but to improve their family relationships as a result. The fact that at previous and historically recorded times of famine, actual instances of cannibalism, including child-eating, had occurred in Ireland (about which Swift certainly knew), adds hideous and tragic overtones to the insinuation.[20] Swift's compassion would certainly have been mixed with a very uppish revulsion, for the fact was clearly in accord with his notions of the barbaric squalor of 'the poor Popish Natives' (IX, 209). In *An Answer to . . . A Memorial* (1728) Swift noted, from a certain ironic distance, 'that our Ancestors, the *Scythians*, and their Posterity our Kinsmen the *Tartars*, lived upon the Blood and Milk, and raw Flesh of their Cattle; without one Grain of *Corn*; but I confess myself so degenerate, that I am not easy without *Bread* to my Victuals' (XII, 19). In 1729, newspaper reports were saying that the unemployed Dublin weavers were forced to feed 'on Grains, and Blood from the Slaughter-Houses'.[21] In 1730, in the 'Answer to the

Craftsman', Swift returns to the modern Irish descendants of the Scythians, and their diet, as '*Virgil* describeth it':

Et lac concretum cum sanguine bibit equino.

> Which, in *English*, is Bonnyclabber, mingled with the Blood of Horses, as they formerly did, until about the Beginning of the last Century Luxury, under the Form of Politeness, began to creep in, they changed the Blood of Horses for that of their black Cattle; and, by Consequence, became less warlike than their Ancestors.
> (XII, 178)

Behind the pained compassion of such passages lies a whole tradition of contempt for the Irish and their barbarous ways. The link between the Irish and the Scythians was a popular tradition,[22] and many authors (notably Spenser) noted the diet of boiled blood, sometimes adding to this some cannibal variants. Spenser and others noted not only that the Irish in times of famine nourished themselves on human bodies, but that like the Scythians they were given (for various ritual reasons) to drinking human blood.[23] Long before, Strabo had spoken of both the Irish and the Scythians as cannibals or reputed cannibals.[24] There was also a tradition that the Scythians made mantles out of the skins of their enemies,[25] which gives a doubtless fortuitous additional irony to the *Modest Proposal*'s notion that the skins of cannibalized babies 'will make admirable *Gloves for Ladies*, and *Summer Boots for fine Gentlemen*' (XII, 112).

There are also, in the background to Swift's Scythian parallel, Swift's own frequent references to the Scythians in the *Tale of a Tub*, the 'Mechanical Operation of the Spirit' and elsewhere, as prototypes of the many 'modern' madnesses of Britain: a reverence for asses and '*True Criticks*' (*Tale*, III; I, 60–1) and allied zaninesses in the domain both of 'learning' (VII; I, 93–4), and of religion, notably Roundhead or Puritan enthusiasm, and 'artificial Extasies' ('Mechanical Operation'; I, 175–6, 178).[26] The Scythians were often thought of as a generalized type of barbarian, rather than as a very precisely defined race.[27] For Swift, in particular, they clearly meant not only barbarism, but certain archetypal forms of human folly which he felt to be very close at hand. Such radical folly, for Swift, is both 'modern' and atavistic, and thus poses a perennially immediate threat of disruption, in which man, either by simple primitive reversion, or (as in the *Tale*) through excesses of arrogant intellect, brings himself back to an animal state. The descriptions of Scythian barbarisms among the Irish in the tracts of the late 1720s are shot through with pity, but the pity is an angry one, mixed with many kinds of resentment and contempt. And the same inextricable amalgam of fierce compassion and contemptuous fury lies behind Swift's description of himself in 1732 as soured and dispirited by 'fighting with Beasts like St. Paul, not at Ephesus, but in Ireland' (*Correspondence*, IV, 79).[28] As Ferguson says of the *Modest Proposal*: 'Swift is saying to the Irish, in effect, "You have acted like beasts; hence you no longer deserve the title of men." '[29]

Swift's ways of animalizing Ireland and the Irish are clearly not ironic in that simple compassionate sense presupposed by many readers of the *Modest Proposal*. In an essay of the same date, 'A Proposal that All the Ladies and Women of Ireland should appear constantly in Irish Manufactures', Swift wrote:

> the three seasons wherein our corn hath miscarried, did no more contribute to our present misery, than one spoonful of water thrown upon a rat already drowned would contribute to his death; . . . the present plentiful harvest, although it should be followed by a dozen ensuing, would no more restore us, than it would the rat aforesaid to put him near the fire, which might indeed warm his fur-coat, but never bring him back to life.
>
> (XII, 122)

In the following year, on 21 March 1730, Swift wrote to Bolingbroke: 'I would if I could get into a better [world than Ireland] before I was called into the best, and not die here in a rage, like a poisoned rat in a hole' (*Correspondence*, III, 383). In the Drapier's second letter, it is William Wood, exploiter of the Irish, who is described as a rat: 'It is no Loss of Honour to submit to the *Lion*: But who, with the Figure of a *Man*, can think with Patience of being devoured alive by a *Rat*?' (X, 20). The latter usage is close to Pope's in a note of 1729 to *Dunciad* A.III.337, warning us not to underestimate the power of the dunces: 'the *Dutch* stories somewhere relate, that a great part of their Provinces was once overflow'd, by a small opening made in one of their dykes by a single *Water-Rat*'. In 'A Proposal that All the Ladies . . .' it is Ireland herself that is a dead rat, and it is a characteristically teasing coincidence that he should on separate occasions have used the same image to describe a victimized Ireland, one of her more contemptible oppressors, and himself to boot. The drowned rat which is Ireland evokes a mixture of feelings. If the passage includes exasperation at the Irish, it also angrily mimics the contemptuous way in which the condition of Ireland is normally spoken of, and it contains an obvious gruff compassion on Swift's part, itself partly contemptuous.

The same compassion is clearly present in 'An Answer to Several Letters', also of 1729. Swift angrily answers those who explain or justify Ireland's troubles by the primitive and vicious squalor of the 'poor native Irish': 'supposing the size of a native's understanding just equal to that of a dog or a horse, I have often seen those two animals to be civilized by rewards, at least as much as by punishments' (XII, 88). Swift hints eloquently here at 'how easily those people may be brought to a less savage manner of life'. But Swift was often as pessimistic as any of his objectors about the prospects of any improvement in Ireland through practical expedients; and if his Modest Proposer is mimicked as referring to the native Irish as '*our Savages*' (XII, 111), Swift himself spoke without irony of 'the savage old Irish' (*Correspondence*, V, 58), and often thought of them as sub-human Yahoos.[30] Ferguson quotes a mid-century Lord Chancellor of Ireland as saying '"The law does not suppose any such person to exist as an Irish Roman Catholic"', and adds that 'In 1709, Swift could write of them with an easy callousness, "We look upon them to be altogether as inconsiderable as the Women and Children"'.[31] Ferguson later points out that it was in the late 1720s that Swift's sympathies and commitment were extended beyond the Anglo-Irish interest to '"the whole People of Ireland"'.[32] It is, however, sometimes held that this last phrase applies only to the Protestant Irish.[33] Oddly, moreover, Swift's point in the passage of 1709, from the *Letter . . . Concerning the Sacramental Test* (II, 120), was actually to minimize the supposed dangerousness of the Irish Catholics, compared with that of Protestant Dissenters, whilst in the tracts of the 1720s and after we find many expressions by Swift of the kind of harsh contempt which he was at the same time, as in 'An Answer to Several Letters', quick to resent in others.

Swift's celebrated, proto-Malthusian use of dehumanized economic jargon must be seen in the light of these complexities. It is not simply, perhaps not even mainly, an ironic protest at the statistical reduction of human beings, in the manner of, say, Auden's 'The Unknown Citizen'.[34] The statistician's hard depersonalizing vocabulary, 'males', 'females', 'couples', 'breeders', 'souls', is mimicked with a kind of aggressive playfulness, as though Swift were flaunting his ability to play the statisticians' game with the best:

> The Number of Souls in *Ireland* being usually reckoned one Million and a half; of these I calculate there may be about Two hundred Thousand Couple whose Wives are Breeders . . .
> (XII, 110)

It is very like Swift, consciously or otherwise, to seize on the incongruous fact that the incorporeal term 'Soul' should be making the same point as the solidly animal 'Breeders', and the whole passage tingles with an unsettling, deadpan humour. But Swift had no disrespect for economic surveys as such, and his over-riding concern here is in any case well beyond parody. The warm, direct ballad protest of Auden's displaced person:

> Say this city has ten million souls,
> Some are living in mansions, some are living in holes:

> Yet there's no place for us, my dear, yet there's no place for us,
> ('Twelve Songs', I)[35]

is far removed from Swift's hard cold note. If there is, in Swift as in Auden, a complaint about inhumane attitudes as expressed through language, it has relatively less place in Swift's total effect. And his tendency to talk of the Irish Catholics as 'things' and 'beasts' is almost as great in his direct utterances as in the parodied voice of the Modest Proposer. Dehumanized terminology ('Females', 'Couples' etc.) and an insulting use of animal terms occur plentifully, for example, in the *Proposal for Giving Badges to the Beggars.* Thus Swift says of the beggar who stays within his own parish:

> If he be not quite maimed, he and his Trull, and Litter of Brats (if he hath any) may get half their Support by doing some kind of Work in their Power, and thereby be less burthensome to the People.
> (XIII, 133)

When a resident beggar becomes a strolling beggar, he becomes a still greater object of distaste:

> But, when the Spirit of wandring takes him, attended by his Female, and their Equipage of Children, he becomes a Nuisance to the whole Country: He and his Female are Thieves, and teach the Trade of stealing to their Brood at four Years old.
> (XIII, 134)

A little later, Swift says about the marriage-customs of the Catholic poor:

> many thousand Couples are yearly married, whose whole united Fortunes, bating the Rags on their Backs, would not be sufficient to purchase a Pint of Butter-milk for their Wedding Supper, nor have any Prospect of supporting their *honourable State* but by Service, or Labour, or Thievery. Nay, their *Happiness* is often deferred until they find Credit to borrow, or cunning to steal a Shilling to pay their Popish Priest, or infamous Couple-Beggar.
> (XIII, 136)

But Swift is equally harsh about the English Protestant beggars whom England exports to Ireland – in 'large Cargoes' (XIII, 136–7). And as to the wealthier, ruling Protestant Interest (the section of Ireland with which Swift, in the last analysis, identified himself) they are no more spared than the poorer classes. All the insulting exploitations of the *mythe animal* may occur just as fiercely when Swift has reason to complain of them. The

'Answer to Several Letters' says of Swift's favourite bugbear, the women who use foreign rather than Irish manufactures, that they are

> a kind of animal suffered for our sins to be sent into the world for the Destruction of Familyes, Societyes, and Kingdoms; and whose whole study seems directed to be as expensive as they possibly can in every useless article of living, who by long practice can reconcile the most pernicious forein Drugs to their health and pleasure, provided they are but expensive; as Starlings grow fat with henbane: who contract a Robustness by meer practice of Sloth and Luxury: who can play deep severall hours after midnight, sleep beyond noon, revel upon Indian poisons, and spend the revenue of a moderate family to adorn a nauseous unwholesom living Carcase.
>
> (XII, 80)

(One grotesque piquancy of the *Modest Proposal*, it may be noted in passing, is that it is a perverse application of Swift's insistently reiterated view that the Irish should consume their own, rather than imported, products).

The famous onslaught on the dead Lord Chief Justice Whitshed in *An Answer to . . . A Memorial* justifies itself by saying that though the memories of people like him 'will *rot*, there may be some Benefit for their Survivers, to smell it while it is *rotting*' (XII, 25). In the *Vindication of . . . Lord Carteret* (1730), Swift describes himself as a 'political *Surgeon*' opening up the carcase of Lord Allen before his death, and displaying his noisome innards (XII, 157–8). The same Lord Allen (nicknamed Traulus) is the subject of some of Swift's angriest verse:

> Traulus of amphibious Breed,
> Motly Fruit of Mungril Seed:
> By the *Dam* from Lordlings sprung,
> By the *Sire* exhal'd from Dung.
>
> (*Poems*, III, 799)

The Modest Proposer, who thinks of the Irish as part statistical objects and part beasts, who speaks of children dropped from their dam, of carcases, of couples and breeders and the rest, is not mainly parodying other pamphleteers, so much as giving vent to a certain side of Swift himself. Part of what parody there was would have, characteristically, to turn on himself, and on acts of verbal aggression of which he was as guilty as any real statistician, and which he shows no evidence of wanting to recant. There is a further coil of self-mockery which is never far from the surface, a wry sense (not always allowed to become fully conscious) that the predicament of those unhappy Irishmen he most pitied and despised was an image of his own. The *Modest Proposal*'s 'Child, *just dropt from its Dam*' who might later regret that he had been allowed to live on in wretched Ireland instead of being 'sold for Food at a Year old' (XII, 110, 117) may not seem much like the Dean of St Patrick's. But was Swift half-remembering these phrases from the *Proposal* when he wrote to the Earl of Oxford in 1737 of his personal feelings about the 'wretched Kingdom' of his birth: 'I happened to be dropped here, and was a Year old before I left it, and to my Sorrow did not dye before I came back to it again' (*Correspondence*, V, 46–7)?

The 'other Expedients' passage in the *Modest Proposal* (XII, 116–17) and similar passages elsewhere confirm, as Ferguson has shown, that Swift was 'not concerned with satirizing the proposals of other writers on Irish affairs', many of whose schemes he had himself championed.[36] The genuinely sane and practical suggestions included in the list of 'other Expedients' divert whatever mockery of economic projectors there may have been wrily back to Swift himself. The self-mockery is here one of Swift's ways of emphasizing not the culpability of economists but the hopeless incurability of the human material whose lot they are trying against odds to improve. The 'malicious Pleasure' he is half-tempted to feel, in *An Answer to . . . A Memorial* (XII, 22), at the dire realization of all his past warnings, is part of the same charge of hostility which makes him so ready to talk of the Irish as mere *material*, economists' fodder, cattle. But even such element of protest as there nevertheless was, on Swift's part, at the fact that people were being treated, or thought of, as animals, or as mere economic commodities, certainly does not mean (as Wittkowsky thought) that he was objecting to such specifically reifying doctrines of the economists as that 'people are the riches of a nation'.[37] Louis Landa has made it clear that Swift does not 'attack' this maxim 'because he thinks it false', but because the Irish situation is so unnatural that even such a universally valid economic law 'does not apply to Ireland'.[38] Nor is there evidence to suppose that he rejected such hard-headed mercantilist corollaries of the maxim as that large dense populations kept wages low and manufactures cheap, provided that the people were made productive and that idleness or beggary were kept to the minimum. Nor was he in favour of depopulation (e.g. through emigration).[39] Some statements in support of this are in fact bitter upside-down ironies, expressing a deep dismay at how Ireland's unnatural economy made it a grimly special case. This irony he expressed very clearly in the 'Letter . . . Concerning the Weavers':

> I am not in the least sorry to hear of the great Numbers going to America, though very much so for the Causes that drive them from us, since the uncontrolled Maxim that People are the Riches of a Nation is

> no maxim here under our Circumstances. We have neither [manufactures] to employ them about, nor food to support them.
> (XII, 66–7)

Actually, Swift is very 'sorry' indeed. Again, in 'Maxims Controlled' he felt driven to say that the poverty and unemployment in Ireland had

> made me often wish, for some years past, that, instead of discouraging our people from seeking foreign soil, the public would rather pay for transporting all our unnecessary mortals, whether Papists or Protestants, to America, as drawbacks are sometimes allowed for exporting commodities where a nation is over-stocked.
> (XII, 136)

And yet there is another irony than the obvious one. Many of the emigrants to America were Ulster Presbyterians who 'found the enforced payment of tithes to an Anglican clergyman not only an economic burden but also something that went against their consciences'.[40] Swift would be no friend to them, and part of him, for reasons which cut across any economic maxims about population, would not be sorry to see them go. The recruitment of Papists by foreign armies introduced further complexities still. Swift opposed the idea, which he ironically made his Modest Proposer advocate in the 'Answer to the Craftsman'. But again it seems possible to feel that he was not wholly and unequivocally dissociated from his callous Whig spokesman. The latter produces the following piece of political arithmetic based on the supposition, first, that the kings of France and Spain take away for their armies 6,000 'Bodies of healthy, young, living Men' from Ireland:

> by computing the Maintenance of a tall, hungry, *Irish* Man, in Food and Cloaths, to be only at Five Pounds a Head, here will be Thirty Thousand Pounds *per Annum* saved clear to the Nation, for they can find no other Employment at Home, beside begging, robbing, or stealing.
> (XII, 174)

He then contemplates a more large-scale project:

> But, if Thirty, Forty, or Fifty Thousand, (which we could gladly spare) were sent on the same Errand, what an immense Benefit must it be to us; and, if the two Princes, in whose Service they were, should happen to be at War with each other, how soon would those Recruits be destroyed, then what a Number of Friends would the Pretender lose, and what a Number of Popish Enemies all true Protestants get rid of.

The glimpse of Papist hordes of Irishmen destroying each other abroad is three parts mimicry of cynical Whigs, but also one part Swiftian animus. (The Papists in question would, after all, be allowing themselves, and had in the past illegally allowed themselves, to be bought, like cattle, into the service of potential enemies of Protestant Britain).[41] It is one of a whole series of black jokes in which a mock-cynical compassion shades unsettlingly into a certain exasperated velleity for 'final solutions',[42] a velleity which encompasses Papist slave and Protestant ruler alike. The country-beggars in Dublin are 'fitter to be rooted out off the Face of the Earth, than suffered to levy a vast annual Tax upon the City', he was to say in *A Proposal for Giving Badges to the Beggars* (XIII, 139), having first made the point that shopkeepers ought to order the whipping of 'every Beggar from the Shop, who is not of the Parish, and doth not wear the Badge of that Parish on his Shoulder', a practice which would quickly get rid of all the 'sturdy Vagrants' from other parishes.[43] 'As for the Aged and Infirm, it would be sufficient to give them nothing, and then they must starve or follow their Brethren' (XIII, 138).

Similar outbursts occur against the ruling Protestant society, notably, as we should expect, against the women who do not use Irish manufactures. The Modest Proposer's extension of the cannibal project to include them is much more literal, and carries a much simpler hostile animus, than the rest of the work's exploitation of the cannibal formula. Indeed, the irony momentarily ceases to work *in reverse*, according to the formula, and moves instead in some kind of direct parallel with Swift's own feelings:

> Neither indeed can I deny, that if the same Use were made of several plump young girls in this Town, who, without one single Groat to their Fortunes, cannot stir Abroad without a Chair, and appear at the *Play-house*, and *Assemblies* in foreign Fineries, which they never will pay for; the Kingdom would not be the worse.
>
> (XII, 114)

To this may be added this outburst against Bankers in the *Short View*: 'I have often wished, that a Law were enacted to hang up half a Dozen *Bankers* every Year; and thereby interpose at least some short Delay, to the further Ruin of *Ireland*' (XII, 11), and a similar passage in the 'Answer to the Craftsman' (XII, 177).

The 'malicious Pleasure' at Ireland's plight in the *Answer to . . . A Memorial* (XII, 22) is surely also one of the ingredients of that later, eloquent and compassionate sarcasm in 'Maxims Controlled', when, immediately after expressing a wry approval of the emigration of Papists and Protestants to America, Swift continues:

I confess myself to be touched with a very sensible pleasure, when I hear of a mortality in any country-parish or village, where the wretches are forced to pay for a filthy cabin and two ridges of potatoes treble the worth, brought up to steal or beg, for want of work, to whom death would be the best thing to be wished for, on account both of themselves and the public.

(XII, 136)

NOTES

1. All quotations from Swift's prose works are from the edition of Herbert Davis and others (Oxford: Blackwell, 1939–68, 14 vols), unless otherwise noted. References are to volume and page of this edition, and are generally given immediately after citation in the text or notes: sometimes to avoid a local ambiguity, the title is given in abbreviated form as *Works*, but in general volume and page only, without title, are given. *Correspondence* and *Poems* refer to the editions by Harold Williams (Oxford: Clarendon Press, 1963–5, 5 vols; and 2nd edn, Oxford: Clarendon Press, 1958, 3 vols, respectively).
   Oliver W. Ferguson, *Jonathan Swift and Ireland* (Urbana, 1962), is referred to as Ferguson throughout.
2. George Wittkowsky, 'Swift's *Modest Proposal:* the biography of an early Georgian pamphlet', *Journal of the History of Ideas*, IV (1943), 88–9. This important article is full of valuable information, on which I have drawn, whilst not always agreeing with its conclusions. It is referred to as Wittkowsky throughout.
3. Wittkowsky, *loc. cit.*
4. The notion that beggars and vagabonds were above all a social nuisance was widespread; see Christopher Hill, *Puritanism and Revolution. Studies in Interpretation of the English Revolution of the 17th Century* (1968), 218, 222–30; *Society and Puritanism in Pre-Revolutionary England* (1969), 251, 258, 262–87 *passim* (the whole chapter on 'The Poor and the Parish', pp. 251–87, surveys the sixteenth- and seventeenth-century debate on the duty of charity and the opposite need for severity towards beggars. Hostility to beggars was a feature of Puritanism, but it was by no means confined to the Puritans.)
5. Wittkowsky, 83–4. See also R. H. Tawney, *Religion and the Rise of Capitalism* (1948), 193; Hill, *Puritanism and Revolution*, 218, 226–30, *Society and Puritanism*, 264–87, *passim*.
6. Wittkowsky, 84.
7. Wittkowsky, 88n.
8. Cited Wittkowsky, 84n. See Dorothy Marshall, *The English Poor in the Eighteenth Century* (1926), 24.
9. Swift's qualified advocacy of charity schools (he 'actively assisted in founding a charity school', IX, 129n) distinguishes him from the much more hostile attitude which Mandeville expressed in his 'Essay on Charity and Charity-Schools', printed in the 1723 edition of the *Fable of the Bees*. But there are many similarities between Swift's and Mandeville's thinking, and some of Mandeville's harshness will also be found in Swift.
10. On the possible date of the sermon, see IX, 136, where Louis Landa suggests various possibilities, and inclines to 1724–5.
11. On the common notion that poverty and beggary are evidence of unrighteousness, and deserve harsh treatment, see Tawney, *op. cit.*, 262–5; Hill, *Puritanism and Revolution*, 215, 218–19, 225, *Society and Puritanism*, 276–7 and 251–87 *passim*. Max Weber identified this attitude with the Puritan ethic (*The Protestant Ethic and the Spirit of Capitalism*, trs.

Talcott Parsons, 1971, 163, 177–8, 268nn), but it was by no means confined to Puritans or to dissenting sects. For some similar views to mine on the question of Swift's attitude, see David Nokes, 'Swift and the beggars', *Essays in Criticism*, XXVI (1976), 218–35, which appeared after this essay was sent to press.

12. See also the sermon 'On the Poor Man's Contentment': 'there is hardly one in a hundred who doth not owe his Misfortunes to his own Laziness or Drunkenness, or worse Vices' (IX, 191).
13. Ferguson, 174, shows that actual cruelty to children, among the Irish poor, was a known fact of the time, reported on by non-ironic observers. More generally, the Irish seem to have had a reputation for outlandish family life and marriage customs, including unusually early disposal of daughters in marriage, the eating of their dead parents' flesh, the feeding of male infants on the point of a sword, incest, easy dissolution of the marriage-bond and intense enmities arising from unhappy marriages (see, for example, William Camden, *Britannia*, facsimile of 1695 edn, 1971, cols 965, 1041, 1046).
14. In a letter dated July – 2 August 1732, however, Swift wrote to Charles Wogan, an Irish Catholic Jacobite exile who had served in Dillon's regiment in France and later took service with the Spanish army:

> Although I have no great Regard for your Trade, from the Judgment I make of those who profess it in these Kingdoms, yet I cannot but highly esteem those Gentlemen of *Ireland*, who, with all the Disadvantages of being Exiles and Strangers, have been able to distinguish themselves by their Valour and Conduct in so many Parts of *Europe*. I think above all other Nations, which ought to make the *English* ashamed of the Reproaches they cast on the Ignorance, the Dulness, and the Want of Courage, in the Irish Natives; those Defects, wherever they happen, arising only from the Poverty and Slavery they suffer from their inhuman Neighbours, and the base corrupt Spirits of too many of the chief Gentry, *&c*.

He goes on to say that 'the poor Cottagers' of Ireland 'have much better natural Taste for good Sense, Humour, and Raillery' than their English counterparts, although 'the Millions of Oppressions they lye under, the Tyranny of their Landlords, the ridiculous Zeal of their Priests, and the general Misery of the whole Nation, have been enough to damp the best Spirits under the Sun' (*Correspondence*, IV, 51). Allowance must be made for Swift's desire to compliment his addressee. But the letter also shows the tendency to ambiguity and to fluctuation of emphasis in Swift's feelings about Ireland.

15. An official letter to the Duke of Dorset, who became Lord Lieutenant of Ireland in 1730, argued that in view of Protestant emigration, the scheme to permit recruiting of Irish Catholics for the French army 'might have the appearance of right policy, to diminish, on that account, the Number of the Popish Inhabitants' (cited by Ferguson, 177).
16. On this, see Ferguson, 19–23.
17. Calling England 'an Habitation of Saints in Comparison of *Ireland*' seems to be a pointed irony. See Camden's *Britannia*, col. 969: 'St. *Patrick*'s disciples in Ireland were such great proficients in the Christian Religion, that in the age following, Ireland was term'd *Sanctorum Patria*, i.e. the Country of Saints'.
18. Ferguson, 21. For a summary of the historical facts about Henry II's intervention in Ireland, see J. C. Beckett, *A Short History of Ireland* (1952), 17ff., and, for a more detailed treatment, A. J. Otway-Ruthven, *A History of Medieval Ireland* (London and New York, 1968), 42–65, esp. 48ff. The 'Voluntary Submission' was not unmixed with military conquest, of course. In his by no means original account of Henry's reign in the 'Fragment of the History [of England] from William Rufus', Swift notes that Henry II requested the Pope's 'licence for reducing the savage people of *Ireland* from

their brutish way of living, and subjecting them to the crown of *England*' (V, 76: see V, 73–8 for Swift's overall account of Henry II). In his 'Essay upon the Advancement of Trade in Ireland', Temple had spoken of Henry II's 'conquest' of Ireland (*Works of Sir William Temple*, 1770, III, 7).

19. I am indebted to Professor J. C. Beckett for some valuable comments on this whole question.

20. Wittkowsky, 91–3, and Thomas B. Gilmore, Jr, '*A Modest Proposal* and *Intelligencer* Number XVIII', *The Scriblerian*, II.i (Autumn 1969), 28–9, draw attention to the fact that Thomas Sheridan had in 1728 cited in the *Intelligencer*, No. XVIII, an account from Fynes Moryson's *Itinerary* (1617), of Irish women eating children, and in one case children eating the flesh of their dead mother (see *The Intelligencer*, 1729, 195–6). Several numbers of the *Intelligencer*, including one by Swift himself (No. XIX), dealt with the condition of Ireland. No. XV contained a reprint of Swift's *Short View of the State of Ireland*. See also Spenser's *View of the Present State of Ireland*, in *Spenser's Prose Works*, Variorum Edition, ed. Rudolf Gottfried (Baltimore, 1949), 158, and (for other sources) annotation, 382. Spenser is advocating measures for subduing the Irish so that they will 'quicklye Consume themselues and devour one another', having already displayed their cannibal propensities anyway. Critics differ as to whether this is 'a terrible proposal, uttered with cold deliberateness', or more neutral or compassionate (p. 381).

    In Swift's own time, cannibal jokes and associated ironies about, for example, flaying the Irish and selling their skins, were evidently not uncommon, whether in a contemptuous or a compassionate or other context: see the examples cited in Clayton D. Lein, 'Jonathan Swift and the population of Ireland', *Eighteenth-Century Studies*, VIII (1975), 436 (also cited in *Works*, IX, XX) and 452.

21. Ferguson, 170.

22. Spenser alludes to this throughout much of his *View*, and for other authorities see the Variorum Edition, 309–11, 320 etc. Sir William Temple devoted a whole section of his essay 'Of Heroic Virtue' to a (not altogether unfavourable) account of the Scythians, noting that those who conquered Scotland and Ireland 'retained more of the ancient Scythians . . . both in their language and habit' (*Works of Sir William Temple*, 1770, III, 347–68, 351; also III, 78–80, a passage from *An Introduction to the History of England*, which notes the habit of 'eating blood they brew from living cattle'). For hostile analogies, see Donald T. Torchiana, 'Jonathan Swift, the Irish, and the Yahoos: the case reconsidered', *Philological Quarterly*, LIV (1975), 195–212, esp. 197 (special number published separately as *From Chaucer to Gibbon. Essays in Memory of Curt A. Zimansky*, ed. William Kupersmith, Iowa City, 1975). Strabo reports that the Scythians used to castrate their horses like English Yahoos (Strabo, *Geography*, VII.iv. 8, Loeb edn, III, 249; *Gulliver's Travels*, IV. ix, *Works*, XI, 272–3).

23. Spenser, Variorum Edition, 108, 112, and annotation, 340, 343–4. On the Scythians, see Herodotus, IV. lxiv, lxx.

24. Strabo, *Geography*, IV.v.4; VII.iii.6–7 (Loeb edn, II, 259–61; III, 189, 195, 199).

25. Noted by Johannes Boemus (1571), and cited in annotation to Spenser, Variorum Edition, 328. For the manufacture by the Scythians of various objects out of the parts of human bodies, see Herodotus, IV, lxiv, lxv; Strabo, *Geography*, VII.iii.6–7 (Loeb edn, III, 189, 197). Cf. the passage of 1716 by Archbishop William King, adapting these motifs to the sad predicament of the Irish poor: 'I cannot See how any more can be got from them, except we take away their potatoes and buttermilk or flay them and Sell their Skins' (cited Lein, *op. cit.*, 452).

26. At I, 178 it is also said that the 'noble [Irish] Nation, hath of all others. . . degenerated least from the Purity of the Old *Tartars*'. On Tartars and

Irishmen see also XII, 19 and the quotations from Berkeley in Torchiana, *op. cit.*, 197.

27. E.g. as 'a vague "northern nation"' (annotation to Spenser, Variorum Edition, 327). It is presumably as generalized Barbarians that the Scythians and Tartars are referred to in Blackmore's *Satyr Against Wit* (1699), ll.277–8 (*Poems on Affairs of State*, VI, ed. Frank H. Ellis, New Haven and London, 1970, 149).
28. For scriptural echoes and allusions in Swift's Irish writings, see C. A. Beaumont, *Swift's Use of the Bible* (Athens, Georgia, 1965), 36–52. Beaumont, p. 66, says that the *Modest Proposal* 'ignores the Bible' because Biblical allusions would be inappropriate in a work purportedly written by 'a modern economic projector', but Robert A. Greenberg has suggested in a persuasive note that a source of the cannibal formula might have been the frequent and 'almost conventional Old Testament admonition that unless the Hebrews mend their ways they will be reduced (amongst other extremities) to the eating of their children' ('*A Modest Proposal* and the Bible', *Modern Language Review*, LV (1960), 568–9). For Swift's sarcastic exploitation of the cannibal formula, there may also have been a patristic model in Tertullian's *Apology* (see Donald C. Baker, 'Tertullian and Swift's *A Modest Proposal*', *Classical Journal*, LII (1957), 219–20, and J. W. Johnson, 'Tertullian and *A Modest Proposal*', *Modern Language Notes*, LXXIII (1958), 561–3).
29. Ferguson, 173.
30. For a fuller recent discussion of this point, see Torchiana, *op. cit.* For the widespread view of the Irish as savages, see especially *ibid.*, 196–202.
31. Ferguson, 17. See *Works*, II, 120, and cf. X, 104. I think Ferguson may here be exaggerating the 'easy callousness', which, in so far as it is evident, is partly ironic. But the general point that Swift often took a harsh view of the native Irish is undoubtedly right.
32. Ferguson, 150.
33. J. C. Beckett, 'Swift and the Anglo-Irish tradition', *Focus: Swift*, ed. C. J. Rawson (1971), 161–2.
34. Auden, *Collected Shorter Poems 1927–1957* (1966), 146–7.
35. *Ibid.*, 157. Compare with the first line a late eighteenth-century prose usage in John Howard's *State of the Prisons*, about Amsterdam: 'In this city they compute 250,000 souls . . .' (Everyman edn, London and New York, 1929, 54). Both the cold statistical and the compassionate usages were common long before Swift and remained common long after (see *Oxford English Dictionary* Soul 12 and 13; for some examples with a close bearing on Swift see *Letters to and from Persons of Quality. Being the Third Volume of Irish Writings from the Age of Swift*, ed. Andrew Carpenter (Dublin, 1974), 18, and passages cited in Lein, *op. cit.*, 435, 441). Howard and Auden are perhaps merging the two usages, creating compassionate connotations by charging the statistical usage with bitterness or irony in varying degrees. Perhaps to some extent Swift does so too. For a specialized irony, exploited in Gogol's *Dead Souls*, see T. E. Little, 'Dead Souls', in *Knaves and Swindlers. Essays on the Picaresque Novel in Europe*, ed. Christine J. Whitbourn (London, New York and Toronto, 1974), 115.
36. Ferguson, 175.
37. Wittkowsky, 90ff. It has been suggested that an immediate source for Swift's reference to this maxim might have been Sir William Temple's essays 'Upon the Advancement of Trade in Ireland' and 'Of Popular Discontents' (F. V. Bernard, 'Swift's maxim on populousness: a possible source', *Notes and Queries*, CCX (1965), 18). The first of these essays has also been suggested as a possible source of the *Modest Proposal* in other respects (Thomas B. Gilmore, Jr, 'Swift's *Modest Proposal*: a possible source', *Philological Quarterly*, XLVII (1968), 590–2).

38. Louis Landa, reviewing Wittkowsky in *Philological Quarterly*, XXIII (1944), 179. See also Landa's '*A Modest Proposal* and populousness', *Modern Philology*, XL (1942), 161–70, and (for the larger question of Swift's general attitude to mercantilism) 'Swift's economic views and mercantilism', *ELH: A Journal of English Literary History*, X (1943), 310–35.
39. Landa, review of Wittkowsky, 179, and the more complex discussions of the question of emigration in '*A Modest Proposal* and populousness', *passim*, and Ferguson, 161ff. For two discussions of emigration by Swift himself, see XII, 58–61 and 75–7.
40. Ferguson, 162. For Swift's concern 'about the danger of depopulation' and useful accounts of his attitude to the question of emigration, see Ferguson, 161–4, and Lein, *op. cit.*, 431–53, esp. 443–5 (on emigration).
41. See Ferguson, 176–7.
42. It was not unprecedented for writers on Irish affairs to toy more or less ambiguously with notions of large-scale extermination. See n.20 above, and 'A Brief Note of Ireland', possibly also by Spenser, Variorum Edition, 240, 244, and cross-references at 439 n.328–9.
43. On the legal basis, developed in the preceding century and a half in England, for whipping beggars back to their own parish, see *Hudibras*, ed. John Wilders (1967), 377 (note to II.i.817), and Hill, *Society and Puritanism*, 261.

3

Swift's Comic Poetry

COLIN J. HORNE

Swift was not habitually a gloomy, bitter, or even an angry man, and he was certainly not unsociable. On the contrary he much enjoyed the company of a variety of friends, was generally welcome among them, and had a strong propensity to mirth and a declared preference for 'laughing'. He liked to think that he could 'encounter Vice with Mirth' and admitted that his women friends were more amenable to his 'merriment' (his own word for his playfulness with them) than his 'scolding'.[1] Pretending that he was already dead by 1731, he could present himself, not altogether distorting the truth about his life up to that time, as one who in the memory of his acquaintances 'Was cheerful to his dying Day'.[2]

Though to plead, as he does, that he 'Hardly can be grave in Prose'[3] is an obvious quibble, there are nevertheless frequent passages in *A Tale of a Tub* and *Gulliver's Travels* that are genuinely funny. One need only cite Gulliver's resourceful method of quenching the conflagration in the royal palace of Lilliput, his soberly farcical account of his escapade with the monkey at the court of Brobdingnag, or his circumstantial accounts of the ludicrous projects in the Grand Academy of Lagado.[4] Swift's lively comedy of clothes and manners in the parable of the three brothers, Peter, Martin, and Jack, in *A Tale* is an extension in robuster spirit of Restoration drama. This flair for comic situation and dialogue was maintained throughout his life in the collection of observed instances that he accumulated over the years for *Polite Conversation* (1738) and *Directions to Servants* (1745). Arbuthnot was not being disingenuous when he wrote admiringly to Swift, 'Gulliver is a happy man that at his age can write such a merry work'.[5] But it is only in Swift's poetry, and intermittently in his letters, that this lighter, more genial side of his nature is clearly evident.

In the poetry there are abundant instances of his love of fun and nonsense, of jokes and amusing trifling, never wholly nonsensical, for it is always charged with intellectual acuity as well as verbal wit, and mostly has some moral concern in view. We often see him there among his friends, quizzically jolly rather than radiantly genial, and in his poetry we become more intimate with the man than we do in his prose. Writing verse was necessary to him for relaxation and relief from his cares and his indignation with the world. Though much of it was directed to those political and moral issues that find fuller expression in his prose, he nevertheless was more at ease, often even gay, in his verse. It is precisely this 'easiness and gaiety' that Dr Johnson singles out as most characteristic of Swift's poetry,[6] and indeed Swift's own age was more aware of his jesting, more responsive to his humorous and downright comic spirit, than subsequent readers have been. In the remarkable range and variety of his poetry there is ample scope for his rendering of the comic view of life in a serious and even profound way. Nevertheless his always keen sense of the ridiculous attitudes struck by designing and conceited men, and of the general absurdity of human behaviour, provides many occasions for overt laughter in his poetry. This readiness to laugh and jest needs to be set over against the bitter, more tragic strain that so often darkens his prose.[7] So it is that I want to direct attention to some of the poems that are truly comic in the more popular sense of that term as being funny, those that provoke in the reader the sense of pleasing amusement in the form of entertainment that disposes one to laughter, or at least to a smile of complicity and approval.

I am all the more disposed to emphasize Swift's jocularity because the main defect of Swift criticism has been to take him too solemnly as 'the gloomy Dean' who never let up in his hatred of human folly. I wish to take a corrective view. Many readers today find it difficult to assent to Arbuthnot's verdict that Swift was a 'happy man' who had written 'a merry work'. Yet scarcely anyone in his day knew Swift better than this early and constant friend; nor was he the only contemporary who had this more balanced view of Swift's nature. It is significant, though not generally known, that his verse was well represented in one of the most popular of eighteenth-century collections of comic verse, *The Muse in Good Humour*, an anthology so much to the taste of the age that it passed through at least eight editions from 1744 onwards.[8] In those volumes Swift's poems about drabs and whores and fine ladies, prattling and posing, painting, pissing and shitting, the very poems that the complacent modern reader of *Ulysses* and *Portnoy's Complaint* finds too indecent to be funny, are well represented. Eighteenth-century readers, up to the mid-century at least, often found them matter for a good hearty laugh and did not think Swift, or the women he wrote about, any the less human because of that.

There were of course objectors, but some of their retorts on behalf of women were little different in manner. Lady Mary Wortley Montagu, in seeking to discredit Swift, proved herself as much an adept in coarseness and obscenity without the grace of an equal wit, but with a resort to bawdiness such as Swift habitually eschews.[9] At worst, Orrery and Delany and Hawkesworth charge him with a 'general want of delicacy and decorum'. 'The subjects of his poems', says Orrery, 'are often nauseous', but against this he commends the performances as 'beautifully disagreeable'. The others conclude that the poems are censured 'with no better reason than a medicine would be rejected for its ill taste'.[10] Johnson's later condemnation of the grossness of the images was more scathing. It was an aberration, he found, common to Pope and Swift, both of whom 'had an unnatural delight in ideas physically impure, such as every other tongue utters with unwillingness, and of which every ear shrinks from the mention'.[11] Whatever Johnson's sense of humour, and his acquaintances were not agreed about it, his revulsion was in part a reflection of the developed sentimentalism and accompanying prudery that emerges in the later eighteenth century. It was just such attitudes of false delicacy and unreal refinement, in their earlier manifestations in the literature of romantic love, that Swift had mocked in these very poems. Significantly this queasy sensibility appeared first in Richardson, whose Clarissa Harlowe and Harriet Byron were revolted by the offence given to pure minds by Swift's indecency and 'dirty imagination'.[12] It must equally be recognized that robustness, and even coarseness, in both subject and expression were not only tolerated in Swift's time but accepted and enjoyed as genuinely comic, even funny. It is precisely for this lack of seriousness and moral design that Richardson reprehends Swift's comic poetry.[13] The grosser features of human nature were neither blinked nor found improper matter for art, as witness Hogarth and the caricaturists. Coarseness was accepted as irremediably natural and, as one might observe in a Swiftian kind of pun, fundamental to man, and woman too.

The so-called scatological poems, especially those on women, are now taken too soberly. There are at least passages in one of the most notorious of these poems, 'A Beautiful Young Nymph Going to Bed', at which it is difficult to resist a laugh, and that not unkindly:[14]

Then, seated on a three-legg'd Chair,
Takes off her artificial Hair:
Now, picking out a Crystal Eye,
She wipes it clean, and lays it by.
Her Eye-Brows from a Mouse's Hyde.
Stuck on with Art on either Side,
Pulls off with Care, and first displays 'em,
Then in a Play-Book smoothly lays 'em.
Now dextrously her Plumpers draws,
That serve to fill her hollow Jaws.
Untwists a Wire; and from her Gums
A Set of Teeth completely comes.
Pulls out the Rags contriv'd to prop
Her flabby dugs and down they drop.
(ll. 9–22)

It is not disgust, much less pathos, but the visible grotesqueness that hits us in reading that passage, with its lively, graphic, and unexpected details. Such is the battered chair with a missing leg, not a properly commodious three-legged stool but a decrepit, unstable seat befitting a 'nymph' whom hard and long wear have similarly deprived of many of her more commodious parts. The 'Crystal Eye', stock image of poetic amorists, is here, most piquantly, literally glass, a physical fact. The emphatic alliteration of the last line has the same effect of intensified reality and invites a sudden gust of surprised laughter, exactly like the jolt given by the conclusion of a witty joke or 'dirty' story. In comparison the account in *Clarissa* of the dishevelled strumpets gathered round the deathbed of the bawd, Mrs Sinclair, singularly lacks the vividness and comic energy of Swift's poem.[15] Though Richardson's language is more temperate his intention, nevertheless, is harsher. The declared purpose of this sordid, macabre scene is, in Belford's words, to make Lovelace and the reader 'hate a profligate woman', and specific comparison is made with a proper hatred of the Yahoos. Richardson allows no possibility of pity or pathos. The presence of such sentiments in 'A Beautiful Young Nymph' is largely a discovery of the modern age. The basic difference between Swift and Richardson is not here but in the lack of hatred and the dominance of the comic mode in the poem. Gusto dispels disgust; the verve of the realized details of her toilette transforms potential horror and pity into a rich apprehension of the ludicrous plight of the 'nymph'.

Similarly jocular is the less physical but equally adept depiction of feminine flightiness in a passage of pure comedy of manners from 'The Furniture of a Woman's Mind':[16]

> If chance a Mouse creeps in her Sight,
> Can finely counterfeit a Fright;
> So, sweetly screams if it comes near her,
> She ravishes all Hearts to hear her.
> Can dext'rously her Husband teize,
> By taking Fits whene'er she please:
> By frequent Practice learns the Trick
> At proper Seasons to be sick;
> Think nothing gives one Airs so pretty;
> At once creating Love and Pity.
> (ll. 33–42)

Here the comic effect arises not so much from the ludicrous depiction of objects reflecting the situation as from the double value given to the metrically emphatic key-words, 'counterfeit', 'sweetly', 'ravishes', 'dext'rously', 'proper Seasons', 'pretty', 'Pity'. The ironical rhyme 'pretty-

Pity' precisely sums up the feeling of amused scorn for this flighty young minx.

In Swift's earlier poetry there is a more unalloyed and gentler sense of fun, prevalent in such pieces as 'The Humble Petition of *Frances Harris*', 'The History of Vanbrug's House', 'Baucis and Philemon', and the poems that promulgated the announcement of a fictitious death for the unfortunate astrologer Partridge. In 'The History of Vanbrug's House'[17] Swift approaches his theme through an analogy with the self-consuming life-cycle of the silkworm:

> There is a Worm by Phœbus bred,
> By Leaves of Mulberry is fed;
> Which unprovided where to dwell,
> Consumes it self to weave a Cell.
> Then curious Hands this Texture take,
> And for themselves fine Garments make.
> Mean time a Pair of awkward Things
> Grew to his Back instead of Wings;
> He flutters when he Thinks he flyes,
> Then sheds about his Spaun, and dyes.
> Just such an Insect of the Age
> Is he that scribbles for the Stage.
> (ll. 29–40)

He proceeds to use this analogy to exhibit Vanbrugh's ineptitude as both architect and dramatist, all of it a fairly good-humoured jeer at the small, pretentious house Vanbrugh had built himself on the ruins of Whitehall Palace. It is at the same time a comment by a true wit on the falsity 'of Modern Witt and Style' (l. 83). Similarly in 'Baucis and Philemon'[18] the dexterous manipulation of a witty analogy accomplishes the metamorphosis of a humble cottage in Kent into the village church:

> The Groaning Chair was seen to crawl
> Like an huge Snail half up the Wall;
> There stuck aloft, in Publick View,
> And with small Change, a Pulpit grew.
> (ll. 85–8)

Through the intermediary of the sluggish snail, the chair in which pregnant women were confined during labour is transformed, grotesquely but appropriately, into the pulpit. Swift's comment on a kind of ranting preaching to which he always took exception had been made more specifically in the earlier version of the poem,[19] where the pulpit,

mindfull of it's antient State,
Still Groans while tatling Gossips prate.
(ll. 109–10)

Further on, with the same entertainingly inventive fancy, and by a parallel analogy that similarly depicts behaviour in church,

A Bedstead of the Antique Mode,
Compact of Timber many a Load,
Such as our Grandsires wont to use,
Was Metamorphos'd into Pews;
Which still their antient Nature keep;
By lodging Folks dispos'd to Sleep.
(ll. 101–6)

As so often with Swift, the 'pay-off' comes as apt anticlimax in the last line.

This fertile, one might almost call it highly imaginative, exploitation of the comic effects lurking in analogies is akin to the metaphysical conceit, here converted to a comic role. Not far-fetched, but homely, images are brought together by an unusual insight into the natural essence of objects in order to promote simple truths by the revealed likeness of things seemingly unlike. By means of this metamorphic or transformational method Swift sets static objects in motion, seeing them as it were from the other side as 'through the looking glass'. His later delight in riddles, a primitive activity where superior knowing is magical power, and in which 'there lurks the profoundest wisdom concerning the origins of existence',[20] has something of the same basis. Normally, in looking at objects and people we attach to them their attributes as such, and appearance cuts us off from recognition of the reality. In a riddle the process is reversed, and from a collection of attributes we deduce the thing itself, its basic substance and form. These are the processes at the core of Swift's comic art of transposition and reversal.

While these basic methods remained permanent in Swift's comic poetry, the tone changed markedly and much of the geniality was lost in his later work. The Irish milieu and the society to which Swift was both committed and confined in that country, colonial and parochial as it was, had something to do with this. The humour becomes more often tainted with a caustic wit and a sour view of society, though jesting and high spirits kept breaking through his many frustrations of spirit and purpose. Much of the poetry remains personal and social and he is himself his own best subject, pre-eminently so in the well-known 'Verses on the Death of Dr. *Swift*', but also in many other poems such as those written during his country-house visits to Gaulstown and Market Hill. He was a difficult, demanding, but not unacceptable guest, and he at least, if not always his hosts, enjoyed his visits to Sheridan's dilapidated dwelling at Quilca and the country houses of the Irish gentry. One such visit is recounted in 'The Journal', written when he was staying with the Rochforts in 1721 at Gaulstown House.[21] He records with relish and almost exuberant enjoyment, and with genuine wit, the commonplace events of a day in his life there:

Begin, my Muse, first from our Bowers,
We issue forth at different Hours;
At Seven, the *Dean* in Night-gown drest,
Goes round the House to wake the rest:
At Nine, grave *Nim* and *George* Facetious,
Go to the *Dean* to read *Lucretius*.
At Ten, my Lady comes and Hectors,
And kisses *George*, and ends our Lectures:
And when she has him by the Neck fast,
Hawls him, and scolds us down to Breakfast.
(ll. 3–12)

The Dean *en déshabillé du matin*, though always imperious and no doubt something of a trial, was not lacking in charm, even though he did outstay his welcome on this, and other visits.[22] With a few sharp strokes he depicts, later in the day,

How *Dan* caught nothing in his Net,
And how the boat was over set,

adding wryly,

For brevity I have retrench'd
How in the Lake the *Dean* was drench'd.
(ll. 61–4)

One gathers that the misadventure was received mirthfully rather than rancorously.

It is relevant to observe, in a consideration of the mirthful strain in Swift, that another of these country-house poems, 'The Grand Question debated',[23] was written in the summer of 1729, much about the time when he was composing his sardonically grim *Modest Proposal*. It is a rollicking poem in colloquial dialogue between Sir Arthur Acheson, his lady, and her maid Hannah on their domestic dispute whether to turn Hamilton's Bawn into a malt-house, which would be profitable to its owner, or a barracks mainly to indulge the fancy of the women for military company. Though not lacking a caustic strain, its unflagging jollity is clear evidence that Swift, then exactly in the situation where he could observe the distresses of the country poor and vagrant beggars that prompted his own more weighty 'Proposal', had become neither morbidly depressed nor unrelievedly bitter.

His vein of humour was unchanged when, a year later, he was again staying at Market Hill. In 'A Panegyrick on the Dean',[24] as supposedly delivered by his hostess, Lady Acheson, he gives an invigorating, graphic account of the roles he played there and his energetic participation – perhaps we should call it intermeddling – in the routine activities of the house and estate as 'Dean, Butler, Usher, Jester, Tutor'; or out among the menials as 'Our Thatcher, Ditcher, Gard'ner, Baily', quite absorbed in building two outside privies, with an appropriate address to the 'Goddess Cloacine':

Here, gentle Goddess *Cloacine*
Receives all Off'rings at her Shrine.
In sep'rate Cells the He's and She's
Here pay their Vows with *bended Knees*:
(For, 'tis prophane when Sexes mingle;
And ev'ry Nymph must enter single;
And when she feels an *inward Motion*,
Comes fill'd with *Rev'rence* and Devotion.)
(ll. 205–12)

The transposition effected here recalls the witty exploration in *The Mechanical Operation of the Spirit* of the link between body and spirit, the material explanation that can be given for intellectual and spiritual attitudes. The passage is, in lighter vein, a parallel statement about the comic dilemma that lies at the root of the human condition. Denis Donoghue has reminded us that, contrary to the supposedly perverted 'excremental vision', Swift had a genuine respect for the body and the facts of nature that its functions impress on man.[25] To this I would add Swift's profound awareness of the truths of the physicality of objects, animals, and men. For all his scoffing at projectors and virtuosi, he was very alert to the implications of the new age of the physical sciences in which he wrote. It is one of the reasons for the markedly dramatic reality of Swift's comic writing.

In his social encounters he kept up, above all, a flow of ingenious, inventive jesting which – so at least he claimed in this same poem – 'never yet a Friend has lost you' because, again on his own view of himself,

You judge so nicely to a Hair,
How far to go, and when to spare.
(ll. 113–16)

His friends did at times feel the strain of Swift's untiring badinage and he was unsparing with mere acquaintances whose impertinence invited rebuke. Thus, of the earlier occasion at Gaulstown, with a cutting shift of tone from the companionably jocose to a disdainful contempt for humbug, he records the call upon the Rochforts of the pompous Dean Percival and his silly, chattering wife:[26]

I might have told how oft *Dean Per*[*civa*]*l*
Displays his Pedantry unmerciful,
How haughtily he lifts his Nose,
To tell what ev'ry School Boy knows:
And with his Finger on his Thumb,
Explaining strikes opposers Dumb;
And how his Wife that Female Pedant,
But now there need no more be said on't,
Shews all her Secrets of House keeping,
For Candles, how she trucks her Driping;
Was forc'd to send three Miles for Yest,
To brew her Ale, and raise her Paste:
Tells ev'ry thing that you can think of,
How she cur'd *Charley* of the Chincough;
What gave her Brats and Pigs the Meazles,
And how her Doves were kill'd by Weezles.

Both speech and mannerisms are observed with precision and deployed unmercifully, with a comic heightening of triviality and a virtuosity of rhyming that is in every sense killing. Percival was at least sufficiently wounded to charge Swift in print with a gross breach of the Rochforts' hospitality, not without some justification, it would seem.[27]

With his chosen friends, and particularly women with some pretensions to good sense and a readiness to respond to his chidings, Swift was indulgent and affectionate. Even such friends, notably the facetious, feckless, and indiscreet Rev. Thomas Sheridan and the querulous, sharp-nosed Lady Acheson, are subjected to reproaches, at times hectoring, that could be hurtful. He is most amusing and sympathetic where he can combine genuine affection and friendship with teasing censure, and his domineering manner rarely lost him a coveted friend. Those closest to him apparently knew how to take it; 'Dr. Swift', said Pope, 'has an odd, blunt way that is mistaken by strangers for ill-nature'.[28] We, on our part, can now recognize it as a form of over-compensation against the prevailing mode of fulsomely polite panegyric. Furthermore, it is a question how often Swift was deliberately playing the part expected of him, that of the irritable, irascible, censorious dignitary, and whether his companions were not genuinely entertained by the exaggeration to the point of virtuosity of what he described as 'my own hum'rous biting way'.[29] Johnson divined this when he observed, 'This authoritative and magisterial language he expected to be received as his peculiar mode of jocularity.'[30] His friends, Swift said, 'would let him have his way'.[31] Perhaps they accepted it as a mark of trust and mutual understanding, even a way, however perversely seeming, of conveying his affection for them.

However exaggerated by the power of sharp observation and the focussed physicality of his rendering of action and situation in words, both so typical of Swift's genius, this rough handling was an accepted mode of raillery in the period and his friends were rarely as outraged by it as we might be in similar circumstances. Though he did not always observe it in practice, Swift himself understood better than most the distinction between railing and raillery and was quite sincere in his abhorrence of

> that senseless Tribe,
> Who call it Humour when they jibe.[32]

An honest man, with too much self-knowledge for his own comfort, he was correspondingly uneasy that he could himself fairly be censured for lapsing on occasion into 'Gibes' and 'Jeers'.[33] He did not want to be, as he observed his thoughtlessly volatile friend Sheridan too often was, one of those 'pert Dunces of Mankind' who,

> Whene're they would be thought refin'd,
> Because the Diff'rence lyes abstruse
> 'Twixt Raillery and gross Abuse,
> To show their Parts, will scold and rail,
> Like Porters o'er a Pot of Ale.[34]

In this same poem '*To Mr.* Delany' he selects 'Humor, Raillery and Witt' as the 'Three Gifts for Conversation fit' and sets about defining each. Humour, he found, was incapable of exact definition, except that it is a natural gift and gives delight, while wit surprises:

> Humor is odd, grotesque, and wild,
> Onely by Affectation spoild,
> Tis never by Invention got,
> Men have it when they know it not.

Raillery is not a crude matter of 'the Horse-laugh and dry Rub' because it requires delicacy of feeling to achieve its proper function as 'an obliging Ridicule', a jest that is rightly received as a transparent compliment. It must never reproach a friend 'For those Defects he cannot mend': that is railing, and railing is gross and objectionable.[35] Though no one was more subtle than Swift, nor more brilliant, in his flashes of friendly raillery, from the opposite fault of grossness in personal address he was not however entirely immune. His naturally passionate spirit too often inflamed him to an excess of anger and contempt that would sweep him beyond the bounds of urbane raillery into scathing attack and lampoon. That strain, however, is more often to be found in his political verse than in his truly comic poems.

Even in the latter it is open to question whether Swift was not too much obsessed with outward behaviour and the observable actions no less of his friends than his victims. It is all part of his unceasing and unresolvable preoccupation with the relation of appearance to reality. Whether he was being serious or comic, there was always in his disposition, it seems fairly obvious, a defective sensitivity for other people's feelings (as distinct from his own) and a failure to recognize that the motives behind their seemingly objectionable behaviour might not be entirely unreasonable, at least if considered from their own point of view. In fairness it must be allowed that, if he had little sense of empathy, he did at times acknowledge himself to be not entirely free from offence, and even offensiveness. The comic poems already instanced, and notably 'Verses on the Death of Dr. *Swift*', his serio-comic apologia, contain knowledgeable self-portraits in which his characteristic traits are no less justly than humorously delineated. He could laugh wryly at himself because he understood himself only too well. He mocks and castigates in others what he has first discovered, and disliked, in himself. That is one good reason why he could maintain that 'Malice never was his Aim'.[36]

His tartness, I believe, was often a protective covering for his acute self-sensitivity and he was never put out by frank, natural vulgarity. In his Rabelaisian gusto for the vulgar joke there is nothing very sinister or revolting. The animal functions of humans, where they do not tend to lewdness, he was capable of translating into witty images of man's captivity to his body. It is the mirror image of his obsession with cleanliness, another aspect of the process of reversal in his art, which tries to arrive at reality through a dialectic of opposites, each of which has to be recognized and accepted. Such were the riddles that he bandied in bouts of merriment and a frenzy of rhyming exchanges with Sheridan. The innocent amusement that Coleridge derived from these riddles attaches no less to specimens like '*The* Gulph *of all* human Possessions', the solution to which is a privy.[37] The appositeness of the implications that Swift discovers in this necessary, lowly object reminds us once again of the conceits and emblem literature of the seventeenth century, though the ingenious twists and surprising parallels are contrivances entirely his own. The poem is indeed a glass in which the beholder may observe every *face* but his own, yet see himself as he truly is:

Come hither and behold the Fruits,
Vain Man, of all thy vain Pursuits.
Take wise Advice, and *look behind*,
Bring all *past* Actions to thy Mind.
Here you may see, as in a Glass,
How soon all human Pleasures pass.
How will it mortify thy Pride,
To turn the true impartial Side!
How will your Eyes contain their Tears,
When all the sad *Reverse* appears!
(ll. 1–10)

Swift was particularly at ease with common, lowly people, and for them he had an unaffected liking, prompted by an affinity with their simple humanity and even their failings. As a young man on his journeys to Leicester he chose to put up at rough 'penny lodgings', a preference which Lord Orrery imputed to 'his innate love of grossness and vulgarity' but which Johnson more perspicaciously attributes to 'his desire of surveying human life through all its varieties'.[38] Though he could be overbearing towards them, he was on easy terms with his own servants and those of his hosts at Quilca, Gaulstown, and Market Hill. He represents Lady Acheson as 'lamenting' his familiarity with them:[39]

He's all the day saunt'ring,
With labourers bant'ring,
Among his colleagues,
A parcel of Teagues,
(Whom he brings in among us
And bribes with mundungus.)
Hail fellow, well met,
All dirty and wet:
Find out, if you can,
Who's master, who's man;
Who makes the best figure,
The Dean or the digger;
And which is the best
At cracking a jest.

These are jovial Skeltonics, where the swinging rhythms and gaily 'bant'ring' rhymes echo the complete relaxation he found in the company of homely labourers. In this and other comic verse of the kind there appears to be a direct link with the tradition of Gaelic humour, as emerges further in 'A Pastoral Dialogue' between Dermot and Sheelah.[40] The Irish dialogue is not primarily parody of the artificiality of pastoralism so much as indulgence in positive, even boisterous, enjoyment:

DERMOT

No more that Bry'r thy tender Leg shall rake:
(I spare the Thistle for Sir *Arthur*'s sake.)
Sharp are the Stones, take thou this rushy Matt;
The hardest Bum will bruise with sitting squat.

SHEELAH

Thy Breeches torn behind, stand gaping wide;
This Petticoat shall save thy dear Back-side;
Nor need I blush, although you feel it wet;
Dermot, I vow, 'tis nothing else but Sweat.
(ll. 17–24)

There can be no doubt that he had a genuine affection for these simple creatures and felt for them as people, much more perhaps than for their betters. This again is the reverse image of *A Modest Proposal* and was written at the same time: it is only in the poem that life is affirmed, as it is in the thumping energy of 'The Description of an *Irish-Feast*', itself 'translated almost literally out of the Original *Irish*':[41]

They dance in a Round,
Cutting Capers and Ramping,
A Mercy the Ground
Did not burst with their stamping.
The Floor is all wet
With Leaps and with Jumps,
While the Water and Sweat,
Splish, splash in their Pumps.
(ll. 37–44)

For all his insistence on his Englishness (a frequent stance of the colonist) Swift took on a good deal of the quality of the country in which he was actually born. 'In one or other of his writings', observes Vivian Mercier, 'Swift displays all the most strongly marked features of the Gaelic comic tradition' and seems to fit comfortably into it.[42] My own residence of ten years in Ireland prompts me to the view that Irish humour, very like Swift's, is both boisterous and slily personal, sardonic and physical, even to the point of cruelty. The Irishman's fun is apt to end in fighting, and what he does in fun can all too readily become brutally serious. By temperament, as in the cast of his humour, Swift was very much akin to the Irish and they have always claimed him, with affection and admiration, as a genuine Irishman.

Swift's sympathy for simple, ordinary people extended to their vernacular speech, for the nuances of which he had an amazing ear. He saw its potential for comedy of a kind that is neither mocking nor condescending because it is felt and rendered through the mind of the putative speaker. His comic poetry is enlivened with passages of this kind and 'The Humble Petition of *Frances Harris*', 'Mary the Cook-Maid's Letter', and 'The Grand Question debated' are classic renditions in this manner:[43]

> So the *Chaplain* came in. Now the Servants say, he is my Sweet-heart,
> Because he's always in my Chamber, and I always take his Part;
> So, as the *Devil* would have it, before I was aware, out I blunder'd,
> *Parson*, said I, can you cast a *Nativity*, when a Body's plunder'd?
> (Now you must know, he hates to be call'd *Parson*, like the *Devil*.)
> Truly, says he, Mrs. *Nab*, it might become you to be more civil:
> If your Money be gone, as a Learned *Divine* says, d'ye see,
> You are no *Text* for my Handling, so take that from me.

It is not just the vocabulary and idiom that he recaptures, but the intonation, tempo, and total tonality of the speech. This is so perfectly right as spoken verse that one is astounded to learn from Swift's own report, confirmed by Deane Swift, that he 'was famous for reading verses the worst in the world'.[44]

It is obvious that Swift's comic poetry is in most respects at odds with the Meredithean view of the Comic Spirit.[45] In his later residence in Ireland Swift was cut off from the politer society that he had frequented earlier in London, and after 1714

> In Exile with a steady Heart,
> He spent his Life's declining Part;
> Where, Folly, Pride, and Faction sway,
> Remote from ST. JOHN, POPE, and GAY.
>
> His friendship there to few confin'd,
> Were always of the midling Kind.[46]

The world of his comic poetry is not, in Meredithean terms, the truly polite society that provides a congenial habitat for the urbane and cultured spirit of comedy. Swift's life in Ireland coarsened his poetic spirit and blunted the finesse displayed in his earlier poems; at the same time it became more full-bloodedly funny. Meredith observed that

> Contempt is a sentiment that cannot be entertained by comic intelligence. What is it but an excuse to be idly minded, or personally lofty, or comfortably narrow, not perfectly humane?
>
> (p. 63)

In some measure Swift is guilty of all these failings. It is only at times, mostly in his comic verse, that he escapes the pressures and irritations of his world and defuses them with a jest. His detachment is not emotionally or intellectually neutral but a stance of superior wisdom and haughty contempt for failings so prevalent in human behaviour that to most people they seem merely natural. Yet he is perhaps not so much haughty and unfeeling as plagued by a sense of loneness, of not having the general opinion of society behind him. He was a lonely, isolated man. That is why he is most light-hearted, humorous, and likeable when he is among friends or common people.

A comic genius, though not of the serene, refined kind postulated by Meredith, Swift undeniably had, and in the poems here dealt with there is to be found an engaging sense of fun, and a love of the people, of various ranks and natures, in whose company he could energetically indulge it. With 'that vigilance of minute attention' that Johnson noted,[47] he is unsurpassed in his gift of rendering people, objects, and situations with an extraordinary physical actuality. Transfixed under the cold stare of his pale blue eyes, which could suddenly dissolve into merriment, seemingly trivial and commonplace things, as we have seen, take on an excitingly novel and meaningful reality. Unsuspected implications are revealed in seeming ordinariness. The constant flow of energy and dynamic exuberance is at the same time wonderfully controlled and is applied to throw up surprising, novel turns of speech and meaning, often leaving his reader 'bit'. His comic skill is the art of exposure by transformation and reversal. Much of the poetry is designedly anti-poetic as well as anti-romantic. The product is none the less genuine poetry which, though its models can be found in popular as well as classical literature, was, as his contemporaries recognized, of a quite new kind. In his poetry, at least as much as in his prose, Swift was a genuine original. He brought new matter into poetry and had a great gift for inventing, by the renovation of old forms or the devising of new ones, the exquisitely right mode for it. This is particularly true of his comic poetry.

NOTES

Except where otherwise indicated the text of Swift's poems is quoted from *Poetical Works*, ed. Herbert Davis (1967), Oxford Standard Authors edn, cited hereafter as *Poetical Works*.

1. 'An Epistle to a Lady, Who desired the Author to make Verses on Her, in the *Heroick Stile*', 561, ll. 236, 144, 214. Swift's own statements contradict the tradition that he rarely gave way to laughter and are indeed confirmed by Pope's representation of him as a relaxed and convulsive laugher: 'laugh and shake in Rab'lais' easy chair' (*Dunciad* 1742, I.22).
2. 'Verses on the Death of Dr. *Swift*', 496, l. 481.
3. 'An Epistle to a Lady, etc.', 561, l. 140.
4. *Gulliver's Travels*, I, ch. 5; II, ch. 5; III, chs. 5–6.
5. *The Correspondence of Jonathan Swift*, ed. Harold Williams, III (1963), 179, 5 November 1726.
6. Johnson, *Lives of the English Poets*, ed. G. B. Hill, 3 vols (1905), III, 65.
7. On the subject of Swift's 'enormous gaiety' see Bonamy Dobrée, 'The Jocose Dean', in *Fair Liberty Was All His Cry. A Tercentenary Tribute to Jonathan Swift*, ed. A. Norman Jeffares (1967).
8. *The Muse in Good Humour: Or, A Collection of Comic Tales. By the most Eminent Poets* (1744); 8th edn, 2 vols, 1785). The collection, which also contains pieces by Pope, Prior, Congreve, King, Gay, etc., includes 12 poems and several riddles by Swift, among which are all those that later came to be deprecated as scatological.
9. Robert Halsband, 'The Lady's Dressing-Room "Explicated by a Contemporary" ', in *The Augustan Milieu. Essays Presented to Louis A. Landa*, ed. H. K. Miller, *et al.* (1970), 225–31.
10. *Swift. The Critical Heritage*, ed. Kathleen Williams (1970), 116, 120, 121, 137, 155.
11. Johnson, *op. cit.*, III, 242.
12. Williams, *op. cit.*, 103–5.
13. In a footnote (omitted by Williams, *loc. cit.*) added by Richardson to the letter from Belford to Lovelace (*Clarissa*, Everyman edn, 1932, IV, 381).
14. *Poetical Works*, 517. It is worth noting that Swift thought prostitutes less despicable than termagant women, 'a Tribe of bold, swaggering, rattling Ladies, whose Talents pass among Coxcombs for Wit and Humour'. He would have the latter not only stripped, but kicked downstairs as well. ('A Letter to a Young Lady on her Marriage', *Prose Works*, IX, ed. H. Davis, 1948, 93.)
15. *Ed. cit.*, IV, 380–1.
16. *Poetical Works*, 328.
17. *Poetical Works*, 55.
18. *Poetical Works*, 77.
19. *Poetical Works*, 61.
20. Johan Huizinga, *Homo Ludens. A Study of the Play Element in Culture* (1970, first published 1944), 127–8.
21. *Poetical Works*, 216.
22. The wonder is not so much that Swift eventually tried the patience of his hosts as that, for most of the time, he managed to maintain the appearance of cheerfulness. During his visit he was worried about Vanessa and was suffering from attacks of giddiness and deafness. Cf. *Correspondence*, ed. Williams, II, 407ff.
23. 'The Grand Question debated whether *Hamilton*'s *Bawn* should be turned into a *Barrack* or a *Malt House*', 396.
24. *Poetical Works*, 452.
25. D. Donoghue, *Jonathan Swift. A Critical Introduction* (1969), 96–8.
26. Quoted from the fuller broadside version in *The Poems of Jonathan Swift*, ed. Harold Williams (2nd edn, 1958), I, 281–2, ll. 79–94.
27. Cf. Aubrey Williams, 'Swift and the Poetry of Allusion: "The Journal" ', in *Literary Theory and Structure. Essays in Honor of William K. Wimsatt*, ed. F. Brady *et al.* (New Haven and London, 1973), 228–30. Williams finds in the poem a 'seriocomic conversion' of the genre of Epicurean poems on the bliss of rural retirement.

28. Joseph Spence, *Observations, Anecdotes, and Characters of Books and Men*, ed. James M. Osborn (1966), I, 53.
29. 'Verses on the Death of Dr. *Swift*', 498, l. 54.
30. Johnson, *op. cit.*, III, 60.
31. 'Verses on the Death of Dr. *Swift*', 512, l. 482.
32. *Idem*, ll. 469–70.
33. 'The Grand Question debated', 401, l. 198.
34. '*To Mr.* Delany', 158, ll. 46–50.
35. Ll. 13–14, 25–8, 57, 36, 68.
36. 'Verses on the Death of Dr. *Swift*', 512, l. 463.
37. Coleridge, *Biographia Literaria*, ed. J. Shawcross (1907), I, 44; *Poetical Works*, 621.
38. Johnson, *op. cit.*, III, 6.
39. 'My Lady's Lamentation and Complaint against the Dean', 364, ll. 159–72.
40. *Poetical Works*, 393.
41. *Poetical Works*, 195.
42. Vivian Mercier, *The Irish Comic Tradition* (1962), 76, 188. See also his 'Swift and the Gaelic tradition', in *A Review of English Literature*, III, 3 (1962), 69–79.
43. *Poetical Works*, 49, 163, 396; the ensuing passage is quoted from 'The Humble Petition', ll. 50–7.
44. *Journal to Stella*, ed. Harold Williams (1948), I, 146.
45. George Meredith, *An Essay on Comedy and the Uses of the Comic Spirit*, (1919, Standard Edition), originally delivered as a lecture in 1877.
46. 'Verses on the Death of Dr. *Swift*', 511, ll. 435–40.
47. Johnson, *op. cit.*, III, 56.

4 The Elegy as Exorcism: Pope's 'Verses to the Memory of an Unfortunate Lady'

IAN JACK

From the very beginning too much has been written about the lady, and too little about the poem. 'Pray in your next tell me who was the Unfortunate Lady . . .', John Caryll wrote on 16 July 1717. 'I think you once gave me her history, butt tis now quite outt of my head.'[1] It is clear that Pope did not answer the question,[2] and Caryll's curiosity about the lady was soon shared by a great many other readers. 'What would I not give to know who she was', wrote a correspondent from Boston in 1728, 'and the remarkable circumstances of her History. But I presume too far, and must ask Your Pardon for my Impertinance.'[3] If Spence ever 'presumed' so far as to raise the question we must conclude that he received no answer, as his *Anecdotes* do not contain a single reference to the poem. It is hardly surprising that the problem of identification became something of an obsession with subsequent writers on Pope, and it is necessary to glance at their conjectures before we consider the poem itself.

'This Lady seems to have been a particular Favourite of our Poet,' wrote the unreliable William Ayre, in the *Memoirs* which he rushed out in 1745, 'whether he himself was the Person she was remov'd from I am not able to say, but whoever reads his Verses to her Memory, will find she had a very great Share in him.'[4] His account of her appears to be no more than a fanciful summary based on the Elegy itself: his embellishments include the information that 'Spies being set upon her it was not long before her Correspondence with her Lover of lower Degree was discover'd' and a description of how 'some Young People of the Neighbourhood, who saw her put into common Ground . . . strew'd her Grave with Flowers', a circumstance which 'gave some Offence to the Priesthood, who would have buried her in the Highway, but it seems their Power . . . did not extend so far.'[5]

In 1751 a curious note was appended to the poem, in Warburton's edition:

> See the Duke of Buckingham's verses to a Lady designing to retire into a Monastery compared with Mr. Pope's Letters to several Ladies, p. 206. She seems to be the same person whose unfortunate death is the subject of this poem. P.[6]

While there is no justification for rejecting Warburton's claim that this note is Pope's own, or derives from information supplied by Pope, the word 'seems' is disconcerting. We must assume either that the first sentence is Pope's and the addition Warburton's, or (as would appear more probable) that the whole note is Pope's, and that he is teasing his readers. In any event, neither the poem nor the letter proves helpful. The poem, as printed in the first volume of Pope's edition of *The Works of His Grace The Duke Of Buckingham* in 1723, begins with a rhetorical question which forms a fitting introduction to a thoroughly conventional set of verses:

> What Breast but yours can hold the double Fire
> Of fierce Devotion, and of fond Desire?

There is no reason to believe that these lines have any autobiographical or even historical basis. As for the letter, it had been printed in 1735, in the section of the 'Surreptitious' edition of Pope's letters which contained 'Letters to Several Ladies'. It is undated, but described in the Contents as '*To an unfortunate Lady*'. Pope assures her that she is 'the most valuable thing I know', and congratulates her on the fact that her brother 'will at last prove your relation, and has entertain'd such sentiments as become him in your concern'. He seems to be urging her not 'to rob the world of so much example as you may afford it', but maintains that 'even in a Monastery your devotions cannot carry you so far toward the next world as to make This lose the sight of you'.[7] There is nothing in the letter to prove the reality of the addressee: it could perfectly well be a purely literary composition mischievously inserted to encourage further speculation about the Unfortunate Lady. A few months later, after all, the poem was to be reprinted in the first volume of a new edition of Pope's *Works*, the edition in which (incidentally) the title was changed from 'Verses' to the now familiar 'Elegy'.

If the note was designed to provoke speculation, it succeeded admirably. In *An Essay on the Writings and Genius of Pope*, published in 1756, Joseph Warton admits that 'We are unacquainted with her history, and with that series of misfortunes, which seems to have drawn on the melancholy catastrophe', but continues: 'She is said to be the same person, to whom the Duke of Buckingham has addressed some lines', referring to the poem and letter mentioned in the 'P.' footnote. A page or two later he commits himself to a statement of the dogma which lies behind a great deal of subsequent criticism of the poem:

> If this ELEGY be so excellent, it may be ascribed to this cause; that the occasion of it was real . . . Events that have actually happened are, after all, the properest subjects for poetry.[8]

In the second edition of *An Essay*, six years later, Warton elaborates on the biographical background. He will now only admit that 'We are unacquainted with *the whole of* her history', while he adds an important passage at the end of the penultimate paragraph of the book. Whereas in the first edition he had censured the last eight lines of 'Eloisa to Abelard' and commented that 'They might stand for the conclusion of almost any story', he now writes:

> They might stand *it should seem* for the conclusion of almost any story, were we not informed, that they were added by the Poet in allusion to his own case, and the state of his own mind. For what determined him in the choice of the subject of this epistle, was the retreat of that lady into a nunnery, whose death he had lately so pathetically lamented, in a foregoing Elegy, and for whom he had conceived a violent passion. She was first beloved by a nobleman, an intimate friend of POPE, and, on his deserting her, retired into France; when, before she had made her last vows in the convent, to which she had retreated, she put an end to her unfortunate life. The recollection of this circumstance will add a beauty and a pathos to many passages in the poem, and will confirm the doctrine delivered above, concerning the choice of subject.

In 1796 Owen Ruffhead was content to rely on Ayre, from whom he takes the picturesque detail that the dead lady had been found 'yet warm upon the ground': appropriately enough, as he considers that the poem 'came warm from the heart, and does honour to [Pope's] sensibility'.[9] Johnson clearly wished to be more specific, but failed. 'The lady's name and adventures I have sought with fruitless enquiry,' he observes in his Life of Pope, 'I can therefore tell no more than I have learned from Mr. Ruffhead.' Failing to notice Ruffhead's indebtedness to Ayre, Johnson describes him as a man 'who writes with the confidence of one who could trust his information'. He complains that 'the tale is not skilfully told: it is not easy to discover the character of either the lady or her guardian . . . On such an occasion a poet may be allowed to be obscure, but inconsistency never can be right.' While he allows the Elegy some merit, his irritation at the absence of biographical information and his strong disapproval of suicide – 'Self-murder; the horrid crime of destroying one's self' – leads him to the unworthy observation that 'her desires were too hot for delay, and she liked self-murder better than suspence' and to the well-known conclusion that 'Poetry has not often been worse employed than in dignifying the amorous fury of a raving girl.'[10]

In the year of Johnson's death a pseudonymous correspondent wrote to the *Gentleman's Magazine* to record what he had heard 'long ago, from a very worthy, but obscure, country parson':

> That the lady's name was *Scudamore*; that she and her family were Roman Catholics; that, having fixed her affections on a person not suitable to her, the match was steadily opposed by her uncle and guardian. This created such uneasiness between them, that it was agreed they should separate, and the lady go abroad to a convent. It was to Antwerp, as well as I can recollect, that she was sent; not with a view of taking the veil, but to stay as a boarder, her friends hoping that, by the time she was of age, she might come to better judgement; that she was soon after seized with a fever, which ended in a state of melancholy; and that she some how or other procured a sword, and put an end to her life.[11]

Horace Walpole immediately commented on this 'pretended discovery' in a letter to Joseph Warton, expressing his belief that the writer was 'quite mistaken': 'at least, my Lady Hervey, who was acquainted with Pope, and who lived at the time, gave me a very different name, and told me the exit was made in a less dignified manner – by the rope. I have never spread this . . .'. He promised to give Warton the lady's name when they next met. By that time, as it would appear, Walpole may well have given the name to at least one other enquirer, as Sir John Hawkins wrote in 1787 that he had in his possession

> a letter to Dr. Johnson, containing the name of the lady, and a reference to a gentleman well known in the literary world for her history. Him I have seen, and, from a memorandum of some particulars to the purpose communicated to him by a lady of quality, he informs me that the unfortunate lady's name was Withinbury, corruptly pronounced Winbury; that she was in love with Pope, and would have married him; that her guardian, though she was deformed in her person, looking upon such a match as beneath her, sent her to a convent, and that a noose, and not a sword, put an end to her life.

It seems clear that the gentleman in question was Walpole (and the lady of quality Lady Hervey), since in his MS. notes on Pope Walpole had written:

> The name of this Lady was Withinbury, pronounced Winbury: the seat of her family was Chiras Court, Vulgarly Cheyney's Court, situated under Fromehill, & forming nearly a triangle with Home-Lacy & Hampton-Lacy. It is said that she did not stab, but hang herself.[12]

This information was duly passed on to Warton, who wrote as follows in his edition of Pope:

> The true cause of the excellence of this elegy is, that the occasion of it was real; so true is the maxim, that nature is more powerful than fancy, and that we can always feel more than we can imagine; and that the most artful fiction must give way to truth, for this Lady was beloved by Pope. After many and wide enquiries I have been informed that her name was Wainsbury, and that – which is a singular circumstance – she was as ill-shaped and deformed as our author. Her death was not by a sword, but, what would less bear to be told poetically, she hanged herself.

This is all remarkably circumstantial, and it is certain that Lady Hervey had been in an excellent position to catch such rumours, while Walpole is a reliable retailer of gossip. 'Chira's Court' appears on Isaac Taylor's *Map of the County of Hereford* (1754), about a mile north of Castle Frome, and at the time in question it was occupied by a Roman Catholic family (the Scudamores being the principal aristocrats of the neighbourhood). Unfortunately, however, their name was not any variant of Withinbury, Winbury or Wainsbury, but Slaughter, and an exhaustive search of the County Council Records of Hereford and Worcester has failed to reveal anyone with the name required; while enquiries in the Public Record Office have proved equally fruitless.[13] We must assume that Lady Hervey gave Walpole a more or less accurate account of an old rumour, but the question of the truth of the rumour is another matter. If a lady with some such name as Withinbury had in fact lived at Chiras Court it seems unlikely that she was more than just one of various unfortunate ladies whose fates may have been in Pope's mind as he wrote his poem.

In 1806 a slightly farcical postscript was provided by William Lisle Bowles who, after conceding that 'It is in vain ... perhaps, to attempt further elucidation', nonetheless continues:

> but I should think it unpardonable not to mention what I have myself heard, though I cannot vouch for its truth ... The story which was told to Condorcet by Voltaire, and by Condorcet to a gentleman of high birth and character, from whom I received it, is this: – "That her attachment was not to Pope, or to any Englishman of inferior degree;" but to a young French Prince of the blood royal, Charles Emmanuel Duke of Berry, whom, in early youth, she had met at the court of France.

Bowles concludes, a little tartly, by observing that 'it is most probable that incipient lunacy was the cause of her perverted feelings, and untimely end'.[14]

Incipient lunacy is certainly the danger threatening any scholar who presses too far in this particular enquiry, and one is tempted to comment that criticism has not often been worse employed than in pursuing the shadowy identity of a largely imaginary girl. After more than a century of fruitless conjecture that admirable scholar, Charles Wentworth Dilke, pointed this out. 'All we are told by the biographers', he wrote in *The Athenæum*, 'no matter how circumstantially, is merely conjectural, made up from hints in the Elegy, fanciful interpretations of passages in Pope's letters, assumption of dates, changes of persons, and traditional or original nonsense.'[15] Fortified by his example, Victorian critics proved harder-headed in this matter than their predecessors. In 1871 the Rev. Whitwell Elwin, in his edition of Pope's *Works*, gives copious extracts from earlier writers (though not from Dilke) and comments: 'At variance in nearly every particular, the conflicting histories of the unfortunate lady have the common quality, that they are unsupported by a single circumstance which could warrant the smallest measure of belief... The biographers and editors... had no suspicion that she might be altogether a poetical invention.' It is his conclusion that 'there was no real victim in the case'.[16] In *The Life of Alexander Pope*, published in 1889 as the last volume of the same edition, W. J. Courthope adopts a similar point of view. Although he claims that Pope's sympathy with Mrs Weston provided a 'basis of sincere emotion' for certain passages, he concedes that 'there is scarcely a line in the poem founded on the actual circumstances of the case' and censures earlier critics for believing that 'such an animated expression of feeling could only have been evoked by a series of facts corresponding with the story suggested in the poem'. It is revealing to juxtapose his statement that 'What the "Elegy" really establishes... is Pope's right to be considered a creative poet of genuine pathetic power'[17] and Warton's assumption that the powerful expression of pathos in the poem 'may be ascribed to this cause; that the occasion of it was real'.[18]

Although he is rather less than fair to Elwin and Courthope, George Sherburn comes to a conclusion which is substantially theirs. While he allows that 'the woes of various ladies with brutal parents or husbands may have been sublimated into the tragedy of Pope's lady' (who could allow less?), he concludes that 'no one alone among all those suggested notably parallels her woes'.[19] In his edition of the *Correspondence*, 22 years later than *The Early Career*, he comments somewhat impatiently that the letter to which 'P.'s' note refers was addressed 'to Mrs. Weston, Mrs. Cope, or some other worthy but hitherto unappreciated lady'.[20] Tillotson dutifully repeats the names of Mrs Weston and Mrs Cope, and suggests that the poem may constitute a highly imaginative expression of Pope's love for Lady Mary Wortley Montagu, but he clearly appreciates that the literary context is more important than the biographical or historical, although he refrains from pursuing the matter.[21] The most stimulating discussion of the Elegy is that of Reuben Arthur Brower, who is content to leave the question of the lady's identity unresolved[22] and stresses (perhaps following a hint of Sherburn's) that in the poem she 'is cast as a Roman lover' and that 'the accent of the poet in addressing her is Roman-elegiac'.[23]

As soon as we take the Elegy rather than the lady as the focus of our attention we are reminded that there was an element of fiction in the tradition of the funeral elegy as developed from the poets of antiquity through the neo-Latin and vernacular poets of the Renaissance, as there had been (more prominently) in the tradition of the love elegy from the earliest times. The experience of 'E.K.' with Spenser, almost a century and a half before the publication of Pope's Elegy, was similar to that of Caryll with Pope. 'In this xi. AEglogue', he wrote, 'he bewayleth the death of some mayden of greate bloud, whom he calleth Dido. The personage is secrete, and to me altogether unknowne, albe of him selfe I often required the same.'

The handsome folio edition of his Works which Pope published in 1717 contains the Pastorals and a brilliant collection of other poems in various genres more exacting than the pastoral but less ambitious than the epic to which he already aspired. Nothing could be more appropriate than the presence among such poems of a fine example of the classical elegy. It is true that the fourth Pastoral, 'Winter', is elegiac in form (and we notice that whereas in 1709 it is simply 'To the Memory of a Fair Young Lady', with nothing to prove the reality of the lady, in 1717 Pope yielded to the persuasion of Walsh and headed it 'To the Memory of Mrs. Tempest'[24]); but that was early work. He decided to write another elegy, an elegy (as I believe) which is no more about a particular lady than 'Winter' is about Mrs Tempest, an elegy which is the product of his imagination working upon his reading. A brief consideration of the art which he displays in it may help us to set it more firmly in the tradition to which it belongs.

In his introduction to the Elegy Tillotson did well to quote Pope's observation to Spence: 'Most little poems should be written by a plan. This method is evident in Tibullus and Ovid's elegies, and almost all the pieces of the ancients.'[25] An outline plan for a funeral elegy is provided in the *Poetics* of Julius Caesar Scaliger, which Pope described as 'an exceeding useful book in its kind, and extremely well collected'.[26] For Scaliger the constituent parts of an elegy are the Praise, the Narration, the Lamentation, the Consolation and the Exhortation. He stresses the importance of appropriateness – 'The treatment is different according to whether the song is for an emperor . . . for a private citizen, a man, a woman . . . each one of whom must be treated in the appropriate way' – and points out that whereas an elegy sometimes 'begins with a calm proem' it may also commence 'with an exclamation or interrogation'. He insists on the need for 'A discourse of consolation . . . which restores the mind of the mourner to tranquility'.[27]

Pope's Elegy was clearly 'written by a plan', and elements of Scaliger's scheme may be found in it – though less (one may conjecture) because of Scaliger's precepts than because of the examples of the poets from whose work Scaliger deduced his rules. The centre of Pope's plan is remarkably simple, but also remarkably audacious. His 'Elegy' is a rite of exorcism.

As Thomas Warton pointed out, the opening lines of the poem may well have been suggested by those of Ben Jonson's 'Elegy on the Lady Jane Pawlet',[28] but we notice that the ghost in Pope's poem requires more than the 'garland' which is sought in Jonson's. The Unfortunate Lady, like the ghost of Hamlet's father, cannot rest until a wrong has been righted. This is the principal business of the poem, and it is accomplished by line 68.

If we wish to understand how Pope came to make so uncanonical a use of a Christian rite we shall do well to turn to the discussion of 'Elegy' in Joseph Trapp's *Praelectiones Poeticae*. I quote from the English translation of a book which Pope knew in the Latin, and referred to in a characteristically precise instruction about the printing of *The Rape of the Lock*.[29] 'The chief Subjects to which Elegy owes its Rise', Trapp points out, 'are Death and Love', and he concludes that 'That Elegy, therefore, ought to be esteem'd the most perfect in its Kind, which has somewhat of both at once: Such, for Instance, where the Poet bewails the Death of his *Corinna*, his *Delia*, or *Lycoris*, or of some Youth or Damsel falling a Martyr to Love'.[30] It seems likely that this passage contributed more to the inspiration of Pope's poem than the misfortunes of any particular lady, however 'beauteous', however 'friendly'.

The part of the poem which owes its structure to the rite of exorcism consists of five verse-paragraphs. In the first (ll. 1–10) the poet describes the ghost which has appeared to him, and wonders whether there is

> no bright reversion in the sky,
> For those who greatly think, or bravely die?[31]

The second (ll. 11–22) deals briefly yet powerfully with the traditional topos of Ambition, with a glance at the sluggish souls that lack this 'glorious fault'. In the third (ll. 23–8) the poet speculates that Fate has snatched the lady away because she was superior to 'her Race', while the fourth (ll. 29–46) constitutes a curse on her 'false guardian' and his family. The final paragraph consists of two parts: in the first (ll. 47–62) the poet demands what can atone for the lady's 'fate unpity'd, and [her] rites unpaid', while in the second (ll. 63–8) he astonishingly asserts that the ground in which she was buried has been rendered 'sacred' by the very fact of her interment there. The brief penultimate paragraph ('So peaceful, rests . . .') reminds us that the exorcism has been completed, prepares us for a noble rendering of one of the great commonplaces – 'pulvis et umbra sumus' – and allows the poet to introduce himself in the double role of mourner and future subject for elegy.

To analyse the poem in this way is to become aware that part of Pope's 'plan' must have been a variation of tone and tempo as one movement of thought and emotion succeeds another. In a letter to Cromwell in 1710 he had written that 'there is (if one may express it so) a Style of Sound'.[32] While he seems to have had something relatively simple in mind (as a reference to 'Alexander's Feast' suggests), we may perhaps extend the meaning of the phrase as we consider the architectonics of the Elegy. It opens, as Warton observed, 'with a striking abruptness':[33] the initial rhetorical question is followed, in rapid succession, by four others, with two exclamation marks thrown in for good measure – so exemplifying one of the modes of beginning an elegy which had been mentioned by Scaliger. The effect is dramatic, verging on the melodramatic. A further exclamation, and a further rhetorical question, introduce the paragraph in which the poet extols ambition and satirizes the spiritually lethargic. As we read lines 17–20 –

> Most souls, 'tis true, but peep out once an age,
> Dull sullen pris'ners in the body's cage:
> Dim lights of life, that burn a length of years
> Useless, unseen, as lamps in sepulchres

– it is interesting to recall Pope's observation, in the same letter, that 'Monosyllable-Lines, unless very artfully manag'd, are stiff languishing, & hard'. Elsewhere he explains what he means by 'artfully managed' by conceding that they 'may be beautiful to express Melancholy, Slowness, or Labour'.[34] Lines 17 and 19 'express [a] Slowness' which is spiritual rather than physical.

The movement of the third paragraph might be marked 'Andante', as the poet uses an image from chemistry to express the notion that the lady may have been 'snatch'd . . . early to the pitying sky' from a world which is unworthy of her. By way of contrast, the paragraph in which her guardian and his family are cursed opens with a mark of exclamation and advances with cumulative ferocity as couplet succeeds to couplet. Rhetorical questions and exclamations again characterize the paragraph on the lady's burial, and lead up to the climax in which the poet asserts that the ground has now been rendered 'sacred' by her 'reliques'. In the two paragraphs which form the coda the tone becomes much quieter (in spite of the exclamation mark at the end of each). At the same time the diction becomes strikingly simple, while 'Monosyllable-Lines' are skilfully used 'to express Melancholy':

'Tis all thou art, and all the proud shall be!

and:

And the last pang shall tear thee from his heart.

The quietly controlled conclusion contrasts strikingly with the rhetorical uncertainty of the opening: the speaker remains deeply sorrowful, but his passion has been brought under control, just as the ghost of the lady has been exorcized by his lines.

Pope's poem incorporates one element of which Trapp might have disapproved. 'With this Kind of Poem', he had written, 'every Thing that is epigrammatical, satirical, or sublime, is inconsistent. Elegy aims not to be witty or facetious, acrimonious or severe, majestic or sublime; but is smooth, humble, and unaffected.'[35] While the Elegy contains nothing 'epigrammatical . . . or sublime' and is certainly not 'witty or facetious', the fourth paragraph is undoubtedly 'acrimonious' and 'severe'. Yet this does not indicate any departure from the tradition of the classical funeral elegy as it had been interpreted by the poets and critics of the Renaissance: if the poem had lacked a satirical passage it would have departed from the elegiac tradition as exemplified by poets as different from each other as Donne and Milton, a tradition psychologically justified because the death of a beloved person predisposes the mourner to search for a scapegoat, a world unworthy of a soul as pure as that of a deceased girl, a Church the corruptions of which do not deserve an upright minister. And so Donne commemorated the first anniversary of the death of a young woman by writing *An Anatomie of the World* 'Wherein, By occasion of the untimely death of Mistris Elizabeth Drury, the frailty and the decay of this whole World is represented', and the second anniversary by writing a poem *Of the Progresse of the Soule* 'Wherein . . . the incommodities of the Soule in this life, and her exaltation in the next, are contemplated'; while in 'Lycidas' Milton not only 'bewails a learned Friend' but also 'by occasion foretels the ruine of our corrupted Clergy then in their height'. Unlike the elegies by Donne and Milton, Pope's is not a Christian poem: a fact which makes his use of exorcism as a structural principle the more striking. His satirical passage is less comprehensive than Donne's two sermons *de contemptu mundi* and different in focus from Milton's attack on the 'Blind mouthes' of the contemporary church. The miscreants on whom he turns are sluggish souls to whom passion and true ambition are alike unknown and in particular the lady's guardian and family, whom he takes as examples of the proud and pitiless among mankind:

Thus, if eternal justice rules the ball,
Thus shall your wives, and thus your children fall:
On all the line a sudden vengeance waits,
And frequent herses shall besiege your gates.
There passengers shall stand, and pointing say,
(While the long fun'rals blacken all the way)
Lo these were they, whose souls the Furies steel'd,
And curs'd with hearts unknowing how to yield.
Thus unlamented pass the proud away,
The gaze of fools, and pageant of a day!
So perish all, whose breast n'er learn'd to glow
For others good, or melt at others woe.

The angry satire of this paragraph recurs for a moment in its successor, in the lines describing the conventional 'mockery of woe' and the meaningless way in which the 'hallow'd dirge' is habitually 'mutter'd o'er [the] tomb'; but the principal part of this, the triumphant climax of the poem, is a brilliantly original version of the *consolatio*. While he excludes the Christian faith from this Roman elegy, Pope turns unhallowed ground to hallowed by the very intensity (as it were) of his admiration of a beautiful and courageous woman. His use of anaphora in lines 51–3 compels our admiration:

By foreign hands thy dying eyes were clos'd,
By foreign hands thy decent limbs compos'd,
By foreign hands thy humble grave adorn'd,
By strangers honour'd, and by strangers mourn'd![36]

The withdrawal from anaphora in the fourth line is particularly striking. Whereas a lesser poet would have continued the figure, Pope avoids the obvious yet enhances our sense of the rhetorical unity of the four lines by the repetition of the word 'strangers' and by the near-assonance of 'honoured' and 'mourned'.

A further reason for the variation in the fourth line was no doubt a desire to avoid rhythmical monotony. In his letter to Cromwell Pope pointed out that 'in any smooth English Verse of ten Syllables, there is naturally a Pause either at the fourth, fifth, or sixth Syllable', and continued: 'Now I fancy, that to preserve an exact Harmony & Variety, none of these Pauses shou'd be continu'd above three lines together . . .; else it will be apt to weary the Ear with one continu'd Tone'.[37] Since the caesura or pause occurs after the fourth syllable in the two lines immediately preceding the passage just quoted, the rejection of anaphora in line 54 avoids an even more flagrant violation of Pope's own principle. In lines 19–22 we find another possible instance:

Dim lights of life,/that burn a length of years
Useless, unseen,/as lamps in sepulchres;
Like Eastern Kings/a lazy state they keep,
And close confin'd in their own palace sleep.

The pause in the last line must either occur after the fourth syllable or after the ninth: in either case Pope is obviously intent on creating a sense of mindless monotony. At lines 63–6 we have an undoubted example of four successive lines with the pause after the fourth syllable:

What tho' no sacred earth allow thee room,
Nor hallow'd dirge/be mutter'd o'er thy tomb?
Yet shall thy grave/with rising flow'rs be drest,
And the green turf/lie lightly on thy breast:
There shall the morn/her earliest tears bestow
(ll. 61–5)

Here no defence can be offered, or required: one has only to remember one of the most important injunctions in *An Essay on Criticism*:

If, where the rules not far enough extend,
(Since rules were made but to promote their end)
Some lucky Licence answers to the full
Th' intent propos'd, that Licence is a rule.
(ll. 146–9)

The Elegy contains no example of the pause after the sixth syllable 'continu'd above three lines together'.

Returning to the paragraph on the lady's burial, we notice that the movement towards the resolution of conflict is marked by a less concentrated use of the figure of anaphora, in lines 55–62:

What tho' no friends in sable weeds appear,
Grieve for an hour, perhaps, then mourn a year,
And bear about the mockery of woe
To midnight dances, and the public show?
What tho' no weeping Loves thy ashes grace,
Nor polish'd marble emulate thy face?
What tho' no sacred earth allow thee room,
Nor hallow'd dirge be mutter'd o'er thy tomb?

So we come to the hinge or turning-point of the poem –

Yet shall thy grave with rising flow'rs be drest,
And the green turf lie lightly on thy breast

– with just the hint of an anaphora in the following couplet –

There shall the morn her earliest tears bestow,
There the first roses of the year shall blow

– to prepare for the final statement that angels will

o'ershade
The ground, now sacred by thy reliques made.

In a widely-used American anthology we are assured that whereas 'Pope speaks in his own person' in the last eight lines of the Elegy, in the preceding 74 lines he 'imagines the lover to be addressing the ghost of the unfortunate lady',[38] but surely few readers have sensed any change of voice (as distinct from the beautifully managed modulation of tone) in these concluding lines. The poem as a whole may be regarded as a dramatic monologue in which the speaker is a poet, but not necessarily the historical Alexander Pope. Writing of the Latin love elegists, Colin Macleod has recently reminded us that when they 'suggest they are speaking of their own experience' we should not allow ourselves to be misled: 'This does not mean the elegists are describing real events or even real persons; but their manner as love poets is autobiographical, however fantastic their matter'.[39] Exactly the same is true of Pope's Roman elegy, which is a triumphant variation on a number of classical themes. It is ironical that the poet who had exorcized a ghost so unforgettably in a poem should have raised it again in a mischievous footnote.

NOTES

1. *The Correspondence of Alexander Pope*, ed. George Sherburn, 5 vols (1956) (hereafter cited as *Correspondence*), I ,416. 'Butt now I have named such a person', Caryll continues, 'Mrs. Cope occurrs to my mind.' Cf. above, p. 74.
2. *Ibid.*, I, 419.
3. *Ibid.*, II, 528.
4. *Memoirs of the Life and Writings of Alexander Pope, Esq.* (1745), I, 75.
5. *Ibid.*, 75, 76.
6. *The Works of Alexander Pope Esq.* (1751), I, 265n.
7. *Correspondence*, II, 367–8.
8. Pp. 249, 253. The passages quoted from the 2nd edn (in which the title becomes *An Essay on the Genius and Writings of Pope*) are from p. 247 and pp. 333–4. The italics are mine.
9. *The Life of Alexander Pope, Esq.*, 135, 133.

10. *Lives of the English Poets by Samuel Johnson*, ed. George Birkbeck Hill (1905), III, 100, 226, 101. The definition of suicide is from the *Dictionary*.
11. *The Gentleman's Magazine*, LIV (November 1784), 807. Walpole's comment occurs in a letter first published by Cunningham and not yet included in the Yale edition. It is given in vol. XIII (1905) of Mrs Paget Toynbee's edition, pp. 230–2. The passage from Hawkins is to be found in his edition of *The Works of Samuel Johnson*, IV (1787), 113n.
12. Photograph and transcription most kindly provided by Mr W. S. Lewis. Warton's note is in vol. I (1797) of *The Works of Alexander Pope, Esq., with notes and Illustrations by Joseph Warton and others*, 336n.
13. I am very much indebted to Miss Meryl Jancey, the Deputy County Archivist, for searching the Hereford records for me, and to my friend Dr Nicholas Cox for his investigations at the Public Record Office.
14. *The Works of Alexander Pope*, ed. William Lisle Bowles, I (1806), xxxi–ii, xxxiv.
15. 'The Life of Alexander Pope', second part, *The Athenaeum*, 15 July, 1854 (no. 1394), 876c: reprinted in *The Papers of a Critic, selected from the writings of the late Charles Wentworth Dilke* (1875), I, 128.
16. *The Works of Alexander Pope*, with introductions and notes by the Rev. Whitwell Elwin, II (1871), 203–4.
17. Pp. 133–4.
18. *An Essay*, 253.
19. *The Early Career of Alexander Pope* (1934), 202–3.
20. *Correspondence*, II, 367n.
21. The Twickenham Edition, II (1940), 331–4.
22. 'Who she was outside the poem (if she existed) will perhaps never be known', he remarks in *Alexander Pope: the poetry of allusion* (1959), p. 64, while on p. 66 he writes: 'Pope's difficulties . . . may have come from trying to write a heroic epistle about a private affair, or perhaps about no affair whatever.'
23. Brower, *op. cit.*, 64.
24. The Twickenham Edition, vol. I (1961), ed. E. Audra and Aubrey Williams, 47.
25. *Joseph Spence, Observations, Anecdotes, and Characters of Books and Men*, ed. James M. Osborn (1966), I, 226. The word 'elegy' is often ambiguous, as most writers on the subject point out, notably Joseph Trapp (see n.30, below). None of the elegies of Tibullus deals primarily with death, and only one or two of Ovid's do.
26. *Ibid.*, 234.
27. *Poetices Libri Septem* (1561), Book III, cxxii–iii, as translated in *Milton's 'Lycidas'*, ed. Scott Elledge (1966), 109–10.
28. *Observations on the Faerie Queene* (1754), 166n., cited by Tillotson. Cf. lines 19–22 of Jonson's poem:

    Shee was the Lady *Jane*, and *Marchionisse*
    Of *Winchester*; the Heralds can tell this:
    Earle *Rivers* Grand-Child – serve not formes, good Fame,
    Sound thou her Vertues, give her soule a Name

    with lines 69–72 of Pope's 'Elegy':

    So peaceful rests, without a stone, a name,
    What once had beauty, titles, wealth, and fame.
    How lov'd, how honour'd once, avails thee not,
    To whom related, or by whom begot.
29. 'I desire . . . that you will cause the space for the initial letter to the Dedication to the Rape of the Lock to be made of the size of those in Trapp's Praelectiones': *Correspondence*, I, 394. The letter seems to have been written early in 1717.
30. *Lectures on Poetry . . . Translated from the Latin* (1742), 165. Trapp's lectures were first published in Latin, in three volumes, in 1711, 1715 and

1719. The lecture 'De Elegia' occurs in the second volume (pp. 66–75), and first appeared, therefore, a year or two before Pope seems to have written this poem.

31. My quotations are from the Oxford Standard Authors edition, edited by Herbert Davis (1966). When I quote line 39 I correct the obvious misprint 'These' to 'There'.

32. *Correspondence*, I, 107. As Sherburn points out (*ibid.*, 22 n.3), a letter which Pope printed as addressed to Walsh, in 1735, seems to have been 'fabricated' from the Cromwell letter which is genuine. The letter addressed to Walsh slightly elaborates certain points.

33. *An Essay*, 250.

34. *Correspondence*, I, 24. The same is true of the other monosyllabic line, 33:

    Cold is that breast which warm'd the world before.

35. *Lectures*, 169.

36. It has usually been taken for granted that 'foreign' has its most common modern meaning, as it sometimes has in Pope (e.g. *Epilogue to the Satires*, I, 155, 'foreign Gold'), Elsewhere, however, he uses the word to mean 'belonging to or coming from another district, county, society, etc.' (*Oxford English Dictionary*), 6.b), as in the second Moral Essay, *To A Lady*, ll. 223–4:

    For foreign glory, foreign joy, they roam;
    No thought of peace or happiness at home.

    The proximity of the words 'friends', 'domestic' and 'strangers' could support the older meaning of the word. The *Oxford English Dictionary* notes that the word is often 'opposed to *domestic*'.

37. *Correspondence*, I, 107.

38. *Eighteenth Century Verse & Prose*, ed. Louis I. Bredvold, Alan D. McKillop and Lois Whitney, 3rd edn prepared by John M. Bullitt (New York, 1973), 542. My objection to the view that there are two speakers in Pope's poem is not that it is inherently improbable but that it is not true. Minturno distinguishes between three types of elegy on the basis of the speaker of the poem: 'sive se ipsum poeta, sive alterum fingit, qui queratur, et quod triste, luctuosumve est, exprimat . . . Mixtum autem hoc dicendi genus cum sit, poeta nunc suam tenet, nunc alienam summit personam . . . Quod vero plerumque fit, est ubi nemo alius, quam poeta ipse loquatur': *De Poeta* (Venice, 1559), 407–. The speaker of the last eight lines of 'Lycidas' is different from the speaker of the rest, so that it is to be considered as belonging to the mixed kind. In the elegies of the Italian Latinist Ioannes Iovianus Pontanus, *De Tumulis*, which Pope is certain to have known (three of his poems are included in the second volume of *Selecta Poemata Italorum*, which he edited in 1740, although none of them happens to be an elegy in our sense of the word), there are sometimes several speakers within a single poem. I.v, for example, is divided between Viator, Genius and Sacerdos.

39. Colin Macleod, *Times Literary Supplement*, 7 November 1975, 1326. Scaliger observes that 'A discourse of consolation . . . can proceed only from a friend. For this reason the rule of the ancient writers was that the comforter also must show grief and must magnify the atrocity of the event' (Elledge, *op. cit.*, 110). Critics who believe that Pope's Elegy is 'about' Mrs Weston, Mrs Cope or Lady Mary have made him 'magnify' matters to an unusual degree, as none of these ladies was dead.

I should like to thank Dr Howard Erskine-Hill for his kindness in reading and commenting on this essay.

5

Pope's 1717 Preface with a Transcription of the Manuscript Text

MAYNARD MACK

[1]

Pope's preface to the first collected edition of his works, published in folio and quarto in 1717,[1] is a fascinating document when considered in the context of his activities at the time. It was evidently written in the late autumn of 1716, following a flying October visit with Lord Burlington to York and Bath: in the 1736 reprint, he actually assigns it to 'NOV. 10'.[2] If this date means anything, he also wrote on that day one of the most entertaining of his letters to Lady Mary Wortley Montagu, then in progress across Europe with her husband to the court of the Turkish bashaw at Adrianople;[3] had published only three days earlier a piece of high jinks entitled *God's Revenge against Punning*, of which the climax is the 'punishment' of his friend John Gay for a particularly bad pun by a fall from his horse;[4] and must already have been meditating a second piece of high jinks in his *Further Account of the Most Deplorable Condition of Edmund Curll, Bookseller*, which seems to have appeared not later than the first days of December.[5] As always during these years, he was also at work on the Homer, polishing the verse of the translation (this, for each successive volume, was hammered out during the summer) and composing and arranging the notes. Volume III would issue from the press on 3 June 1717 simultaneously with the *Works*. The coincidence can hardly have been accidental.

The prose of Pope's letter to Lady Mary is a prose that reads like this:

> I doubt not but I shall be told, (when I come to follow you thro' those Countries) in how pretty a manner you accomodated yourself to the Customes of the True-Believers. At this Town, they will say, She practised to sit on the Sofa; at that village, she learnt to fold the Turbant; here she was bathd and anointed; & there she parted with her black Full-bottome. At every Christian Virtue you lost, and at every Christian Habit you quitted, it will be decent for me to fetch a holy Sigh, but still I shall proceed to follow you. How happy will it be, for a gay young Woman, to

live in a Country where it is a part of Religious worship to be giddy-headed? I shall hear at Belgrade, how the good Basha receivd the fair Convert with tears of joy, how he was charm'd with her pretty manner of pronouncing the words Allah, and Muhammed, and how earnestly you joind with him in exhorting Mr. Wortley to be circumcised. But he satisfies you by demonstrating, how in that condition, he could not properly represent his Brittannick Majesty.

(*Corr.* I, 369)

The prose of *God's Revenge* differs markedly:

Manifold have been the Judgments which Heav'n from Time to Time, for the Chastisement of a Sinful People, has inflicted on whole Nations. For when the Degeneracy becomes Common, 'tis but Just the Punishment should be General: Of this kind, in our own unfortunate Country, was that destructive Pestilence, whose Mortality was so fatal, as to sweep away, if Sir *William Petty* may be believ'd, Five Millions of Christian Souls, besides Women and Jews.

And the prose of *A Further Account* (in this paragraph, Curll's alleged madness impels him to imagine all the bad books he has published coming down alive from their shelves to flutter their leaves and flap their covers at him) differs yet more:

Now *G-d damn* all *Folio's*, *Quarto's*, *Octavo's* and *Duodecimo's*! Ungrateful Varlets that you are, who have so long taken up my House without paying for your Lodging? – Are you not the beggarly Brood of fumbling *Journey-men*; born in *Garrets*, among *Lice* and *Cobwebs*, nurs'd upon *Grey Peas*, *Bullocks Liver*, and *Porter's Ale*? – Was not the first Light you saw, the *Farthing* Candle I paid for? – Did you not come before your Time into *dirty Sheets* of brown Paper? – And have not I cloath'd you in double *Royal*, lodg'd you handsomely on *decent Shelves*, lac'd your *Backs* with *Gold*, equipt you with splendid *Titles*, and sent you into the World with the Names of *Persons of Quality*? Must I be *always* plagu'd with you? – Why flutter ye your Leaves and flap your Covers at me? Damn ye all, ye *Wolves* in *Sheeps Cloathing*; *Rags ye were, and to Rags ye shall return*. Why hold you forth your *Texts* to me, ye paltry *Sermons*? Why cry ye – at every Word to me, ye bawdy *Poems*? – To my Shop at *Tunbridge* ye shall go, by *G* – and thence be drawn like the rest of your Predecessors, bit by bit, to the *Passage-House* . . .

(Ault edn, 284–5)

Unlike as these passages are, the 1717 Preface differs from all of them more than they differ from each other:

> If anyone should imagine I am not in earnest [in insisting that my work falls short 'not only of what I have read of others but even of my own Ideas of Poetry'], I desire him to reflect, that the Ancients (to say the least of them) had as much Genius as we; and that to take more pains, and employ more time, cannot fail to produce more complete pieces. They constantly apply'd themselves not only to that art, but to that single branch of an art, to which their talent was most powerfully bent; and it was the business of their lives to correct and finish their works for posterity. If we can pretend to have used the same industry, let us expect the same immortality: Tho' if we took the same care, we should still lie under a farther misfortune: they writ in languages that became universal and everlasting, while ours are extremely limited both in extent, and in duration. A mighty foundation for our pride! When the utmost we can hope, is but to be read in one Island, and to be thrown aside at the end of one Age.
>
> (TE, I. 6–7; ll. 115–29)

Though so nearly contemporary with these other writings, every reader will recognize that the style of the Preface is notably impersonal and 'philosophical' where they are engaged, abstract and general where they are circumstantial, and spare where they are elaborate – 'written with such simplicity', said Joseph Warton, 'that scarcely a single metaphor is contained in it'.

Some of the more obvious considerations governing this style leap immediately to mind. In the Preface, Pope is taking the high road of sober reflection with a large reading public, the public by whom his standing as a writer and the sales of his book will be determined. He is not addressing a correspondent in private, as with Lady Mary, or, as in the other instances, writing in the assumed identity of a pious evangelical and then in the assumed character of Edmund Curll. He is also, we may justly infer, offering an appraisal of the London literary situation and his own concerns in it that will correspond, in classic clarity and detachment, to the poems it introduces and the elegant format in which it appears, especially perhaps the newly fashionable quarto in the manner of the French editions of La Fontaine (1668) and Boileau (1674) and, perhaps most important, the editions of ancient authors issued in this format *in usum Delphini.*[6] The Preface's first word, one notices, flaunts in type an engraved pictorial initial (it is appropriate but doubtless accidental that the initial is 'I') which shows Pegasus striking Helicon with a hoof and so opening the spring of Hippocrene.[7] As John Butt has reminded us, Pope 'never doubted that he was a classic',[8] and here he is at age 28 (29 when the volume appeared) taking pains that his public not doubt it either.

Perhaps there were other motives at work too. The year had been a trying one for a young Roman Catholic poet, especially one so concerned as Pope was to keep alive an appearance of being above the battle, whether political or literary. The preceding 23 January had been the last day for non-jurors to take the oaths under the new regime, and he had not taken them – though already, two weeks before, on 5 January, a notice in *The Flying-Post* had lumped him with Ormonde and Sacheverell among the retainers of James III and therefore among so-called traitors to their country. Insinuations of a similar sort, some obscure, others alarmingly pointed – 'This Day is Publish'd, The Second Part of Mr. Pope's *Popish* Translation of Homer' – continued through the spring, to culminate on 31 May with Oldmixon's *The Catholick Poet* and Dennis's *A True Character of Mr. Pope and His Writings*, two of the most distressing attacks on his person, poetry, and religion ever to be made.

Meantime the irrepressible vein of mischief in his own make-up had been flowing. On 26 March that spring, Curll had published, under the sensation-seeking title *Court Poems*, three satyrical 'town eclogues', implicating Pope, Gay, and (by innuendo) Lady Mary Wortley Montagu in their authorship. Publication of the poems offered no threat to Pope personally. Presumably, it did offer some to Gay, who was soliciting court preferment, and also to Lady Mary, who as a noblewoman frequented the personages and gatherings that the eclogues ridiculed. In any case, moved either by concern for Gay, who could not protest the publication himself without seeming to accept the attribution, or by his romantic attachment to Lady Mary and the wish (how much intensified in a dwarf and cripple) to assume the role of Beauty's Defender, or by both, Pope ill-advisedly took the disciplining of Curll into his own hands. At some sort of gathering at Lintot's (publisher of the Homer and soon of the 1717 *Works*) he gave Curll an emetic disguised in a glass of sack. Worse, he promptly wrote up his exploit in an exulting and sometimes very funny pamphlet entitled *A Full and True Account of a Horrid and Barbarous Revenge by Poison on the Body of Mr. Edmund Curll, Bookseller. With a Faithful Copy of His Last Will and Testament*, which he published within a matter of days.[9]

The gauntlet was down. From this time forward, in Curll's view (for which there is much to be said!), Pope would deserve whatever irritations he could be forced to suffer, and the surest route to such satisfaction for a bookseller would be to publish in his victim's name whatever came to hand that would most embarrass him, spurious as well as genuine. In this mood, Curll published (7 April) the mock advertisement of Mr Pope's 'Popish' Homer; announced (10 April) the preparation of a volume in which any gentleman's animadversions on that translation would be accepted; procured (31 May) the attacks above-mentioned by Dennis and Oldmixon; and kept alive his earlier attributions of *Court Poems* by publishing (15 September) *More Court Poems. Part 2d.* More vexing for Pope, he managed to get hold of a copy of the high-spirited and sometimes off-colour lines *To Mr. John Moore, Author of the Celebrated Worm Powder,* which he gave to the world on 1 May, and a piece of amusing bawdy (in parody of Sternhold and Hopkins) mischievously titled *A Roman Catholick Version of the First Psalm. For the Use of a Young Lady,* which he made public on 30 June. With the former, he probably hoped to embroil Pope further with Addison's Little Senate at Button's, who had disparaged his undertaking Homer; for its final stanza read:

Our Fate thou only can'st adjourn
Some few short Years, no more!
Ev'n *Button's* Wits to Worms shall turn,
Who Maggots were before.
(TE, VI, 161–4)

With the latter, he not only sought to capitalize again on the anti-Catholic feelings of the public, for whom the Jacobite uprising of 1715 was only a few months gone by, but also (perhaps an even more effective gambit at this particular moment) to expose the dignified British Homer as a scurrilous rhymer. Its operative stanzas ran:

To Please her shall her Husband strive
With all his Main and Might,
And in her Love shall Exercise
Himself both Day and Night.

She shall bring forth most Pleasant Fruit,
He Flourish still and Stand,
Ev'n so all Things shall prosper well
That this Maid takes in Hand.
(TE, VI, 164–6)

Pope was sufficiently alarmed to print an equivocating advertisement in two London newspapers a month later, repudiating the Psalm, along with 'certain scandalous Libels, which I hope no Person of Candor would have thought me capable of'.[10]

[2]

It is against this background, I believe, that the 1717 Preface should be read. It shows Pope putting off, at least for the time being, the mountebank part of himself that had already proved to be only too capable of knavish devices and lying advertisements, yet was also capable, as some of these quotations may have shown, of a true Hogarthian delight in the homely undersides of life, and indeed of experience generally, and could command, when it wanted to, a remarkable range of prose from high romantic to low farcical. His society having no established outlets for this sort of impulse in a reputable man of letters, it seems to have kept pressing for a suitable vehicle, finding it eventually, as we all know, in a succession of brilliant *Dunciads*, not to mention such other colourful improprieties as *Sober Advice* (his imitation of Horace's second satire of the first book) and the Byzantine machinery by which he would ultimately tease Curll into pirating his letters so that he could publish them himself.

But all this, in late 1717, lay ahead. What had to be managed now was a self-presentation that would sweep the mountebank quite under the rug – in fact, for the sake of success with the Homer, repudiate him altogether – and this, I think, is what the 1717 Preface sets out to accomplish. Partly in so many words, asking readers to accept as his only the contents of the volume it inaugurates:

> For what I have publish'd, I can only hope to be pardon'd; But for what I have burn'd, I deserve to be prais'd. On this account the world is under some obligation to me, and owes me the justice in return, to look upon no verses as mine that are not inserted in this collection.
> (TE, I, 8; ll. 162–70)

But partly too, I would suggest, the claims to high responsibility are incorporated in the book itself. There is the stateliness of the formats; their resemblance, as we have seen, to the formats of other 'works' of unquestionable respectability and consequence, including his own Homer; the publication of the *Works* on the same day as one of the volumes of that translation – the volume, in fact, that saw his obligation to his subscribers half finished; and, though here economic considerations must have been decisive, the affinity established between the two undertakings by use of many of the same initial letters and tailpieces (the Pegasus-Helicon initial, for instance, by which the Preface is introduced, appears first in the Homer) – all these features seem calculated to invest the author with authority and respectability. And then there is the lofty austerity of matter and manner in the Preface itself.

Just here, the manuscript text can be useful to us. Worth printing, in any case, as the original of a composition that Atterbury was to praise for its 'modesty and good sense',[11] Johnson for its 'great spriteliness and elegance',[12] and Warton (though most of us will agree that he protested too much in calling it 'one of the best pieces of prose in our language') for its 'clearness', 'closeness', and 'elegance' as well as for the metaphorless simplicity mentioned earlier,[13] the manuscript has the virtue of clarifying the role that at this point in his career the poet evidently felt called on to play. The very fact that our own literary norms are better met by the relaxed, conversational, and confessional essay that we discover to be buried in the manuscript and its marginalia enables us to appreciate the strength of the inhibiting forces at work on the formation of the printed text. Some of these would of course arise from conventions of prefatorial decorum, as Pope and his age understood them, and some, it may be, from a genuine diffidence on his part, less about the quality of the offering, perhaps, than about the boldness or, as his enemies would be sure to say, the effrontery of the venture, on so sumptuous a scale, by a writer not yet 30. In spite of his well-attested vanity – or should we say because of it? – there is every reason to believe that Pope was no stranger to the 'fear and trembling' which he attributes to himself in the manuscript (ll. 220–1), and especially no stranger to that dread of 'being ridiculous' (again how much keener in one who already so often had been held up to scorn for his size and shape) which he imputes to every young author in his final text (TE, I, 5; l. 61).

Further inhibitions, I suspect, sprang from his sense of his situation at the time. Though we cannot now know what considerations operated at what point, it seems safe to say that the plan of making the Preface confessional had to be abandoned, at least in part, in view of what Curll and his minions could make of such materials: those little vignettes, for example, of a boy-poet whose 'first productions were the children of Self Love upon Innocence' (MS., n.11), who wrote easily because he wrote badly and was careless about fame because he knew it would come (MS., n.16), who, with a juvenile epic and 'panegyrics on all the Princes of Europe' in hand, thought himself 'the greatest genius tht ever was' (MS., n.15), and who, even now at age 30 – a violent trespass against all the codes to which the age paid lip-service – could express regret for childhood experiences: 'those visions of my childhood wch like the fine colours I then saw when my eyes shut are vanished for ever' (MS., n.15). An appealing side of Pope, we are inclined today to think, but not a glimpse of it is allowed to appear in the printed text of 1717. As for the playful phrase by which in the manuscript he was to introduce this material – 'a general Confession of my real Thoughts of my owne Poetry' (MS., ll. 130–1) – it took very little imagination to foresee what a syllabub of Popish blasphemies a Gildon or Dennis or Tom Burnet could whip up out of that.

In several other alterations between the manuscript and the printed Preface, I am inclined to think Pope's appraisal of his current circumstances may have played some part. The personal dimension of his assertion of a poet's right to attend to other matters besides pleasing the public – 'I therfore hope the Witts will pardon me if I reserve myself some of my time to save my soul' (MS., ll. 162–4 and n.32) – quite disappears, not impossibly because so many changes could be rung at that sensitive political moment on the theme of a papist's 'salvation'. His manuscript allusion to 'the pleasures of the Head, the only pleasures in wch a man is sufficient to himself, & the only Part of him wch he can employ to his satisfaction all day long' (MS., n.15) may have been blotted merely as belonging to a body of confessional material judged indecorous or too vulnerable as a whole; but he may have been sensitive, in addition, to the opportunities it offered for comment on his crippled body. Likewise, his witty similitude about the professional tenacity of poets and whores – a similitude not owned but shrugged off as an 'undoubted maxime' (MS., ll. 104–6) – may have been thought too undignified for the translator of Homer, or too demeaning of a craft whose products were at the same time to be presented with such strong claims of authorial solicitude; but they may also have been thought just too dangerously reminiscent – like 'Flams' (MS., l. 128)? – of the realms of discourse Pope had been occupying in his succession of anonymous warfaring pamphlets. That particular similitude was in any event tied up with another that might bring down laughter on a poet who was at this very instant receiving an excellent monetary return for his attentions to Calliope: 'The Muses are Mistresses without Portions, & whoever has once made his Court to them, can hardly sett up afterwards for a Fortune.' (MS., ll. 102–4.) For as with most revolutions in merchandising, Pope's shrewd subscription arrangements for the *Iliad* had stirred up in Grub Street many a cry of greed and fraud.[14]

An additional degree of detachment in the printed Preface is obtained by careful omission of all references that might seem to have been prompted by private resentments. Dennis's name (MS., l. 201) vanishes. The sentence about critics who 'blame us so much for Borrowing' from the ancients (MS., ll. 206–7) also vanishes. Though general in intention, it could easily be read as a direct response to the charge of 'servile Deference' that Dennis had lodged against the *Essay on Criticism*.[15] When it comes time, moreover, for the prefacer to disclaim all attributed pieces not found in this 1717 volume, he quite removes the manuscript imputation that the fault lies with 'the present Liberty of the Press' by which 'a Man is forced to appear as bad as he is, for fear of being thought worse' (MS., ll. 237–9), ascribing it instead to individual 'malice' (a much vaguer and more conciliatory complaint) and leaving room even for unmalicious 'ignorance'. Furthermore, a phrasing that might suggest that the volume itself is to be seen as simply a response to an unhappy set of personal experiences is softened. That nothing should be accounted his which is not contained in this collection is said, in the manuscript text, to be his 'chief View' in making it.[16] In the printed text, the relation of cause to effect has been reconstructed more obliquely and is considerably depersonalized: 'And perhaps nothing could make it worth my while to own what are really so [i.e. mine] but to avoid the imputation of so many dull and immoral things as partly by malice, and partly by ignorance, have been ascribed to me.' (TE, I, 8; ll. 167–70.)

Thus in a variety of ways and degrees, though none is precisely measurable today, the 1717 Preface became an exercise in image-making. Pope's ego possibly required this after the attacks he had been subject to for five years. His credit as a man of learning equal to the task of translating the greatest of epic poets certainly required it. And, if there is any merit in the present argument, his moral situation in late 1716 required it too: the disreputable figure he had been made to appear in by Curll and company, not without a reckless assist from himself, could only be neutralized by assuming a grave posture.

This is far from saying that an essay admired by so many sound critics is an empty charade. Postures make part of every authorial act by definition (as Henry James among others reminds us) and need not prevent the expression of genuine concerns. Certainly they do not in this instance. Almost every sentiment that Pope utters in the Preface, he will reiterate again and again in the course of his life; and when he speaks of the trials of authorship (TE, I, 5; ll. 57ff.), which for him had been extreme, or of the near hopelessness of matching the perfections that he and his contemporaries were equipped to find in the writers of Greece and Rome (TE, I, 6–7; ll. 115ff.), who were always before him as a beacon, or, with some pride, of the care with which he has exercised 'The last and greatest art, the art to blot' (TE, I, 8; ll. 152ff.), we know we are in the presence of his deepest convictions. The idiom, tone, and manner have been qualified for the occasion; the matter remains: a poet's lot, even a successful poet's lot, is not a happy one – or at any rate is not the felicity it is imagined to be by others: 'In a word, whatever be his fate in Poetry, it is ten to one but he must give up all the reasonable aims of life for it'. (TE, I, 5; ll. 81–3.) Like so much else in Pope's work, both at this time and later, this is an attitude to be struck. It is also a felt truth.

[3]

The manuscript of the 1717 Preface[17] consists of four small quarto pages that Pope has numbered 1, 2, 3, 4; four additional small quarto pages, of which he has numbered the first 5 and the last 8; and two unnumbered small quarto pages that a later hand has marked with pencil 9 and 10: five leaves in all. The contents of pages 1–8 correspond approximately to the contents of lines 1–185 of the 1717 printed text as found in TE, I, 3–9; for the remainder of the printed text, no manuscript original is known to survive. Page 9 of the manuscript recapitulates in a working copy roughly lines 172–87 and 257–82 of the earlier manuscript text; page 10 recapitulates in a fair copy lines 133–71 of that same text. As in most of his surviving manuscripts, Pope sets down his first rough efforts in a column at right or left that occupies approximately three-fifths of the width of the page, reserving the rest for insertions and rewriting. Above this column, on page 1 of the manuscript, he has written in capitals in his printing hand, 'PREFACE', and, at the right of this: 'To the Whole Collection/of my Works./A. P.' Above this, at top of the same leaf, he has repeated: 'Pope's preface to all his Work./A.P.'

In transcribing the manuscript, I have lowered all raised letters ('w^{ch}', 'wth', and so on), but have retained the abbreviated forms. I have modernized OE 'y' to 'th', thus converting 'y^{e}' to 'the', 'y^{t}' to 'tht', and so on again, except where the result would be ambiguous or misleading, as with 'thn, (then or than?) for 'y^{n}' or 'thy' (they or thy?) for 'y^{y}'. I have also modernized his scribal form of the double letter with macron or tilde, common for comon. Pope's lineation in the main body of the text has been indicated by dividers, and the marginal line numbers refer to the lines of type in this transcript. Extensive cancellations are identified in the footnotes, as are over-writings of words. Smaller cancellations made during the process of composition are shown by the use of small capital letters. Insertions appear between single brackets (< >), insertions within an insertion between double brackets (≪ ≫), except in the notes to the transcript, where these symbols are replaced by single and double minute marks. Through these signals, a careful reader should be able to reconstruct the manuscript of the Preface with some accuracy.

NOTES TO THE INTRODUCTION

1. R. H. Griffith, *Alexander Pope: A Bibliography*, 2 vols (Austin, Texas, 1922), Nos. 79–86.
2. The 1717 text, with the revisions of 1736 and later, is printed in the Twickenham Edition of Pope's *Poetical Works* (hereafter cited as TE), I, 3–10. All quotations are from this edition and are accompanied by the line numbers provided by the TE editors. These should not be confused with the line numbers I have applied to the manuscript text, which are always preceded by 'MS.'
3. *The Correspondence of Alexander Pope*, ed. George Sherburn, 5 vols (1956) (hereafter cited as *Corr.*), I, 367–70.
4. *The Prose Works of Alexander Pope*, ed. Norman Ault (1936), cx–cxiv and 267–72.
5. Ault edn, xcviii–cvi and 273–85.
6. On the relatively new vogue of the quarto format at this time, and its backgrounds, see David Foxon's lively and informative *Pope and the Early Eighteenth-Century Book Trade* (forthcoming), ch. II.
7. Interestingly, too, the headpiece above shows Apollo in a glory among the nine Muses.
8. John Butt, 'Pope's poetical manuscripts' (Warton Lecture on English Poetry), in *Proceedings of the British Academy*, XL (1954), 23.

9. More circumstantial accounts of the above matters may be found in George Sherburn, *The Early Career of Alexander Pope* (1934), 159–85, and in Ault, *ed. cit.*, xcivff.
10. Sherburn, *op. cit.*, 181.
11. Atterbury to Pope [December 1716], *Corr.*, I, 378.
12. *Lives of the Poets*, ed. G. B. Hill, 3 vols (1905), III, 135.
13. See his edition of Pope, 10 vols (1797), I, 1n.
14. A valuable account of Pope's innovations at this time and later will be found in the work by David Foxon cited above in n.6.
15. In his *Reflections Critical and Satyrical upon a late Rhapsody, call'd An Essay upon Criticism* (1711).
16. That this is a fair statement may be seen in the terms of Pope's agreement with Lintot of 28 December 1717, which exacts a penalty of £20 if Lintot prints any pieces as Pope's other than those contained in the 1717 volume or those for which he has Pope's permission signed and sealed. Pope may have been protecting his canon against the juvenilia he had published in his miscellany of 1717, as Ault argues (*Pope's own miscellany*, 1935, xxvii); but he surely also had in mind embarrassing items like his parody of the Sternhold and Hopkins psalm. See Foxon, *op. cit.*, ch. I, pt vi.
17. Now part of the C. B. Tinker collection in the Beinecke Library at Yale.

Preface

I am inclined to think that the Dispositi / on both of those who write Books and of / those who read them is generally not a lit- / tle unreasonable. For Writers seem to fancy / that the world IS OBLIGED TO <must> approve what- / ever they PUBLISH <produce> and Readers to imagine / that Authors are BOUND <obliged> to please them at / any rate. Methinks, as NO ONE <on the one hand no single> man is born / with a Right of controuling the Opinion s of ANOTHER S <all the rest>,[1] / so <on the other> the World has no title to de- / mand OF ANY ONE that ALL HIS <the whole> care and time <of any particular person> / should be sacrificed to its entertainment. & / I cannot but believe that the writing and / unwriting Parts of mankind are EACH under / AN equal obligation s OF ACCEPTING WITH CAN / DOUR WHAT THE OTHER AFFORDS THEM. <for as much FAME OR AS MUCH Pleasure ≪or Fame≫ as each affords ≪AS ONE AFFORDS≫ [2] the other.>

Every one acknowledges it a wild Notion / to expect Perfection in any work of Man; / AND YET <BY THE> JUDGMENT IS <COMMONLY> PAST UPON POEMS AS IF <and yet one would / think> the contrary were taken for granted <by the judgment commonly past upon Poems.> / A Critick is thought to have done his part, if / he proves a writer has faild in an Expression / or err'd in a particular point. <and can> IS it then TO / be wonderd at, if the whole Body of Poets / seem resolved never to own themselves in / an error? For as long as one Side despi- / ses a well-meant Endeavor, the other will / not be satisfyd with a moderate Appro- / bation. Indeed they both proceed in such / a manner as if they really believed that

Leaf 1 : verso

Poetry was immediate Inspiration. IT WERE / TO BE WISHED THEY WOULD REFLECT, THAT THIS EX- / TRAORDINARY ZEAL AND FURY IS ILL-PLACED: PO-/ ETRY AND CRITICISM BEING BY NO MEANS THE U- / NIVERSAL GRAND CONCERN OF THE WORLD, BUT ON- / LY <'TIS ONLY> THE AFFAIR OF IDLE MEN WHO WRITE IN THEIR / CLOSETS, AND OF IDLE MEN WHO READ THERE. I / DO NOT SAY THIS TO <I would not> imitate those people, who / make a merit of undervaluing the Arts and / Qualifications without which they had never / been taken notice of; I think Poetry as use / ful as any other Art, because it is as enter / taining, AND THERFORE AS WELL <in that respect as> deserving of / mankind.[3] HOWEVER IT IS <I am afraid this extreme zeal AND ≪on≫ both sides is ill-placed, Poetry and Criticism being> by no means the u- / niversal grand Concern of the world; IT IS / <but> only the affair of idle men that write in / their closets, and of idle men that read / there.

I CONFESS <But sure> upon the whole, I THINK a bad / Writer deserves better treatment than a / bad Critick. <For> A man may be the former, meer- / ly thro' the misfortune of an ill Judgment, / but he cannot be the latter without both / that, and an ill Temper. AND <FOR THE MOST PART> A WRITERS EN / DEAVOR FOR THE MOST PART IS TO PLEASE <GRATIFY> HIS / READERS, BUT A CRITICKS TO PUT THEM OUT / OF HUMOUR.[4] <I think a good deal may be said to extenuate the fault of bad Writers.> What we call a *Genius* is / hard to be distinguishd by a man himself / from a strong Inclination: FOR MANY (IT IS / PLAIN) HAVE THE LAST <ONE> ALL THEIR LIVES, WI- / THOUT THE LEAST SHARE OF THE FIRST <OTHER>.[5] And if / a person's Genius, be never so great, he / can AT FIRST DISCOVER IT NO OTHER WAY <NO WAY find it out AT FIRST ≪no other way at first≫> than / THAN BUT by that Prevalent Propension, which makes / him the more liable to be mistaken. / The only method he has is to make the Ex / periment by writing, and appealing to the

Leaf 2: recto

judgment of others: And if he does not write well, / (which is certainly no Sin in itself) he is im- / mediately made an Object of Ridicule. I wish / we had the humanity to consider, that even / the worst Authors at first endeavord to please / us, and might in that endeavor deserve some-[6] / thing at our hands: We have no cause to quar- / rel with them but for their obstinacy in / persisting, and this CRIME too may BE ALLEVI / ATED BY SOME <admit of SOME alleviating> Circumstances. Their particular / Friends may be ignorant, or unsincere; and the rest of / the world IN GENERAL IS too well-bred to shock / them with a Truth, which generally their / Booksellers first inform them of. This is not / TILL THE TOWN HAS LAUGHD AT THEM, AND till they / have spent too much of their time to apply / to any profession that better suits their / Talents: AND EVEN <and till> what Talents they may / have are BY THIS TIME <MEANS> so far discredited, / as to be of small service to them. For (wt / is the hardest case imaginable) the Repu- / tation of a man commonly depends upon THE <his> / first Appearance HE MAKES in the world; / and people will establish their opinion of / us, ON

<from> what we do at that season, when / we have least judgment to direct us.

On the other hand, a good Writer no soo- / ner communicates his works with the same / desire of Information; but it is imagined / he is a vain Creature, given up to the am- / bition of REPUTATION <Fame>, when perhaps the poor / man is all the while trembling with the / fear of being ridiculous. If he is made / to think he HAS A GENIUS, <TALENT TO ≪may≫ please the world> & INDUCED TO / HOPE HIS WRITINGS MAY PLEASE, he falls / under very unlucky circumstances; for / from the moment he prints, he must ex- / pect to hear no more truth than if he

Leaf 2: verso

were a Prince, or a Beauty. If he has not very / good Sense, (and indeed there are twenty men / of Wit for one man of Sense) his living, thus / <from his youth> in a course of flattery, WILL <may> put him in no / small danger of becoming a Coxcomb. If / he has understanding, he will consequently / have so much Diffidence WITH IT, as not to / reap any great Satisfaction from his SUC- / CESS: SINCE Praise,[7] <since> if given to his face <it> can / hardly be distinguishd from Flattery, and if / in his absence, how can he be certain of it? / Were he sure of being commended by the / best and most knowing, he is as sure of / being envy'd by the worst & most ignorant, / which are the Majority: For 'tis with a fine / Genius, as with a fine Fashion, all those / are dis- pleasd at it, who are not able to / follow it: And 'tis to be feard that Esteem / <will> seldom does any man so much good, as Ill- / will does him harm. Then there are a / third Class of people, who make the greatest / part of mankind, those who are betwixt / Wits and Fools; who (to a man) will sus- / pect or hate him: A hundred honest Gen- / tlemen will dread him as a Wit, and a / hundred innocent Women as a Satyrist. / Upon the whole, whatever be his fate in / Poetry, it is ten to one but he must give / up FOR IT all the reasonable Aims of Life. / <for it>.[8] THE MUSES ARE MISTRESSES WITHOUT PORTIONS, & / WHOEVER HAS ONCE MADE <HIS> COURT TO THEM, CAN / HARDLY SETT UP <AFTER- WARDS> FOR A FORTUNE: FOR ONCE / A POET & ALWAYS A POET, IS THOUGHT AS UN / DOUBTED A MAXIME, AS ONCE A WHORE AND / ALWAYS A WHORE. TO SAY THE TRUTH, <In a word,> the / <INDEED THE> <only advantage I KNOW ≪can think of≫ accruing from THE CHARAC- TER OF A MAN OF WIT, IS THAT IT GIVES / HIM THE PLEASURE OF BEING ADMITTED INTO THE / a Genius to Poetry is the agreable [AMUSEMENT ?] Power of Self-amusement in THE INTERVALS ≪any≫ ≪vacant≫ Inter- vals OF LIFE, the pleasure of being admitted into the

Leaf 3: recto

best Conversation, and the freedom[9] of saying as FOO- / LISH <many idle> things as other people, without being so severely / remarkd upon.[10]

I believe, if ANY <a> man <shoud> early in his life SHOULD / contemplate the many dangerous fates of Authors, / he would scarce be of their number on any con- / sideration WHATEVER. The Life of a Wit is a War- / fare upon earth; and <indeed> the present Spirit of the / LEARNED World is such, that no man should <attempt to serve it, any way,> BE / AN ACTOR IN IT without the constancy of a Martyr, / and a resolution to suffer for its sake. And for / my part, had I seen things at first in this view, / the publick had never been troubled either with / my Writings or with this Apology for them. / <Perhaps had I thought of this in time, I had never been OBLIGED, ≪reducd≫ as I now am, to make apologies.>[11]

TIS INDEED VERY DIFFICULT <Tis hard> to speak of oneself / with ANY Decency; but when a man must speak / of himself, the best way is to speak Truth of / himself, FOR ALL MANNER OF FLAMS WILL BE DISCO- / VERED. <or he may depend upon it, others will do it for him.> I will therfore make this Preface a / general Confession of <ALL> my <real> Thoughts OF <CONCERNING> of my owne / POETRY, <Poetry> resolving with the same freedom to ex / pose myself, as it is in the power of any other / to expose THAT. <them>.[12]

I could wish people would believe what I am / pretty certain they hardly will, that I have been / much less concernd for Fame than I durst declare / till this occasion. METHINKS I SHOULD NOW FIND MORE / CREDIT THAN I COULD HERETOFORE SINCE[13] <in wch may be had the more credit because> my Writings / have had their fate already, & 'tis too late to / think of prepossessing the reader s in their favor. / I WOULD PUT THEM IN MIND THAT THESE[14] ARE THINGS / FOR WHICH <TILL THIS PRESENT> THEY WERE <The world was> never prepared <for them> by Prefaces, / byass'd by PROCURED Recommendations, dazzled with / the names of great Patrons, wheedled with fine / REASONS AND pretences, NOR troubled with Excuses.[15] / And upon this consideration, I hope to be believd wn / I say that I had never written but to amuse my / self, <FINDING MY FAULTS,> never corrected but that it was as pleasant[16]

Leaf 3: verso

<it was as pleasant> to me to correct as to write; AND NEVER PUBLISHD / IF I HAD NOT BEEN <I was then> made to hope THEY <I WAS THEN

TOLD my verses> were / correct enough to please others, & that made me publish 'em.

I fairly own that I have USED <done> my best Endeavours to[17] / THE FINISHING OF THESE PIECES finish these pieces ; THAT I MADE WHAT / USE OF I COULD <that I have servd myself> of the judgment of Authors, dead / and living; that I omitted no means in my pow- / er to be informed of my Errors, both by my / Friends and Enemies; and that I expect no[18] FA / VOUR <to be excused> on account of MY Youth, Business, want / of Health, or any other idle EXCUSES <allegations>. But the / true reason they are not YET more correct, is / owing to the consideration how short a time / they, and I, have to live. A man who can ex- / pect but sixty years, may be ashamed to em- / ploy THIRTY <half his Life> in bringing Sense and Ryme together. / I therfore hope the Witts will pardon me if I leave <reserve> / myself <some of my> time ENOUGH to save my soul, and that / there will be some wise men of my opinion, even / <tho'> IF I should think a Part of it better spent in / the Enjoyments of Life than in pleasing the Criticks.[19]

I <must> next confess, I am very ignorant to what / degree I have succeeded. TIS UNHAPPY ENOUGH, / THAT AT FIRST, we have too much fondness for our / works to judge of them <at first,> and AT LAST WE HAVE / too much judgment to be pleas'd with them. <at last.> / <But> I ONLY know, that WHATEVER <THESE they can have no> reputation THEY MAY / HAVE IT CAN NEVER LAST <that will continue> long, NOR <that> deserves to do so. / For they have always fallen short, not only of what / I have read of other s MEN, but even of my own / Ideas of Poetry.

That my Cotemporaries may think me in ear- / nest, IN THIS DECLARATION, I beg them to reflect / on those surprizing Genius's which were perhaps / the gift of Nature only to better Climes and / better Ages: on That Thirst of Fame and Spirit / of Knowledge which urg'd theM <Ancients> thro so many Tra-

Leaf 4: recto

vels and Labours, to break open the fountains of / all Sciences; their unwearyd diligence and ob- / stinate pursuit of them;[20] THAT CONSTANT APPLI- / CATION <THAT They constantly applyd themselves not only to that one Art,[21] but to that sin-/ gle Branch of an Art, to which their GENIUS Talent / was most powerfully bent; and <THAT they employed> their whole Lives / EMPLOYED in THE correcting and finishing THEIR those / Works for Posterity. Let us REFLECT ON ALL <SERIOUSLY consider> this, / AND BE VAIN IF WE CAN. <and if> IF we are conscious / to have used the same Industry, let us expect / the same Immortality.

But <I fear> tis far otherwise with modern Poets; THEY We / must bring THEIR <our> Wit to the Press, as Gardiners / do their Flowers to the market, which if they / cannot vend in the morning are sure to die be- / fore night. Were THEY <we> animated by the same / noble Ambition, and ready to prosecute it with / equal Ardor, THEIR <our> Languages are not only BO[22] / confined to a narrow Extent of Countries, but / in a perpetual Flux, not so much as fixd by / an acknowledgd Grammar: while THOSE OF THE / ANCIENTS <Theirs> were such, as Time and Fate conspird / to make BOTH universal and everlasting. A migh- / ty foundation for our Pride![23] when the utmost / we can hope is but to live TWENTY <a few> years longer / than QUARLES OR Withers! Or Dennis.

All that is left us, TO DO, is to recommend our / WRITINGS Productions by the imitation of the Anci- / ents: and it will be found true, that in every / Age the highest reputation[24] has been attained / by those who have been most indebted to their[25] / PREDECESSORS. THE CRITICKS THINK BUT LITTLE OF / THIS WHEN THEY BLAME US SO MUCH FOR BORROWING. / For whatever is very good Sense must have been / common Sense in all times, and what we call / Learning is but the knowledge of the Sense of

Page 4: verso

our ANCESTORS. <Predecessors> Therfore they who say our Thoughts / are not our own because they resemble the An- / cients, may as well say our Faces are not our / own because they are like our Fathers. And / indeed 'tis very unreasonable, that people will / expect we should be Scholars, and yet are an- / gry to find us so.

I confess then I have[26] assisted myself as much / as I could by Reading; BEING OF OPINION THAT / THOSE AUTHORS WHO NEVER READ, WILL NEVER BE / READ. <FOR> I have always been fearful of making / an ill Present to the World, for which I have / as great a Respect, as most Poets have for / themselves. What I thought incorrect, I suppressd; & / what I thought most finishd, I never publishd but / with fear and trembling. For what I have prin- / ted, I can only[27] hope to be pardon'd; but for what / I have burnt, I deserve to be prais'd. IF IT WERE / CONSIDERED, HOW <COMMONLY> most[28] authors <can> forgive themselves some / particular lines for the sake of a whole Poem, / and again a whole Poem for THE some particu- / lar lines; AND ON THE OTHER HAND, <But if IT WERE KNOWN my Readers knew,> HOW MANY TO / LERABLE THINGS I HAVE BEEN ASHAMED TO PUT UPON / THE PUBLIC, AND HOW MANY BAD ONES I HAVE SAVD / IT FROM, <how many vile things of mine I have saved them the trouble of, and how many AS

WELL AS tolerable ones I have thought too bad for them> I THINK NO <EVERY CANDID> READER THAT IS A GENTLE- / MAN BUT <they> would think himself[29] OBLIGD <under some obligation> to me for / so many Sacrifices to him of my own Self-love. I HOPE / FOR SO MUCH <It will be but> justice in <them in> return, THAT NOTHING WILL <as THAT NOTHING MAY> be lookd[30] upon <nothing> as / mine WHICH <that> is not inserted in this Collection, wch / indeed WAS IS was my chief View in making it: For / in the present Liberty of the Press, a Man is / forced to appear as bad as he is, for fear of / being thought worse.

IF ANY ONE THINKS I HAVE WRITTEN WELL, <In this> I / entreat him to consider that <it is what> no Man can WRITE <do> / well without Good Sense: a quality which makes[31]

Leaf 5: recto

And I would hope upon this consideration, to be / credited, when I say that I had never written / but to amuse myself, never corrected but that / it was as pleasant to me <to correct> as to write, and ne / ver published BUT THAT <if> I WAS <had not been> made to hope / they were correct enough to please others. I / fairly own I have usd my best endeavors to / make them so, & <THINK IT NO EXCUSE TO ALLEDGE> expect no favor on account / of my Youth, want of Health, Time, or any / other <USUAL idle> excuses.[32] I have ever been fearful[33] of ma / king an ill Present to the World, for which I / have as much respect as most AUTHORS <Poets> have / for themselves. I have really sacrificed much / of my own Self love to this Veneration for the / publick, in doing justice on several other / Things of mine; WHICH <THAT> DID NOT WANT MANY OF / THOSE QUALIFYING LINES <of which> I was natural / ly as fond OF AS OTHER POETS <any of my> Brethren. I / hope IN RETURN my readers will be so grateful / as not to impute any such triffling pieces / to me, which out of regard to them, I would / not suffer to be inserted in this Collection. / <Those pieces wch were most finished> I never published but with fear & trembling / AND IF I DESERVE TO BE PARDOND for[34] what I / have printed, I DESERVE TO BE PRAISD <can only hope to be pardond but> for what / I have burnt. I deserve to be praised. Most / authors <will> forgive IN <in> thmselves <IN> MANY <some> particular lines for the / sake of THE <a> whole poem, & agn MANY <a> whole poem for the / sake of MANY <some> particular lines. I HAVE SACRIFICED <Whereas if it were known how much of> / my own Selflove I have sacrificed to this respect <veneration> for the publ<ick,> / how many tolerable things I woud not trouble them wth / & how many

VERY bad ones I <have> savd 'em from, no readr / tht is a gentleman but woud think himself obligd to / me. They owe me in return, the justice of looking upon no / thing as mine wch is not inserted this collection. IT / <THAT> WAS CHIEFLY MY <which indeed was my chief> view in making <it> THIS COLLECTION THT NOTHING / MIGHT [*Here Pope leaves space to be filled in*] WCH IS NOT CONTAIND IN IT. For in the prest [present] / Liberty of the press, I AM <ONE ≪a man≫ is> forcd to appear as bad as I AM <≪one≫ he is> / not to be thought worse.

If any MAN <one> thinks I have

Leaf 5: verso

best Company, and the freedom of saying as / many foolish things as other people, with- / out being so severely remarkd upon.

I believe if any man, early in his life, / shou'd contemplate all the dangerous fates / of Authors, he would scarce be of their num- / ber on any consideration whatever. The Life / of a Wit is a Warfare upon Earth, & the pre- / sent Spirit of the learned world is such that / no man should be a Party in it without the / constancy of a Martyr and a resolution to / suffer for its sake. For my part I confess, / had I seen things in this view at first, the / publick had never been troubled <either> with my wri- / tings, or <with> this Apology for them.

I am sensible how difficult it is to speak / of one's self with decency: but when a man / must speak of himself, the best way is to / speak truth of himself, for all manner of / Tricks will be discoverd. I'll therfore make / this Preface a general Confession of all my / Thoughts of my own poetry, resolving with the / same freedome to expose myself, as it is / in the power of any other to expose that.

I could wish people would believe what I / am pretty certain they will not, that I have / been much less concernd about Fame, than I / durst declare this occasion; when methinks / I should find more credit than I could heretofore; /since my Writings have had their fate al- / ready, and 'tis too late to think of prepos- / sessing the reader in their favor. I would / plead it as some merit, that the world has never / been prepard for these things by Prefaces, / byast by procured recommendations, dazled / with the names of great Patrons, wheedled / with fine reasons & pretences; or troubled wth / Excuses.

NOTES TO THE TEXT

1. *Pope first wrote* Opinion, *then pluralized it to* Opinions, *struck out* an *in* another *and pluralized it also, then struck* others *out in favour of* all the rest.

2. *Pope's caret calls for these three words to follow* what, *but it is unclear how they are to be integrated into the sentence at that point. They seem rather to be alternative to* as each affords.
3. Indeed . . . that (*ll. 24–5*) *is marked for deletion with a marginal delta.* Poetry . . . mankind (*ll. 26–35*) *is struck out.*
4. And . . . Humour (*ll. 43–6*) *is struck out.*
5. for . . . other (*ll. 48–50*) *is struck out.*
6. *In the margin opposite* us . . . some- (*ll. 59–60*): qu – *apparently for* quaere. (*This is a common marginalium in Pope's poetical MSS., signifying an intention to consult about the appropriateness of a passage*).
7. *After* Praise, *Pope has altered the comma to a semicolon.*
8. *After* 'for it' *Pope writes between the lines*: There is indeed one advantage accruing from a Genius to poetry and tis all I can say for it. I mean tht agre [able].
9. *Marginally Pope tries out a further version of this passage*: Notwithstanding all 'After all' these discouragemts, there is one [*Pope overwrites* one *with* some] real happiness accruing from a Genius to Poetry: it gives a man the agreable Power of Self-Amusement in all the 'idle' Intervals of Life; it procures him THT PL [*Pope evidently started to write* pleasure] 'an' admission into the best Conversation; & it gains him the freedom *The entire passage is struck out.*
10. *An additional sentence is proposed in the margin*: This IS A REAL 'REALLY "indeed is" some advantage and THIS is [*Pope subsequently prefixes a* t *to* is] 'INDEED' all I can say for Poetry.
11. *Marginally Pope has another go at this idea – a* 3 *before* too young, a 2 *before* & I, *and a* 1 *before* wn I *indicate a proposed later rearrangement.* Perhaps, had I thought of this in time, I SHOUD NOT HAVE NEEDED 'I had never been reducd' to apologize for my FAULTS 'sins' in poetry. But I was too young to resist temptations & I was very innocently in love with myself wn I began to write & my first productions were the children of Self Love upon Innocence. *Below this, Pope inserts an additional sentence that looks forward to ll. 168–70*: I had then too much fondness to judge of my productions and had too much judgmt to be pleasd.

    Two additional treatments of this idea appear, the first one looking forward as far as ll. 144–50: (*1*) The Muses are amicae omnium horarum, & like our gay acquaintance the best 'It must be allowd of the Muses that they are the most agreable' company in the world as long as one expects no real service from em. BUT I was so innocent 'in my childhood' as to 'WRITE BECAUSE IT PLEASD ME' think of nothing but pleasing myself, and writing DID 'happened to do this' as effectually as any other calling, & therfore I writ. (*2*) Perhaps had I thought of this in time, I had never been obligd as I now am to make apologies [*cf. ll. 123–5*]. Tis indeed very difficult [*l. 126*] – to – do it for him [*l. 129*]. I will therfore [*l. 129*] – to – Poetry [*l. 131*]. *These are Pope's abbreviated indications of passages to follow. All passages recorded in this note are struck out.*
12. *A marginal cue here* – in wch I may HOPE FOR 'find' the more credit [*cf. l. 137*] [. . .] all day long [*cf. n. 15 below*] *indicates a passage that was evidently intended at one time to follow directly on the word* Poetry. *The cue was struck out along with the material mentioned in n. 13.*
13. resolving . . . since (*ll. 132–7*) *is struck out.*
14. *Pope overwrites* these *with* They.
15. *A cancelled passage of* 'confession' *apparently intended to follow at this point appears in the margin of this page and continues in the margin of the next:* In the first place I thank God & Nature tht I was born wth a Love to THIS STUDY 'Poetry'. 'For' Nothing SO AGREABLY 'CAN more conduce s to' fills up the intervals of ones time, or 'if' rightly usd MORE CONDUCES TO 'to' make the whole course of Life so 'MORE' entertaining. Cantantes licet usque minus via laedat eam [us] [Virgil, *Eclogues*, ix 64: *modern texts usually read* laedit]. Tis a SERIOUS 'vast' happiness to HAVE 'possess' the pleasures of the Head, the only pleasures 'in wch' a Man is sufficient to himself, & the only Part of him wch he can employ 'to his satisfaction' all day long. It was this tht made me a writer. I confess there was a time wn I was innocently in love wth myself; wn I had WRIT 'made' an Epic poem & panegyrics on all the Princes of Europe & thought MYSELF 'I had' the greatest Genius tht ever was. [*Illegible words*] 'I cant but regret' those DELIGHTFUL DREAMS ARE VANISHD 'visions of my childhood' wch like the 'fine' Colours I 'we' then saw [*Pope has altered* saw *to* see] wn MY 'our' Eyes shut, are vanishd for ever. Many trials & sad experience have 'so' undeceivd

me by degrees TILL 'that' I am utterly at a loss at wt rate to value myself. As for fame, I shall be glad of any I can get & not repine at any I miss, & AS FOR VANITY I have <vanity> enough to keep me from hanging myself & even from wishing those hangd who wd take it away.

16. And . . . pleasant (*ll. 144–7*) *is struck out. Below it Pope inserts but then also strikes out:* I writ with great Ease for I writ very ill, & I was not SOLICITOUS 'uneasy' for Fame, for I thought my self sure of it.

17. *Marginal tentatives beside ll. 148–58 are only partly decipherable. Sentences that can be made out follow in order of appearance:* (*1*) I think in saying this I have given the best reason FOR WRITING 'why I writ'. (*2*) We are too fond of our works to judge of em at first, & have too much judgmt to be pleasd with em at last. (*3*) I afterwards corrected partly out of a sense of my faults & partly because I was then told they were correct enough to please others, & that made me publish em. (*4*) It was this tht made me write. I AFTERWD FOUND OUT THE 'A sense of my' faults OF MY WRITINGS made me correct (besides it was as pleasant to me to correct as to write). *In his editions, Warburton quotes the sentences in* (*4*) *as if they related directly to the final sentence of the 'confession' in n. 15. I believe they actually relate to ll. 145–53 of the text, like the other sentences above.*

18. *Pope has later added* a t *to* no.

19. A . . . Criticks (*ll. 160–6*) *is struck out. Marginally, Pope revises:* THESE THINGS 'They' have 'already' layn by me some years, and a [*all the preceding is struck out*] 'A' man may be ashamd to spend half his life in bringing Sense & Ryme together. & WHY WOULD THE 'and can any' Criticks be so unreasonable as not to leave ME 'an author' time enough to save MY 'his' Soul, or take MY 'his' pleasure s.

20. on . . . them (*ll. 177–82*) *is struck out.*

20. *Pope recapitulates marginally from* reflect *to* Art (*ll. 177–84*): that the Ancients (to say the least of em) had as much genius as we, that they took AS MUCH 'more' pains and travelld AS far 'ther' for their Knowledges, that they constantly applyd themselves not only to that one *On the following page, he works this over three times more:* (*1*) that the Ancients (to say the least of them) had as much Genius as we: and that to take much more pa [*evidently Pope started to write* pains] time, and employ much more pains WILL 'must' certainly make MUCH more finishd Pieces. (*2*) that they traveld & were educated as carefully & travelld as far for their Knowledge (*3*) twice as much time will certainly make twice as finishd a piece in people of equal capacities, & the Ancients were 'VIRGIL WAS' at least as learned as we. I

22. *Pope evidently began to write bounded.*

23. But . . . Pride (*ll. 196–9*) *is struck out. In the margin, a summary version:* BUT IF WE HAD TAKEN THE SAME PAINS, 'But if we had equal "WHATEVER MAY BE OUR" merits' we want the same happinesses. They writ in Languages that became universal & everlasting, while ours are extreamly limited both in DURATION AND Extent 'and duration'. LET US BE VAIN IF WE CAN 'A mighty foundation for our vanity' when the utmost we can hope is but to be read in an island, and to last a few years longer than W— or D—.

24. *A marginal note adds:* for Sence & Learning.

25. *Pope alters* their *to* them *and inserts a period before* Predecessors.

26. *Pope overwrites* have *with* having.

27. *Marginally Pope tries an alternative version of ll. 215–21:* The only PRETENCE I HAVE 'Plea I shall use TO PLEAD' TO FAVOR FROM 'for the favor of' the public is tht I have as REAL 'great a' respect for it as most Authors have for themselves; THAT I HAVE 'NOT ONLY SUP [*Pope started to write* suppressed] FOR ITS SAKE' SUPPRESSED MANY VILE THINGS & 'BUT' MANY THAT I THOUGHT TOLERABLE that 'for its sake' I have sacrificed much of my self-love, TO in the suppression of 'not only' many vile things & 'but' many tht I thought tolerable. For wt I have publishd I can only *This version was apparently to finish with* hope . . . prais'd (*ll. 221–2*) *and then, omitting all that intervenes in the main text about the* whole poem *and* particular lines, *turn immediately to the author's plea for justice:* It will [BE] BUT JUSTICE IN THE READER in return, be but justice in the reader to look upon *The plea seems intended to finish with* nothing . . . worse (*ll. 235–9*).

28. *Pope alters* m *to* M.

29. *Pope alters to* themselfs.

30. *Pope alters* be lookd *to* to look.
31. If . . . makes (*ll. 240–2*) *is struck out.*
32. *Pope draws a line around this sentence apparently to indicate that it is to be replaced by the following marginal insertion:* 'In the first place' I 'fairly own' WILL NEXT CONFESS tht I have usd my best utmost endeavor to MAKE THEM CORRECT 'the finishing these pieces'; 'that' I made wt advantage I cou'd BOTH FROM READING 'of the judgment' of DEAD authors, & ADVICE OF THE 'dead and' living; tht I omitted no means in my powr to be informd of my Errors, either by my friends or 'OR by' my Enemies; I THERFORE CAN 'and tht I' expect no favor on acct of 'my Youth', business, want of health, or any 'sad' idle Excuses. THAT I MAKE ONE OF IT NOW 'But the true reason they are not yet more correct' is owing to the consideration [of] THT LITTLE 'of how short a' time they, and I, have to live. A man tht can expect but sixty years may be ashamd to employ 30 IN MEASURING SYLLABLES in [REUNITING? RECASTING?] 'bringing' sense & ryme together. We spend our youth in the pursuit of MONEY 'riches' or fame in hopes to enjoy em wn we are old, & wn we are old we find THERE'S NO ENJOYING 'tis too late to enjoy' any thing. I HAVE GOT OVER THE MISTAKE PRETTY EARLY SOON & 'I therfore hope to be excusd' if I SPEND 'shoud think' the rest of my time 'better spent' either in saving my soul or enjoying the amusements of life. thn in pleasing a few Criticks.

    Pope follows this immediately with a second version of the final sentence: I therfore hope TO BE PARDOND 'SOME WISE MEN "the Witts" will pardon me' If I leave myself time enough to save my Soul 'some wise men will be [will be *overwrites* are] of my opinion if I think a part of it' EVEN IF I SHOUD THINK IT better spent in the COMMON AMUSEMENTS 'Enjoyments' of life thn in pleasing A FEW the criticks. *After this the passage continues:* 'I KNOW PRETTY WELL' I will next confess I am very ignorant AS TO THE DEGREE OF SUCCESS to wt degree I have succeeded. Tis unhappy enough (*l. 168*) . . . pleasd wth em (*l. 170*). I am only certain that I can have no reputation tht will last 'long' or tht deserves to do so (*l. 173*). For they have always (*ll. 173–5*) – poetry (*l. 175*). That my Cotemporaries (*l. 176*) – &c – to angry to find us so (*l. 214*). *The fragments again indicate the proposed progress of ideas.*
33. *In a marginal note, Pope introduces this sentence differently:* I confess then, I have assisted my self ALL 'as much as' I coud by READING & 'the' forein Helps of Reading, being always of opinion tht those Authors WILL 'who' never read, will never be read. I have EVER 'always' been fearful (*cf. l. 217*).
34. *Pope has altered* f *to* F.

Addendum: In l. 172 can never *is altered from* cant ever; *in l. 302,* these *is altered from* them; *in n.9 above,* gains *is altered from* gives.

6 Pope's Rambles

PAT ROGERS

The urge towards self-exploration figured strongly in the Augustan world. As A. R. Humphreys finely puts it, 'the great houses were not only private residences but showplaces to be publicised by admiring tourists and artists (the eighteenth century is the first great age of guide-books and scenic drawings).'[1] Suitably for an epoch much addicted to definition, boundary-beating and enclosure, men and women began to make their own survey of Britain. They witnessed at first hand what previous generations had left to specialist authorities, and topography moved from the hands of antiquaries or civil servants into those of travellers and trippers. 'The common sightseer or connoisseur was the effective public for a lot of artistic activity,' Humphreys points out: more and more art presumed what might be called a speculative audience, who might arrive casually on the day, rather than a prepacked court gathering. Everyone knew who was to attend a masque at Ludlow Castle in 1634; practically anyone could (and did) turn up at Shakespearian festivities in Stratford not much more than a century later. And as people became more mobile, the pleasures of scenery were attached to local piety, property and the order of rural society. Where Leland had seen remnants of a battle-scarred feudal world, the eighteenth-century traveller saw views – and views inescapably meant the present day and the current owner, even where Sanderson Miller or one of his kind had been brought in to supply an evocative ruin.

The picturesque moment may have dawned after Pope's death, but the taste for inland journeys started in the high Augustan era.[2] The most famous travellers of this early period are generally regarded as businesslike rather than aesthetic in their outlook, whether local historians like Ralph Thoresby, mettlesome explorers like Celia Fiennes (that adventurous ur-Victorian), or journalists and compilers like Defoe or John Macky. Nevertheless the first quarter of the new century already brought its crop of travellers, as it were, for the sake of it – people who went about the country for private and arbitrary reasons, who took holidays on the road, who set out to test a theory or to win a bet. Camden's *Britannia* was translated, re-edited, abridged, augmented, modernized, beset by rivals actual and potential. It is a profound mistake to think that tourism was simply a child of the picturesque movement. Long before the Lakes were in fashion, people made their peregrination of the northern counties. Half a century before Tintern and Llangollen came into their own, there was a tourist itinerary based on Blenheim, Castle Howard and Wilton. Mansions like Houghton and Holkham became objects of pilgrimage as soon as they were half up: Charles Lyttelton, a bishop who was also a Fellow of the Royal Society and a noted antiquarian, wrote to Sanderson Miller in 1758 that 'very few strangers' would visit a county as unattractive as Norfolk if it had not been for the showplaces in its northern half.[3] For the genteel, a round of country houses and (even more important) their gardens was a well-established custom at a time when the beautiful remained in assured dominance over the sublime or the picturesque.

It is not surprising that Alexander Pope, even so early, should exhibit many full-blown characteristics of the tourist. With his fanatical dedication to the art of landscape gardening, he possessed one prime qualification. A connoisseur's interest in the visual arts gave him the awareness of *contemporary* architecture which was an appropriate ingredient at this period. On the other hand, his weakness for 'romantic' moods allowed him to anticipate in some measure the mid-century taste for evocative twilight scenery and Gothic (not yet truly Gothick) appurtenances. Moreover, his feeling for the loss and mutability of things was deeply implanted in his instincts as a writer: it derived from Virgil rather than from currently modish verses on the ruins of Rome. The poet who could compose a passage such as this needed little instruction in the proper technique of musing over broken pillars:

All vast Possessions (just the same the case
Whether you call them Villa, Park, or Chase)
Alas, my BATHURST! what will they avail?
Join *Cotswold* Hills to *Saperton's* fair Dale,
Let rising Granaries and Temples here,
There mingled Forms and Pyramids appear,
Link Towns to Towns with Avenues of Oak,
Enclose whole Downs in Walls, 'tis all a joke!
Inexorable Death shall level all,
And Trees, and Stones, and Farms, and Farmer fall.[4]

Finally, Pope had some of the older tourist equipment. He was more of an antiquarian than has generally been recognized; and, to take a single example, *Windsor-Forest* embodies a sustained allusion to patriotic 'meeting of the waters' themes set out in Camden, Spenser, Drayton and Milton.[5] Lacking only good health and freedom from family ties, Pope had almost all the proper attributes of an eighteenth-century traveller.

Yet he never quite became such an animal, and the practical disabilities do not account for the whole omission, though they do for some of it. Pope's own preferred term, 'ramble', is indicative here. While the word was by no means idiosyncratic (Prior and Berkeley amongst others use it to describe their journeys), Pope developed a special fondness for *ramble* and often employs it to the exclusion of more likely synonyms. The *Oxford English Dictionary* gives the verb as the basic mode with the noun as a derivative: 'An act of rambling; a walk (formerly any excursion or journey) without definite route or other aim than recreation or pleasure.' Similarly with the verb: 'To wander, travel, make one's way about . . . in a free unrestrained manner and without definite aim or direction.' In both cases the first example cited is from the seventeenth century. Now it is immediately clear that Pope's rambles invariably *did* have a definite route, however jagged or irregular owing to changes in plan. It is fair to conclude, I think, that the term as he employs it carries a certain disingenuous quality of freewheeling or spontaneity: it reflects a level of aspiration, something Pope would like to associate with his travels, rather than just the bare reality. And 'recreation [and] pleasure', though no doubt a large part of Pope's aim, can scarcely be called an accurate or full description of his motives; they included elements of self-education, renewal both nervous and physical, compliance with social obligations, and so on. As with most aspects of his life, Pope took his rambling fairly seriously. And as with many other things, he invented a vocabulary for talking about it in jocose or dismissive accents.

Whenever the word appears in his letters (it never figures in his poetry, outside the early imitations of Chaucer), the tone is one of slight disparagement. It is as though Pope wishes to belittle his own sense of enjoyment, or to suggest he ought to be doing something more worthwhile. Sometimes the ramble is seen as interrupting business or social contracts: 'I hope all health will attend you till we meet again which I fear will now not be till after my Rambles in the Country.'[6] It is often an excuse for not writing letters: 'The same cause that commonly occasions all sorts of negligence in our Sex to yours, has hinder'd thus long my answering your most obliging Letter; I mean A Rambling way of Life which I have run into these two months & upwards.'[7] Again, Pope writes to John Caryll of a plan with Lord Jersey 'to have run away to see the Ile of Wight and Stanted. He thought it a mere ramble, but my design lay deeper, to have got to you.'[8] The overtones of the word are interestingly suggested by a letter from London to Sir William Trumbull at Easthampstead, written at the date of *Windsor-Forest*: 'I daily meet here in my Walks with numbers of people who have all their Lives been rambling out of their Nature, into one Business or other, and ought to be sent into Solitude to Study themselves over again.'[9]

Yet all the time it is clear that Pope derived a good deal of sustenance from his journeys, and looked forward to them with keen anticipation. This relish shows through the perpetual complaints about bad roads or constitutional upsets: as in a message to Martha Blount from Stowe in 1739.

> Your next direction is to Sir Tho. Lyt. at Hagley near Stowerbridge, Worcestershire, where I hope to be on the Tenth, or Sooner if Mr Lyt: come: Mr Grenville was here & told me he expected him in 2 or 3 days, so I think we may travel on the 8th or 9th tho' I never saw this Place in half the beauty and perfection it now has, I want to leave it to hasten my return towards You, or otherwise I could pass three months in agreable Rambles & slow Journies. I dread that to Worcester & back, for every one tells me tis perpetual Rock, & the worst of rugged roads; which really not only hurt me at present, but leave Consequences very uneasy to me.[10]

Again and again in the later years one comes on similar worries regarding the state of the roads: 'If ever you draw my affections nearer Devonshire than the Bath, you will have cause to think your self very Powerfull; for there's no Journey I dread like it, not even to Rome, tho both the Pope & Pretender are there. The last ten miles of Rock, between Marlborow & Bath almost killed me once, & I really believe the Alps are more passable than from thence to Exeter.'[11] There is nothing here of the mixed horror and excitement with which picturesque travellers negotiate the dizzy route past the cliffs of Penmaenmawr; Pope never makes any pretence to enjoyment where travelling rough is concerned. As he told Ralph Allen, 'the Journies I have now made will disqualify me from making more, till I become almost a New Body . . . I am really otherwise Sore & sick of a Journey so many days after it, that it deprives me of all the Enjoyment & Quiet I propose by it & can only give my Friends Pain & no pleasure.'[12] A different kind of hazard from Cotswold stone was provided by Sussex mud, and like every traveller of the time Pope would have understood the comment by Horace Walpole that 'Sussex is a great damper of curiosities'.[13] For Pope, particularly after his coach accident in 1726, the better roads which the turnpike system promised, and which Defoe welcomed so effusively in his *Tour*, came into the category of a necessity rather than a luxury.

Pope's addiction to travel became a byword with his friends. The Duchess of Buckingham wrote urging him to make his peace with his mother 'for staying abroad soe long she will probably describe You by the Gadder as she did Mr [Speaker] Compton by the Prater.' A few years later Swift told the Earl of Oxford, 'I am glad to hear Mr Pope is grown a Rambler; because I hope it will be for his Health.'[14] There was perhaps some covert flattery intended here, because Oxford himself nurtured the same inclinations: 'Mrs caesar tells me I have got such a habit of Rambling that she supposes I shall be like Teague never stand still.'[15] His journeys of the 1720s and 1730s have been printed from the Portland manuscripts, and they make mildly entertaining reading with some nicely prejudiced remarks on the subject of Palladian architecture. As for Pope, he was of course never to write any finished account of his trips; indeed he wrote nothing quite as self-conscious and elaborate as the description of 'a tedious ramble of six weeks through South and North Wales' (mainly South, in fact) which David Mallet sent to him in August 1734, while he was himself away on a visit to Bevis Mount.[16] Pope's own masterpieces of description relate to single occasions or to a sojourn in one place: notably, those devoted to Stonor (1717), Stanton Harcourt (1718), Sherborne (?1724) and Netley (1734).[17] In most cases the letter in question was not published in Pope's lifetime, as though he wished to avoid a return volley of similar descriptive sketches – understandable for a man whose every moral essay produced half a dozen essays on taste in confirmation or rebuttal.

Exactly when 'the Spirit of Rambling', a phrase he used to Allen,[18] descended on Pope it is hard to be certain. His first extended visit was to William Walsh, at Abberley in Worcestershire, during the summer of 1707. This occasioned Trumbull's often-cited remark that the young man had undertaken 'a dreadful long journey' – an indication of his visible frailty – and a strenuously witty letter from Pope to Anthony Englefield.[19] In this he speaks of a 'change of *Air*', again reminding us of the recuperative aim of travel and at the same time hinting at a desire for novelty – something Pope was often forced to suppress, but which emerges in his later years as a flight from *ennui*. One function of the annual jaunt was to take the poet out of himself and to avoid deadening routine (see his comments on Martha Blount in the letter to Hugh Bethel of 25 September 1737). He more than once regretted not being able to take sea-trips, which would allow him to visit Swift in Ireland or Bolingbroke in France. But his chest disorder forbade it, and he was forced to confine himself to more gradual changes of air – such as the temperate champaign districts of southern England could afford him.

After the visit to Abberley, while the young poet was busy establishing himself in London, he seems to have strayed very little outside the region between Berkshire and the capital. He went to visit Caryll at Ladyholt in the early summer of 1711, returning to his own 'Hermitage' in May; and the following year spent a matter of two months there. He went down to see Swift in his windy refuge on the Downs near Wantage in July 1714; and the following month made the first of at least a dozen visits to Bath. By this time he was taking regular trips to Oxford, principally in order to consult books for use in his *Iliad* translation, but also to extend his acquaintance with University figures like Dr George Clarke. Oxford lay on the axis of much of his travelling, and could be reached in reasonable comfort if a stop was made at Mapledurham or Whiteknights, both of which lay adjacent to Reading. Despite the proximity of Wimpole to Cambridge, Pope never made anything like the same penetration into the academic life of the sister university, a fact he came to rue when seeking subscribers to the *Odyssey* in 1724. It was a fact that Oxford showed itself 'much forwarder in this affair',[20] and indeed (whether the reason was political, or personal, or what) the same disparity had appeared in the *Iliad* subscription lists – both as regards institutional 'sales' to houses and those to individuals. Pope is a prime case of a writer whose outlook and affinities seem to have been strongly conditioned by geographical accidents. If he had had as good a friend as Allen living near Tunbridge Wells around 1740, he would probably have made that spa rather than Bath his main resort; and had the Earl and Countess of Burlington spent more time at Londesborough he might well have made more than the one visit to York in 1716. Admittedly he found the roads 'terrible', but his friendship with Hugh Bethel and other Yorkshiremen offered a regular inducement to brave the inclement northern air.[21] And though he told Swift that they were the only two among their circle 'qualify'd for the Mountains of Wales',[22] the most he attempted was what must have been a very short trip across the Bristol Channel in 1743. His habitual ports of call changed over the years, but the area of operation was always the same. Friendships burgeoned and fell away, loyalties developed and cracked, suspicions arose and were allayed, literary politics took one turn or another, and Pope's gardening consultancies required his presence here or there – none the less, year after year Pope took coach along the same highroads and traversed the same prosperous shires. The Whigs in time were to acquire their Dukeries: Pope had earlier rambled through the earldom of the Thames Valley.

The houses where he stayed can be roughly divided into three. First, there were family homes, those belonging to lesser Catholic gentry around Berkshire – Binfield, Hall Grove, Mapledurham, Whiteknights. These became less important as Pope established himself and as an older generation died off, but to begin with they were essential bases to which Pope could retreat from London. Second, there were homes of less intimate acquaintances, to which Pope was invited on specific occasions. In this group we could put Holm Lacey in Herefordshire, where Pope seems to have been a guest of Lady Scudamore in 1725 (a trip to the same county in 1717 had been planned but put off). Comparable is Leighs, the Essex home of the Duchess of Buckingham, where Pope was bidden three or four times and where he actually stayed on at least one occasion. In the same county, some way further from the capital, was Gosfield, home of the Knight family; it is not certain that Pope went there, despite legend and odd bits of circumstantial evidence, and despite a promise in 1727. West Wickham in Kent, where the minor poet Gilbert West lived, may also have received a single visit, in the early part of 1743. Several other such houses lay in the ambit of the major itineraries fanning out westwards from Reading, in Oxfordshire, Gloucestershire or Wiltshire. These include Tottenham, belonging to Lord Bruce, Burlington's brother-in-law (1734); Middleton, home of Lord Carleton (1716); Rentcomb, seat of Sir John Guise (1721); and Dodington, belonging to Sir William Codrington (1728).

The most important of these categories is that of Pope's regular stopping points: for the most part substantial houses at the centre of large estates, owned by men of considerable local (if not national) significance. A further subdivision here would mark off 'suburban' from rural seats. Bolingbroke's Dawley was too near Twickenham to be regularly used for sleeping in, though it was of great avail for talking and philosophizing. On the other hand Riskins was far enough from London to be the occasion for a minor ramble or to be the last stage of a longer journey. Pope was frequently there in the mid 1720s, though not as often as Lord Bathurst would have desired. Pope certainly knew other great houses just outside London (Chiswick, perhaps Canons, Marble Hill of course), but in such cases he would be paying a call for a limited period during the day. His rambles involved more extended periods as a house-guest, and it was these privileged sojourns around which the rambles were built. Pope was far from indifferent to natural beauty, but his routes were chosen not to maximize spectacle: they were intended to be pleasant and efficacious ways of getting from one centre of civilization to another.

It is in this light that we should consider the proud announcements of journeys under way or in prospect. Of course there is some vanity displayed – the sickly disadvantaged boy had come a long way, and was not averse to parading his familiarity with the great:

> I have been indispensably obliged to pass some days at almost every house along the Thames; half my acquaintance being upon the breaking up of the Parliament become my neighbours. After some attendance on my Lord Burlington, I have been at the Duke of Shrewsbury's, Duke of Argyle's, Lady Rochester's, Lord Percival's, Mr Stonor's, Lord Winchelsea's, Sir Godfrey Kneller's (who has made me a fine present of a picture) and Dutchess Hamilton's. All these have indispensable claims to me, under penalty of the imputation of direct rudeness, living within 2 hours sail of Chiswick. Then I am obliged to pass some days between my Lord Bathurst's, and three or four more on Windsor side. Thence to Mr Dancastle, and my relations on Bagshot Heath. I am also promised three months ago to the Bishop of Rochester for 3 days on the other side of the water... In a word, the minute I can get to you, I will,

> tho' Lintot's accounts are yet to settle, and three parts of my year's task to do.[23]

In fact the leading strategy here is to placate Caryll for not having made a promised visit. The same thing happened in other years, and one suspects that Pope was often glad of an excuse not to go to Ladyholt. In the letter cited, from 1717, Pope continues, 'I had forgot to tell you in my list of rambles (which if it goes on at this rate will shortly exceed in dimension the map of the children of Israel) that I must necessarily go some time this season to my Lord Harcourt's in Oxfordshire.' It was in this summer that his rambles became really complicated, so that he had to work out routes and times of arrival in careful detail. His correspondence starts to read like an annotated Bradshaw: 'Indeed I have of late had a smaller share of Health than ever, & in hope of amending it, I shall ramble about the Kingdom, as you are to do, most part of the Summer [1734]. I wish it may so happen as we may meet in our progress. If you go to Down Amney, I go to Ciceter, if you go to Portsmouth, I shall be at Southampton, if you ramble near Oxford, I shall be at Stowe: in any of which places I can entertain you, a day or two. If I can, I will return from Stowe to Oxford, but this cannot be till July or August.'[24] The trips begin to generate their own paper-work: 'It was a very great Pleasure to me to hear from you, after a long Intermission . . . which partly my Rambles and intended Rambles occasioned. I put them off with almost as much difficulty as I might have made them, & at the Expence of writing Letters in folio to Lord Bathurst about his Plans. I went only to Southampton, where the Roads are good, the accomodation good, Friends all the way, & a most agreable Retreat at the End, with a very valuable Person to crown all the Satisfaction of it.'[25]

The claims of friendship certainly ranked high among Pope's inducements. But he went for something more than convivial small talk. As Horace Walpole kept up acquaintance with people for their utility as letter-recipients, so Pope seems to have been drawn to men whose territorial influence and rural vocation answered his own poetic needs. It has been recently observed of the *Epistle to Burlington* that 'Pope's concern with houses and estates expands into a concern with the country, indeed with civilization, as a whole'.[26] This is not the place to explore what the country house ideal or the image of the planned garden meant to Pope: the attitudes that went to make his literary and private personality have been sensitively described by Maynard Mack, Howard Erskine-Hill, Peter Dixon and others. I wish to remark only that Pope's rambles were a way of keeping him in intimate contact with those places where the art of living was cultivated in opulent (but rarely ostentatious) surroundings. Pope could act as environmental designer, could escape from the cramping limitations of

Twickenham, could view antiquities and local showplaces, and could share in the daily round of those whom he celebrated in poetry. The ramble made actual a familiarity and social inwardness which were otherwise to some degree a fiction.

It was in a handful of great houses that dream and reality could be brought most closely together. There was Cirencester, at least ten times between 1718 and 1743; Stowe, eight or more occasions between 1725 and 1741, with other projected visits prevented by special circumstances; and Prior Park, regular annual visits in the last part of Pope's life. Slightly more intermittent was attendance at Rousham, perhaps five or six times over 15 years. In the same part of the country lay Adderbury, where Pope could rely on 'a little Bed' to be available;[27] Cornbury, an occasional point of call over 25 years; and, further south, Marston. Stanton Harcourt and the adjacent Cockthorpe seem to have dropped from the itinerary after a famous stay in 1718, when Pope made excellent progress with his Homer. By contrast Wimpole and its humbler sister-house Down Hall, on the other side of England, saw little of Pope, despite the longevity of his friendship with the second Earl of Oxford. Where Matthew Prior had been a habitué, Pope came occasionally as a welcome but perhaps stiffly received house-guest.

Outside this region one thinks of Sherborne, which surprisingly in view of his links with the Digby family Pope may only have visited on one long-heralded occasion.[28] It is possible that the death of Robert Digby in 1726 may have deterred further journeys to Dorset, just as the loss of Simon Harcourt in 1720 may have explained Pope's absence from the Harcourt home. In both cases he kept in touch with an older generation and continued to exercise his literary gifts on behalf of the family, but without an easy friendship between contemporaries the habit of visiting dropped away. And then there is Bevis Mount, not perhaps a great house exactly, but a charming and impressive seat where Pope obviously felt entirely at home – his stay there was generally protracted, and his letters bespeak his delight in the surroundings. In part this may be put down to the character of his host, the Earl of Peterborough, whom Pope admired for his wit, vivacity and magnanimous spirit. A spell at Bevis Mount inevitably meant a special detour, or at least a ramble in itself: Pope often came home through Basingstoke and thence into Berkshire. Like the topographical writers he liked to make a 'circuit' rather than a straight linear out-and-return journey. It added to the improvisatory quality he sought to give his highly organized rambles.

Towards the end of his life, when he no longer had an aged mother to look after, Pope made more of a ceremony of his rambling. An added ingredient now, carrying with it both pain and pleasure, was supplied by nostalgic reflection. 'In the Summer,' he told Swift in 1739, 'I generally ramble for a Month, to Lord Cobham's, the Bath, or elsewhere. In all those Rambles, my Mind is full of the Images of you and poor Gay, with whom I travell'd so delightfully two Summers.'[29] The years in question were 1726 and 1727; Swift had spent a fair amount of time, before and after this date, in wandering over Ireland; while Gay became more willing to carry his plump frame round the countryside to places like Holm Lacey in the late 1720s. Again, Pope writes to Martha Blount of a planned excursion to Mapledurham and Windsor Forest, 'This may be the last time I shall see those Scenes of my past Life, where I have been so happy, & I look upon one of them in particular in this Light, since it was there I first knew you.'[30] The memory of the Forest was never far from Pope's consciousness: 'I often give a Range to my Imagination, & goe a strolling with . . . you, up & down Binfield Wood, or over Bagshot Heath.'[31] His rambles took him to favourite haunts, as well as to new scenes and much-desired spectacles like Netley Abbey. The refreshment he gained need not entail a long journey, provided there was a change of company and atmosphere. The picturesque somehow required a degree of remoteness, but Pope's aesthetic senses sharpened as soon as he was well clear of Hounslow Heath.

In the final years any kind of travel became even more of an effort. Paradoxically, as the quest for health grew more urgent, so the discomforts of each spell away from home increased. In 1740 Pope wrote to the Earl of Orrery of 'having been myself upon a wild Winter Ramble (not unlike a Scythian expedition) for near three months, essaying the Virtue of Waters when they were almost Ice'.[32] As well as Bath and Bristol, he may have tried the spa at Holt, which his physician Dr John Burton had purchased from the Lisle family (themselves commemorated in the Crux Easton poems). It was all to no avail, but Pope clung to his itinerant ways. Less than a year before he died, in September 1743, he embarked on an ambitious round-trip covering Cornbury, Rousham, Oxford, Amesbury and Salisbury. He had not been to the last two before, though Gay had often stayed with the Queensberries in Wiltshire. Unabated in will and curiosity, he submitted only to bodily decay.

Perhaps the most remarkable inland voyager of Pope's day was the antiquarian William Stukeley. His *Itinerarium Curiosum* (1724) begins with a sounding defence of travel in Britain, at a time when 'the genteel and fashionable *tours* of France and Italy' arrogated a young man's attention. In terms that might have appealed to the author of *The New Dunciad*, Stukeley deplored the fact that 'our own country lies like a neglected province'.

> Like untoward children, we look back with contempt upon our own mother. The antient Albion, the valiant Britain, the renowned England, big with all the blessings of indulgent nature . . . is postponed to all

> nations . . . And if I have learnt by seeing some places, men and manners, or have any judgment in things, it is not impossible to make a classic journey on this side the streights of Dover.[33]

Pope could not attempt the Grand Tour, and his health made Stukeley's kind of strenuous fact-finding expedition physically impossible, even supposing his temperament had led him that way. But taken together his rambles do merge into something that might fairly be described as 'a classic journey'. Their declared aim was escapist, but in truth they engaged the same imaginative faculties as his own poetry. 'You are much a superior genius to me in rambling,' he wrote to the lawyer Fortescue, then on the circuit. 'You, like a Pigeon . . . can fly some hundred leagues at a pitch; I, like a poor squirrel, am continually in motion indeed, but it is about a cage of three foot: my little excursions are but like those of a shopkeeper, who walks every day a mile or two before his own door, but minds his business all the while.'[34] We may be glad that Pope, too, 'minded his business' while upon his little excursions. He was never more imaginatively alive than when he was rambling.

NOTES

1. A. R. Humphreys, *The Augustan World* (1954), 238.
2. For the topographic tradition, see Esther Moir, *The Discovery of Britain* 1964), and my introduction to Daniel Defoe, *A Tour through the Whole Island of Great Britain* (1971), 18–29.
3. *An Eighteenth-Century Correspondence*, ed. Lilian Dickins and Mary Stanton (1910), 397.
4. *The Second Epistle of the Second Book of Horace Imitated by Mr. Pope*, ll. 254–63.
5. That he consulted Camden from his travels is evident from references in his letters, e.g. Pope to Oxford, 1 September 1734, *The Correspondence of Alexander Pope*, ed. George Sherburn, 5 vols (1956) (hereafter cited as *Corr.*), III, 430.
6. *Corr*, III, 482.
7. *Corr.*, I, 180–1.
8. *Corr.*, I, 411.
9. A. Coyle Lunn, 'A new Pope letter in the Trumbull correspondence', *Review of English Studies*, XXIV (1937), 310–15.
10. *Corr.*, IV, 185.
11. *Corr.*, IV, 156.
12. *Corr.*, IV, 190.
13. Quoted by Moir, *op. cit.*, 6.
14. *Corr.*, II, 303; III, 429. See also Bolingbroke's report of Pope's travels, III, 413.
15. *Corr.*, II, 315.
16. *Corr.*, III, 421–3.
17. *Corr.*, I, 429–30; I, 505–7; II, 236–40; G. S. Rousseau, 'A new Pope letter', *Philological Quarterly*, XLV (1966), 439–48. For comments on the Stanton Harcourt letter, see my *Introduction to Pope*(1976), 146–9. For the Sherborne letter, see Howard Erskine-Hill, *The Social Milieu of Alexander Pope* (1975), 287–90.

18. *Corr.*, IV, 347.
19. George Sherburn, 'Letters of Pope', *Review of English Studies*, IX (1958), 388–406.
20. *Corr.*, II, 271.
21. *Corr.*, III, 61. For the Yorkshire connection, see 'The Burlington Circle in the Provinces', *Durham University Journal*, LXVII (1975), 219–26.
22. *Corr.*, II, 395.
23. *Corr.*, I, 417–8.
24. *Corr.*, III, 408.
25. *Corr.*, IV, 39.
26. Erskine-Hill, *op. cit.*, 304.
27. *Corr.*, IV, 189.
28. Likewise there is evidence only of one visit to Hagley (*Corr.*, IV, 185), a residence much more familiar to James Thomson.
29. *Corr.*, IV, 179: cf. II, 388.
30. Rousseau, *op. cit.*, 418.
31. *Corr.*, I, *393*.
32. *Corr.*, IV, 231.
33. William Stukeley, *Itinerarium Curiosum* (2nd edn, 1776), I, 3. This opening journey is dedicated to Maurice Johnson, the antiquarian friend of Gay, who introduced Pope to the Gentlemen's Society of Spalding (admission was on 31 October 1728). A colleague and fellow-traveller of Stukeley was Roger Gale, who subscribed to Pope's edition of Shakespeare in 1725. It is exceedingly probable that that Pope was familiar with *Itinerarium Curiosum*, but I have not been able to establish this positively.
34. *Corr.*, II, 521. For useful comments on Pope's rambles as a young man, see George Sherburn, *The Early Career of Alexander Pope* (1934), 210–14.

7 Pope and Homer

GEORGE FRASER

In the mid-1950s, I took part in a Third Programme series in which a number of poets translated important passages from the *Iliad*. It was not very successful: but the sharpest comment I heard was from Constantine Trypanis, at once a distinguished poet and Professor of Byzantine Greek studies at Oxford. 'There is', he said to me, 'a quality in Homer which none of these young men has conveyed. I would call it *epic monotony*.' Certainly Pope, in the years between 1715 when he sampled the public's taste by producing his version of the first four books of the *Iliad* and 1726, when he produced the last two volumes of the version of the *Odyssey* which he had 'undertaken' with Broome and Fenton as his assistants, did not aim at epic monotony. For all his eloquence in *An Essay on Criticism* about Homer and Nature being the same thing, and regularity being something needed by poets, and appealing to critics, of the second order, Pope knew instinctively that a baldly literal version of Homer was out of the question. Virgil would have been quite another thing: Virgil, like Pope, was writing for an audience that was enjoying peace and the sense of dominance after a long period of internal strife and threats from other nations. The Romans under Augustus were not so very different from the English under Queen Anne and the early Georges. But Dryden had pre-empted Virgil; and the case against Dryden's Virgil is that it has a boisterous and rough energy, which is very much Dryden's own, whereas Virgil's lingering pathos and continuing sense of accepted loss are almost if not quite (there is the elegy on Oldham and the very moving epistle to Congreve on *The Double-Dealer*) beyond the reach and touch of Dryden. Pope's *Eloisa to Abelard* is, of course, deliberately Ovidian, modelled on the *Heroides*, which means that its sentiment has some cleverly false flashiness; but there is a sad Virgilian tenderness, too. Yet Pope had a fiery temperament to which, in fact, the heroic and the awesome in Homer made a special appeal; invalids like to think about heroes: and, as Matthew Arnold noted, Pope had one quality essential to any translator of Homer, swiftness. For the rest, as the actors say, Pope deliberately played against the text: against Homer's card of formulistic repetition, he played his own card of elegant variation.

Pope's old bad name (the reproach has died down now) for having invented an ornate and unreal 'poetic diction' rests mainly on his versions of Homer: elsewhere he is our great master, in verse, of the style of easy, vivacious conversation. But where Homer is powerfully bare and bald, Pope's only resource is to deck him with garlands. Peter Quennell, in his vivid and sympathetic biography of Pope up to 1728, gives a graceful example of this bedecking. Quennell quotes a line of Pope's about a gallant squire, Clytus, killed by Teucer's 'thrilling arrow':

> In youth's first bloom reluctantly he dies

The pathos comes from the apt choice and beautiful placing of the movingly reticent adverb 'reluctantly'. But (reluctantly himself, perhaps) Quennell adds

> we owe [this] to the translator's unaided fancy: Homer's hero is described neither as reluctant to leave the world, nor, indeed, as very young.

Dr Johnson, a much finer classical scholar than Pope (whose religion deprived him of a regular education), felt that such licences in Pope were not only defensible but necessary: a modern reader, he told Boswell, would find a literal version of Homer unreadable. Gibbon and Ruskin, Quennell tells us, both acquired their first delight in Homer from Pope's translation. Modern readers who have had the chance to compare both might often admit that they find more pleasure, and less of a sense of reading from duty, in Pope's *Iliad* than in the accentual hexameters of Professor Richmond Lattimore, though the latter is not merely a fine scholar but an American poet of some reputation. Lattimore's comparative failure, *poetic* failure, may be due to the inhospitality of the English language to what used to be called the fourteener. The accentual or quantitative hexameter is not, of course, an iambic fourteener but it has a very similar awkwardness in English. Only Auden has used it well, with strict syllable count and free stress movement, in 'In Praise of Limestone'. The pre-Audenic accentual hexameter was used in a manner half-serious, half-humorous by Clough, and to tell a sentimental tale by Longfellow, but at its best it remains what an amateur of metrics would call a 'curiosity'. The last thing it ever sounds like is a trumpet. H. A. Mason, in his fascinating *To Homer through Pope* (1972) nevertheless thinks Lattimore's the best modern version, but not as verse – merely as what he calls a 'creeping translation', the sort of line-for-line crib a scholar might make to help him in his re-readings. It cannot be poetry, Mason says, for he can write such lines himself.

Pope was always an invalid, and he always loved society – the society, it must be admitted, of lords and ladies and gentlefolk with a weakness for poetry rather more than the society of his fellow men of letters, except a select few, notably Swift, Gay, Arbuthnot. His disease was a progressive curvature of the spine, and weakening of it, called Potts' disease. He had acquired this by drinking infected milk at his father's farm; his being trampled on by another cow, brought round by a milkmaid to his father's London home and warehouse, when Pope was much smaller, was responsible for his stunted height, less than five feet. His beautiful intellectual face and fine hands, his vivid and dominating eyes, his sheer genius (which must have displayed itself in conversation in a way Spence fails to record), made people forget these disadvantages.

Up to the triumph of his first volume of 1717 (which contains no poem mainly satirical except *The Rape of the Lock*, and that poem itself satire so good-natured that he was able to dedicate it to its heroine, Arabella Fermor), Pope led a very social life and even affected gallantry, and perhaps felt for Martha Blount an affection mixed with sensuality and certainly about Lady Mary Wortley Montagu admiration for wit and beauty combined with erotic daydreams. By 1726, he had completed Homer but with a painful and sustained labour that affected permanently both his temper and his health. He then undertook a labour for which he was ill fitted, the editing of Shakespeare; was attacked on sound scholarly grounds, by Lewis Theobald, a drudge, but a scholar; and in 1728, with Theobald as the hero (we hate our sound critics far more than the fools who miss the point), launched on his enemies the most ferocious and merciless verse satire in the English language, *The Dunciad*. He was much hated: he was the greatest poet of his age, and he moved in the best society, and for his fellow writers, then as now, these were very adequate motives for hatred. He was a Papist also, tiny and almost hunch-backed: it was a brutal age.

The men who attacked him did not realize that the little man would bother to strike back: to strike them where they were most vulnerable; they were bad writers, they were self-deceiving failures, they were uneducated, they lived in sordid poverty. His attack on their poverty seemed to his enemies unforgivable. But Pope gave more money, year after year, than he could properly afford to charity (this, indeed, is in itself a definition of monetary charity). No man has a duty to write, and it would have been possible for Pope's enemies to earn an honest living as clerks, say, in shops or offices . . . Yet when one has said all that, one still wonders whether, for all the fame and independence it brought him, Homer put a heavier weight on that sick body and affectionate but irritable soul than they could bear. I would have preferred the friendship of the younger to that of the older Pope. With his sleepless nights while translating, and nightmares of an endless journey, at which every halting place opened on a new vast prospect of wilderness, Pope too might have preferred his youthful self.

When Pope settled into his Homer routine, he could rely, with the help of the commentators, of the Dacier version in French and the Chapman versions in English, on producing about 40 lines a day. The hours or so of pleasure came when he thrust Homer, Dacier, Chapman aside and polished what he now felt to be his own verses. Though Broome and Fenton did the groundwork of 12 of the 24 books of the *Odyssey*, he gave these, also, this final polish, and their work, reworked by him, cannot be distinguished from his own. They felt he should have paid them more: but he was never grudging about money. They felt he should have brought forward their names more prominently: like all poets, he was a little grudging about fame, but the sales of the *Odyssey* were lagging after the great success of the *Iliad* and Pope knew that his name, not Broome's or Fenton's, would sell the volumes. They were obviously competent scholars and versifiers, but they have left nothing of their own that has lived.

It is pleasant to turn from such topics to Pope's *Iliad* and the *Odyssey*, which is half his and wholly under his supervision and revision, as great Popeian poems. Pope's labours never, as his introductions and footnotes show, diminished his enthusiasm for his idea of Homer. 'Homer', he tells us, 'is universally allowed to have had the greatest *Invention* of any writer whatever.' For Homer's invention we might perhaps today say his creative imagination, drawing directly on nature (the natural shaping spirit in Homer himself, not merely the actual and describable world around him), rather than on art, rules, judgment. Homer is, for Pope, the fount of all literature, perhaps (though Pope does not say so) in secular literature what the Bible is in sacred. Virgil may equal Homer in judgment but no author at all equals him in natural power; and, in the end, all that Art, as distinct from Nature, can do is 'as in the most regular gardens . . . reduce the beauties of Nature to more regularity, and such a figure, which the common eye may better take in, and is therefore more entertained with.'

Pope, as we know from the 'Epistle to Burlington', had not the 'common eye' which is 'entertained with' 'such a figure':

His Gardens next your admiration call,
On every side you look, behold the Wall!
No pleasing Intricacies intervene,
No artful wilderness to perplex the scene;
Grove nods at grove, each Alley has a brother,
And half the platform just reflects the other.

'And perhaps', Pope concludes this introductory paragraph to his preface to the *Iliad*, 'the reason why common criticks are inclined to prefer a judicious and methodical genius to a great and fanciful one, is, because they find it easier for themselves to pursue their observations through the uniform and bounded works of art, than to comprehend the vast and various extent of Nature.' This high disdain for 'common criticks' and their sterile wish to have everything tidy is a splendid contradiction of what used to be the common critics' idea of Pope himself.

But with that enthusiasm, there was still that slavery. Between 1717 and 1726, Pope wrote only one poem of the first order, outside Homer, the noble 'Epistle to Robert Earl of Oxford, and Earl Mortimer', written in 1721 and in 1722 used as a dedicatory epistle to the poems of Thomas Parnell. Parnell had been a close friend both of Robert Harley and of Pope and Pope had found time to edit his poems. The opening lines are among Pope's most musically melancholy:

Such were the notes thy once-loved Poet sung,
Till Death untimely stop'd his tuneful Tongue.

Perhaps it is Pope's work on Homer that gives this tribute to a sick old Tory, permanently out of office like his party, a heroic note. Robert Harley, Lord Treasurer in the last years of Queen Anne, and created Earl of Oxford and Earl Mortimer, had been imprisoned in the Tower on suspicion of treasonable correspondence with the Pretender, been released for lack of evidence or from the dying away of old enmities, and had retired to his country estates ('In vain to Desarts thy Retreat is made'). Since all his political schemes in his days of power had been muddled (so much so, that he rarely came to court sober, and this was one of Queen Anne's motives for depriving him of the Treasurer's staff on her death-bed) and since he loved books, these last few years of exclusion from politics and comfortable leisure may, in fact, have been the happiest of Harley's life.

But a great poet is not concerned with prosaic facts of this sort, and Pope's Harley is Homerically sublime:

And sure if aught below the Seats Divine
Can touch Immortals, 'tis a Soul like thine:
A Soul supreme, in each hard Instance try'd,
Above all Rage, all Passion, and all Pride,
The Rage of Pow'r, the Blast of Publick Breath,
The Lust of Lucre, and the Dread of Death.
  In vain to Desarts thy Retreat is made,
The Muse attends thee to the Silent Shade:
'Tis hers, the Brave Man's latest steps to trace,
Re-judge his Acts, and dignify Disgrace.
When Intrest calls off all her sneaking train,
And all th'Oblig'd desert, and all the Vain;
She waits, or to the Scaffold, or the Cell,
When the last ling'ring friend has bid Farewel.

Harley knew he hardly deserved a word of this (though he was in fact, though without any clear policy, incorrupt, full of calm passive courage, and very good-natured) and was properly touched and grateful. Wearying as these long Homeric labours were, they had touched Pope's soul with fire. His gift for steady loyalty to old friends in distress was perhaps his noblest single quality: one does not blame him that the friends, Harley, Bolingbroke, Swift morosely exiled in Ireland, were all great men, in rank, genius, or both. The great are naturally drawn to each other and Homer would strengthen Pope in his wish to find even in this world gods and heroes.

But let us look in some detail at one quite short and yet self-contained passage from Pope's Homer, to be precise from Book XI of the *Odyssey* where Ulysses describes how he arrived at the land of the Cimmerians and performed sacrifices to raise the spirits of the dead, particularly that of the prophet Tiresias. But the first ghost who appears to Ulysses is that of Elpenor, Ulysses' companion, who explains that having drunk too much in Circe's house, he had needed to get off his bunk, missed his footstep on a ladder, and broken his neck: he asks Ulysses to come back to Circe's island when he can, build him a tomb, and set up his oar as a trophy. Ulysses promises to do so.

The passage is very well known because it appears in Ezra Pound's first *Canto,* translated in an Anglo-Saxon style (coming from Pound's own early version of *The Seafarer*) from a Renaissance Latin version of the *Odyssey.* Like much of Pound, it is so vividly written that it appeals to young students of poetry who are quite unaware of its context. I do not think Pope's version would have the same sort of appeal, to the same sort of audience: yet in my own mind I have decided it is finer poetry, even though there are implications in the Elpenor passage that Pound responds to instinctively and that leave Pope exceedingly puzzled. I would say that Pope works with more care but within a more rigid moral and imaginative framework.

Here is Pound's version:

But first came Elpenor, our friend Elpenor,
Unburied, cast on the wide earth,
Limbs that we left in the house of Circe,
Unwept, unwrapped in sepulchre, since toils urged other,
Pitiful spirit. And I cried in hurried speech:
'Elpenor, how art thou come to this dark coast?
'Cam'st thou afoot, outstripping seamen?'
'Ill fate and abundant wine. I slept in Circe's ingle.
'Going down the long ladder unguarded,
'I fell against the buttress,
'Shattered the nape-nerve, the soul sought Avernus.

'But thou, O King, I bid remember me, unwept, unburied,
'Heap up my arms, be tomb by sea-bord, and inscribed:
'*A man of no fortune, and with a name to come.*
'And set my oar up, that I swung mid fellows.'

Let us see how Pope treats the same passage (the reader will find it at line 65 of Pope's *Odyssey*, Book XI):

There, wand'ring thro' the gloom I first survey'd,
New to the realms of death, *Elpenor*'s shade;
His cold remains all naked to the sky
On distant shores unwept, unburied lye.
Sad at the sight I stand, deep fix'd in woe,
And ere I spoke the tears began to flow.
O say what angry pow'r *Elpenor* led
To glide in shades, and wander with the dead?
How could thy soul, by realms and seas disjoyn'd,
Out-fly the nimble sail, and leave the lagging wind?
The Ghost reply'd: To Hell my doom I owe,
Daemons accurst, dire ministers of woe!
My feet thro' wine unfaithful to their weight,
Betray'd me stumbling from a tow'ry height,
Stagg'ring I reel'd, and as I reel'd I fell,
Lux'd the neck-joint – my soul descends to hell.
But lend me aid, I now conjure me lend,
By the soft tye and sacred name of friend!
By thy fond consort! By thy father's cares!
By lov'd *Telemachus* his blooming years!
For well I know that soon the heav'nly pow'rs
Will give thee back to day, and Circe's shores:
There pious on my cold remains attend,
There call to mind thy poor departed friend.
The tribute of a tear is all I crave,
And the possession of a peaceful grave.
But if unheard, in vain compassion plead,
Revere the Gods, the Gods avenge the dead!
A tomb along the wat'ry margin raise,
The tomb with manly arms and trophies grace,
To shew posterity *Elpenor* was.
There high in air, memorial of my name
Fix the smooth oar, and bid me live to fame.
  To whom with tears: These rites, oh mournful shade,
Due to thy Ghost, shall to thy Ghost be paid.

Pope is not padding here, more than the couplet forces him to: Pound, as often, is cutting drastically. Here from a very accurate version by Professor Ennis Rees (New York, 1960) is a passage that Pope paraphrases and Pound simply leaves out:

> 'Now I have something to ask in the name
> Of those at home, your wife and the father that raised you
> And your only son Telemachus, for I'm sure that after
> You leave this kingdom you'll stop for a while at that
> Aegean island with your excellent ship'

Rees goes on again at the point where Pound picked up after his omission:

> 'There,
> O King, I beg you, remember me, do not
> Leave me behind unwept and unburied, for then
> You'll surely have me to haunt you.'

Pound leaves out the passage about the threat of haunting for his Odysseus is too grand to be threatened by anyone: Pope wraps it in periphrasis, so that it becomes a tactful reminder of how the Gods punish impiety, rather than a direct threat. It is interesting that all three translators use the words 'unwept' and 'unburied': we need not imagine Pound borrowing from Pope, or Rees from Pound: they are simply the directest words for the meaning and have also (or therefore) proper dignity. It is sad that Professor Rees, whom one feels one can trust as a crib, should hardly read at all like poetry. 'The father that raised you' too clearly suggests the American Middle West. The lines, ranging in a sample count from 11 to 15 syllables, aim at six strong stresses each but one needs the capital letters at the beginning of each line to tell limping verse from limping prose. Does all successful *poetic* translation involve a sort of transformation – a rethinking, refeeling, rewording of the raw material in (in our case) English? Are Pope's and Pound's Homers versions of Pope and Pound? And is what one feels the lack of in Professor Rees's version exactly the specific tone, character, and flavour of Professor Rees? ('It is magnificently primeval, Homer, but you must not call it Pope!')

Pope has some very interesting footnotes, making up a kind of running commentary, on the Elpenor passage. He was clearly very puzzled both by its function in the general narrative and by its tone:

> 73. How could thy soul, by realms and seas disjoyn'd,
> Out-fly the nimble sail?

Eustathius is of the opinion that Ulysses speaks pleasantly to *Elpenor*, for were his words to be literally translated they would be, *Elpenor, thou art come hither on foot, sooner than I on a ship.* I suppose it is the worthless character of *Elpenor* that led that Critic into this opinion; but I would rather take the sentence to be spoken seriously, not only because such railleries are an insult on the unfortunate, and levities perhaps unworthy of Epic Poetry, but also from the general conduct of *Ulysses*, who at the sight of *Elpenor* bursts into tears, and compassionates the fate of his friend. Is there anything in this that looks like raillery? If there is, we must confess that *Ulysses* makes a very quick transition from sorrow to pleasantry.

Such quick transitions, however, *are* very common in great poetry. They illustrate admirably Freud's theory of jokes: that these are safety valves, through which painful feelings find a harmless and even superficially pleasurable outlet. Shakespeare's Hamlet often 'speaks pleasantly' in this way, as in his 'Very like, very like!' when told that the spectacle of the ghost would have much amazed him. Or consider the first stanza of Donne's 'A Feaver' which 'speaks pleasantly' and also speaks in agony:

Oh doe not die, for I shall hate
All women so, when thou art gone,
That thee I shall not celebrate
When I remember, thou wast one.

It suggests some kind of limitation in the Augustan sensibility that Pope, unlike Homer, unlike Shakespeare, unlike Donne, unlike Pound, cannot respond to this special fusion of grief and wit. Perhaps the only contemporary of Pope's who did respond to it was Swift, a survival from the seventeenth century. The old example will serve: 'Last week I saw a Woman *flay'd*, and you will hardly believe, how much it altered her Person for the worse.' But I am afraid there is also in Pope's notes here just a touch of Addisonian priggishness. Elpenor is such a low and absurd person to thrust himself into the front of the story just when we are expecting awe and horror! But is there a moral perhaps? A moral always helps. Pope leans heavily on Le Bossu:

But it may be asked what connection this story of *Elpenor* has to do with the subject of the poem, and what it contributes to the end of it? *Bossu* very well . . . answers that the Poet may insert some incidents that make no part of the fable or action: especially if they be short, and break not the thread of it: this before us is only a small part of a large Episode, which the Poet was at liberty to insert or omit, as contributed most to the beauty of his Poetry: besides, it contains an excellent moral, and shows us the ill effects of drunkenness and debauchery. The Poet represents *Elpenor* as a person of a mean character, and punishes his crime with sudden death, and dishonour.

The effect of the sudden appearance of Elpenor, with its homeliness and pathos, almost its tragic absurdity, is to set us down in the real, vulnerable yet moving human world before we encounter the nightmare horrors of Hades: passages that occur to me as relevantly similar in their effect are the porter's speech and the knocking on the gate in *Macbeth* (in De Quincey's classical account of them) or Barnardine's stubborn and drunken refusal to be executed in *Measure for Measure*. Elpenor is our bridge between two worlds, the 'human, all too human' and the chillingly preternatural. He is on the verge not only of comedy but of low farce (no doubt he was groping about for the ladder he missed, or slipped on, to find a quiet corner to relieve his bladder of 'abundant wine'). But he is also the kind of hopeless character whom people like. Odysseus responds most sympathetically to Elpenor's request to be given the sort of tomb he would have deserved *if* he had been a hero. After all it was bad luck ('ill fate') that Elpenor never had a chance to show whether he could have been a hero or not. That Homeric or Shakespearian largeness of sympathy is outside Pope's range.

But he must do what he can with Elpenor and he aims, through a musical expressiveness, first of all at pathos:

His cold remains all naked to the sky
On distant shores unwept, unburied lye.
Sad at the sight I stand, deep fix'd in woe,
And ere I spoke the tears began to flow.

Notice the use of *l*'s, *r*'s and *d*'s – trilled liquids and voiced dentals; of alliterative sibilants, '*S*ad at the *s*ight I *s*tand'; and of long open diphthongs for end-rhymes, 'sky', 'lye', 'woe', 'flow'. The consonants within the line sometimes seem to clench the feeling back (the voiced dentals) and sometimes to let it ripple forwards (the trilled liquids): but the grief opens out and bursts like a great wave at the rhymes.

Yet such a smoothness could become monotonous (though not in Trypanis's sense of 'epic monotony') and suddenly we get a line that veers and jogs like a small boat in a sea-swell:

Out-fly the nimble sail, and leave the lagging wind . . .

Pope, however, faced problems of sense as well as sound. After studying these three versions, I remain rather in the dark about the exact mechanics of Elpenor's death. Pound makes him sleep 'in Circe's ingle', which means her hearth, which would be on the ground floor. There would be no height to fall from (if Pound's 'ingle' is 'house' by metonymy, the figure is used in a clumsy and confusing way). Pound also makes Elpenor break his neck on a 'buttress', which suggests that he was sleeping on a flat roof, with a ladder up to it, missed the ladder and broke his neck on a buttress outside the house. Homer, we must remember, according to the most recent speculations, was shaping into two great poems, say in the seventh century B.C., traditions dating from around the twelfth century B.C. Chariots are part of his inherited material but he does not seem to know how they might be used in battle; spears are sometimes flung from them, but mostly they bring the heroes up to the front line, where they dismount for single combat. Similarly, if we could call him like Tiresias from the grave, it would be silly to ask him for an architectural drawing of Circe's house. The useful Professor Rees seems to confirm my own guess of sleeping on a flat roof which one climbed up to by an outside ladder (perhaps only a specially honoured guest like Odysseus would sleep inside the house):

> When I woke up in the house
> Of Circe, I did not remember that long ladder
> By which I came up, and proceeded to fall headlong
> From the roof, fatally breaking my neck.

Even there it is a puzzle that Elpenor is '*in* the house' but falls '*from* the roof'. Of the three versions, Pound's ('ingle', 'buttress') sounds most physically solid but holds architecturally least coherently together. Pope, very brilliantly, makes no attempt to plan the house for us but instead concentrates on the psychology of falling:

> My feet thro' wine unfaithful of their weight,
> Betray'd me tumbling from a tow'ry height,
> Stagg'ring I reel'd, and as I reel'd I fell,
> Lux'd the neck-joynt – my soul descends to hell.

The dizzying mimesis of

> Stagg'ring I reel'd, and as I reel'd I fell,

is beyond admiration. The deliberate vagueness of 'a tow'ry height' gets us inside a drunk man's scared, bewildered consciousness. Pope, of these three translators, is the only one who for a moment makes us *become* Elpenor.

Perhaps also in these four lines, and in these only, Pope wished to skirt the edges of comedy. H. A. Mason points out that the earliest recorded *literary* use of 'lux' (a surgical term, short for 'luxate', to dislocate) alongside, also, the less unusual but not common 'neck-joynt' is in a passage about Elpenor in John Philips' *Cyder* (1708), a comic though admiring parody of Milton's heroic blank verse:

> What shall we say
> Of rash *Elpenor*, who in evil hour
> Dry'd an immeasurable Bowl, and thought
> T'exhale his Surfeit by irriguous Sleep,
> Imprudent? Him, Death's Iron-Sleep opprest,
> Descending careless from his Couch; the Fall
> Luxt his Neck-joint, and spinal Marrow bruised.

It would be probable, in any case, that the young Pope had read *Cyder*, a very popular poem: the Elpenor passage from his *Odyssey* makes this certain.

In the four lines of his falling, Pope has made Elpenor frighteningly real to us. But Elpenor, as an individual person, embarrasses him, and as the passage progresses Elpenor is deliberately de-particularized, becomes any person of high rank, seeking some memorial:

> There high in air, memorial of my name,
> Fix the smooth oar, and bid me live to fame.
>
> To whom with tears: These rites, oh mournful shade,
> Due to thy Ghost, shall to thy Ghost be paid.

There is a certain briskness, perhaps, in Ulysses's military courtesy: 'Request granted, Elpenor! Elpenor, dismiss!' And there may have been a thought in Pope's mind (though he allows no sarcasm to tinge his voice) that the rites were due to Elpenor the Ghost rather than Elpenor the Man. What is worth noting especially is the triumph Pope made of an episode which, as his footnotes show, he found essentially pointless and undignified. The poet's instinct – and perhaps this happens quite often with Pope – triumphed over the critic's, and the man's, limitations.

8

On Earth as it Laughs in Heaven: Mirth and the 'Frigorifick Wisdom'

J. S. CUNNINGHAM

The God of Genesis, and the God of *Paradise Lost*, saw that it was good; and perhaps the creator of both tigers and lambs did 'smile his work to see', hard though it is to interpret that smile in its darkly momentous context,

> When the stars threw down their spears
> And watered Heaven with their tears.

The English Hymnal's serener image of divine creation is 'The world that smiled when morn was come' (no. 777) – to which, across Time, or across three score years and ten, another hymn answers:

> In the joy which His smile shall afford
> My soul shall her vigour renew.
> (no. 778)

Between that first smile and this last, we may trust, with William Cowper, that

> Behind a frowning providence
> He hides a smiling face,
> (no. 373)

or, with Pope, that a benevolent human spirit mirrors divinity:

> Earth smiles around, with boundless bounty blest,
> And Heav'n beholds its image in his breast.[1]

Christian piety may look to the revelation of a smiling beatitude, perhaps in this world, chiefly or even wholly in the next, through the cloud of temporal adversity, sinfulness, even despair; Cowper's faith loads the rifts of mystery with ore:

Deep in unfathomable mines
Of never-failing skill
He treasures up his bright designs,
And works His sovereign Will.
(no. 373)

Trust in a reverent rational optimism, by contrast, envisages a smile which irradiates *this* world wholly, once man's deforming propensities, and the inequities of terrestrial experience, have been rightly understood – or their right understanding recognized as the prerogative of Providence, a mystery. At a more exalted level, to the ecstatic spirit the luminous Paradisal vision seems *un riso dell' universo.*[2] We might think of a rising scale, from the clearly-known countenance of a devotional father-figure, through the benignity of a dispassionate Providence, to the radiant abstract face of peace and love. As the tone and impress of that smile alter, the spaces open and close between God and man: it may suffuse the understanding as a full revelation of His nature; it may register as the expressive tone of a Being whose nature and purposes remain enigmatic or inscrutable; it may seem an awesome possibility whose implications (as in Blake's poem) oppress the finite mind. Our response to the smile of God changes, too, according to whether we think of it as man's imaging of God, however full or approximate that image might be, or as God's revealing himself to the creature made in his likeness. Deities whose pleasure is pain lie awaiting personification outside the Christian range, as with Thomas Gray's Adversity

Whose iron scourge and tort'ring hour,
The Bad affright, afflict the Best!

or his mock-epic godship who drowns favourite cats:

Malignant Fate sat by, and smil'd.

When we turn from the smile of deities to their laughter, the distances between cultures are almost constantly borne in upon our attention, whether in comedy or tragedy or satire, and whether we are represented as laughable because of our own perversity, or as essentially ridiculous creatures, or as arousing divine pleasure in the moment of our destruction. God's laughter, or the laughter of the gods (an interestingly durable phrase), commonly retains in the Christian era more or less audible – and more or less disturbing – traces of the mirth of Zeus or the derision of Jehovah. In consequence, it exerts a special influence wherever it occurs, extending the frame of allusion, testing the tolerances of belief, unsettling assumptions and chastening conceit. Two texts which seek to accommodate divine mirth within a (variously) Christian argument are *Paradise Lost* and *An Essay on Man*. Learning to 'love with fear the only God' (XII. 563), Milton's Adam encounters the foreknowledge of a derisive laughter in Heaven roused by the spectacle of human arrogance. Pope's provident skies are jovial at the cost of mankind's perpetual cupidity and self-deceit:

Oh sons of earth! attempt ye still to rise,
By mountains pil'd on mountains, to the skies?
Heav'n still with laughter the vain toil surveys,
And buries madmen in the heaps they raise.
(IV. 73–6)

Within these lines, the chastisement of man unregenerate by sagacious man – the peripatetic gentleman-satirist – is corroborated by Olympian laughter at the cost of Titanic pointlessness, with echoes of God's mirth at Babylon in *Paradise Lost*. Pope is blending Jehovah's tone of righteous anger with a broadly classical-satiric sense of man as essentially foolish. Seen from the high perspective of 'the gods', our theatrical vanity provokes eternal amusement and suffers a continual apt retribution. When God, or 'the gods', or a 'heav'n' more or less Christian, emerge as prototype comedians in passages such as these, we are to understand the joke and, simultaneously, suffer the laughter. As men, we are at once the jest and the partisan audience of the jester – whether we are open to derision as fallen creatures, after Adam, or funny by ancient birthright. But in *Paradise Lost* and in Pope's 'vindication' of God we are afforded cover against what Rasselas will experience (at the hands of his fellow-men) as 'the horrour of derision' (ch. xvii). Milton's God will, ultimately, redeem the erring and castigated sons of Adam. For Pope, our folly is peculiarly illustrative of God's benignity:

See! and confess, one comfort still must rise,
'Tis this, Tho' Man's a fool, yet God is wise.
(II. 293–4)

The satiric sense of human nature, supported by the rhetorical figure of heaven's laughter, is gathered into the benevolent smile, equally godlike, at the end of Pope's poem. A preference for benignity over mockery had been declared at the outset:

Laugh where we must, be candid where we can.

Elsewhere, more disturbingly, we are killed in play by gods as wanton boys, or toyed with by such an imposing figure of speech as 'the President of the Immortals', and little, if any, consolation is available to the victims of the joke. In such examples, we are not drawn to participate in the laughter: it stirs in us, as part of its complex effect, dread or even revulsion in face of the figurative Authors of the jest – if, indeed, the contexts allow us any confidence that the sportive deities are there at all, unequivocally. The mirth might echo in a problematic or an empty heaven, itself as remote to our understanding as the laughing God of Homer or Hesiod or the psalmist.[3] Some unease, at the least, about what is disclosed of God through his laughter, is present even in those cases where we share the joke as well as accept its meaning at our expense. But our perspectives on the laughter alter at a touch: what God's mirth reveals of him is a question rivalled by our asking what prompts man to image God as a jester at man's own cost. We are laughable in God's eyes; alternatively, God (in our eyes) finds us laughable. God's ridicule might lend authority to satire – but ridicule human or divine sorts ill with Christian belief and ethics. The mind moves to and fro between what we can bear to know of God and what to think of man, ourselves. And the laughter might betoken a mystery: the expressive manifestation of a consciousness which sees and knows more than man ever could. Repeatedly, our feelings will include dread of becoming the object of an all-knowing mirth, and awe of the being which is able to laugh at what we ourselves find painful or murky. A passage from *Measure for Measure* dextrously, and painfully, catches some of the implications of this laughter. If we are incorrect to heaven, in our strutting neglect of spiritual values, we might hope that mockery is human, but to weep divine:

man, proud man,
Dress'd in a little brief authority,
Most ignorant of what he's most assur'd –
His glassy essence – like an angry ape
Plays such fantastic tricks before high heaven
As makes the angels weep; who, with our spleens,
Would all themselves laugh mortal.
(II. ii. 118–24)

That we are laughable, and that we are able to laugh ourselves to death at this, are seen in these lines as equal, and related, aspects of our mortal state. A clear (angelic) view of man would permit no stomach for such mirth. We see what is funny about our arrogant vanity, but are rebuked for seeing it as something to laugh at.

More simply impulsive than splenetic; more laughing than laughing *at*: the glee broadly associated with the Homeric gods is festive, ebullient, and sustained. Kerenyi reminds us that they laugh, not at man, but 'at their own kind'.[4] 'Unextinguish'd laughter' (in Pope's version) is called forth by the clowning of Hephaistos and by his trapping of the divine adulterers under his net. The laughter appears to emanate from glorious fulness of being, and to confer a kind of splendid recognition upon its object:

> among the blessed immortals uncontrollable laughter
> went up as they saw Hephaistos bustling about the palace.[5]

This mirth is drawn upon himself deliberately by the cup-bearer as a comedian concerned to achieve reconciliation. As such, it associates readily with the divine laughter which echoes the healing concord at the end of a human comedy:

> Then is there mirth in heaven,
> When earthly things made even
> Atone together.[6]

This divine laughter closes the distances between earth and heaven: godly derision, by contrast, opens them – except that we might feel at one with heaven in finding man derisory. With reference to either sphere, celestial or sublunary, it is often convenient to conceive of an ideal laughter as the integration of two kinds of mirthful response to life: one, the lofty scrutiny whose long perspective clarifies and penetrates and tends to belittle; the other, the felt conceiving of what is laughable, a vision intimately in touch with what it contemplates. To match Johnson's phrase for the first – the 'philosophic eye' – we might call the second the 'risible heart'. Risibility, as a buoyant inclination to laugh, is what Colley Cibber, preening himself to Pope's delight, shares with Jove. In a secondary sense, too, 'risible' has an aptness for our theme: man finds himself risible, laughable. The 'risible' makes for pleasure, the delight of finding or making laughable things, an infectious impulse which may feel curiously affirmative even of the objects it mocks. The 'philosophic' makes for scorn, asperity – at its bitterest, inhibiting laughter even while exposing the objects of scrutiny to ridicule. The antithesis is, roughly, between looking *at* or *into*, on the one hand, and seeing *through*, on the other. The balance between the two outlooks or incitements is changeable, and it is hard to find either in its pure state. Among the most articulate expressions of a blending of the two is Johnson's invocation of the laughter of Democritus in *The Vanity of Human Wishes*. This exemplary comedian laughs with his whole being, and by evoking laughter he brings home invigoratingly a sense of life which might otherwise merely depress us with the conviction of our folly:

> Once more, Democritus, arise on earth,
> With chearful wisdom and instructive mirth,

See motley life in modern trappings dress'd,
And feed with varied fools th'eternal jest.
(ll. 49–52)

Hypocritical mourning, sycophancy, political chicanery, social caprice: this comic vision sees through all we do 'with philosophic eye', with an undeviating accuracy and an Olympian capacity for generalization. Cheering, but uncompromising; scornful, but enlivening and wholesome – it is a godlike scorn which

fill'd the sage's mind,
Renew'd at ev'ry glance on humankind.
(ll. 69–70)

The lines offer well-established satiric types. That they *are* enduring types is, of course, part of the satiric point. But the laughter feeds on them, rather than just defining them, and is entertained richly by the fashionable innovations which disguise them, unavailingly, from one age to the next. It is almost as if the mocked connived at mockery:

All aid the farce, and all thy mirth maintain,
Whose joys are causeless, or whose griefs are vain.
(ll. 67–8)

But the laughter hurts. An Olympian penetration exposes those who, among men, grieve or rejoice over empty things: but perhaps this is virtually an inclusive description of human experience, as is insinuated in the insistent 'all' and in the scope of the second line's antithesis. The 'philosophic' sense of the laughter could soon impede the risible impulse, in the reader if not in the poem's prototype comedian. As Johnson explores the grounds of Democritus' laughter, its meaning tends to transfer from the comedian to the human beings who display folly or contemplate it within, not outside, the sphere of our vanity – it becomes the sting of 'remember'd folly' (l. 119), or the vindictiveness of 'detestation' (l. 90), 'derision' (l. 253), and 'hissing Infamy' (l. 342). This mirth is, of course, contaminated. Even if it were not, the poem has found the burden of a godlike scorn intolerable, whether to him who exercises it or to him who reads its meaning at our cost. The notion of heaven ringing with dismissive laughter is not available, as it was in support of the Christian conclusion of *Troilus and Criseyde*:

And in hymself he lough right at the wo
Of hem that wepten for his deth so faste;
And dampned al oure werk that foloweth so

The blynde lust, the which that may nat laste,
And sholden al oure herte on heven caste.
(V. 1821–25)

Perhaps the philosophic eye is at its coldest, the distance longest between mocker and mocked, in Swift's poem 'The Day of Judgement':

While each pale Sinner hangs his Head,
Jove, nodding, shook the Heav'ns, and said,
"Offending Race of Human Kind,
By Nature, Reason, Learning, blind;
You who thro' Frailty step'd aside,
And you who never fell – *thro' Pride*;
You who in different Sects have shamm'd,
And come to see each other damn'd;
(So some Folks told you, but they knew
No more of Jove's Designs than you)
The World's mad Business now is o'er,
And I resent these Pranks no more.
I to such Blockheads set my Wit!
I damn such Fools! – Go, go, you're bit."

Even 'the laceration of laughter at what ceases to amuse'[7] has been purged in this dismissal of man's vanity from a consciousness to which Swift's poem denies us any further access. Not to have fallen is as culpable as to fall; all sectarian allegiances are hypocritical. The comprehensiveness of these judgments destroys our capacity to judge – but we are in any case created, and educated, into total ignorance. We are tiresome absurdities in the eyes of a bored God, and cease to be there to consider, let alone there to laugh at. We are seen through, totally – but the full sense of this mirthless exposure is essentially beyond the understanding of its victims. A merrier version of this philosophic scorn is offered by Erasmus:

> It's hardly believable how much laughter, sport and fun you poor mortals can provide the gods every day. For they allocate their sober morning hours to settling altercations and listening to prayers, but once the nectar is flowing freely they want a change from serious business, and that is when they settle down on some promontory of heaven and lean over to watch the goings-on of mankind, a show they enjoy more than anything.[8]

As the fools in that theatre, we (by definition) do not know our folly. On the other hand, identifying with the mirthful audience (though alarmed by alcoholism in High Places), we find that the comic vision which sees *through* us balances with a delight that is sustained by looking *at* us, abundant folly generating an abounding mirth. And the balance tips further towards the risible, away from the piercingly philosophic, in Sterne's witty by-play with the myth of Momus's window. Lucian relates how Momus, the licensed railer of Olympus, judged a competition to which Hephaistos contributed a model man:

> and the fault he found with Hephaestus, was this: he should have made a window in his chest, so that, when it was opened, his thoughts and designs, his truth or falsehood, might have been apparent.[9]

The speaker in Lucian's dialogue uses the story banteringly, for his own forensic purposes. Sterne develops the sense of man's opacity, with a skilfully mock-portentous tone, 'wrapt up here in a dark covering of uncrystallized flesh and blood' – and he looks through the window, disclosing the true nature of the self, a riotous and swarming liveliness which intrigues and confuses:

> If the fixture of *Momus's* glass in the human breast, according to the proposed emendation of that arch-critick, had taken place, – first, This foolish consequence would certainly have followed, – That the very wisest and very gravest of us all, in one coin or other, must have paid window-money every day of our lives.
>
> And, secondly, That had the said glass been there set up, nothing more would have been wanting, in order to have taken a man's character, but to have taken a chair and gone softly, as you would to a dioptrical beehive, and look'd in, – view'd the soul stark naked; – observed all her motions, – her machinations; – traced all her maggots from their first engendering to their crawling forth; – watched her loose in her frisks, her gambols, her capricios; and after some notice of her more solemn deportment, consequent upon such frisks, etc. – then taken your pen and ink and set down nothing but what you had seen, and could have sworn to: – But this is an advantage not to be had by the biographer in this planet.
>
> (*Tristram Shandy*, I, ch. xxiii)

Here, the insight into man's nature wished for by the Olympian satirist reveals materials said to be plain and manageable, but seen to be infinitely complex and delightful.

The risible world of *Tristram Shandy*, 'big with jest', can accommodate the sense of man as made for some deity's sport. An inconsequential, but kindly disposed, gaiety tends to defuse explosive ideas: 'if ever malignant spirit took pleasure, or busied itself in traversing the purposes of mortal man, – it must have been here' (I. xix). The philosophic definition of

Gulliver, seen from the sage altitude of Brobdingnag, is isolated by Swift as ridiculously ponderous: '*Relplum Scalcath*, which is interpreted literally *Lusus Naturæ*' (ch. iii). The joke turns back at the cost of those who avail themselves of the potent idea of man's freakishness simply as a grandiose way out of an intellectual difficulty. Sterne keeps the anatomizing of his *relplum scalcath* within the turbulent, untidy ambience of tragi-comic rhetoric:

> Unhappy *Tristram!* child of wrath! child of decrepitude! interruption! mistake! and discontent!
>
> (IV. xix).

Pope, too, keeps the Momist concept within the frame of humour when he playfully disowns it in the urbane opening of *Epistle III. To Bathurst*:

> You hold the word, from Jove to Momus giv'n,
> That Man was made the standing jest of Heav'n.

He is then free to proceed, deftly, to acknowledge that a contemplation of human folly, even by one more forgiving than Momus –

> And surely, Heav'n and I are of a mind –

leads eventually to agreement with the main sentiment:

> Like Doctors thus, when much dispute has past,
> We find our tenets just the same at last.

This manoeuvre draws attention to, and wittily softens, the rivalry between Christian views of man and the classical concept of the laughable creature.

Milton's Adam has to bear the burden of the stated meaning of God's laughter at man's cost – but not, of course, mirth occasioned by the sense that man is essentially laughable. Disdain and contempt emerge first in Satan when the Father decrees the Son viceregent, and God responds to the rebel angels with scorn:

> 'Mighty Father, thou thy foes
> Justly hast in derision, and secure
> Laugh'st at their vain designs and tumults vain.'
>
> (V. 735–7)

Satan, himself adept at mockery, is partly laughable because he acts as if his machinations could work unseen before the omniscient gaze. Man, in his turn, will occasion God's amusement when he seeks to know and to accomplish more than, in God's decree, he should. Adam learns this on two occasions, one before the Fall, one after: and each time he understands the laughter fully in the meaning that it holds about God's Providence. Men will be wise, he is told, to check their eagerness 'to know at large of things remote from use':

Or, if they list to try
Conjecture, he his fabric of the Heavens
Hath left to their disputes – perhaps to move
His laughter at their quaint opinions wide
Hereafter, when they come to model Heaven,
And calculate the stars; how they will wield
The mighty frame; how build, unbuild, contrive
To save appearances; how gird the sphere
With centric and eccentric scribbled o'er,
Cycle and epicycle, orb in orb.
(VIII. 75–84)

Adam does not laugh at this himself, but the lines do more than (speculatively) assert God's laughter. They give lively definition to the source of the entertainment. Though the laughter emanates from the heart of a mystery 'above all height', it is delightedly attentive and close to what it contemplates. More painful is the mirth caused by God's own satiric joke, an absurdist's Pentecost, at Babylon, where He

in derision sets
Upon their tongues a various spirit, to rase
Quite out their native language, and, instead,
To sow a jangling noise of words unknown:
Forthwith a hideous gabble rises loud
Among the builders; each to other calls,
Not understood – till, hoarse and all in rage,
As mocked they storm; great laughter was in Heaven,
And looking down to see the hubbub strange
And hear the din; thus was the building left
Ridiculous, and the work *Confusion* named.
(XII. 52–62)

Here, again, the laughter is defined by lively representation of the antics of those God mocks: the poetry reflects the scornful vigilance of a satirist gratified by the results of his retributive prank. The mirth is sharper than that aroused by man's funny errors in astronomy. Human aspiration, at

Babel, has threatened to 'obstruct heaven-towers', being at once ridiculously futile in God's eyes and significant enough to deserve severe poetic justice. Adam does not share the laughter, but angrily interprets its moral sense:

> 'O execrable son, so to aspire
> Above his brethren, to himself assuming
> Authority usurped, from God not given.'
> (XII. 64–6)

He is reminded that this fault, like all others, stems from his own Fall – but the Fall could never be, in God's eyes, laughable. God's laughter at Babel does not exceed the explicit definition of its meaning. Relatedly, it is not treated as the expression of a consciousness which infinitely outreaches that of man: it is, rather, the function of superior height – exaltation 'looking down'. It carries, in itself, no mystery; alerts us to no mystery in the human behaviour to which it is a response; and it exercises, as mirth, no redemptive influence. It is not a central revelation of the nature of the poem's God: in the poem's time-span it relates, of course, to the Old Testament period. These limitations on the scope and implication of the laughter, in this context, soften the disturbing impact it naturally has, especially in the Babel episode. Conversely, the laughter and (emphatically) its moralized meaning register all the more sharply because of their separation from the sense of God's mystery and transcendence.

Milton lends impetus to the justification of laughter in terms of its directly interpreted meaning, with consequences not just for the theodicy of *An Essay on Man* but for the discussion of satiric mirth. In *The Dunciad*, heavenly laughter recurs, as a simple rhetorical figure, at the contemplation of Curll's whirlwind of stolen verse and other bric-a-brac – and Dulness preens herself on giving such high amusement:

> Songs, sonnets, epigrams the winds uplift,
> And whisk 'em back to Evans, Young, and Swift.
> Th'embroider'd suit at least he deem'd his prey;
> That suit an unpay'd taylor snatch'd away.
> No rag, no scrap, of all the beau, or wit,
> That once so flutter'd, and that once so writ.
> Heav'n rings with laughter: Of the laughter vain,
> Dulness, good Queen, repeats the jest again.
> (II. 115–22)

The laughter is expansive, Homeric, and moves with the breathless flutter of the mock-epic events, the controlled tumble of the verse. Similarly, Codrus displays, in *An Epistle to Dr. Arbuthnot*, an absurd heroic fortitude in face of a momentous mirth which he draws upon himself – and his unconcern is rendered as a comic misunderstanding, with ironic praise:

> Let Peals of Laughter, *Codrus!* round thee break,
> Thou unconcern'd canst hear the mighty Crack.
> Pit, Box and Gall'ry in convulsions hurl'd,
> Thou stand'st unshook amidst a bursting World.
> (ll. 85–8)

At such points, we rejoice in the poetry, however pointed its mockery, as the dance of a creative sensibility among its materials:

> All aid the farce, and all thy mirth maintain.

The laughter wells up from, and excites, delight. In 'instruction' and its 'cheer' are indivisible. At intervals in the poetry elsewhere, Pope justifies his activity as the victimized and disinterested defence of Virtue. Such descriptions of his role enhance our sense of dramatic circumstance, but they commonly seem simplistic: the philosophic apologia tends to exclude the risible impulse. But we are likely to feel that the range and precision of incitements to laughter constitute the real creative vitality and value of the poetry. And if the mirth is often cruel, this is better defended by appeal to the effects of laughter, the way it sharpens attention, purges feeling, generates pleasure, than by claiming for the satirist an invariable, high-minded righteousness – or, even more tenuously, a comprehensive rightness about the times and people of whom he writes. *The Dunciad* accomplishes as comedy lively blends of delight and ridicule; but some passages and editorial notes in Book IV translate this into pompous general convictions about the nature of intellectual error in Pope's time. Relatedly, Pope prefaces the poem with the rather austere claim that the human objects of satire 'are not ridicul'd because Ridicule in itself is or ought to be a pleasure; but because it is just'. There is something regrettably defensive, similarly, in the assertion that the poet's motives are pure:

> I shall conclude with remarking what a pleasure it must be to every reader of humanity, to see all along, that our Author, in his very laughter, is not indulging his own Ill nature, but only punishing that of others.[10]

A better model for discussion of much satiric laughter may be found in Kerenyi's discussion of the laughter provoked by Hephaistos in Book I of *The Iliad*. Zeus and Hera, quarrelling, are displaying 'the darker Titanic side of the characters of these two children of Cronos':

> Quarrelling and tension, fighting and bloodshed are in their nature Titanic. Their Titanic *seriousness* is destroyed in this laughter. That is the sense of it. The laughter, too, of course, wells up from an original Titanic source, from the very nature of the gods.[11]

The concept of 'the essential unity of its two components – the laughter itself and the object of its relieving power, the Titanic' is applied also by Kerenyi to the more mysterious mirth shown by Zeus when he sees the gods joining in the fight for Troy. In Lattimore's version of *The Iliad*, this delight keeps its secret completely:

> Zeus heard it
> from where he sat on Olympos, and was amused in his deep heart
> for pleasure, as he watched the gods' collision in conflict.
> (XXI. 388–90)

Pope's translation goes nearer to defining the nature of Jove's pleasure, but he introduces a powerful combination of disinterest and 'sport':

> *Jove*, as his Sport, the dreadful Scene descries,
> And views contending Gods with careless Eyes.
> (XXI. 454–5)

For Kerenyi, discussing this deep movement of pleasure, it is the laughter of a Titan's heart, awakened by 'memories of the old battle of the Titans'.[12] The Titan laughs in Pope's satiric laughter, as he makes and kills for his sport and for ours.

Man killed in sport for pleasure by the gods or by some beings intermediate between himself and God – the intolerable notion has a varied history in English contexts, deriving its chief impetus from Gloucester's despairing words in *King Lear*:

> As flies to wanton boys, are we to the gods;
> They kill us for their sport.
> (IV. i. 36–7)

In the play, this view of man's destiny competes with many other emphatic but partial illuminations, but it has gained a kind of choric prestige like that of Hardy's sentence on Tess of the d'Urbervilles:

> 'Justice' was done, and the President of the Immortals, in Æschylean phrase, had ended his sport with Tess.
> (ch. 59)

This is, of course, elaborately protected against simple acceptance as a bitter statement of authorial belief. But its sardonic skill, its distancing, tend to enforce the very notion they ironically frame – the remote and calculated sport of Zeus, so much less open to the understanding than the wanton cruelty of boys. Hardy took pains to argue that the sentence had the force of a rhetorical figure, and it has manifold aptness in the total context of the novel.[13] It stands, for instance, among many ghostly metaphysical ideas which impose a superstitious burden on the benighted human consciousness. When the concept recurs in Beckett's *Watt*, it is lingeringly developed in a perplexing narrative environment in which the reader strives in vain to separate fantasy from actuality:

> But our particular friends were the rats, that dwelt by the stream. They were long and black. We brought them such titbits from our ordinary as rinds of cheese, and morsels of gristle, and we brought them also birds' eggs, and frogs, and fledgelings. Sensible of these attentions, they would come flocking round us at our approach, with every sign of confidence and affection, and glide up our trouser-legs, and hang upon our breasts. And then we would sit down in the midst of them, and give them to eat, out of our hands, of a nice fat frog, or a baby thrush. Or seizing suddenly a plump young rat, resting in our bosom after its repast, we would feed it to its mother, or its father, or its brother, or its sister, or to some less fortunate relative.
>
> It was on these occasions, we agreed, after an exchange of views, that we came nearest to God.[14]

Johnson had, similarly, made the exercise of cruelty by higher beings exquisitely circumstantial, atrociously fastidious:

> Many a merry bout have these frolic beings at the vicissitudes of an ague, and good sport it is to see a man tumble with an epilepsy, and revive and tumble again, and all this he knows not why. As they are wiser and more powerful than we, they have more exquisite diversions, for we have no way of procuring any sport so brisk and so lasting as the paroxysms of the gout and stone which undoubtedly must make high mirth, especially if the play be a little diversified with the blunders and puzzles of the blind and deaf.[15]

Beckett's narrator rises through malicious kindness to a sense of cruel divinity ('give them to eat'). Johnson is drawing on humane revulsion from the notion of a providential hierarchy of beings who derive delight from inflicting pain. Jenyns had advanced the concept with the pointless safeguard that it was plausible but 'inconceivable' – not in the least because he thought cruelty acceptable. In doing so, he had debased both the mystery of God and the intellectual currency.

Johnson's resistance to the idea relates to his response to the laughter of Democritus, and engages his convictions about the use of literature and therefore, too, his Christian faith. He prays to a God who 'afflictest not willingly the children of Men'.[16] He recoils from, but reluctantly accepts, the observation that human beings can derive pleasure from pain:

> That he delights in the misery of others no man will confess, and yet what other motive can make a father cruel?[17]

He shuns man's idea of an unforgiving God as 'an enemy infinitely wise, and infinitely powerful, whom he could neither deceive, escape, nor resist'.[18] God might withdraw favour – and there is the pressing fear of damnation – but not gratuitously, and He could not conceivably mock. Doubt and ignorance are allayed by patience and humility:

> Let me rejoice in the light which thou hast imparted . . . and wait with patient expectation for the time in which the soul which Thou receivest, shall be satisfied with knowledge.[19]

Much of Johnson's thinking turns upon questions of what we can and cannot know, what we can bear to think, and what knowledge we can offer others that they may live by or draw endurance from. Faith trusts a God who bestows grace, and who will ultimately illuminate the spirit. The proposition that human ignorance is 'a cordial administered by the gracious hand of providence' is rebutted by opening questions of motivation – in human terms, but not, of course, implying a presumptuous analogy between man and God:

> The privileges of education may sometimes be improperly bestowed, but I shall always fear to with-hold them, lest I should be yielding to the suggestions of pride, while I persuade myself that I am following the maxims of policy; and under the appearance of salutary restraints, should be indulging the lust of dominion, and that malevolence which delights in seeing others depressed.[20]

Particularly resilient, and decisive, is Johnson's confrontation of those generalized disparagements of man which owe much of their prestige in the eighteenth century to the laughter of god-satirist or satirist as god. *Rambler* 129 singles out part of the moralized sense of Democritean laughter, beginning from a restatement of that prudent advice which is transmitted from one age to the next. This is, Johnson declares, a secondary knowledge which saves writers the pains of 'casting their eyes abroad in the living world':

> Among the favourite topicks of moral declamation, may be numbered the miscarriages of imprudent boldness, and the folly of attempts beyond our power. Every page of every philosopher is crouded with examples of temerity that sunk under burthens which she laid upon herself, and called out enemies to battle by whom she was destroyed.[21]

Johnson castigates the hubristic folly which the philosophic eye discovers –

> a ridiculous perseverance in impracticable schemes, which is justly punished with ignominy and reproach –

but he does not let this endorsement of derision blind him to the justification of less blatant strayings from the middle way:

> in the wide regions of probability which are the proper province of prudence and election, there is always room to deviate on either side of rectitude without rushing against apparent absurdity; and according to the inclinations of nature, or the impressions of precept, the daring and the cautious may move in different directions without touching upon rashness or cowardice.[22]

This moderate scale of virtue could itself look foolish – as what could not? – in the light of a disposition to see humanity as if with God's eyes. But Johnson, in this *Rambler*, finds himself able to celebrate temerity itself:

> It is the vice of noble and generous minds, the exuberance of magnanimity, and the ebullition of genius; and is therefore not regarded with much tenderness, because it never flatters us by that appearance of softness and imbecillity which is commonly necessary to conciliate compassion.[23]

Prudence itself comes under scrutiny. In that it all too readily discourages enterprise and disables effort, it emerges as a folly of its own: 'the folly of presupposing impossibilities, and anticipating frustration'. Equally important is the objection 'that it is impossible to determine without experience how much constancy may endure, or perseverance perform'. The disabling weight of moralized satiric mirth is being lifted in these sentences. Ardour, which compounded human folly in *The Vanity of Human Wishes* unless turned to a life of prayer and Christian love, is here greeted as a means of overcoming difficulty honourably. Conversely, to live in the light of the (admittedly just) moralisms at the cost of our folly is to incur

> some danger lest timorous prudence should be inculcated, till courage and enterprize are wholly repressed, and the mind congealed in perpetual inactivity by the fatal influence of frigorifick wisdom.[24]

Rasselas has, in part, the look of a fable in which the frigorifick wisdom of laughter moralized is borne in upon the human consciousness, and confirmed by experience, until it is completely disabling. We hear, for instance, the overt Olympian sententiousness of Imlac's rebuke of those who indulge fantasy:

> Whoever thou art that, not content with a moderate condition, imaginest happiness in royal munificence, and dreamest that command or riches can feed the appetite of novelty with perpetual gratifications, survey the pyramids, and confess thy folly!
> (ch. xxxii)

What may be discovered, truly, by an empirical inspection of the world, is balanced by scepticism about the trustworthiness of reason itself and about the whole ground on which the inquiry is conducted. Those who learn how incorrigibly man clings to his cherished fantasies of total power also see one of their number, the astronomer, retrieved from his version of this delusion. And they achieve a capacity not merely to see the errors and confusions of others, but to turn risibility in upon themselves, in a social frame of laughter:

> they diverted themselves with comparisons of the different forms of life which they had observed, and with various schemes of life which each of them had formed.
> (ch. xlix)

Laughter *at* man has been acknowledged *by* man, rather than indulged under the authority of a laughing, satiric heaven: mockery of the mad astronomer was decisively rebuked by Imlac himself, the prototype wise Augustan. And the sense lingers that an infinite number of things, more than Imlac knows, are true about human experience: the philosophic eye has not imposed its findings at the cost of curiosity, even though the quest of those curious for truth has itself been shown to be hazardous, wasteful of energy, and partly laughable. Seen one way, in the terms of this discussion, the laughter of heaven has here been thoroughly humanized, issuing as the converse of the traditional appeal by the satirist to godlike laughter as a validation of his own seeing through his fellow-men. Ortega y Gasset contrasts the sense of God as an old high-minded rationalist, looking at human life from far outside it, with God as the sum of all imaginable views of experience.[25] *Rasselas* mediates what it inspects through a prose balanced yet incisive, austere yet amused: we come into the presence of a music of consciousness which has a distinctive tonal behaviour but does not offer a particular viewpoint as a key to interpretation.

Contemplating the Eton College schoolboys, from the vantage point of a nostalgic and bitter melancholy, Thomas Gray expounds a chilling wisdom. Youth is blissful because it is ignorant, pursuing objectives which 'we' know, in the world of experience, to be 'less pleasing when possest'. The analogy is clear with part of the import of *Rasselas* as a story of incremental disillusionment. Gray's pessimism is thoroughgoing, and dourly melodious. 'Thought would destroy their Paradise': it would reveal, as life does all too soon, that the world is ruled by grotesque avenging deities who inflict suffering from within and without, and who totally characterize adult life – Anger, Fear, Shame; Unkindness, Falsehood, Scorn; Disease, Poverty, Age. The poem depends, for its simple rhetoric of doom, on a blend of sentimental nostalgia and melancholic fatalism – not opposites, of course, but each the obverse of the other. For Blake, illustrating the poem, this vision is presided over by that gloating President of the Immortals, Urizen. Gray's own *Ode to Spring* looks critically at the sententious pessimism of eighteenth-century contemplation. The received wisdom of the world is rehearsed, the speaker discounting with elegant triteness the beauty of evanescent things. He is suspiciously 'reclin'd in rustic state', brooding on the imminent destruction of all men, as flies to those twin deities, bad luck and mortality:

> To Contemplation's sober eye
> Such is the race of Man:
> And they that creep, and they that fly,
> Shall end where they began.
> Alike the Busy and the Gay
> But flutter thro' life's little day,
> In fortune's varying colours drest:
> Brush'd by the hand of rough Mischance,
> Or chill'd by age, their airy dance
> They leave, in dust to rest.

This Mischance is, in Blake's illustration, an atavistic, brutish figure who crushes the winged beings fallen from the cowled, white-bearded Contemplation: the spirit of the moralist's attention to life feeds catastrophe with innocent victims. It is a powerful point: sagacity tending, the more inclusive its range, to pre-empt conclusions about life. But when Contemplation is rebuked at the end of Gray's poem, the rebuke is still grounded within the antitheses dear to worldly sententiousness – youth and age, bud and blown rose, life and death:

> We frolick, while 'tis May.

From 'Such is the race of Man' we arrive readily, as Blake knew, at 'The Fly' in *Songs of Experience*. Gray's Mischance had crushed the fly unthinkingly (not for his sport). Blake's human agent plays and destroys thoughtlessly – not pausing to reflect on the momentary event, not having taken care to prevent its happening. Man is to God as fly to man:

> For I dance
> And drink and sing,
> Till some blind hand
> Shall brush my wing.

Blake's poem is in part repudiating the life of contemplative reflection and consideration – if such thought is 'life' – in favour of instinctive, joyous living. So far, this is close in sentiment to Gray's *Ode to Spring*. But 'thought' also sets up in Blake's poem a more inclusive, and more radical, affirmation: the happy fly images a full, energetic identity, a consciousness – 'thought' now in the sense of a totally awake selfhood, which *is* life and strength and breath, almost tautologically. This break with frigorifick wisdom has affinities with Johnson's affirmation of magnanimity and enterprise – and both Blake and Johnson register the force and oppressive weight (for Johnson, the justice) of satiric sagacity.

That the calorific and the chilling stand close together in the tradition we have been briefly visiting can be asserted one way by returning to the sense of the Homeric laughter, in its context of heroic, tragic action:

> Human Existence . . . is miserable and from the divine point of view ridiculous, unimportant, in a way which cannot be further explained. But it becomes tragic, in its nothingness inexplicably important, in relation to the divine laughter. Zeus laughs aloud, the quarrel of indestructible forms becomes a divine comedy. Zeus let the gods quarrel but men moved him to pity. The seriousness of the strife and tension, the fights and bloodshed of the unhappy sister-race of the gods attains, in comparison with the unseriousness of a 'blessed' fight, an enormous importance, and grows into a tragedy which demands divine spectators.[26]

In Tennyson's version of the theme,[27] the gods 'smile in secret' at the comprehensive picture of man's sufferings and conflicts and intercessions –

> Clanging fights, and flaming towns, and sinking ships, and praying hands.

The vision is turned to account by the lotos-eaters as a model of sensuous disinterest – but the human spectacle, though resistant to understanding, registers as a congenial harmony in the divine mind:

> But they smile, they find a music centred in a doleful song
> Steaming up, a lamentation and an ancient tale of wrong,
> Like a tale of little meaning tho' the words are strong.

Perhaps the fullest creative inheritance from Homer for our time – if we except the admirable translations by Lattimore – is to be found in Yeats. The contemplatives of *Lapis Lazuli* register their ancient gaiety to the touch of sad melodies played by accomplished fingers, as if in recall of the Tennysonian gods. But their impressive, sympathetically tuned detachment is only one among many vibrant responses to human tragedy, in this one poem and in *Last Poems* as a whole. To 'laugh in tragic joy' does not, in Yeats, exorcize human dread, or the sense of oppressive mystery, or the frightening images of human nullity; but the sustained, calorific emphasis is on the heroism of man's own capability for facing, and expressing, this range of feelings – a heroism seen in the light of 'the great song' of Homer, itself at once obsolete and permanent, like the figure of the laughing Zeus.

NOTES

1. *An Essay on Man*, IV. 371–2.
2. Dante, *Paradiso*, canto xxvii.
3. 'The Works and Days', *Hesiod*, tr. Richmond Lattimore (Ann Arbor, 1925), 25: Zeus 'laughs out loud' on sending Pandora as a punishment for the Promethean theft of fire. *Psalm 2*, in Milton's version (8–11):

   > He who in Heaven doth dwell
   > Shall laugh; the Lord shall scoff them, then severe
   > Speak to them in his wrath, and in his fell
   > And fierce ire trouble them.
4. C. Kerenyi, *The Religion of the Greeks and Romans* (1962), 193.
5. *The Iliad of Homer*, tr. Richmond Lattimore (Chicago, 1951), 75 (I. 599–600).
6. *As You Like it*, V.iv. 110–12.
7. T. S. Eliot, *Little Gidding*.
8. Erasmus, *Praise of Folly*, tr. Betty Radice (1971), 141.
9. Lucian, *Herotimus*, *Works*, tr. H. W. and F. G. Fowler (1905), II, 52.
10. *The Dunciad Variorum*, 'To the Publisher'.
11. Kerenyi, *op. cit.*, 198.
12. *Ibid.*, 199.
13. See Florence Emily Hardy, *The Life of Thomas Hardy* (1965 edn), 243–4.
14. *Watt* (Calderbook edn 1976), 153. The book also carries a mock-scholarly grammar of laughter, culminating in a definition of 'the laugh of laughs, the *risus purus*, the laugh laughing at the laugh, the beholding, the saluting of the highest joke, in a word the laugh that laughs – silence please – at that which is unhappy' (p. 47).
15. Samuel Johnson, 'Review of *A Free Enquiry*', *Prose and Poetry*, ed. Mona Wilson (1963), 365–6.

16. Johnson, *Diaries, Prayers, and Annals*, ed. E. L. McAdam, Jr (Yale, 1958), 390.
17. *Rambler*, 148 (*The Rambler*, ed. W. J. Bate and Albrecht B. Strauss, Yale, 1969, V, 25).
18. *Rambler*, 110 (ed. Bate and Strauss, IV, 221).
19. *Diaries, Prayers, and Annals*, ed. McAdam, 384.
20. 'Review of *A Free Enquiry*', *Prose and Poetry*, ed. Wilson, 359.
21. *Rambler*, 129 (IV, 321).
22. *Rambler*, 129 (IV, 322).
23. *Rambler*, 129 (IV, 323).
24. *Rambler*, 129 (IV, 322).
25. Ortega y Gasset, *Meditations on Quixote*, ed. Marias (New York, 1963), 172.
26. Kerenyi, *op. cit.*, 199.
27. *The Lotos-Eaters.*

9 Colley Cibber: the Fop as Hero

LOIS POTTER

It is to Pope that most readers owe their image of Colley Cibber the careless coxcomb, but it was Cibber himself who created that image. He wrote and acted the parts of fops; he was a highly successful speaker of prologues and epilogues 'in character' as a fop; most of his non-dramatic writings, even such unlikely-sounding ones as *The Character and Conduct of Cicero*, deliberately make use of theatrical imagery and the digressive, flippant style of the fop persona. Above all, the *Apology* and the controversy with Pope reveal a total agreement between Cibber and his opponents as to the kind of man he was supposed to be. He himself suggested that critics might demolish the *Apology* by saying, for instance, that 'I want nothing but Wit, to be as accomplish'd a Coxcomb here, as ever I attempted to expose on the Theatre.'[1] In lifting such sentences as this into the footnotes of the *Dunciad*, Pope and Warburton were doing no more than accepting Cibber on his own terms.

That the image was a false one hardly needs proving. It is contradicted by the sheer amount of writing, acting, and indeed litigation in which the supposedly frivolous Cibber was engaged during his 50 years in the theatre.[2] Even his man-about-town pose needs re-examining. Sometimes it seems merely silly, as in the dedication to *Richard III*, with its unabashed gloating over the author's privileged relationship with the dedicatee.[3] But the dedication of *The Careless Husband* to the Duke of Argyll has more serious implications. When he claimed that any improvement over the dialogue of his earlier comedies was due to 'the many stolen Observations I have made from your Grace's manner of conversing',[4] Cibber must have been aware that he was echoing Dryden's dedication of *Marriage à la Mode* to the Earl of Rochester, and thus associating himself with an important attitude towards patronage. Behind both Cibber and Dryden, moreover, stands Ben Jonson, with his still more strongly defined view of the relationship between poet and aristocrat as a means of asserting the dignity of both. Like some of Jonson's prologues, Cibber's sometimes lecture the audience on the fine points of dramatic construction so that, as he said apropos of *She Would and She Would Not* (1702),

they,
Who only us'd to *like*, might learn to *taste a Play*.

Perhaps there is a similar source for Cibber's notorious 'impudence'. Take, for instance, the epilogue to *The Non-Juror*, where Mrs Oldfield is supposed to be reporting her conversation with the author:

These Blows I told him on his Play would fall,
But he, unmov'd, cry'd – Blood! we'll stand it all.

Along with an only half-facetious parody of Horace's 'Integer vitae' standing unmoved amid the storms, the couplet recalls the end of *Cynthia's Revels*, where a boy actor quotes the author's comment on his comedy: 'By——, 'tis good, and, if you like't, you may.' The apparent frivolity is quite consistent with 'a moderate Mixture of the *Merry* and *Wise*'.[5] As dictator of one half of London's theatre life, author of pro-government propaganda, and finally poet laureate, Cibber was a man who ought to have been taken very seriously indeed.

Why, then, did he and his contemporaries so readily accept the fop image? One reason, no doubt, was that it served both as a defence against, and an excuse for, the complementary image of the satirist: just as Cibber pretended not to be hurt by satire, so his satirists ('No creature smarts so little as a Fool') pretended that they did not really want to hurt Cibber. But the very irritation which inspired their attacks shows genuine bewilderment as to how to deal with him. Images of the world as a stage have always been common enough, but an actor who writes parts for himself is 'role-playing' in the fullest sense of the word, and fully conscious of the fact. He may, at the same time, be fulfilling less conscious needs, not only in himself but in his audience. In examining the most important parts which he wrote for himself, I hope to show how Cibber's particular situation as an actor contributed to the transformation of a familiar comic type (the fop), and how this in turn enabled him to manipulate his audience's response towards him as a human being.

We may take it for granted that every actor wants to be liked, and prefers to play likeable characters. Cibber makes this point many times in the *Apology*. At the beginning of his career, he says, he wanted to play romantic comedy heroes opposite the beautiful Mrs Bracegirdle, but soon realized that his skinny physique and weak voice were going to be permanent disqualifications from such roles (*Apology*, p. 102). What remained, for any actor who rose above mediocrity, were villains and old men in tragedy, fops and grotesques in comedy. Cibber observed the personae adopted by his fellow actors and the pleasure which audiences got from recognizing a familiar style of performance. His first stage successes were the result of impersonating, not a character, but another man's way of playing that character: Kynaston as Lord Touchwood in *The Double Dealer*, Doggett as Alderman Fondlewife in a production of *The Old Bachelor* – whose purpose, incidentally, was to give another actor a chance to imitate Betterton in the title role (*Apology*, p. 104 and pp. 114–16). Cibber does not seem to find anything odd in this approach to acting. But, although he admired the actors whose success with the audience depended on the recognition of easily imitable mannerisms, his favourite models appear to have been those with greater range. In particular, he praises William Mountfort, a good-looking actor with a pleasant speaking and singing voice, for the ease with which he could 'at once throw off the Man of Sense for the brisk, vain, rude and lively Coxcomb' (*Apology*, p. 76). This double ability released Mountfort from the restrictions of type-casting. His public would accept him as both hero and fop, Dorimant and Sir Fopling.

In 1693 Mountfort was killed in a street brawl. Cibber wrote his first play, *Love's Last Shift*, in 1695, and insisted on playing Sir Novelty Fashion, thus staking a claim to the foppish half of Mountfort's repertoire. The resulting triumph – for Cibber the actor as well as Cibber the author – set the pattern of his subsequent career. But a full understanding of his development must take account also of his second play – *Woman's Wit, or the Lady in Fashion*, whose subtitle was obviously intended to link it with *The Fool in Fashion*. *Woman's Wit* (1696–7) was a failure which Cibber clearly wanted to forget; he barely refers to it in the *Apology* and omitted it from the 1721 edition of his plays. A reading of the play shows why it was such a painful memory. It is possible that he originally had Betterton in mind for the part of the hero Longville, since they were both with the breakaway company at Lincoln's Inn Fields when he began the play, but when Cibber decided to rejoin the Drury Lane actors he took over the part himself. It is a vehicle for a versatile actor – a second Mountfort, in fact. To remind the audience of his previous success as Sir Novelty, Cibber makes Longville not only talk about fops but also, like Etherege's Dorimant, impersonate one. To succeed in this double role, the actor had to be a convincing hero in the first place. Longville can best be described as a watered-down, moralized Dorimant, who shows his culture not by repeating scraps of verses but by mentioning that he has a volume of Milton in his closet. The other characters adopt a uniformly admiring attitude towards him, which he accepts as his due. 'Virtue ever is the secret Care of Providence,' he remarks (V. i), when all the plots against him have been foiled and the heroine has given him her hand.[6] What made this conclusion impossible to take was not simply its smugness but the fact that the speaker was the author and the heroine his offstage wife. Whether or not the audience found Cibber a believable hero, they could not accept his attempt to present himself as one. He must have recognized his mistake, because he never again wrote any part for himself which explicitly demanded the admiration of his audience. He was, therefore, confined to the less attractive half of Mountfort's repertoire, along with the elderly and villainous characters for which his weak voice was no liability.

Unfortunately, the audience's awareness of the actor behind the role did not prevent them from viewing the former in terms of the latter. The *Apology* tells how Sandford – a small, deformed actor who usually played villains – once had to take the part of an honest statesman:

> the Pit, after they had sate three or four Acts, in a quiet Expectation, that the well-dissembled Honesty of Sandford (for such of course they concluded it) would soon be discover'd . . ., at last, finding no such matter, but that . . . Sandford was really an honest Man to the end of the Play, they fairly damn'd it
>
> (*Apology*, pp. 77–8).

This anecdote, which he may well have invented, gives Cibber an excuse to defend Sandford's morals and, by implication, his own. Despite what he says about the advantages of villains' parts (e.g., they are 'thicker sown, with sensible Reflections' than heroic ones: *Apology*, p. 124), his frequent harping on the subject suggests that he was uncomfortable about them; Steele mentions the actor's reluctance to revive *Othello* at Drury Lane because it would mean playing Iago.[7] To understand this apparently far-fetched concern, we need only look at what John Dennis wrote about him in 1720:

> The Truth of the Matter is, that he acts nothing at all well. He sometimes appears pretty well upon the Stage, when he is the real Thing which the Poet designs, as a ridiculous, incorrigible, impudent Fop in Comedy; and a bold, dissembling, dangerous, undermining Villain in Tragedy. And sometimes in Tragedy he blends the Fop and the Villain together, as in *Jago* for Example, in the *Moor of Venice*.[8]

This anonymously-published attack obviously disturbed Cibber greatly. Contrary to his usual custom, he advertised in an effort to find the author. He still remembered it ten years later. When he became poet laureate, and satires rained down upon him, he joined in the fun with some anonymous verses of his own. They were meant to prove him a good sport, but they also show the impression Dennis had made:

> Who sees thee in *Iago*'s Part,
> But thinks thee such a Rogue?
> And is not glad, with all his Heart,
> To hang so sad a Dog?

'When *Bays* thou play'st, Thyself thou art,' he added (*Apology*, p. 32). The verses differ from Dennis's libel in that they accuse the actor of foppery but not of villainy; the connection between Cibber and Iago is shown to exist only in the spectator's mind. Cibber may well have felt that, given the alternatives, he preferred to be fool rather than knave. It is noticeable that, in his generally unsuccessful attempts at tragedy, even the villains are uninteresting. This can hardly have been deliberate, but it does suggest inability or unwillingness to think himself into roles with which he did not want to be identified.

The exception, of course, is his adaptation of *Richard III* (1700). A comparison of Shakespeare and Cibber not only throws light on the latter's practice in creating other starring roles for himself, but also makes clear why actors for so long preferred the Cibber version.[9] The fact is that Cibber's Richard differs from Shakespeare's in one respect that is particularly gratifying for an actor: he never loses control of the action. Though more obviously villainous than his Elizabethan predecessor, by Augustan standards he is the nobler of the two. His imagery is more elevated: Shakespeare's 'But yet I run before my horse to market' (I, i) becomes 'But soft – I'm sharing Spoil before the Field is won' (I. ii). He is a man of sensibility, shown when he first sees Lady Anne

> Darting pale Lustre, like the silver Moon!
> Thro' her dark Veil of rainy Sorrow!
> (II. i)

and when he stands before his tent, on the eve of Bosworth Field, breathing in the scent of new-mown hay. Shakespeare's character gets rattled when bad news is brought him (IV. iv); in Cibber's play, this scene was the point when 'the actor, after having thrown aside the hypocrite and politician, assumed the warrior and the hero.'[10] The character who in Shakespeare's play dies silently and is summed up with 'The bloody dog is dead' gets the conventional heroic treatment from Cibber: an exchange of defiances with Richmond, a death speech, and a respectful farewell from his conqueror.

Still more important, in view of Cibber's other plays, is his expansion of the hero's relationship with Lady Anne. Although Shakespeare's Richard puts on the manner of a lover, there is no reason to believe he ever feels anything for the woman he deceives. But Cibber's character, though he speaks the lines about how 'love forswore me in my mother's womb' (*3 Henry VI*, III. ii), is not cut off from common humanity. He apparently does love Anne at the beginning, and when he decides to discard her it is not simply to make a more politically advantageous marriage: 'The fair *Elizabeth* hath caught my Eye' (III. i). Cibber's most original (and most deplored) contribution is the scene where Richard tries to break Anne's heart by suggesting that she commit suicide so that he can remarry. Marital unhappiness was not of much interest to Shakespeare in his histories, but post-Restoration comedies like those of Congreve, Vanburgh and Farquhar are obsessed with the subject, and it is one on which Cibber himself was to become something of an expert: the husbands of *The Careless Husband* (1704) and *The Lady's Last Stake* (1707) are scarcely less cruel to their wives than Richard is to his. But Richard's scenes with Anne are even more indebted to Restoration comedy of the old school, where the rake hero first exaggerates his passion to gain his purpose and then, with brutal honesty, lets the woman know what a fool she has been. Compare:

L. ANNE. Thy Vows of Love to me were all dissembled.
RICH. Not one – for when I told thee so I lov'd:
Thou art the only Soul I never yet deceiv'd;
And 'tis my Honesty that tells thee now,
With all my Heart I hate thee
(III. i)

and the language of Cibber's favourite model, *The Man of Mode*:

LOVEIT. Think on your Oaths, your Vows and Protestations, perjur'd Man!
DORIMANT. I made 'em when I was in love.
LOVEIT. And therefore ought they not to bind? O Impious!
DORIMANT. What we swear at such a time may be a certain proof of a present passion, but to say truth, in Love there is no security to be given for the future.[11]

Having given himself courage, absolute self-control, and the ability to inspire love and admiration in others, Cibber could afford to let himself be *called* a villain. He had in fact assimilated Richard to the type he most wanted to play: the Restoration comedy hero.

He applied the same treatment to the fops he created. In early Restoration comedy (take *The Man of Mode* again) fop and hero were often contrasted as rivals in love; at the end the hero captured the beautiful heiress while the fop was either left isolated or married to someone's discarded mistress or chambermaid. This punishment was particularly appropriate for an effeminate character who, it was hinted, would rather talk about an affair than have one. Even before Cibber began writing, the fop-hero balance had already begun to shift. After 1688, the more sober mood of the country, now intermittently at war with France, was reflected in the emergence of a new comedy hero: less rakish, more polite, more self-consciously *English* than his predecessors. By contrast, the fop began to be more of a rake himself. The reversal of roles was to culminate in Steele's famous moralistic attack on *The Man of Mode*, which called Dorimant 'more of a coxcomb than . . . Fopling.'[12] As an author, Cibber was astute enough to realize that giving rakish characteristics to a fop would allow him to exploit, without seeming to condone, a still-existing taste for dashing rascality. It is evident that this would also have been extremely satisfying to him as an actor.

At first sight, Sir Novelty Fashion seems a copy of Sir Fopling Flutter: he is an unsuccessful suitor to a girl who, like Etherege's Loveit, pretends to encourage him in order to rouse the jealousy of the man she really loves. But Sir Novelty also has a mistress of his own, who is passionately jealous of him. Mrs Flareit is the counterpart of other revengeful discarded mistresses of comedy – Loveit herself, or, more recently, Mrs Termagant in Shadwell's *Squire of Alsatia* (1688) – but these ladies had been in pursuit of the hero, not the fop. Indeed, Shadwell's Termagant goes so far as to draw a pistol on her lover. Similarly, Mrs Flareit, exasperated by the nonchalance of Sir Novelty, runs at him with a sword. His response is to draw his own and stand on guard. One of the other women questions the gallantry of this action, but he replies quite sensibly, 'Why, what wou'd you have had me done, Madam, complemented [*sic*] her with my naked Bosom? No! No!' (IV. i).

Sir Novelty's coolness had a few precedents, notably that of Sir Nicholas Dainty in Shadwell's *The Volunteers* (1692), who sets off to war in Flanders with eight waggons of baggage, a cook and a confectioner. Vanbrugh's Lord Foppington (*The Relapse*, 1696) takes the commonsense approach still further, fighting with Loveless when he sees no alternative but refusing to be provoked by his penniless younger brother who has everything to gain from a duel. His reasoning was evidently considered valid enough to be acceptable in the mouth of the popular comedy hero Sir Harry Wildair (*The Constant Couple*, 1699), though this was a Wilks, not a Cibber, part. Cibber completed the fop-hero reversal in *Love Makes a Man* (1700). The part he played, Clodio, was a composite of two quite different Fletcher characters, which may explain why this egregious silly-ass is able to defeat the biggest bully in Lisbon. 'Take that, Peasant!' shouts Don Duarte, striking the fop. 'I can't, upon my Soul, Sir,' Clodio replies; '*Allons*!' The fight ends with his running his opponent through, murmuring, 'Never push'd better in my Life, never in my Life, split me' (III. iii). He later marries the bully's beautiful sister.

Oddly enough, the first person to realize what was happening to the fop stereotype was Jeremy Collier. In his earliest attack on the stage, many of the lines which he condemned as immoral were those of Lord Foppington in *The Relapse*. Vanbrugh retorted that the fop's manner, 'together with the Character he represents, plainly and obviously instructs the Audience (even to the meanest Capacity) that what he says of his Church-Behaviour, is design'd for their Contempt, and not for their Imitation.'[13] But 'As the Poet has manag'd the business, this Lord is not so contemptible,' was Collier's answer;[14] he had already noticed that the fop had been given 'some of the most Gentile raillery in the whole *Play*' and that, in III. i, he 'discovers nothing of Affectation for almost a *Page* together.'[15] Collier was of course judging *The Relapse* entirely on the basis of the printed text, not Cibber's performance. All the indications are, however, that Cibber took as much care as Vanbrugh to see that Foppington was 'not so contemptible'. There is nothing ridiculous about his costume in the Grisoni portrait (now in the Garrick Club); his fop periwig for *Love's Last Shift* had actually been bought by a spectator who wanted to wear it himself. So Collier may have been right in thinking that Foppington was attractive enough to inspire imitation.

The Relapse was a sequel to *Love's Last Shift* and *The Careless Husband* was a sequel, though a much more tenuous one, to *The Relapse*. Cibber's presence in the one role which all three plays have in common must have given them a greater sense of continuity than emerges from a reading. If Vanbrugh's fop is much profounder than Sir Novelty, it may well be because Vanbrugh was basing his character on Cibber's performance rather than Cibber's writing. *The Relapse* is the first comedy in which a fop is described as 'a man whom Nature has made no Fool' (II. i), and it has been said that this Lord Foppington differs from all his predecessors in that 'he seems to be perfectly conscious of what he is doing'.[16] It is likely that Vanbrugh had observed the same quality in Cibber. In creating the still more genteel Lord Foppington of *The Careless Husband*, Cibber profited from the lesson in self-awareness. Now, we learn, the fop is no longer a contemptible rival:

> The Women now begin to laugh *with* him, not *at* him: for he really sometimes rallies his own Humour with so much Ease and Pleasantry, that a great many Women begin to think he has no Follies at all.
> (I. i)

Though in both plays the fop loses the lady to a rival, his defeat is in no way humiliating and he is able to accept it with good grace – sarcastic in Vanbrugh, apparently genuine in *The Careless Husband*. Miss Hoyden is clearly no real loss, and in Cibber's play we discover that Foppington has a wife at home; little is said about her, for fear of complicating the moral situation, but it appears that she is ample compensation for his defeat in the earlier play. That Cibber's Foppington should be a philandering husband rather than an unsuccessful suitor is in keeping with the theme of marital infidelity in *The Careless Husband*, but it also shows the extent to which the character is now a part of society rather than an outsider.

Fops enter still further into high society in Cibber's later plays. In *The Lady's Last Stake* he played Lord George Brilliant, who is described as a 'strange Piece of wild Nature' and a 'silly affected Rogue' but is nevertheless given some of the most frankly sexual love scenes of the period. The play's most recent editor has wondered whether 'the audience, so accustomed to Sir Novelty Fashion and Lord Foppington, could support Cibber's portrayal of Brilliant's appeal as the romantic hero and good-natured man.'[17] But in fact Cibber wrote, or rather adapted, two other plays in that prolific year (1707), giving himself the same kind of part in each. Celadon in *The Comical Lovers* is based on a Dryden character who had originally been played by Charles Hart, a romantic comedy actor; Atall in *The Double Gallant* is designed as much for a light comedian as a fop. In two of the three plays, moreover, Cibber was able to play love scenes opposite his favourite actress, Mrs Oldfield, which must have been as satisfactory as his earlier dream of acting opposite Mrs Bracegirdle. Though in all three plays the Cibber character is described in strictly comic terms, he never suffers the usual fate of the Restoration fop: to be rejected and unpartnered at the end. This does happen to Witling – Cibber's last fop part – in *The Refusal* (1721), but his good-natured attitude again converts defeat into a sort of triumph. 'Since thou has Wit enough to laugh at thyself,' says the victorious hero, 'I think nobody else ought to do it' (V. i).

This line indicates the paradox underlying Cibber's fop persona. His constant admission of his own folly is a way of defending himself against ridicule by anticipating it, but the effect most constantly aimed at is one of total self-awareness which makes nonsense of his claims to impenetrable stupidity. The *Apology* constantly plays off apparent frankness and naivety against remarks which show the author's awareness of precisely what impression he is making:

> A very natural Vanity! Though it is some sort of Satisfaction to know it does not impose on me. Vanity again!
> (*Apology*, p. 20)

The author of *The Laureat* (1740) was one of the few to recognize Cibber's strategy, arguing 'that you are not so great a Fool as you are pleas'd to say you are, and that you tie up your Wit, as a Beggar does his Limbs, to excite our Compassion and our Charity, and to be forgiven your Errors by this pretended Confession of them.'[18] Cibber agreed with this, as he agreed with everything said about him. When Pope ridiculed his laureateship in an epigram which described him as combining the roles of court fool and poet, Cibber replied,

Those Fools of old, if Fame says true,
Were chiefly chosen for their Wit;
Why then, call'd Fools? because, like you,
Dear *Pope*, too bold in shewing it.[19]

The point of displaying so obviously exaggerated a persona is to make the reader wonder what is 'really' behind it. Cibber seems deliberately out to tantalize in his dialogue, *The Egotist* (1743), which allows a 'Friend' to raise a number of awkward questions about the accuracy of the self-portrait in the *Apology* ('Ay, but no Blockhead is so dull, as not to be sore when he is called so') but evades answering them.[20] There are hints that he may be a man of sensibility after all, yet Cibber also remarks that he has a good deal of Lord Foppington in himself. It is never clear how much of his mockery is directed at himself and how much at the roles he has played. The constant emphasis on acting eventually makes one willing to believe that the actor is the opposite of his role, like one of the wise fools of Elizabethan drama. It may have been with Cibber's peculiar technique in mind that Fielding (also in 1743) defined the kind of raillery which does no harm to its victims:

True Raillery indeed consists either in playing on Peccadillo's, which, however they may be censured by some, are not esteemed as really Blemishes in a Character in the Company where they are made the Subject of Mirth....

Or, Secondly, in pleasantly representing real good Qualities in a false Light of Shame, and bantering them as ill ones....

Lastly; in ridiculing Men for Vices and Faults which they are known to be free from.[21]

In fact, Cibber's 'bantering' of his supposed folly sometimes makes it look almost like sanctity. Fielding recognized the truly incredible part of the self-portrait when he commented that the *Apology* 'deals in Male-Virtue' and that chastity was 'almost the only Virtue which the great Apologist hath not given himself'.[22] His remarks are borne out by the meaning which Cibber gives to folly in an epilogue which he wrote for himself to speak when he returned to the stage for a few special performances in 1742:

Now worn with Years, and yet in Folly strong,
Now to act Parts, your Grandsires saw when young!
What could provoke me! – I was always wrong....
Mixt, in the wisest Heads, we find some Folly;
Yet I find few such happy Fools – as *Colley*!

So long t'have liv'd the daily Satire's Stroke,
Unmov'd by Blows, that might have fell'd an Oak,
And yet have laugh'd the labour'd Libel to a Joke. . . .
If for my Folly's larger List you call,
My Life has lump'd 'em! There you'll read 'em all.
There you'll find Vanity, wild Hopes pursuing;
A wide Attempt, to save the Stage from Ruin!
There I confess, I have *outdone* my *own outdoing*![23]

The last line quoted here is one of several occasions on which Cibber revives a clumsy phrase which had been extensively ridiculed when he first used it in 1728; it is characteristic of him that he should keep the joke going for 14 years, until the phrase became almost proverbial. Like the rest of the 'folly' in the epilogue, it is an example of amazing endurance. The *Apology*, as described by Cibber, is the account of a heroic career, foolish only in its disinterestedness.

'His very Nakedness is a Disguise,' wrote the author of *The Laureat*; it was true.[24] It was a disguise perhaps more important for its influence on those who believed in it than for those who saw through it. The persona of the harmless, lovable fool can be found again in Goldsmith (who quoted one of Cibber's lines, quite pertinently, about Dr Johnson);[25] for Boswell, who took Cibber's part when the Doctor ridiculed him,[26] the actor provided a useful example of how the mixture of good-nature and honest vanity could win one the friendship of great men. It is also possible that his copying of Cibber's false frankness was one means by which Boswell was able to achieve his extraordinary insights into the workings of his own mind. Cibber may have had similar insights, but he kept them to himself. So long as he could write parts for himself, onstage or off, he could fulfil his real ambition: he could play heroes.

NOTES

1. *An Apology for the Life of Colley Cibber with an historical view of the stage during his own time* (ed. B. R. S. Fone, Ann Arbor, 1968), 29. Cited hereafter, in text, as *Apology*.
2. See Helene Koon, 'The kind Impostor; Colley Cibber's Dramatic Technique' (Ph.D. thesis, UCLA, 1969), 36–7; T. B. Gilmore, Jr, 'Colley Cibber's good nature and his reaction to Pope's satire', *Papers on Language and Literature*, II (1966), discusses the falseness of the image presented during the pamphlet war with Pope.
3. This is printed only with the first edition of 1700; evidently Cibber himself became ashamed of it later.
4. Except where otherwise indicated, Cibber's plays are quoted from *Plays Written by Mr. Cibber* (2 vols, 1721).
5. Cibber, *The Character and Conduct of Cicero* (1747), sig. B2–v.

6. Quoted from vol. I of *The Dramatic Works of Colley Cibber, esq.* (5 vols, 1777).
7. *The Town Talk*, No. 2, 23 Dec. 1715, *Richard Steele's Periodical Journalism* (ed. Rae Blanchard, 1959), 196–7.
8. 'Characters and Conduct of Sir John Edgar', *The Critical Works of John Dennis* (ed. E. N. Hooker, 2 vols, Baltimore, 1939), II, 193. (Society for Theatre Research, 1964), 128–33.
9. See A. C. Sprague, *Shakespeare's Histories: Plays for the Stage* (Society for Theatre Research, 1964), 128–33.
10. Thomas Davies, *Memoirs of the Life of David Garrick, Esq.* (2 vols, 1780), I, 40–1.
11. *The Dramatic Works of Sir George Etherege* (ed. H. F. B. Brett-Smith, 2 vols, 1927), II, i.
12. *The Spectator*, No. 65 (ed. D. F. Bond, 5 vols, 1965), I, 280.
13. 'A Short Vindication of the Relapse and the Provok'd Wife', *The Complete Works of Sir John Vanbrugh* (Plays ed. Bonamy Dobrée, Letters ed. Geoffrey Webb, 4 vols, 1927), I, 199.
14. *A Defence of the Short View of the Profaneness and Immorality of the English Stage* (1699), 108.
15. *A Short View of the Immorality and Profaneness of the English Stage* (1698), 222 and 223.
16. Bonamy Dobrée, 'Introduction', *Works of Vanbrugh*, I, xxiv.
17. 'Introduction', *Colley Cibber: Three Sentimental Comedies* (ed. Maureen Sullivan, New Haven and London, 1973 [Yale Studies in English No. 184]), xvi.
18. [Aaron Hill?], *The Laureat; or, the Right Side of Colley Cibber, Esq.* (1740), 14–15.
19. *A Letter from Mr. Cibber, to Mr. Pope* (1742), 20.
20. *The Egotist: or, Colley upon Cibber* (1743), 12.
21. 'An Essay on Conversation', *Miscellanies by Henry Fielding, Esq., Vol.* 1 (ed. H. K. Miller, 1972), 152.
22. *The History of the Adventures of Joseph Andrews and of His Friend Mr. Abraham Adams* (ed. Douglas Brooks, London, New York and Toronto, 1970), 16.
23. Quoted in *The Egotist*, 57–9. A slightly different text is printed in *The Universal Magazine*, Supplement to vol. LIX (1776), 377.
24. *The Laureat*, 15.
25. James Boswell, *Life of Johnson* (ed. Birkbeck Hill, Rev. L. F. Powell, London, New York and Toronto, [1953] 1961 [Oxford Standard Authors]), 1278.
26. *Boswell: the Ominous Years 1774–1776* (ed. Charles Ryskamp and F. A. Pottle, Melbourne, London and Toronto, 1963), entries for 6 April 1775, and 15 May 1776.

10 Fielding's 'Tom Thumb' Plays

T. W. CRAIK

The Augustan Age, the Age of Reason – as it was once usual to call it – was also a period when the Fancy flourished. To hail it as an Age of Fancy or an Age of Nonsense might be going too far, but it produced some excellent extravagances and absurdities, among the best of which is the 24-year-old Fielding's *Tragedy of Tragedies; or the Life and Death of Tom Thumb the Great* (1731). This is the expanded and revised version of the *Tom Thumb* which he had written in 1730 and to which (as well as making a few verbal changes) he had added the substantial episode of the Bailiff and Follower in the same year. The chief difference between the version of 1731 and these earlier ones is the quantity of additional stylistic parody it contains, parody to which the author's elaborate Scriblerian footnotes call attention; and which, accordingly, has caused *The Tragedy of Tragedies* to be regarded by many as essentially a work of ridicule.[1] If, however, one compares it with Buckingham's *Rehearsal*, or with *The Dunciad*, it is clear that the play is not written with animosity but with a gusto which – remembering the mechanicals' play in *A Midsummer Night's Dream* – can be called Shakespearean. That the passages from Dryden (who had been dead for over 30 years) and from the rest provide a satirical target is of little importance; what is of greater importance is that they provide artistic inspiration.

The play, in all three versions, is essentially an enthusiastic play. Parody of passages and the more general burlesque of dramatic situations and dramatic style are elements in that expansive delight in the ridiculous which is so important a feature of Fielding's work in general. It places him in a great English comic tradition that embraces Chaucer, Shakespeare, and, nearest to Fielding's own time, Congreve. Two short examples of Squire Western's dialogues with his sister may illustrate the abundance of the ridiculous when it is present:

> 'It is by living at home with you that she hath learnt romantic Notions of Love and Nonsense.' – 'You don't imagine, I hope,' cries the Squire, 'that I have taught her any such Things.' – 'Your Ignorance, Brother,'

returned she, 'as the great *Milton* says, almost subdues my Patience.' 'D—n *Milton*,' answered the Squire, 'if he had the Impudence to say so to my Face, I'd lend him a Douse, thof he was never so great a Man.' (*Tom Jones*, Bk VI, ch. xiv)

In their next dialogue, some dozen pages later (Bk VII, ch. iii), being blamed for teaching his daughter disobedience,

'Blood;' cries the Squire, foaming at the Mouth, 'you are enough to conquer the Patience of the Devil!'

In the preface to *Joseph Andrews* Fielding says that the source of the true ridiculous is affectation, but this hardly accounts for the ridiculousness of Squire Western, who may fairly be called the least affected of men. Incongruity and truth to nature count for far more. In this second extract, the Squire has heard of 'the Patience of a Saint', but in his present mood 'the Devil' comes more readily to his tongue, let the ensuing sense be what it will. Fielding writes for readers who can imaginatively entertain impossible ideas (of the devil exercising patience, or of Squire Western teaching romantic notions of love) as well as heartily enjoy the Squire's more obviously amusing reference to Milton.

In his *Tom Thumb* plays he invites a similarly imaginative response to the ridiculous:

KING. Let nothing but a Face of Joy appear.
The Man who frowns this day shall lose his Head,
That he may have no Face to frown withal.*
(1731, I. ii) *withal] again 1730

Thus King Arthur, proclaiming Tom Thumb's victory over the Giants. Commanding joy on pain of death is funny in itself, but there is more to delight us in the lines. In the previous scene the courtiers Noodle and Doodle, conscientiously delivering the exposition to each other, have made the *cliché* 'All Nature smiles' unusually concrete: originally Fielding ended Doodle's opening speech with

All Nature, O my *Noodle!* grins for Joy;

but in 1731 he improved even this into

All Nature wears one universal Grin

– where the noun, so conspicuously placed, makes the grin as substantial, and almost as self-sufficient, as the Cheshire Cat's. This image is still printed on our minds when we reach the 'Face of Joy', which therefore becomes much more than a synonym for 'cheerful looks'; and the concreteness of all this enforces the logic of the King's decree to remove any frown by removing the face that wears it. The change in the text of 1731, directing his decree not against future frowns but against present ones, shows that Fielding was very much alive to this kind of verbal detail.

When Tom Thumb now enters, to receive the public thanks of the King (and the private admiration of the Queen), Fielding again improves on his first thoughts; the dialogue (1730) continues:

> But say, my Boy, where didst thou leave the Giants?
> THUMB. My Liege, without the Castle Gates they stand,
> The Castle Gates too low for their Admittance.
> KING. What look they like?
> THUMB. Like twenty Things, my Liege;
> Like twenty thousand Oaks, by Winter's Hand
> Strip'd of their Blossoms, like a Range of Houses,
> When Fire has burnt their Timber all away.
> KING. Enough: The vast Idea fills my Soul;
> I see them, yes, I see them now before me.
> The monst'rous, ugly, barb'rous Sons of Whores,
> Which, like as many rav'nous Wolves, of late
> Frown'd grimly o'er the Land, like Lambs look now.
> (I. iii)

In 1731 he omitted Tom Thumb's reply to the King's second question and substituted:

> THUMB. Like Nothing but Themselves.
> QUEEN. And sure thou art like nothing but thy Self. [*Aside.*

He also omitted the King's last two lines and ended the sentence with the preceding line. It is interesting to conjecture Fielding's train of thought. Composing the passage he seems to have been concentrating on the over-worked device of the simile in serious drama: the King is presumably asking for a description of the Giants (how many heads has each got, for example); but, having unfortunately used the word 'like' in his question, he is answered by two instant similes (with the remaining 18 in prospect) of which the gist is 'They look defeated'. If this was Fielding's point, he somewhat blunted it by giving the King himself a similar simile directly afterwards; it is a trite one, even when we admit the incongruity between giants and lambs, and neither of Tom Thumb's has the vivid badness that similes in burlesques should have. He was right to prune them (when re-modelling the scene to introduce Glumdalca, the captive Queen of the Giants, with whom the King is to fall involuntarily in love); and he then dealt brilliantly with the gaps they left. Tom Thumb's anti-simile (held up for our further contemplation by the Queen's aside) wins from the King a tribute that would be a fit reply either to eloquence or to the *mot juste*. The effect of the other change, the change in punctuation and hence in syntax and in sense, works along with this: what was a subject clause is now changed to an exclamatory one, as the King, having somehow acquired his vivid mental image of the Giants, recoils in distaste from what he pictures.

Fielding was evidently still in high spirits when revising the play in 1731, as appears from this gratuitous refining of passages which he might have used again in their first form. He cared more for effect than for absolute consistency: he either did not see or did not care that, having introduced Glumdalca in I. iii, he made unreasonable the insinuation by Grizzle (I. v) that Tom Thumb had not really taken any Giants prisoner. It is hard to see why he retained Mustacha's dispraise of Tom Thumb (II. iii), a passage where her two 'comedy-of-manners' speeches alternate with Huncamunca's blank verse reply. It is the only surviving prose in the 1731 version, Fielding having wisely dropped a pair of Molièresque physicians together with the episode in which they occur (1730, II. v–ix). The structural re-modelling which begins here extends to the end of the play. In 1730, the supposed death of Tom Thumb provides the necessary complication between exposition and catastrophe; while the King and Huncamunca are listening to the physicians, Tom Thumb enters (he answers the King's astonished question with '*Tom Thumb* I am, and eke also alive'), having himself heard that Huncamunca was dead (she had fainted in her distress). Noodle reports that the poisoning of a monkey dressed in the hero's clothes led to the mistake, and the King (in the speeches given in 1731 to the Parson) dismisses the happy pair to marriage. After a disconsolate but resilient soliloquy by the Queen (1730, II. x), she is joined by the King and Huncamunca (why the bridegroom is absent is not explained), and after 'Dance, *Epithalamium*, and Sports', Noodle again serves as messenger to announce that the hero has been swallowed by 'A Cow, of larger than the usual Size'. Grizzle (who envies Tom Thumb's triumph but is not in 1730 his rival in love) growls

> Curse on the Cow that took my Vengeance from me;

but almost directly

> *Ghost of* TOM THUMB *rises.*
>
> GHOST. *Tom Thumb* I am – but am not eke alive.
> My Body's in the Cow, my Ghost is here.

GRIZ. Thanks, O ye Stars, my Vengeance is restor'd,
Nor shalt thou fly me – for I'll kill thy Ghost. [*Kills the Ghost.*
HUNC. O barbarous Deed! – I will revenge him so. [*Kills* Griz.
DOOD. Ha! *Grizzle* kill'd – then Murtheress beware. [*Kills* Hunc.
QUEEN. O wretch! – have at thee. [*Kills* Dood.
NOOD. And have at thee too. [*Kills the* Queen.
CLE. Thou'st kill'd the Queen. [*Kills* Nood.
MUST. And thou hast kill'd my Lover. [*Kills* Cle.
KING. Ha! Murtheress vile, take that. [*Kills* Must.
And take thou this. [*Kills himself, and falls.*
So when the Child (*etc.*, as in 1731).

Grizzle's killing of the Ghost is famous as having made Swift laugh for only the second time in his life.[2] Fielding stresses its absurdity admirably by mentioning Grizzle's thwarted vengeance in advance and by making Tom Thumb vary his earlier arrival-line to state that this time he is both dead and bodiless. The lightning-chess effect of the final slaughter – a death a line to begin with, after which the pace is doubled – is also excellent. Fielding was able to keep this, in varied form, but had to abandon Grizzle's killing of the Ghost when he revised the play. It must have cost him a pang to do so.

The sacrifice was justified: structurally, the 1731 version is a great improvement. Apart from the non-event of Tom Thumb's reported death, the earlier version has no development other than its sketch of the Queen's hopeless passion. In 1731 this is retained and to balance it the King is impassioned for Glumdalca; moreover Glumdalca is Huncamunca's rival for Tom Thumb's love, and Grizzle is Tom Thumb's for Huncamunca's. Here is material for a burlesque of Dryden's heroic plays and their eighteenth-century successors, a worthy vehicle for the stylistic parody that is such a feature of the revision. Besides permitting Fielding to write many such speeches, and a whole quarrel scene between the rival ladies which closely parodies that between Cleopatra and Octavia in *All for Love*, this material provides him with a genuine plot. The Queen's passion remains a dead-end, and the King's is another; but Grizzle's motivates his scene with Huncamunca (II. v) in which he tells her that his rival will not make a satisfactory husband and persuades her to marry him instead. In consequence he hurries away to get a licence. Tom Thumb arrives (II. vi) and Huncamunca tells him that she must be another's. No sooner has he begun to declaim than Glumdalca also arrives (II. vii).[3] The ensuing quarrel precipitates the heroine's change of heart:

GLUM. You'd give the best of Shoes within your Shop,
To be but half so handsome.

HUNC. – Since you come
To that, I'll put my Beauty to the Test:
Tom Thumb, I'm yours, if you with me will go.

They are married by the Parson (II. ix);[4] and Grizzle, returning with the licence, is too late, has a stormy scene with Huncamunca (II. x), and departs vowing the vengeance which will be the mainspring of the added third Act, and will allow the introduction of the battle which no heroic play should be without. In the battle Grizzle kills Glumdalca, and Tom Thumb kills Grizzle. It is on his triumphant return to court with the rebel's head that the cow swallows him. Grizzle, being dead, can no longer begin the slaying with Tom Thumb's ghost, so a new starting-point has to be found:

NOOD. Her Majesty the Queen is in a Swoon.[5]
QUEEN. Not so much in a Swoon, but I have still
Strength to reward the Messenger of ill News. [*Kills* Noodle.
CLE. My Lover's kill'd, I will revenge him so. [*Kills the* Queen.
HUNC. My Mamma kill'd! vile Murtheress, beware! [*Kills* Cleora.
DOOD. This for an old Grudge, to thy Heart. [*Kills* Huncamunca.
MUST. And this
I drive to thine, Oh *Doodle*! for a new one. [*Kills Doodle.*
KING. Ha! Murtheress vile, take that. [*Kills* Must.
And take thou this. [*Kills himself, and falls.*

At some stage during this complete reorganization of his plot Fielding must have perceived with glee that though he had to give up the best incident in his original version he did not have to give up the joke on which it was based. Any ghost would serve to hang it upon. Accordingly, taking a hint from Almanzor's encounter with his mother's informative ghost in Dryden's *Conquest of Granada* (Pt II, IV. iii), he introduced the Ghost of Gaffer Thumb to give the King warning of Grizzle's rebellion. Dryden's scene is so ludicrous that parody is supererogatory, but Fielding's original touches are plentiful enough to make an excellent burlesque situation. He allows the Ghost to open the act:

GHOST *solus.*
Hail! ye black Horrors of Midnight's Midnoon!
Ye Fairies, Goblins, Bats and Screech-Owls, Hail!
And oh! ye mortal Watchmen, whose hoarse Throats
Th'Immortal Ghosts' dread Croakings counterfeit,[6]
All Hail! – Ye dancing Fantoms, who by Day,
Are some condemn'd to fast, some feast in Fire;

Now play in Church-yards, skipping o'er the Graves,
To the loud Musick of the silent Bell,
All Hail!

The King, instead of being taken by surprise like Almanzor, arrives on the scene to stop the disturbance which the Ghost is causing by his loud apostrophizings. Thus we reach the joke:

KING. Presumptuous Slave!
Thou diest.
GHOST. Threaten others with that Word,
I am a Ghost, and am already dead.
KING. Ye stars! 'tis well; were thy last Hour to come,
This Moment had been it.

What is lost in action (killing the Ghost) is gained in language (the King's last speech is well worth contemplating).

Again and again, in reading The *Tragedy of Tragedies*, one is pulled up by similarly felicitous ideas and expressions (which make one wonder how Fielding could in the following year write *The Covent-Garden Tragedy*, so deficient in both).[7] Not the least of its pleasures are the proper names and Fielding's use of them.[8] Apart from King Arthur (in whose reign the Tom Thumb story was traditionally set) and Merlin (briefly introduced in 1731 to show the hero an image of his fate) he had a free hand. The names of Dollalolla (1730; in 1731 both this spelling and Dollallolla occur) and Huncamunca are both formed on the 'reduplicated' principle. Perhaps Fielding named the princess before her mother and took 'monkey' as his starting-point: the word, in its familiar personal sense, is applied by Lady Macduff to her son, by Cassio to Bianca, and by Swift to both his lady correspondents in the *Journal to Stella* (2 November 1710). Whatever their origin, both names stand well in a burlesque verse line, even in 1730. But when he developed the element of parody in 1731, Fielding found new resources in the names. His parody of Thomson's

Oh *Sophonisba*, *Sophonisba*, oh!

is the most famous line of his play (as the original was the most famous line of Thomson's), and if the reader turns to the context (II. v) he will see that Fielding has placed the repetitions most skilfully, signalling in advance the third and final return of the line in full by passing from blank verse to rhyme. What he does with the name Dollalolla is more ingenious still. Dryden had written, in *Cleomenes*,

How I could curse my Name of *Ptolemy*!
It is so long, it asks an Hour to write it.
By Heav'n! I'll change it into *Jove*, or *Mars*,
Or any other civil Monosyllable,
That will not tire my Hand.

This becomes (the King is speaking)

Come, *Dollallolla*; Curse that odious Name!
It is so long, it asks an Hour to speak it.
By Heavens! I'll change it into *Doll*, or *Loll*,
Or any other civil Monosyllable
That will not tire my Tongue.

Dryden's characteristic hyperbole is made still more hyperbolical, inasmuch as speaking is faster than writing; the monosyllables even become (one is tempted to say) more *monosyllabic* by being not alternative names but fragments chopped out of the original name itself; one of these fragments, Doll, does happen to be a diminutive already (of Dorothy); and finally, a new tone of peevishness is injected by changing 'How I could curse my Name' into the imprecatory 'Curse that odious Name!'

James T. Hillhouse[9] has pointed out that Noodle and Doodle were names commonly given to characters in the variety shows acted at fairs. Their interchangeable names (the *Oxford English Dictionary* shows that in the seventeenth and eighteenth centuries a doodle meant a noodle) emphasize their supernumerary nature. When Fielding needs a confidant for Grizzle he creates Foodle, and therewithal invents (the language's stock being exhausted) a third rhyming synonym for fool. Incidentally, Foodle is never addressed by name in the dialogue: he is named for Fielding's own pleasure and the reader's. Grizzle himself, an important character, is linked by the form of his name to the court Noodles, Doodles and Foodles, while its sense suggests maturity of years and perhaps also choler of temperament. In 1731 Fielding turned this name also to profit by means of assonance:

Teach me to scold, prodigious-minded *Grizzle*,
Mountain of Treason, ugly as the Devil
(I. v)

and by playing on words:

Aloft he bore the grizly Head of *Grizzle*

There is less to be said about the other names. Mustacha (the literary equivalent of a moustache drawn on a lady's portrait) is chosen for its elementary incongruity with its bearer, a maid of honour; the point (if any) of the other one's name, Cleora, escapes me.[10] The Queen of the Giants naturally has a Brobdingnagian name adjusted to the other names in the play; Glumdalclitch really means 'little nurse', but it was the nearest thing to a proper name that Book II of *Gulliver's Travels* provided.

There is so much to admire and enjoy in the play (especially in its final form) that one is tempted to go into too much detail. It is therefore best to stop. In writing about *Tom Thumb* at all, one is conscious of the amusement Fielding would feel in seeing its beauties held up to admiration, since he had made Scriblerus boast, in his Preface, of being

> more capable of doing Justice to our Author, than any other Man, as have given my self more Pains to arrive at a thorough Understanding of this little Piece, having for ten Years together read nothing else.

NOTES

1. An anonymous contemporary, writing in 1739, blames Fielding for attacking 'all the Great Geniuses *England* has produced, for a Couple of Ages' and for trying to 'provoke our contemptuous mirth' (*Henry Fielding: The Critical Heritage*, ed. R. Paulson and T. Lockwood, 1969, 111–12).
2. *Ibid.*, 73.
3. With a full line of verse, leaving the previous line incomplete. There is, in fact, no join between the two scenes. One could be effected by completing Tom Thumb's last line with the sufficiently theatrical question 'but who comes here?', and I wonder whether this was Fielding's intention and something went wrong with the printing at this point. There is no sign that he personally supervised or corrected any edition. For example, the transposition of Fielding's first two footnotes on III.ii remained uncorrected, as it has remained in every edition since; the most recent editor (L. J. Morrissey, Fountainwell Drama Texts, Edinburgh, 1970) has not perceived it. The pun to which the second footnote refers is 'walk'.
4. In II.viii, Glumdalca is surprised by the soliloquizing King, and they exeunt severally with 'so violent an Affection' that it is 'too big for Utterance' (Fielding's footnote).
5. Fielding has written a similar line earlier (1731, I.iii) as a comic statement of the obvious: after a particularly vehement speech by the Queen against the King's bestowing of Huncamunca on Tom Thumb, Foodle comments: 'Her Majesty the Queen is in a Passion'. Consequently Noodle's line would get a laugh, after which the Queen's utterly unexpected reaction would get a bigger laugh.
6. Fielding could be relied upon to draw upon the Ghost in *Hamlet* (he does so two lines later); he here turns to *Othello* because 'hail' puts him in mind of 'farewell'. His Ghost's soliloquy in its turn must have inspired W. S. Gilbert to write the most famous lyric in *Ruddigore*.
7. Simon Trussler's opinion that the latter play 'is in many ways the better of the two' (*Burlesque Plays of the Eighteenth Century*, 1969, 144) is evidently based on other criteria (cf. his pp. 171–2).
8. So much better than in the later play, where Kissinda and Stormandra are tolerable parodies of such Greek names as Cassandra and Timandra, but

Gallono and especially Lovegirlo are distressingly barren, while Captain Bilkum and Mother Punchbowl come straight from 'humours' comedy.

9. H. Fielding, *The Tragedy of Tragedies*, ed. James T. Hillhouse (New Haven and London, 1918), 155.

10. It is a classical name and belonged to the wife of Agesilaus. It appears in the dialogue only in 1730, where Huncamunca takes two lines to ask Cleora to sing; in 1731 (with *All for Love* in view) the command is 'Give me some Music – see that it be sad.'

11 Fielding in *Tom Jones*: the Historian, the Poet, and the Mythologist

RONALD PAULSON

Reading through *The Jacobite's Journal* in W. B. Coley's fine new edition, I am struck by the coincidence of concerns with the great novel Fielding was finishing at the same time.[1] It is fascinating to watch the historical situation of the *Journal* carried over into the novel and made its central paradigm. What the parable of the Good Samaritan and Fénelon's *Telemachus* meant to *Joseph Andrews* the Rebellion of '45 means to *Tom Jones*. And this fact indicates a fundamental difference between the narrative modes of the two novels, the one based on a literary and the other on a historical nexus.[2]

In 1745, perhaps early in the year, Fielding began writing *Tom Jones*.[3] The Rebellion broke out in the summer and in November he began to produce *The True Patriot*, an alarmist propaganda organ for the government, and at the same time wrote a *History of the Present Rebellion in Scotland*. Three years later, with the '45 quite dead but the unpopularity of the Hanoverians growing and with the need to defend the Pelham ministry's policies at home and abroad, he spent the year 1748 issuing weekly attacks on opponents from the right and left who, he claimed, sought a change in the sovereign. The satiric designation 'Jacobite' was perhaps not so purely propagandistic as has sometimes been thought: for every five portrait prints advertised of Charles I in 1747 there was one of William III and none of George II.

The Jacobite's Journal spends much of its time contrasting the Jacobite mythology with the plain historical facts of 1688, 1715, and 1745. Related to mythology as a type of falsification are all kinds of misunderstandings: some readers take literally his Jacobite mask; the Opposition press casts lies and slanders at him and his ministerial friends, analogous to the Jacobite lies about Stuart genealogy and the succession. The essays treat obsessively such subjects as slander (nos. 8, 26, 28) and personal attacks on Fielding (from serious slanders to the comic mimicry of Samuel Foote, nos. 20, 22) and on his friends (e.g. no. 18 on Lyttelton). The equation between the slandering of the man and his writing, which Fielding develops in *Tom*

Jones, from the chapters on 'mixed character' in Black George and Tom (VIII. i and X. i) to the defence of the good book with some blemishes against the attacks of 'critics' (XI. i), is already laid out in *The Jacobite's Journal*. The application Fielding makes is equally to a *Paradise Lost* and to a Socrates or Brutus: 'to condemn a Work or a Man as vicious, because they are not free from Faults or Imperfections' is contrasted to the alternative, a paragon or 'faultless Monster' (no. 8) of the sort treated in the apparent paragons of, say, Blifil or the king of the gipsies.

False history is the subject of *The Jacobite's Journal*, and so it is of *Tom Jones*, where Jacobite rumours lead to the identification of Sophia Western and Jenny Cameron, the Young Pretender's mistress, and the Jacobite rumours act as a kind of acute symptom for the chronic fabrications that surround Allworthy, Partridge, and especially Tom, recreating 'character' in the forms of the personal fantasies of the rumour-mongers.[4] By Book VIII (pp. 432–3) rumour has Tom getting a servant maid with child, breaking Thwackum's arm, snapping a pistol at Blifil, and beating a drum while Allworthy is sick. Book VIII continues with Partridge's story of a man's fight with a ghost (a drunk encountering a white-faced calf) and ends with the Man of the Hill's conclusion that men must be mad to entertain the possibility of the Stuarts' return. The climax, of course, is Upton, where, we are told, 'they talk, to this Day, of the Beauty and lovely Behaviour of the charming *Sophia*, by the Name of the Somersetshire Angel' (X. viii. 554); and at the Bull's Head at Meriden, the rumour is that 10,000 Frenchmen have landed in Suffolk and that Sophia is Jenny Cameron (XI. iii). In this atmosphere, Rumour herself appears, and a toast to Sophia becomes a toast to the Pretender (p. 441). The Liars' Club's lie that Tom has been killed in a duel (XV. iii) is only the last and most perfectly unfounded rumour.

The narrator of *Tom Jones* is himself in the limited, though privileged, position of an historian who is trying to extricate the true from the false. In VIII. i, as he nears the centre of the narrative, he talks about the historical origins of fictions, telling us that remarkable deeds of humans 'gave Birth to many Stories of the Antient Heathen Deities (for most of them are of poetical Original)' (p. 397). It was the poet who carried out this transformation, whereas 'the Historian will confine himself to what really happened, and utterly reject any Circumstance, which, tho' never so well attested, he must be well assured is false' (p. 401).[5]

The source for the historiography employed in *The Jacobite's Journal* is the Abbé Banier's *Mythology and Fables of the Ancients, explain'd from History* (translated 1739–40). Fielding singles out Banier's volumes (republished in 1748) for praise in the Court of Criticism, and we know that he owned a copy himself.[6] Banier's euhemerist analysis of myths is the basic methodology behind the essays in *The Jacobite's Journal*. Fielding brings it specifically to bear on the Jacobites' constructions in nos. 6 and 12, first as a parallel or comparative mythology linking the story of Bacchus to the Jacobite ethos of hunting, drinking, and dipping into politics; and second as a pursuit of the sources or motivations for such fabulating (vanity, illiteracy, the lies of travellers, etc.).

Fielding cites Banier by name only once in *Tom Jones* (XII. i. 619), but, as in the passage I cited from VIII. i, Banier's methodology is discernible in much of the historical analysis that is carried on. There is, of course, a close relationship between euhemerism or the reducing of mythology to history and the travesty mode Fielding had practised in the 1730s. Banier's explanation 'that the *Minotaur* with *Pasiphae*, and the rest of that Fable, contain nothing but an Intrigue of the Queen of *Crete* with a Captain named *Taurus*' (I, 29) could almost, but not quite, have appeared in *Tumble-down Dick.* The difference is between finding the source of the god in a great man and in a bumpkin. The latter is the strategy of Gay's lines in *The Shepherd's Week*:

> Now plain I ken whence *Love* his Rise begun.
> Sure he was born some bloody *Butcher*'s Son,
> Bred up in Shambles, where our Younglings slain,
> Erst taught him Mischief and to sport with Pain.[7]

The real Mars here is a butcher and Eros the butcher's son. But we also see Gay's melancholy speaker, Sparabella, mythologizing her unhappy love affair.

The euhemerist Banier, to 'fully unravel the History of this God', Mars, relates him to several possible sources: first to the king Belus (the Scriptural Nimrod), 'to whom *Diodorus* attributes the Invention of Arms, and the Art of marshalling Troops in Battle', or perhaps Ninus or Thutas; second to an ancient king of Egypt, third to a king of Thrace named Odin, fourth to a Greek named Ares, and finally to a Roman named Mars, a brother of Amulius Numitor (II, 316). His researches seek a correspondence in dignity to the god, which would explain the magnitude of the fable; no discrepancy is sought, though one emerges; and the mode is scholarship of the historian, not travesty of the satirist.[8] Unlike travesty (or its sister mock-heroic), this mode is concerned with causality and historical relationships, in some sense genealogy and etymology: how *did* the historical ur-Tom become the rake, the Adonis, the 'Angel from Heaven', or the 'murderer'? And what exactly is the relationship, and does it tell us something about the reality, or is it an element without which the reality itself does not signify?

Let us take two battle scenes, Joseph Andrews and the foxhounds (III. vi), and Tom Jones and the attackers of Molly Seagrim in the graveyard (IV. viii). In the first Fielding is merely demonstrating the inadequacy of heroic analogues as literary forms to characterize the real heroism of Joseph: he tells us we have to 'proceed in our ordinary Style' and that no simile, no figure from literature, is 'adequate to our Purpose': 'Let those therefore that describe Lions and Tigers, and Heroes fiercer than both, raise their Poems or Plays with the Simile of *Joseph Andrews*, who is himself above the reach of any Simile' (p. 241). Joseph himself is being made into a literary figure, though he refuses his prototypical potential at the end when he will not sanction a continuation by authors and booksellers.

Tom's battle against Molly's attackers begins as a travesty: Echepolus is in fact a sow-gelder and Myrdon is Kate of the Mill; but there is an additional dimension, already established by all the lies and fabrications that from the start have surrounded Tom, Allworthy, and the others. There is no longer the same kind of adverse comment on the heroic level itself. For there to be, Tom or even Molly would have to be acting foolishly to fight, and they are not (except in so far as Tom is deceived about his relations with Molly); only perhaps the villagers, these pious folk who are outraged by the sight of Molly in Sophia's finery and flaunting her pregnancy in church, retain something of the pretension of the heroic reference. But the villagers are primarily (like Gay's Sparabella) myth-makers, and the narrator is showing that this local scuffle in a graveyard is 'the real truth' or 'what really happened' under the stories the villagers will spread, as under the Homeric description of the Greeks and Trojans in battle. Mars is really Alexander the Great, or the bull is really Captain Taurus; Achilles is a mythologized version, fabricated by the villagers to assuage their wounded self-esteem, of Tom Jones in the graveyard fighting off the mob that is after Molly; and the real Tom can only be known through the myths surrounding him. We are seeing history in the making and in the process of being mythologized, as earlier, in a more literal way, when Partridge's battle with Mrs Partridge was promptly mythologized by their neighbours. What distinguishes such a scene from those in *Joseph Andrews* is the sense of a myth being simultaneously created and analysed.

The analogy with war engendered by the skirmish in the graveyard leads directly to the real war with the Pretender's army. On his way with the troops to meet the Pretender's army, Tom and some soldiers are supping at an inn (VII. xii. 372–6). Tom compares these soldiers to the Greeks on their way to Troy; Ensign Northerton shows his ignorance of the allusion, and one of the soldiers identifies the Greeks and Trojans as 'dey fight for von Woman.' Shortly after, Tom toasts Sophia, Northerton mythologizes her into a notorious whore, Tom calls him a rascal, and he knocks Tom out with a bottle: 'The Conqueror perceiving the Enemy to lie motionless before him, and Blood beginning to flow pretty plentifully from his Wound, began now to think of quitting the Field of Battle, where no more Honour was to be gotten'. Sophia has been turned into a kind of Helen and the inn table into a 'Field of Battle'. The effect is very different from that of Joseph's battle with the hounds, but it is an extension of Tom's with Molly's attackers, and so quite naturally the battle of Upton is based on 'no very blameable Degree of Suspicion' among the people at the inn as to Tom's relations with Mrs Waters, who is a 'Poor unfortunate Helen, the fatal Cause of all the Bloodshed' (IX. iii. 504).[9] The battles progress toward the single combat of Tom and Mrs Waters at the dinner table at Upton, introduced by an allusion to Pasiphae and the bull (a memory perhaps of Banier's amusing euhemerist account), which is presented as an elemental struggle that will be mythologized as a battle – and is literally mythologized in the conversation of the servants in the kitchen.

Banier offers Fielding something the proper historian like Hume does not, and that is the distinction between poet, historian, and mythologist. Banier's title, recall, was *The Mythology and Fables of the Ancients, explain'd from History*: a title which would apply to *The Jacobite's Journal* and *Tom Jones* if we substitute for 'Ancients' the word 'Jacobites' or 'Moderns'. The fundamental point Banier makes is that the stories of the gods are not fables, 'Tales of mere Invention', but 'ancient Facts' (or 'Truths of Importance') 'embellished' with 'numbers of Fables' (I, 21, 26). The form he describes is 'ancient Histories, mix'd with several Fictions': 'those which speak of *Hercules*, *Jason*, &c. instead of telling us in the simple way, that the latter went to recover the Treasures which *Phrixus* had carried to *Colchis*, they have given us the Fable of the Golden Fleece' (I, 30). The poetic fable does not rule out other kinds – philosophical, allegorical, moral – but all carry with them a historical truth, and so consist of two separable elements.

Important inferences can be made from this methodology, both for the narrative mode of *Tom Jones* and for the ontology of its characters. We have noticed the emphasis on history in the introductory chapter to Book VIII; Book IX returns to 'this historic kind of Writing'. Though not like the 'historical Writers' who 'draw their Materials from Records' (Banier identifies inscriptions on monuments as one source of 'ancient Facts'), the author has 'good Authority' for his characters from 'the vast authentic Doomsday-Book of Nature' and so believes his work entitled 'to the Name of History'. By genius, he explains, he means the powers of the mind 'capable of penetrating into all Things within our Reach and knowledge, and of distinguishing their essential Differences'; and by invention he means not 'a creative Faculty' as that of fabulists and romance-writers but rather 'Discovery, or finding out; a quick and sagacious Penetration into the true Essence of all the Objects of our Contemplation.'

Compared with the comic-epic-in-prose writer of *Joseph Andrews*, the historian is a difficult role. As Banier describes it, however much 'the Truths of ancient History . . . may be disguised by the great number of

Ornaments mixed with them, it is *not absolutely impossible* to unfold the historical Facts they contain' (I, 20; italics added).

> The most perplexing Difficulty in the ways of a Mythologist consists in unravelling the Intricacy of different Opinions about one and the same Fable, which is told in so many ways, and so different from one another, that it is impossible to reconcile them all.
>
> (I, 18)

For example, the fable of Tom, Black George, and Molly, as told by Thwackum, Square, Blifil, and Tom, and interpreted by Allworthy, the narrator, and the reader – or by the critical, judicious, or good-natured reader – is a complex knot perhaps never completely capable of being untied.[10] The method 'observed by our best Mythologists', says Banier, is never to adopt a fable 'without having first enquired what might have given rise to it' I, 18), and in both *The Jacobite's Journal* (e.g. no. 12) and *Tom Jones* Fielding's emphasis falls upon the searching out of motives. The awareness of difficulty and uncertainty carries from Banier to *The Jacobite's Journal*, where Fielding writes on the articles of peace: 'Whether we are to impute these Articles (if they are true) to the Intervention of Providence to the reasonable Disposition of our Enemies, or to the Wisdom and Watchfulness of our own Ministers, I will not determine' (*The Jacobite's Journal*, 278). In *Tom Jones* the 'Whether ... or ... I will not determine' construction becomes a virtual refrain of historical probability.[11]

As opposed to the Hume who tries to present demythologized facts for history, or his opposite the Christian weaver of the providential pattern, the Banier sort of euhemerism requires three roles.[12] The poet mythologizes historical facts, the historian tries to establish what really happened, and the mythologist analyses the myth in the light of history. The product is a rich complex of the three stages with the emphasis on the process itself. This is a stage well beyond the role of the travesty-poet, 'to strip it of the Marvellous' (I, 17), which in *Tom Jones* is conveyed by repeated phrases like 'This was the true Reason why', 'To say the Truth', 'the real Truth', or 'what really happened'. But Fielding is showing the simultaneous construction and explanation of myth, showing how it is produced by poets out of historical events.[13]

The historical fact does not exist without its embellishment in fable. Banier asks 'What would the *Aeneid*, *Iliad*, or *Odyssey* be, was it not for the ... perpetual mixture of Truths of small concern, with the most interesting Fictions?' (I, 39.) The 'truth of small concern' that Ulysses and his crew loiter debauching at Circe's court is augmented by the 'interesting Fiction' that Circe is a sorceress who transforms men into swine. Thus we may regard such fictions 'as so many Metaphors and figurative Ways of speaking', and the distinction applies equally to imaginative leaps like the connecting of Captain Taurus (a name only) with a bull. In general, Banier is describing what Cassirer calls the 'mythico-religious Urphenomenon' in which primitive man is confronted by a new and strange thing, and to come to terms with it *names* it, designates it metaphorically, perhaps calling it a god or a spirit. The function of this activity in *Tom Jones* is both instrumental and ontological, partly to express the vanity and other motives of the fabulator and partly to approximate the thing's essential being in the only way possible. I mean that there is a sense in which Sophia *is* Jenny Cameron, just as there is one in which Black George *does* love Tom and Tom *is* both 'so terrible a Rake' and 'an Angel from Heaven' (as Enderson calls him, 720).

'We can only *conceive* being, sidle up to it by laying something else alongside. We approach the thing not directly but by pairing, by opposing symbol and thing.' I am quoting Walker Percy in 'Metaphor as Mistake', where he explores examples 'of an accidental blundering into authentic poetic experience . . . in folk mistakes . . . for what light they may shed on the function of metaphor in man's fundamental symbolic orientation in the world', but I could be quoting a great many contemporary linguistic theorists who see the metaphor's lie as 'not a vagary of poets but a specific case of that mysterious "error" which is the very condition of our knowing anything at all.'[14]

We come to understand Tom Jones or Sophia Western by a number of 'errors' much as we do the beautiful soaring 'Blue Darter Bird' by 'Blue Dollar Bird' or a woman having an affair with a Captain Taurus by the story of Pasiphae and the bull. What Fielding has in *Tom Jones,* that was only glimpsed in *Joseph Andrews,* is the knowledge that the reality of Tom or of Molly in the graveyard, or of Sophia called Jenny Cameron, is the historical figure plus the poeticized one plus the mythologist's relation of the two. Any one of these is inadequate without the others.[15]

Roughly speaking, we can say that Fielding presents the following types of mythologizing:

1. The true character of Tom (perhaps ultimately unknowable) is related to the fables of his enemies and others, reaching from the extreme cases of mistakes (Mrs Fitzpatrick's thinking he is Blifil) to the gradual equation of him with 'so terrible a Rake', 'so very fine a Figure', or 'an Angel from Heaven'.

2. 'Fables of the Historical Kind', writes Banier, 'are easily distinguished, because mention is made in them of People we know elsewhere' (I, 31). One such group would include Lady Ranelagh painted by Kneller and the Duchess of Mazarin by Lely, who are approximations of what Sophia looked like; Hogarth's Bridewell warden for Thwackum, the old lady in

Morning for Bridget, and the servant woman in *Harlot's Progress* 3 for Mrs Partridge. He may have recalled Banier's statement that

> the Painters working upon Poetical Fancies, may be reckoned instrumental in propagating some Fables.... They have even frequently promoted the Credit of fabulous Stories, by representing them with Art; a thing so true... that the Pagans owed the Existence of many of their Gods, to some fine Statues, or Pictures well done.
>
> (I, 44)

Ultimately we come to the scene or character that has no precedent, and he can only specify: 'O, *Shakespeare*, had I thy Pen! O, *Hogarth*, had I thy Pencil!' (555). This is not the exclamation of the author of *Joseph Andrews*, demonstrating the discrepancy between the real and the literary, but an attempt to approximate as best one can the unformulable.[16]

3. On another level there are Ralph Allen and Lord Lyttelton, the actual historical figures of whom Allworthy is a poetic version; Charlotte Cradock Fielding for Sophia; and perhaps Fielding himself for Tom. Fielding is creating his own myth as he analyses those of others, while at the same time admitting the fabrication. The public dimension of 'historical truth' shades off into the private, and this applies especially to the '45 itself, the ultimate fact in process of being mythologized by the Jacobites. The confusion of Tom and Sophia wandering about searching for each other in the wilderness, of families broken up, lovers separated, and allegiances mixed, is the historical reality of the '45.[17] *The Jacobite's Journal* and Abbé Banier come together in Partridge, the garrulous, superstitious Catholic-Jacobite, who believes in the Jacobite 'Mysteries' (that a popish king would defend a Protestant Church) as he believes in prodigies and old wives' tales; and although he concludes of Tom's own story 'that the whole was a Fiction' (427), he proceeds to construct his own on the basis of his self-interest. As in the *Journal*, the time is one of rumours and lies and myths, the greatest being concerned with the virtues of an absolute monarchy (v. a constitutional or mixed form of government) and an absolute paragon (v. at best a 'mixed character', at worst a scoundrel).

We are reminded of the parallels from the outset with the two heirs to Paradise Hall, both as ambiguous as 'the famous Story of the Warming-Pan' and as 'the no more unaccountable Birth of *Bacchus*' Fielding tells in his *Jacobite's Journal* parody of Banier (p. 125). Tom is a bastard, but Blifil is himself conceived out of wedlock, though technically born within. What is clear is that Blifil, despite his technical claim to inheritance, is morally disqualified from his right to carry on the Allworthy-Western line, while Tom demonstrates his right to the title of successor. As any Englishman knew, the Act of Settlement of 1701 had given the reversion of the crown to the Protestant Electress of Hanover and her children, rejecting Jacobite claims of divine right and hereditary succession. The parallels extend from the elaborate lies and plots of Blifil to his behaviour after his exposure, which recalls that of the Prince reported by unsympathetic observers during the rout of Culloden.[18]

4. Another kind of myth is also in process of construction by Fielding the narrator. The similes from about Book V onward push unobtrusively toward the materials of country folklore. In the second battle scene, Tom defending Molly from the interruption of Blifil and company (V. xi. 259–60), the simile links Tom's response to the ritual mating of a stag in 'the Season of Rutting', and Tom becomes the defender of a 'frighted Hind': 'fierce and tremendous rushes forth the Stag to the Entrance of the Thicket; there stands the Centinel over his Love, stamps the Ground with his Foot, and with his Horns brandished aloft in Air, proudly provokes the apprehended Foe to Combat.' The simile remains implicit in the battle that follows, modifying the stated epic terms, and thereafter extends from Partridge's story of the drunk's encounter with a white-faced calf that grows into a battle with a ghost, to the simile with which Book X. ii opens, with frolicking hares, hooting owls, a half-drunk clown in terror of hobgoblins and robbers on the prowl while watchmen are asleep: 'in plain English, it was now Midnight.' We have left behind alien classical similes and are in the world of English country superstitions and folklore, where the absence of Punch and Joan in the puppet show is noticed and the presence of the gypsies' encampment comes as no surprise.

It is in this world that the major characters also function most suggestively. As Pasiphae's bull was a captain named Taurus, so God is in fact a benevolent country squire named Allworthy who lives in Paradise Hall. By Allworthy's errors and pomposities, Fielding makes it clear that he is *not* God; but mythologically the relationship is meaningful. We might say that Fielding never loses sight of the historical reality while mythologizing him – just as his neighbours also mythologize him as atheist, old fool, father of Tom, persecutor of Jenny Jones, and so on. Besides Allworthy of whom God is the fable, there is Tom of whom Adam (expelled from Eden, and sent out in Milton's words into the world) is the fable and Sophia of whom Wisdom is the fable, and so to Molly the latter-day Eve and Blifil, associated with the devil.

In the case of Tom all of the contemporary 'poetry' that he is the son of Jenny Jones and Partridge is swept away and we are left with the fact that he is the son of Bridget (Allworthy) Blifil and, as it happens, a man named Summer. Bridget herself, as her alliance with Hogarth's old woman in *Morning* and Fielding's identification as 'an Emblem of Winter' suggest, is as real and yet projective of myth as her early love named Summer, who is remembered by Mrs Waters (Tom's suppositious mother, whose own married name has the same ambience) as 'a finer Man, I must say, the Sun never shone upon' (XVIII. vii. 940).[19] Blifil, on the other hand, is the son of Winter and whatever we are to make of the swarthy, rough, calculating ungrateful melancholic Captain Blifil. Fielding uses as his example in the opening chapter on 'contrast' (V. i. 212) 'Thus the Beauty of Day, and that of Summer, is set off by the Horrors of Night and Winter', and this is roughly the scheme of the novel's myth. The vigour and fertility in the native Englishman of somewhat confused blood lines versus the paragon of melancholy, the saturnine and scheming Blifil, is the historical reality of the whole imbroglio of 1745.

The hero as nature deity had been broached more straightforwardly in Joseph Andrews, who is employed to serve as scarecrow to keep off birds, 'to perform the Part the Antients assigned to the God *Priapus*.' His cathexis is as ambiguous as Priapus' for his voice 'rather allured the Birds than terrified them' (21), as do his protestations of chastity to Lady Booby. Tom at times recalls one of the gods analysed by Banier. To take, not quite at random, the one Fielding himself analyses in *Jacobite's Journal* no. 6, we notice that Bacchus too came of an obscure liaison: 'the Antients had formed a Design to throw a Veil of Obscurity over the true History of this Prince's Birth and Education' (II, 437), and what follows is the analysis of whether he comes of a human or immortal father, and after that of the myths of bacchic celebration – all those women dancing 'to celebrate the Memory of his Conquests' (p. 446) and carrying aloft the phallus. The main point of debate, indeed, is the nature and meaning of the strange ceremonies that accompanied him wherever he travelled, characterized by 'Debauchery, Lewdness, and Prostitution being carried to the greatest Extremity' (p. 463). Bacchus was 'commonly represented like a young Man, without a Beard' (p. 453), rendered enthusiastic by too deep a use of the vine, and known for his generosity – spreading his mysteries to the world, especially to women. He carried about with him 'a Kind of ambulatory Seraglio', Banier wrily remarks (p. 446). Tom, there can be no argument, attracts both men and women of all kinds, and only repulses sterile figures like Blifil.

I use Bacchus (whose *Jacobite's Journal* caricature is the Jacobite country squire) only as a referent to underline the observation that Fielding has reversed the 'popular' characteristics of the Jacobite myth, making Tom the life-force Bonnie Prince Charlie was portrayed as being, while Blifil has all the Hanoverian-Whig traits attributed by the Jacobites – as by many objective Englishmen. It is certainly the case that the names with which the Jacobite pamphlets commemorated Charles Edward – the Wanderer, the Young Adventurer, the Young Chevalier, and Ascanius – apply to Tom, not to Blifil.[20]

Fielding himself had had a difficult task demythologizing the Prince in 1745, first in *The True Patriot* and then in his *History of the Present*

Rebellion in Scotland. In the latter, where we can juxtapose passages from newspapers and contemporary accounts, Fielding turned the dashing Prince into a Blifil, the spontaneity and expansive gestures into calculation, prudence, and vanity.[21] When the real Prince leads his soldiers across the Forth, his Rubicon, dashing ahead into the historic waters, Fielding's Prince does it to show off:

> Here Charles attempting to give an extraordinary Instance of his Bravery by passing the Water first, and mistaking the Ford, very narrowly escaped drowning, from which he was preserved by Lieutenant *Duncan Madson*, who at the Hazard of his own Life rescued him from the Waves.[22]

His most egregious fabulating of the '45, however, had been in the pages of *The True Patriot*, where he exaggerated the dangers of rape, burning, looting, and terror to the civilian population. And yet even there, true to his own character and preoccupations, Fielding carefully distinguished by headlines between 'The Present History of Great Britain' and an 'APOCRYPHA. Being a curious Collection of certain true and important WE HEARS from the News-Papers.' And once the Rebellion was over, in his final apology for his work on *The True Patriot* (no. 33), he expressed something of a sense of guilt: 'For the Paper principally intended to inflame this Nation against the Rebels, was writ whilst they were at *Derby*, and in that Day of Confusion which God will, I hope, never suffer to have its equal in this Kingdom.' His valedictory was to urge not justice but mercy, human understanding, and a spirit of tolerance toward the defeated – sentiments echoed in his attitude toward Tom throughout the narrative and in Tom's toward Blifil and Black George at the denouement.[23]

It would be interesting to know more about Fielding's response to the undeniably romantic boy who landed in a remote corner of the kingdom with only a few men to win back his father's crown. Whether Tom or Prince Charles Edward came first is, I suppose, an academic question; Fielding may have begun *Tom Jones* before the Prince's landing. But without Squire Western nearby as the pure Jacobite country squire, Tom might have reminded readers of the prince. Either Fielding is turning the myth upside down, or he finds that in an ironic way the myth of the gallant young prince is close to the one he had already adumbrated in *Joseph Andrews*, and for that matter to his own story. This is not to suggest that he is in any way more sympathetic to the Prince's cause than he was in *The Jacobite's Journal*, but only that a common myth of alienation from one's true home and wandering as exile or fugitive tie together these two heroes. Perhaps Tom is the true historical figure beneath the Jacobitish myth, as Sophia is beneath Jenny Cameron.

NOTES

1. *The Jacobite's Journal and Related Writings*, ed. W. B. Coley, 1974). My text for *Joseph Andrews* and *Tom Jones* is also the Wesleyan, ed. Martin Battestin (1967, 1974).
2. I discuss the uses of literary paradigms in *Joseph Andrews* in 'Models and paradigms in *Joseph Andrews*', *Modern Language Notes*, XCI (1976), 1186–1207; but I also clarify the point below, pp.177–8.
3. See Battestin's arguments, *Tom Jones*, introduction, xxxv–xxxix.
4. Fielding's concern with lies and fabrications appear in *Joseph Andrews* (I.iv) in Lady Tittle and Lady Tattle making up stories about Lady Booby and Joseph; but he makes no connection between their activity and the process of historiography.
5. Fielding pretty consistently refers to himself as historian (see, besides the title of the book, pp. 832 and 880). But his use of 'history' was ambiguous and did not lose its older sense of mere 'narrative', as in the titles of most of his books. For the poet-historian contrast, see the preface to *Journal of a Voyage to Lisbon*.
6. Samuel Baker, *A Catalogue of the . . . Library of . . . Henry Fielding*, item no. 219. In the Court of Criticism it is ordered 'that the said Mythology be strongly recommended to the Public, as the most useful, instructive, and entertaining Book extant' (no. 9, p. 146). Although Fielding could have come upon the reissue of 1748, far more likely he had read it at some earlier time in the 1739 edition. I cite the latter.
7. 'Wednesday', ll. 89–92.
8. See Frank Manuel's explanation of the eighteenth-century euhemerist mode in *The Eighteenth Century confronts the Gods* (Cambridge, Mass., 1959), 105; and on Banier, 104–7.
9. By VII.iii Fielding is beginning to show that the Blifil-Sophia 'alliance' or 'treaty' of marriage in the level of personal history is the equivalent of the alliances and treaties in the war of the Austrian Succession that was in 1748 just being brought to a close (p. 333). The myth-maker is Mrs Western, who sees the Blifil-Sophia negotiations in precisely this way (see p. 334).
10. The role of the audience in *Tom Jones* has usually been seen as participatory in the creation of the book's meaning. Certainly the indeterminateness is far less at issue than in *Tristram Shandy*. Fielding wants to create the impression of participation, but I suspect that the centrality of the audience is more nearly due to its part in the myth-making process. I am arguing that the central figure is in fact the historian-mythologist, who is set off somewhat from the audience and the other characters, who are in the same general caetgory of 'poets' or myth-makers.
11. E.g. on Deborah Wilkins's searching out Tom's father (II.iii.81) or Partridge's not offering Tom any of his money (XIII.vii. 712). The either/or construction in *Tom Jones* is also Fielding's version of the doubleness of causality stressed by Virgil in his *Aeneid*, as when Thymoetes urges the Trojans to take the horse into the city – 'whether in treachery, or because/The fates of Troy so ordered,' or when Laocoon's spear fails to break open the horse because 'something/Got in his way, the gods, or fate, or counsel' (Bk II, Humphries trans.). More generally, Aeneas tells us that '[Panthus'] words, or the gods' purpose, swept me on/Toward fire and arms'.
12. I hope that this essay may suggest an alternative meaning of 'history' in *Tom Jones* to that offered by both Leo Braudy and Martin Battestin, the one based on Hume's *History of England* and the other on the pattern of divine providence. See Braudy, *Narrative Form in History and Fiction* (Princeton, 1970), esp. Parts III and IV; and Battestin, *The Providence of Wit: Aspects of Form in Augustan Literature and the Arts* (1974), chs. V and VI.
13. Characteristically he also applies the historian's procedure to literary 'rules'.

A writer does something well, critics then expand these nice details into 'his chief Merit', and then to these 'Time and Ignorance, the two great Supporters of Imposture, gave Authority; and thus, many Rules for good Writing have been established, which have not the least Foundation in Truth or Nature' (211), and these are imposed tyrannically on subsequent writers. This passage points towards the analogy between the character Tom and Fielding's work *Tom Jones.*

14. *Message in a Bottle* (New York, 1975), 72, 81.
15. He was, of course, aware in *Joseph Andrews* that Joseph can only be defined (or understood) in terms of Pamela and the Biblical Joseph, Adams in terms of Cibber and the Biblical Abraham, etc.
16. Banier's historiography explains the basis of *Tom Jones* not only in the '45 but in Fielding's personal 'Experience' (the last of the patron deities invoked in VIII.i): all the references to his friends, enemies, and the political and literary issues of the time. This group would include those whom he invokes as equivalents of the poet's muses: Hogarth for painting, Garrick (or Booth) for acting, Handel for music, Lyttelton for benevolence.
17. See Battestin's essay, 'Tom Jones and "His *Egyptian* Majesty": Fielding's parable of government', *Publications of the Modern Language Association,* LXXII (1967), 68–77.
18. There are the stories that Elcho found Charles in a hut by the river Nairn after the battle, 'in a deplorable state', 'prostrate and without hope, and surrounded only by his Irish friends', believing the Scots officers were going to betray him, speaking to none; etc. See Chevalier de Johnstone, *Memoirs concerning the Affairs of Scotland* (1820), 186 and n.; David Elcho, *A Short Account of the Affairs of Scotland*, ed. Evan Charteris (1907), 94–5, 435–6. Fielding discusses Charles's behaviour during and after the battle in *True Patriot*, no. 27, 1–2. On the varying accounts, see Miriam Locke, ed., *True Patriot* (Alabama, 1964), 222–3.
19. The importance of names was equally thrust upon Fielding by the tradition of epic commentary with its etymological methods. See Thomas E. Maresca, *Epic to Novel* (Ohio, 1974), 33–5.
20. See *Jacobite's Journal*, no. 6, 125; Rupert C. Jarvis, *Collected Papers on the Jacobite' Risings* (1972), II, chs. 16–18.
21. Fielding's emphasis is on Charles Edward's bigotry and such stories as how he executes a Protestant sheep-stealer and pardons the Catholic rapist of an 11-year-old girl. The refrain is 'Such is the spirit of Popery' or 'Such are the Terrors of arbitrary Power'. See also Jarvis, *op. cit.*, II, 134. It is interesting to note that Fielding ends his *History* with the rout of Col. Gardner's dragoons, which in fact is the focal encounter of his account, and even includes a list of casualties. This happens to be the event Hogarth chooses to allude to through the signboard of 'Giles Gardiner' in his *March to Finchley* (1751), his own version of *Tom Jones*. See my *Art of Hogarth* (1975), 55–60.
22. *History*, 35; cited, Jarvis, *op. cit.*, 137.
23. See Locke (ed.), *True Patriot*, 255; cf. e.g. no. 3, 35; cited, Jarvis, *op. cit.*, 137.

12

'Strangers and Pilgrims': Sources and Patterns of Methodist Narrative

ISABEL RIVERS

> These all . . . confessed that they were strangers and pilgrims on the earth. For they that say such things declare plainly that they seek a country.[1]

> They were brought before him and asked, Whence they came? Whither they went, and what they did there in such an unusual garb? The men answered, 'That they were strangers and pilgrims in the world; that they were going to their own country; and that they had given no occasion to the men of the town thus to abuse and stop them in their journey.'[2]

Historians of the rise of the novel have emphasized the importance of seventeenth-century spiritual autobiography, and the secularization of the Puritan motif of life as a pilgrimage.[3] Because interest has been concentrated on the evolution of secular narrative, less attention has been paid to the continuation of the religious tradition. Yet the autobiographies of the early Methodist preachers reveal a distinctive development of the literature of pilgrimage, distinctive because of the nature of Methodist organization and culture. Although some seventeenth-century Puritan autobiographies (for example George Fox's *Journal*) have itinerant heroes, in the majority of Puritan narratives (*Pilgrim's Progress* is the archetype) pilgrimage is a metaphor for the human condition, and the narrator is allegorically, not literally, a pilgrim.[4] Methodist autobiographies, however, are based on actual itinerancy. The patterns of these narratives derive from two main sources: the organization of the travelling preachers, and the literary influences to which they were subject. Literary historians have largely ignored eighteenth-century Methodist culture,[5] yet we can identify with unusual precision the antecedents and assumptions of the self-contained literary tradition that was part of that culture.

[1]

Of the two significant aspects of Methodism, doctrine and organization, it is the second, in its creation of a class of full-time itinerant lay preachers, that is the more relevant to a study of the Methodist literary tradition. Although Whitefield and the Wesleys were not the first eighteenth-century field-preachers, it is from their almost accidental adoption of this method in 1739 that the idiosyncratic Methodist organization developed. Both Whitefield and John Wesley stressed that they only began to preach out of doors when the churches were closed to them. Wesley argued in 1745, 'that I had no desire or design to preach in the open air, till after this prohibition. That when I did, it was no matter of choice, so neither of premeditation . . . nor had I any other end in view than this, – to save as many souls as I could.'[6]

The system that began haphazardly was consolidated when Wesley formed himself into a Connexion with his preachers, and it became essential to Methodism. The importance Wesley attached to it is evident from comments he made after the Leeds Conference of 1755, at which the idea of separating from the Church of England was rejected. Wesley abhorred the prospect of separation, and managed to prevent it during his lifetime, yet he was prepared to accept it rather than abandon his organization. He stated this position in a letter (24 September 1755) to Samuel Walker of Truro, an Evangelical clergyman who approved Wesley's doctrine but not his methods, and who wanted the lay preachers to be either ordained or else fixed in their communities:

> At present I apprehend those, and those only, to separate from the Church, who either renounce her fundamental doctrines, or refuse to join in her public worship. As yet we have done neither; nor have we taken one step further than we were convinced was our bounden duty. It is from a full conviction of this, that we have, (1) Preached abroad: (2) Prayed extempore: (3) Formed societies: And, (4) Permitted Preachers who were not Episcopally ordained. And were we pushed on this side, were there no alternative allowed, we should judge it our bounden duty, rather wholly to separate from the Church, than to give up any one of these points. Therefore, if we cannot stop a separation without stopping lay-Preachers, the case is clear, – we cannot stop it at all.[7]

Wesley was initially reluctant to use lay preachers, just as he had been reluctant to preach outside churches. Yet the extraordinary success of the preachers convinced him that they were called by God, as he explained to Walker the following year:

> So great a blessing has, from the beginning, attended the labours of these Itinerants, that we have been more and more convinced every year, of the more than lawfulness of this proceeding . . . I cannot therefore see, how any . . . Preachers . . . can ever, while they have health and strength, ordained or unordained, fix in one place, without a grievous wound to their own conscience, and damage to the general work of God.[8]

Wesley believed his preachers to be called by God, yet he imposed on them a rigorous human discipline. The *Large Minutes* of the annual Conferences from 1744 to 1789 record the details of this code. Rule 11 of the 'Twelve Rules of a Helper' exhorts: 'You have nothing to do but to save souls. Therefore spend and be spent in this work ... And remember! A Methodist Preacher is to mind every point, great and small, in the Methodist discipline!'[9] Every aspect of this discipline estranged the preacher from his society. He was prohibited from following a trade. The probationary preacher was not allowed to marry; the married preacher spent little time with his wife. Financial responsibility for her was assumed by the circuit, thus releasing him from a material burden. His human attachments were limited; similarly, the yearly change of circuit allowed him no attachment to place. He was an 'extraordinary messenger', single-minded, poor, itinerant, with no recognized social position, and hence frequently feared and abused.[10]

Wesley was determined to be a pattern for his preachers. In 1751 he signed an agreement with his brother Charles: 'We will entirely be patterns of all we expect from every preacher; particularly of zeal, diligence, and punctuality in the work; by constantly preaching and meeting the society; by visiting yearly Ireland, Cornwall, and the north; and, in general, by superintending the whole work, and every branch of it, with all the strength that God shall give us.'[11] Wesley himself practised that Christian indifference to place, possessions, and human affection that he expected of his preachers. He travelled 4–5,000 miles a year, living according to his famous claim of 11 June 1739: 'I look upon all the world as my parish.'[12] When a woman criticized him for leading a 'vagabond life', he answered, 'Why, indeed it is not pleasing to flesh and blood; and I would not do it if did not believe there was another world.'[13] After his marriage in 1751 he wrote: 'I cannot understand how a Methodist preacher can answer it to God to preach one sermon or travel one day less in a married than in a single state.'[14] Wesley's attitudes to the preacher's calling are epitomized in a hymn first published in 1747, beginning 'How happy is the pilgrim's lot':[15]

No foot of land do I possess,
No cottage in this wilderness;
  A poor, way-faring man;
I lodge awhile in tents below,
Or gladly wander to and fro,
  Till I my Canaan gain.

Nothing on earth I call my own;
A stranger to the world unknown
  I all their goods despise;

I trample on their whole delight,
And seek a country out of sight,
A country in the skies.

[2]

Wesley controlled not only the professional organization of his preachers, but what they read and wrote; he thus created a unique literary subculture. He attached enormous importance to the reading of the members of his societies; the 'General Rules of the United Societies' of 1743 warns them against 'reading those books, which do not tend to the knowledge or love of God',[16] and at the end of his life he reaffirmed his belief in the value of proper reading: 'It cannot be that the people should grow in grace, unless they give themselves to reading. A reading people will always be a knowing people.'[17] Wesley's influence is attested by James Lackington, the London bookseller who was himself a lapsed Methodist: 'There are thousands in this society who will never read anything besides the bible, and books published by Mr Wesley.'[18]

The reading of his preachers particularly concerned Wesley.[19] He laid down in the minutes of the Conferences of 1744–7 (revised in the *Large Minutes*) a detailed scheme of study, indicating how, when, and what the preachers were to read. The 'Rules of Kingswood School', first drawn up in 1748 and subsequently enlarged as *A Short Account of the School in Kingswood* (1768), provide a further guide. At the 1746 Conference the question 'In what light should your Assistants consider themselves?' was answered, 'As learners rather than teachers: as young students at the University, for whom therefore a method of study is expedient in the highest degree.' Seven hours of reading a day was recommended.[20] The following year the preachers' obligations were again stressed: 'Might we not particularly inquire, – Do you rise at 4? Do you study in the method laid down at the last Conference? Do you read the books we advise and no other?'[21] In the *Large Minutes* the section outlining the preachers' scheme of study is abbreviated, but there is even greater emphasis on discipline:

> Read the most useful books, and that regularly and constantly. Steadily spend all the morning in this employ, or, at least, five hours in four-and-twenty. 'But I read only the Bible.' Then you ought to teach others to read only the Bible, and, by parity of reason, to hear only the Bible: But if so, you need preach no more . . . 'But I have no taste for reading.' Contract a taste for it by use, or return to your trade. 'But I have no books.' I will give each of you, as fast as you will read them, books to the value of five pounds. And I desire the Assistants would take care that all the large societies provide our Works . . . for the use of the Preachers.[22]

What books did Wesley expect his preachers to read? The 1744 minutes suggest a wide range of Greek and Latin literature, some of it dropped from later lists. The 1745 minutes specify works of practical divinity (including à Kempis, Law, *Pilgrim's Progress*, and the lives of Haliburton and de Renty), doctrinal theology, 'our other Tracts and Poems', *Paradise Lost*, and ecclesiastical history.[23] The *Large Minutes* specify briefly '"The Christian Library", and the other books which we have published in prose and verse, and then those which we recommended in our Rules of Kingswood School.'[24] The significant works in the Kingswood Rules are those of practical divinity and religious biography. The pupils are required to translate the Latin works (Augustine and à Kempis) into English and the English works (Law, Haliburton, and de Renty) into Latin, presumably to fix them indelibly in their minds.[25]

In these reading lists repeated reference is made to 'our tracts', 'our works', 'books which we have published'. Wesley began publishing in the early 1730s, but it was from 1739 onwards that he undertook publishing and distribution on a large scale for the benefit of his preachers and societies, instituting the Book Room at the Foundery, his London headquarters.[26] In 1753 he handed over the management of the Book Room and the national distribution of books to two book stewards. Initially he farmed out book production, but in 1778 he established his own press at the Foundery. The assistants (chief preachers) were responsible for distribution within their own circuits: the *Large Minutes* define one aspect of 'the business of an Assistant' as 'to take care that every society be duly supplied with books'.[27] On his travels Wesley persistently checked that the method was being implemented; he urged members to join together to buy books, and to pay by weekly subscription. Most of his publications were short duodecimo pamphlets, usually selling for 4*d*. In 1782 he began a tract society to distribute some of his works to the poor, with the legend 'This book is not to be sold, but given away'.[28]

Wesley evidently hoped to provide his preachers and societies with a convenient digest of all the literature he thought they needed. Since it was unnecessary for them to obtain books from any other source, he completely controlled their literary environment. He had absolute confidence in his choice of material; he wrote that anyone going carefully through the suggested four-year course of reading, added to *A Short Account of the School in Kingswood*, would 'be a better scholar than nine in ten of the graduates at Oxford or Cambridge.'[29] But Wesley did not intend simply to provide his preachers with a liberal education; they were never to forget their calling. The *Large Minutes* state: 'Gaining knowledge is a good thing; but saving souls is a better... I would throw by all the libraries in the world, rather than be guilty of the loss of one soul.'[30]

Of the hundreds of publications that Wesley issued, four serial works are particularly relevant to the writings of the preachers themselves. Beginning in 1739, and continuing to 1791, the year of his death, Wesley published extracts from his *Journal*. The range of topics covered – social observation, literary criticism, doctrinal disputes, records of religious experience – is too wide to illustrate here. The important point is that the *Journal* provided the preachers with a continuing pattern of a life lived out as a pilgrimage with no fixed resting place on earth; serialization effectively emphasized that Wesley's quest was never complete. From 1749 to 1755 Wesley issued 50 volumes of *A Christian Library*, in which he edited, abridged, and simplified the works of his favourite authors, including Foxe, Jeremy Taylor, Pascal, Bunyan, and Baxter. The series was not a commercial success (his preachers did not consult the *Christian Library* enough for Wesley's satisfaction), yet the continuous emphasis on 'practical divinity', and, in volumes XXVI, XXVII, XLIX, and L, on religious biography, indicates how Wesley hoped to shape his preachers' minds. The emphasis on religious biography continued in the next important publication, *The Works of the Rev. John Wesley*, issued in 32 volumes, 1771–4 (and also in weekly 6*d*. parts).[31] Volumes X, XI, and XII contain the biographies Wesley edited which he valued most highly, those of Haliburton, de Renty, and Brainerd, which had all appeared previously as separate pamphlets. (The other important biography, that of Lopez, appeared first in volume L of the *Christian Library*.) Wesley's last major publication, *The Arminian Magazine* (issued in monthly 1*s*. quarto parts), began in 1778; it continued after his death, although the name was changed in 1798 to the *Methodist Magazine*. Originally designed to counteract Evangelical Calvinism, it had, from a literary point of view, more interesting aims. Wesley's statements of editorial policy in the prefaces to volumes I, IV, and VII show how he regarded his magazine as an educational medium and as a transmitter of a new kind of religious literature. The preface to volume I (p. vi) announces the publication of 'Accounts and Letters, containing the experience of pious persons, the greatest part of whom are still alive.' In a letter Wesley stressed the magazine's originality in this respect: 'Both the letters and the lives, which will make a considerable part of every number, contain the marrow of experimental and practical religion; so that nothing of the kind has appeared before. Therefore, a magazine of this kind is a new thing in the land.'[32] It was in the *Arminian* that Wesley published the autobiographies of his travelling preachers.

[3]

Wesley wanted his preachers to write as well as to read. The 1744 minutes urge all assistants to keep journals 'as well for our satisfaction as for the profit of their own souls'. The 1747 minutes instruct Wesley to ask his preachers: 'Are you exact in writing your journal?'[33] But they were not allowed the right of free publication. The *Large Minutes* warn: 'Print nothing without my approbation.'[34] At successive conferences Wesley insisted that he must revise his preachers' work, and that it must be printed at his own press.[35] Thus the autobiographies were the product of Wesley's disciplinary, educational, and editorial control of his preachers' lives, reading habits, attitudes, and style. The first autobiography to be published in the *Arminian*, that of Peter Jaco, appeared in November 1778, and the tradition of publishing the preachers' lives continued in the *Methodist* until 1811.[36] Though the majority were commissioned by Wesley, there are three exceptions, the lives of John Nelson, Silas Told, and Thomas Walsh. Here Wesley edited previously published accounts.[37] Preachers not in connexion with Wesley, like William Seward, or who had broken with him, like John Cennick, published lives independently of him. In addition, Wesley issued separate editions of lives first published in the *Arminian* (John Haime and Thomas Mitchell). With these exceptions, the standard format of the autobiographies was a monthly instalment of five to ten pages, usually totalling 20 to 40 pages.

When Wesley asked his preachers for accounts of their early lives, conversion, and experience as itinerants, they had a recommended literary tradition on which to draw. Several preachers recognized their own experience in their early reading, the most important authors being Bunyan and Joseph Alleine.[38] 'Happening to read the Pilgrim's Progress,' writes Thomas Taylor, 'I had another powerful visit from the Lord . . . *Allen's Alarm*, now fell into my hands. It described my case as exactly as if it had been wrote on purpose; so that I prized it above rubies' (III, 373, 375). Haime chanced upon *Grace Abounding*, 'and found his case nearly resembled my own' (III, 211). Duncan Wright describes how God sent him 'such books, from time to time, as surprizingly suited my case; particularly *Allien's Alarm*, which proved of wonderful service to me' (IV, 370). Thomas Olivers, Told, and Seward (Whitefield's companion in America in 1740) attribute a similar importance to Bunyan.[39]

However, it is the four religious biographies Wesley repeatedly recommended that indicate best the pattern he wished to impose. In the lives of Haliburton, a Scottish Presbyterian minister, de Renty, a French Catholic nobleman, Lopez, a Spanish Catholic hermit, and Brainerd, an American Presbyterian missionary, Wesley found a standard pattern of Christian perfection for his preachers to imitate. Haliburton explained his object in keeping a journal thus: 'For the work of God in all is, as to the substance, the same and uniform; and as face answers to face in a glass, so does one Christian's experience answer to another's; and both to the word of God.'[40] The life to which Wesley attached most importance was that of Brainerd. Question 56 of the *Large Minutes* reads: 'What can be done in order to revive the work of God where it is decayed?' The answer demonstrates the connexion Wesley saw between literary and moral discipline. 'Let every Preacher read carefully over the "Life of David Brainerd." Let us be followers of him, as he was of Christ, in absolute self-devotion, in total deadness to the world, and in fervent love to God and man. Let us but secure this point, and the world and the devil must fall under our feet.'[41] Brainerd was a missionary to the Indians 1743–7, and died of tuberculosis at Jonathan Edwards's house in Northampton, Mass., in 1747 at the age of 29. Edwards edited and published in 1749 *An Account of the Life of the late Reverend Mr. David Brainerd*, partly as an attack on Arminianism.[42] Wesley read the account that year, and criticized Brainerd's tone.[43] His motive in publishing *An Extract of the Life*... (1768; revised and abridged in *Works*, 1st edn, XII) was obviously different from Edwards's. Brainerd was an ideal model because he was an itinerant, unlike the subjects of the other religious biographies, and he successfully resisted the temptations of place, possessions, and affection which the preachers continually faced. Nine months before he set out as a missionary, he wrote in his diary: 'My soul longs to feel itself a *pilgrim* and *stranger* here below; that nothing may divert me from pressing through the lonely desert, till I arrive at my Father's house.'[44] For four years he lived a life of wandering, self-denial, and loneliness. In 1746 he was strongly tempted to settle down among the Indians he had converted in New Jersey. His account of this temptation is important because of its just assessment of the value of the world he rejected. Brainerd made the traditional Biblical terminology his own; it was both literally and metaphorically accurate, in no way platitudinous:

> It appeared to me, that God's dealings towards me had fitted me for a life of solitariness and hardship; it appeared to me I had nothing to do with earth, and consequently nothing to lose, by a total renunciation of it: and it appeared just [and] right, that I should be destitute of house and home, and many comforts, which I rejoiced to see others of God's people enjoy. The same time I saw so much the excellency of Christ's kingdom, and the infinite desirableness of its advancement in the world, that it swallowed up all my other thoughts; and made me willing to be a pilgrim or hermit in the wilderness, to my dying moment, if I might thereby promote the blessed interest of the great Redeemer... And at the same time I had as quick and lively a sense of the value of worldly comforts, as ever I had; but saw them infinitely overmatched by the worth of Christ's kingdom, and the propagation of his blessed gospel. The quiet settlement, the certain place of abode, the tender friendship, which I thought I might be likely to enjoy, appeared as valuable to me, considered absolutely, as ever before: but considered comparatively, they appeared nothing; compared with an enlargement of Christ's kingdom, they vanished like the stars before the rising sun.[45]

[4]

This pattern of pilgrimage, of life as a spiritual journey through the world in search of the true country, underlies the narratives of the travelling preachers. The preacher's life is also literally a journey. He experiences conversion and the call to preach, gives up his trade, leaves behind his wife and children and takes to the road, is harassed by the justices and the clergy, attacked by mobs, sometimes imprisoned or threatened with impressment, and constantly faces the temptation to give up this arduous life and return to his home, his family, his trade. In resisting temptation he learns the symbolic nature of his experience: his sufferings are providential. In recording this experience, he encourages others to imitate him, just as he himself is supported by a literary tradition.

The sense of being a stranger in the world was often a crucial part of the experience of conversion. When Nelson's friends warned him that following Wesley would spoil his business, he told them, 'I was made sensible that my business in this world was to get well out of it.'[46] Cennick's experience was similar: 'When I looked into the World, all Things seemed to be unnatural and unpleasant, as if I had been banish'd into a Foreign Land.' But he was convinced that he would reach his true home: 'And of this I am well persuaded, that when I have done the Work for which I am sent, I shall be no more a Stranger upon the Earth, but shall be caught up to *Abraham*'s Bosom, and be a Fellow-citizen with the Saints in the Kingdom of my Father, and in the land of *Canaan*.'[47]

The decision to become a preacher required courage. Alexander Mather records that Wesley warned him: 'To be a Methodist Preacher, is not the way to Ease, Honour, Pleasure or Profit. It is a life of much labour and reproach. They often fare hard, often are in want. They are liable to be stoned, beaten and abused in various manners. Consider this, before you engage in so uncomfortable a way of life' (III, 147). Mather could not become a traveller until the stewards provided an allowance for his wife. He continues: 'When I began travelling, I had no end, aim, or design, but to spend and be spent for God: not counting my life, or any thing dear, so I might finish my course with joy' (204). Many became itinerants reluctantly. John Atlay writes: 'I was working in the Field, when *John Manners* came to me, and reproved me for my Unwillingness to give myself up wholly to the Work of God. He told me, I must travel or be damned' (I, 580). When Thomas Hanson refused Olivers's summons, Olivers replied, 'If your Father was dead, and your Mother lay a dying, you must come and preach the gospel' (III, 482). John Mason went through a long struggle before his fellow preachers persuaded him:

I found a stronger and stronger conviction, that it was my duty, to give

> myself wholly up to the work of God and to commence an itinerant Preacher. But I shrunk from the thought. I wept, and prayed, and strove against it with all my might, till I had well nigh lost all the life and peace of God out of my soul. Yet I did not comply: it was so contrary to the plan I had just laid down, having (as I supposed) settled myself for life.
> (III, 654)

Often the hardest task was for the itinerant to leave his wife and home. Nelson, having been threatened with impressment, was advised to give up preaching, to prevent his pregnant wife and family from suffering:

> I said, Let God look to that: if wicked men be suffered to take away my life, for calling sinners to the blood of Jesus; the Lord, whose servant I am, will be a husband to the widow, and a father to the fatherless. And was I assured, I should be banished or put to death for preaching, and my wife and children beg their bread bare-foot, I dare not leave off; for the words of our Lord pursue me, *He that loveth father or mother, wife or children, or his own life, more than me, is not worthy of me.*[48]

After his second marriage Christopher Hopper gave up preaching and returned to a settled way of life. But he could not continue in it:

> I was now favoured with an agreeable, loving companion, a good house, a pleasant situation, and all things to make life easy and comfortable. I must confess I found a desire to settle, but not to leave my dear Master's work. I begun a little business, and had now a fair opportunity to step into the world: but my dear Lord would not suffer me. He shewed me that his good work would bring me far more gain in the end than all the shops in *Newcastle.*
> (IV, 141)

William Green accepted his privation cheerfully: 'Though I have left my wife, and children, and dearest friends, and house, and business, and wander about, chiefly on foot, through cold and rain, I find my mind uninterruptedly happy' (IV, 308). The wife of John Furz accepted her part of the bargain without complaint: 'When I set out as a travelling Preacher, leaving my Children to her care, she never once asked me, When I should come home? But in all her Letters said, "I find difficulties: but let not That distress *you.* I am content. Go strait forward in the work God has called you to" ' (V, 637). When Richard Whatcoat became a travelling preacher in Ireland, he left his mother dying. 'But she knew and loved the work I was engaged in. So she willingly gave me up to the Lord, though she did not expect to see me any more, till we met in eternity' (IV, 193).

Not all were supported by their families. Cennick writes, 'My own House behaved as though they knew me not; and all mine Acquaintance condemn'd me.'[49] John Pawson's father initially threatened to disinherit him: 'I was tempted to think that I was disobedient to my parents; but I clearly saw that I must obey God rather than man' (II, 28). Usually the source of hostility was outside the family, for example the squire, the parson, or the town mob. Violent attacks on the preachers were common during the 1740s and 1750s. Thomas Lee was dragged by the hair, rolled in the common sewer, then thrown over the bridge into the water (III, 30). Thomas Mitchell was covered in white paint, thrown into a pond, and almost drowned; on the minister's advice he was then turned out of town, naked except for his coat (III, 320–1). Some preachers record that their opponents were providentially prevented from harming them. When Furz preached at Wincanton, the Town Clerk read the Riot Act:

> I said, 'Sir, was there any appearance of a Riot here, till you came?' He looked me in the face, and said with the utmost vehemence, '*Thou Rascal.*' Then the blood spouted out in a stream from both his nostrils. He dropt to the earth, crying aloud, 'They will say this is a judgment.' (No wonder if they did.) All possible means were used to stop the bleeding; but in vain. From that time he was lunatic. He was carried to *Bath*, and died soon after.
>
> (V, 574)

Yet privation and suffering were less important than their spiritual interpretation: hardship was providentially ordained. Thomas Hanby, robbed outside Canterbury, asserted: 'I believe this robbery was permitted for good... They were two soldiers who robbed me, and this excited a curiosity in their comrades to hear the Preacher who had been robbed: and it pleased God to convince many of them' (III, 549). Nelson similarly achieved a number of conversions in the North when on military service, and his followers blessed the minister responsible for his impressment as an agent of providence.[50] The preachers emphasized the greater reality of the spiritual world in their accounts of their confrontation with the supernatural, expressing spiritual encounters, Satanic or divine, in terms of acute physical sensation. When Haime tried to pray, Satan interfered: 'A hot blast of brimstone flashed in my face... An invisible power struck up my heels, and threw me violently upon my face' (III, 267). The experience of conversion and of divine anger was often physically painful. When William Ferguson heard a voice threatening him with damnation, his physical response frightened his parents: he was feverish, silent, unable to eat. 'I was filled with horror: I saw myself hanging over the mouth of hell, by the brittle thread of life!' (V, 294). Mather's physical symptoms were more prolonged: 'Meantime my flesh consumed away, like as a moth fretting a garment. And my bones were ready to start through my skin; for I had no rest day or night' (III, 96). Haime's were more acute:

> I could not see the Sun for more than eight months: even in the clearest summer-day, it always appeared to me like a mass of blood: at the same time I lost the use of my knees... I was often as hot as if I was burning to death: many times I looked, to see if my clothes were not on fire. I have gone into a river to cool myself: but it was all the same.
> (III, 266)

Such pain was superseded by feelings of relief, and, in some cases, by heavenly visions. Sampson Staniforth was on guard duty:

> As soon as I was alone, I kneeled down, and determined not to rise, but to continue crying and wrestling with God, till he had mercy on me. How long I was in that agony I cannot tell: but as I looked up to heaven, I saw the clouds open exceeding bright, and I saw Jesus hanging on the cross. At the same moment these words were applied to my heart, 'Thy sins are forgiven thee.' My chains fell off; my heart was free. All guilt was gone, and my soul was filled with unutterable peace.
> (VI, 72)

Told was walking in the fields:

> As I looked up, the heavens seemed to open about a mile in length, and tapered away to a point at each end. The centre of this avenue was about twelve feet wide, wherein I thought I saw the Lord Jesus standing, holding both his hands up, from the palms of which the blood seemed to stream down. Floods of tears now gushed from my eyes, and trickled down my cheeks; and I said, 'Lord, it is enough!'[51]

The experiences the preachers described were never final. Their narratives were a record of a continuing pilgrimage; their readers were denied the satisfaction of a conclusion. This point was stressed by Richard Rodda: 'I have had several offers from the world; but I love it not. I have had the offer of two or three dissenting Congregations... But it is my desire to live and die a Methodist Preacher' (VII, 468). In this respect Methodist literature offers a contrast to the tradition of secular pilgrimage as it developed in the eighteenth-century novel. There are some similarities in the journeys of the Methodist and picaresque traveller. Both undertake a journey of self-discovery, and learn the significance of the events they experience. The threads of coincidence in the picaresque plot lead the hero to his discoveries; they parallel the accumulated recognitions by the Methodist that Providence intervenes in the events of his life. The differences are more striking.

The picaresque hero makes a circular journey; he leaves the place of his origin, uncertain as to his relationships, and journeys back to it, his position now established. He has a fixed point in the existing social order. But the Methodist journeys from this world to the next, leaving behind his worldly position and relationships; the only fixed point for him is eternal and otherworldly. He must remain a stranger.

NOTES

Research for this article was aided by a grant from the University of Leicester Research Board. I am grateful for the help of Dr John Walsh of Jesus College, Oxford, and of Dr John Bowmer, Archivist, and Mrs Jeannette Harkin, Deputy Archivist, of the Methodist Archives and Research Centre.

1. Hebrews 11: 13–14.
2. Wesley's abridgement of *The Pilgrim's Progress*, in *The Works of the Rev. John Wesley*, IX (1772), 94 (hereafter cited as *Works*, 1st edn).
3. For example, G. A. Starr, *Defoe and Spiritual Autobiography* (Princeton, 1965).
4. The development of 'the Puritan epic of wayfaring' is described by William Haller, *The Rise of Puritanism* (New York, 1938), ch. iv. On the assumptions of Puritan autobiography see Owen C. Watkins, *The Puritan Experience* (1972).
5. A recent exception is Valentine Cunningham, *Everywhere Spoken Against: Dissent in the Victorian Novel* (1975).
6. *A Farther Appeal to Men of Reason and Religion*, in *The Works of the Rev. John Wesley*, ed. T. Jackson (3rd edn 1831), VIII, 113 (hereafter cited as *Works*, ed. Jackson).
7. *Works*, ed. Jackson, XIII, 195–6. (Wesley published his correspondence with Walker in *The Arminian Magazine*, II (1779), 368–71, 641–8.)
8. *Ibid.*, XIII, 197, 200.
9. *Ibid.*, VIII, 310. On the itinerants' discipline see also Frank Baker, 'The People called Methodists – 3. Polity,' in *A History of the Methodist Church in Great Britain*, ed. R. Davies and G. Rupp, I (1965), 230–6.
10. The phrase 'extraordinary messengers' appears in a letter of 1763 to Wesley from Jacob Chapman, a sympathetic Presbyterian minister. (Luke Tyerman, *The Life and Times of the Rev. John Wesley*, II (5th edn, 1880), 483), and in *Large Minutes* (*Works*, ed. Jackson, VIII, 309).
11. Tyerman, *op. cit.*, II, 130.
12. *The Journal*, ed. Nehemiah Curnock (1909–16), II, 218.
13. *Ibid.*, IV, 13.
14. *Ibid.*, III, 517.
15. *A Collection of Hymns, For the Use of the People called Methodists* (3rd edn, 1782), 71. This hymn is attributed to J. Wesley by Tyerman, *op. cit.*, I (1st edn, 1871), 529.
16. *Works*, ed. Jackson, VIII, 270.
17. Tyerman, *op. cit.*, III (3rd edn, 1876), 632.
18. *Memoirs of the Forty-Five First Years of the Life of James Lackington, Bookseller* (1827, 1st published 1791), 78.
19. Helpful studies include Frank Baker, 'A study of John Wesley's Readings,' *London Quarterly and Holborn Review*, CLXVIII (1943), 140–5, 234–41; Henry Bett, 'The alleged illiteracy of the early Methodist preachers', *Proceedings of the Wesley Historical Society*, XV (1926), 85–92; T. E. Brigden, 'The reading of Wesley's preachers', *Wesleyan Methodist Magazine*, CXXVI

(1903), 457–65; W. L. Doughty, *John Wesley: His Conferences and his Preachers* (1944).

20. 'John Bennet's Copy of the Minutes of the Conferences of 1744, 1745, 1747, and 1748; with Wesley's copy of those for 1746', *Publications of the Wesley Historical Society* (hereafter *P.W.H.S.*), I (1896), 36.
21. *Ibid.*, 50.
22. *Works*, ed. Jackson, VIII, 315.
23. *P.W.H.S.*, I (1896), 36.
24. *Works*, ed. Jackson, VIII, 314.
25. *P.W.H.S.*, I (1896), 55.
26. R. Green, *The Works of John and Charles Wesley* (1896; 2nd edn, rev., 1906) is an indispensable bibliography. Studies of aspects of Wesley's publishing include Frank Cumbers, *The Book Room* (1956); T. W. Herbert, *John Wesley as Editor and Author* (Princeton, 1940); R. D. Mayo, *The English Novel in the Magazines* (Evanston, 1962); T. B. Shepherd, *Methodism and the Literature of the Eighteenth Century* (1947). See also R. D. Altick, *The English Common Reader* (Chicago, 1957), and M. J. Quinlan, *Victorian Prelude* (1965; 1st published 1941).
27. *Works*, ed. Jackson, VIII, 319.
28. Green, *op. cit.*, 217.
29. *Works*, ed. Jackson, XIII, 289.
30. *Ibid.*, VIII, 304.
31. Green, *op. cit.*, 156.
32. Tyerman, *op. cit.*, III, 284.
33. *P.W.H.S.*, I (1896), 16, 50.
34. *Works*, ed. Jackson, VIII, 317.
35. Doughty, *op. cit.*, 54–5.
36. The majority were collected by Thomas Jackson as *The Lives of Early Methodist Preachers* (4 edns 1837–71; 1st edn, 3 vols, 2nd edn, 2 vols, 3rd and 4th edns, 6 vols). Jackson's text, because of his emendations, is not entirely reliable, hence I quote from *The Arminian Magazine* (citing references in my text), and from Wesley's separate editions of some lives.
37. The following is a brief publishing history of these lives, which illustrates Wesley's methods. Nelson: *The Case of John Nelson Written by Himself* (1st edn, 1745; 6 edns by 1761; included in *Works*, 1st edn, XVIII, 1773). *An Extract of John Nelson's Journal* (1st edn, 1767; not in *Arminian*, but in editions revised by Wesley 1777, 1782; several reprints). Told: *An Account of the Life, and Dealings of God with Silas Told* (1st edn, 1786); heavily revised by Wesley as 'An account of Mr. Silas Told, Written by Himself', *Arminian*, x–xi (1787–8) and reissued separately as *The Life of Mr. Silas Told* (1790). Walsh: James Morgan, *The Life and Death of Mr. Thomas Walsh* (1762); simplified and abridged by Wesley in *Works*, 1st edn, XI–XII (1772), and reissued separately (1782); not in *Arminian*.
38. We do not know what editions were read. Wesley published his abridged *Pilgrim's Progress* in 1743 (many reprints, reissued in *Works*, 1st edn, IX), and Alleine's *An Alarm to Unconverted Sinners* in *Christian Library*, XXIV (1753), reissued separately, abridged (1782). On Wesley's abridgement of Alleine see R. C. Monk, *John Wesley: His Puritan Heritage* (1966), 142–8.
39. *Arminian*, ii, 88; *The Life of Mr Silas Told* (2nd edn, 1790), 63–4; *Journal of a Voyage from Savannah to Philadelphia* (1740), 39.
40. *Works*, 1st edn, X, 261.
41. *Works*, ed. Jackson, VIII, 328.
42. Perry Miller, *Jonathan Edwards* (New York, 1959), 246.
43. *Journal*, III, 449.
44. *Works*, 1st edn, XII, 58–9.
45. *Ibid.*, 270–1.
46. *An Extract from John Nelson's Journal* (1782), 13.

47. *The Life of Mr. J. Cennick ... Written by Himself* (2nd edn, 1745), 11, 39.
48. *An Extract from John Nelson's Journal*, 79. Compare Bunyan's account of parting from his family to go to prison in *Grace Abounding* (Everyman edn), 97–8.
49. *The Life of Mr. J. Cennick ...*, 23.
50. *An Extract from John Nelson's Journal*, 124.
51. *The Life of Mr Silas Told* (1790), 88–9. Compare the first edition (1786), 107, not edited by Wesley:

    As I looked up, the heavens were unclosed about a mile in length, as it appeared to my mortal eyes, and tapered away to a point at each end. The center of this awful and sacred avenue was about twelve feet wide, wherein I saw the Lord Jesus standing in the form of a man, holding both his inestimably precious hands upright, and from the palms thereof the blood streaming down; floods of tears gushed from my eyes, and trickled down my cheeks. I said, 'Lord, it is enough!'

13

Hume: the Historian as Man of Feeling

J. C. HILSON

[1]

There now seems to be general agreement that the eighteenth century was one of those periods in which the 'aesthetic function' was in a state of expansion.[1] Sermons, essays, biography, philosophy – all were conceived and analysed as literary productions. Hayden White has neatly summarized the implications of this state of affairs for historiography:

> Although eighteenth-century theorists distinguished rather rigidly (and not always with adequate philosophical justification) between 'fact' and 'fancy', they did not on the whole view historiography as a representation of the facts unalloyed by elements of fancy. While granting the general desirability of historical accounts that dealt in real, rather than in imagined events, theorists from Bayle to Voltaire and De Mably recognized the inevitability of a recourse to fictive techniques in the *representation* of real events in the historical discourse. The eighteenth century abounds in works which distinguish between the 'study' of history on the one side, and the 'writing' of history on the other. The 'writing' was a literary, specifically rhetorical exercise, and the product of this exercise was to be assessed as much on literary as on scientific principles.[2]

In recent years, the 'writing' and the 'fictive techniques' of David Hume's *History of England* have attracted less attention than its politics.[3] This may be the result of the customary critical placing of Hume in the tradition of 'that special eighteenth-century genre', philosophical history.[4] Most commentators on the period see Hume, Montesquieu, Voltaire and Gibbon as involved in essentially the same enterprise – the enlightening of historiography.[5] But while much has been written about the literary techniques of Voltaire and Gibbon, comment on Hume's artistry in the *History* is sparse, and often perfunctory or dismissive.[6] This, I suspect, is the consequence of a tendency to read Hume through Gibbonian spectacles; to focus on his detachment, irony, or even satire.[7] Some of these qualities are undoubtedly present in Hume's *History*, but to concentrate on them is to blur important distinctions between Hume and Gibbon. Most crucially, a Gibbonian reading of Hume's *History* obscures the fact that the aesthetic impulses behind Hume's work are more heterogeneous than those behind the *Decline and Fall.* One commentator on Gibbon confidently asserts: 'If there was any such thing as an archetypal Neo-Classicist, Edward Gibbon was it.'[8] Good classicist as Hume was, no one would wish to label the man or his work neoclassicist; and indeed, it is difficult to imagine a single classification which would accommodate the elusive diversity of Hume's work as a whole, and of the *History* in particular. Abandoning taxonomy, therefore, I wish in this essay only to suggest a possible alternative context for the study of Hume's *History* as a literary work, namely, the sentimental tradition in mid-century ethics and aesthetics; and with this context in mind, I shall analyse one aspect of Hume's literary technique in the Stuart volumes of the *History.* I begin by examining some of Hume's attitudes towards the aesthetics of historiography, and their relation to mid-eighteenth-century literary theory.

[2]

Towards the end of his life, Hume urged the two sons of his friend, Baron William Mure of Caldwell, to examine the rhetoric of his *History*:

> During the year which my brother and I passed at Edinburgh College in 1775, we attended Dr. Blair's lectures on rhetoric &c., and Hume used often to examine us about them. One day he told us that the Life of Harold was the portion of his *History of England* which he thought the best, and on the style of which he had bestowed the most pains; and he added, 'Now, I wish to submit it to your criticism, that you may apply to it the rules laid down by Dr. Blair. I have given the same task to my nephew David, and I shall compare your several strictures.'[9]

This concern with historiography as a literary activity is apparent from Hume's earliest comments on the subject. His interest in history dates from his youth, as the extant memoranda on his early reading show;[10] but his thinking about the problems of *writing* history develops significantly during the 1740s. Even the early, Addisonian essay 'Of the Study of History', which is primarily concerned with the advantages to be gained from reading history, moves at its close towards a consideration of the role of the historian as writer: 'The writers of history, as well as the readers, are sufficiently interested in the characters and events, to have a lively sentiment of blame or praise: and, at the same time, have no particular interest or concern to pervert their judgment.'[11] Hume's emphasis here is on the historical narrator's stance towards his material, and the reader's response to his narrative. This relationship, in theory and practice, was to preoccupy him throughout his career. It underlies his remarks on the place of sympathy in the reading of history in *A Treatise of Human Nature*, in *An Enquiry Concerning the Principles of Morals*,[12] and, most importantly, in his first (and only) extended treatment of the aesthetics of historiography, in the *Philosophical Essays Concerning Human Understanding*.[13] The inclusion of what Hume calls 'loose Hints' (*PE*, 45) on history as literature is in itself significant. The primary purpose of the *Philosophical Essays* was to recast and clarify the epistemological arguments of the *Treatise*, but at the same time that he began work on it (*c.* 1745–6),[14] Hume also started taking notes for the *History*, as his extant memoranda from this period witness.[15] It is probable, therefore, that his consideration of the art of historical narrative grew as much from first-hand confrontation with the practical problems of historical composition as from abstract speculation on the applicability of associationism to aesthetics.

Hume's main literary concern in Essay III of the *Philosophical Essays*, 'Of the Connexion of Ideas', is with unity in different forms of narrative. Beginning from the premise that there is a propensity towards order in the human psyche, Hume suggests that, whatever the genre, the writer's duty is to strive for unity, if he 'would produce a Work, that will give any lasting Entertainment to Mankind' (*PE*, 36). For, Hume believes, 'The Unity of Action . . . which is to be found in Biography or History, differs from that of Epic Poetry, not in Kind, but in Degree' (*ibid.*, 37). In all of these genres, the 'Imagination, both of Writer and Reader' (*ibid.*,) is the central issue; and the author-reader compact is the matrix of the process of unification in literary composition. In order to attain unity in a work, according to Hume, the author must make a *conscious* extension of the associative process by which the mind spontaneously connects resembling, contiguous, or causally linked ideas. This unification, if successful, will be mirrored in the reader's response to the work, which in turn involves his own associative mechanism. Hume draws one of his examples of this from *Paradise Lost*:

> The strong Connexion of the Events, as it facilitates the Passage of the Thought or Imagination from one to another, facilitates also the Transfusion of the Passions, and preserves the Affection still in the same Channel and Direction. Our sympathy and Concern for *Eve* prepares the way for a like Sympathy with *Adam*: The Affection is preserv'd almost entire in the Transition; and the Mind seizes immediately the new Object as strongly related to that which formerly engag'd its Attention.
> (*PE*, 39)

Reiterating his contention that the difference between history and epic poetry is one of degree, not of kind, Hume concludes that ''twill be difficult, if not impossible, by Words, to determine exactly the Bounds, which separate them from each other' (*PE*, 43); for the judicious author, whether historian or poet, will always aim for 'that Communication of Emotions, by which alone he can interest the Heart, and raise the Passions to their proper Height and Period' (*ibid.*, 45).[16]

Hume's remarks on the literary, or more specifically, the affective aspects of historical composition in his philosophical works align him with other mid-century theorists of historiography, and in particular with such Scottish rhetoricians as Adam Smith, Lord Kames and Hugh Blair.[17] The comments of these and other critics on the writing of history reveal very clearly the ways in which neoclassical literary principles were being married with the emergent psychological aesthetics. Their definitions of history largely repeat the utilitarian, exemplar theories which prevailed in the earlier part of the century.[18] Smith sees its defining characteristics as entertainment and instruction; Blair calls it 'a record of truth for the instruction of mankind'; and for Kames, too, its aims are instruction and veracity.[19] Unlike their predecessors, however, these critics place more emphasis on the affective function of historiography, and attempt to define the proper methods for obtaining emotional effect. Smith sums this up as follows:

> perfection of style consists in expressing in the most concise, proper and precise manner the thought of the author, and that in the manner which best conveys the sentiment, passion or affection with which it affects – or which he pretends it does affect – him, and which he desires to communicate to his reader.[20]

This *rapprochement* of didacticism and feeling is reflected in the way in which mid-eighteenth-century literary theory adapts the neoclassical principle of the orator's or poet's *ethos* to the historian. Early eighteenth-century satire borrows from the rules of classical rhetoric the notion that the satirist must justify his right to criticize society by establishing the essential virtue of his own character. Pope, for example, repeatedly refers to his personal integrity in the Horatian poems.[21] This ethical principle was absorbed into mid-century theories of historiography, undergoing some modification in the process:

> As History is a species of writing designed for the instruction of mankind, sound morality should always reign in it. Both in describing characters, and in relating transactions, the Author should always show himself to be on the side of virtue. To deliver moral instruction in a formal manner, falls not within his province; but both as a good man, and as a good Writer, we expect that he should discover sentiments of respect for virtue, and an indignation at flagrant vice. To appear neutral and indifferent with respect to good and bad characters, and to affect a crafty and

political rather than a moral turn of thought, will, besides other bad effects, derogate greatly from the weight of Historical Composition, and will render the strain of it much more cold and uninteresting. We are always most interested in the transactions which are going on, when our sympathy is awakened by the story, and when we become engaged in the fate of the actors. But this effect can never be produced by a Writer, who is deficient in sensibility and moral feeling.[22]

The *ethos* of the historian, then, differs from that of the satirist in that his moral position should not appear 'in a formal manner': it is communicated to the reader through the medium of 'sympathy', the pervasive benevolent emotion which unites ethical and aesthetic responses. The keywords of this passage (and of those from Hume and Smith quoted above) are drawn from the vocabulary of sentimentalism: 'sentiments', 'sensibility', 'moral feeling' – and, as I shall argue below, such words as 'interest' and 'concern'.[23] The ideal historian, in Blair's view, would therefore be a combination of impartial analyst, moral judge, and man of feeling.

The sphere in which the 'sensibility and moral feeling' of the historian are most exercized, as the quotation from Blair indicates, is the judgment of character. Sentimental historiography, if such a genre may be posited, like sentimental ethics, is essentially a spectatorial experience for both historian and reader; and the ideal spectator is both impartial and sympathetic, rational and feeling. The notion of such a spectator is also the pivot of Hume's ethical theory, which I wish to suggest, is closely related to his attitude towards character in the *History*. For Hume, 'Morality . . . is more properly felt than judg'd of' (*Treatise*, III. i. 2: 522). Virtue, vice, beauty and deformity 'are not qualities in objects, but perceptions in the mind' (*Treatise*, III.i.1:520–1). The function of reason in moral assessments is to discover the facts, to establish as completely as possible the context of any judgment; but,

after every circumstance, every relation is known, the understanding has no further room to operate, nor any object on which it could employ itself. The approbation or blame which then ensues, cannot be the work of the judgment, but of the heart; and is not a speculative proposition or affirmation, but an active feeling or sentiment.

(*Enquiry*, App. 1: 290)

Utility, therefore, is apprehended by reason, but reason has no part in deciding whether utility is good or pleasing. A person may be good without being useful (e.g. to society), or useful without being good.[24]

A historian working within the frame of Hume's theory of moral judgment would therefore begin by collecting all the necessary facts about his subject. Once these were before him, he would analyse the relations between them, and decide which persons or principles have been useful to society or harmful to its interests. This rational conclusion, however, would be followed or accompanied by a feeling of approval or disapproval which, especially in questions of character-judgment, would have no necessary connexion with reason.[25] Both the rational assessments – the political lessons of history, and the felt responses – the moral values of history, must be communicated to the reader: the former by reasoned discussion of the issues; the latter by a transfusion of the historian's feelings into the narrative (e.g. by dramatic heightening or sympathetic description); or, as Hume puts it:

> There is no necessity, that a generous action, barely mentioned in an old history or remote gazette, should communicate any strong feelings of applause and admiration.... Bring this virtue nearer, by our acquaintance or connection with the persons, *or even by an eloquent recital of the case*; our hearts are immediately caught, our sympathy enlivened, and our cool approbation converted into the warmest sentiments of friendship and regard.
>
> (V. II: 230; my italics.)

I do not wish to suggest that the procedure of the hypothetical historian described above is that which Hume consciously adopted in writing his *History*. However, as I hope to show in the next section, Hume's approach to characterization, and his actual presentation of the two central figures in the first two volumes of the *History*, Charles I and Oliver Cromwell, are best understood within this context.

[3]

In the posthumously published autobiographical sketch, *My Own Life*, Hume complains that he was calumniated as 'the man who had presumed to shed a generous tear for the fate of Charles I and the Earl of Strafford' (*Essays*, 611). That this shedding of generous tears was determined as much by literary as by political motivation appears from two of Hume's letters to friends in 1754 and 1755. When his first volume was on the point of publication, he wrote to William Mure of Caldwell: 'The first Quality of an Historian is to be true & impartial; the next to be interesting. If you do not say, that I have done both Parties Justice; & if Mrs Mure be not sorry for poor King Charles, I shall burn all my Papers, & return to Philosophy'.[26] The same note is even more decisively struck in a letter of the following year to the publisher, William Strahan. Remarking on the accusations of political partiality levelled at the *History* ('I am dub'd a Jacobite, Passive Obedience Man, Papist & what not'), he wrote: 'I did indeed endeavour to paint the King's Catastrophe (which was singular & dismal) in as pathetic a manner as I cou'd: And to engage me, needed I any other Motive, than my Interest as a Writer, who desires to please & interest his Readers?' (*Letters*, I, 222). It is clear from statements like these that Hume did not see commitment to literary effect as incompatible with political impartiality. As Duncan Forbes puts it, 'impartiality was a question of avoiding a party "system"',[27] not of scientific objectivity. Indeed it appears that Hume, like Blair, would have advocated that impartiality could and should operate *only* in the political sector of historiography. This is supported by a letter of 1759, in which Hume defended his friend William Robertson's presentation of the character of Mary, Queen of Scots, in his *History of Scotland*:

> Why might not Mary be seducd into many Imprudences & even some Crimes; & yet possess many Accomplishments which, joined to her singular Misfortunes render her a proper Object of Compassion? I know no Story more pathetically wrote than that of Anthony and Cleopatra by Plutarch; yet these were very far from being innocent Persons. It is a singular & a very commendable piece of art in our Friend, to make the Princess an interesting Object, even while he represents her criminal.[28]

There are striking similarities in the vocabulary of the three passages quoted in the last paragraph. In particular, the notion which is common to all three is 'interest'; and 'interest' and its cognates also occur in the extract from 'Of the Study of History' quoted earlier.[29] The primary non-technical modern meaning of 'to interest' would probably be that offered by the *Concise Oxford Dictionary*: 'to excite curiosity or attention'. In the eighteenth-century, however, this group of words seems to have been used in two different senses, indeed, to have been appropriated by diametrically opposed philosophies: *self*-interest on the one hand, and benevolism on the other. Dr Johnson's *Dictionary* offers two meanings for 'interest' as a verb: 'to concern; to affect; to give share in'; and 'to affect; to move; to touch with passion'.[30] The second of Johnson's five definitions of 'concern' is 'to affect with some passion'. These definitions are crucial to an understanding of Hume's use of the vocabulary of interest. When he writes in 'Of the Study of History' that historian and reader 'have no particular interest or concern to pervert their judgment', he means something like 'have no prior attachment to party or faction' (though it is noteworthy that he feels it necessary to add the adjective 'particular' to make this clear). But when he contrasts being 'true & impartial' with being 'interesting', when he talks of his desire to 'interest' his readers, or when he calls Mary, Queen of Scots, 'interesting', he is using the language of sentimentalism. In these contexts, the words are all related to the exciting of emotion and the arousal of sympathetic feelings; and the collocation in two of the above passages of 'pathetic' or 'pathetically' with 'interest' or 'interesting' suggests the proximity of the two concepts for Hume.[31]

The terms of Hume's praise of Robertson, and his deployment of the vocabulary of interest suggest the proper context for the presentation of the character of Charles I in the first volume of the *History*. In the essay 'Of Tragedy', Hume discusses Clarendon's treatment of the death of Charles:

> Lord Clarendon, when he approaches towards the catastrophe of the royal party, supposes that his narration must then become infinitely disagreeable; and he hurries over the king's death without giving us one circumstance of it. He considers it as too horrid a scene to be contemplated with any satisfaction, or even without the utmost pain and aversion. He himself, as well as the readers of that age, were too deeply concerned in the events, and felt a pain from subjects which an historian and a reader of another age would regard as the most pathetic and the most interesting, and, by consequence, the most agreeable.
> (*Essays*, 228–9)

Again, we find 'pathetic' paired with 'interesting'. Clearly, Hume sees himself as sufficiently distanced from the events to transform what was for Clarendon the intolerable pain of reality into the pleasurable pain of art, of tragedy.[32] I shall argue here that Hume did conceive the shape of his first volume, which opens with the accession of James I and ends with the execution of Charles I, as tragic, with Charles as his tragic, or rather 'pathetic' hero: an analysis of Hume's treatment of Charles will, I hope, indicate that Hume's is a sentimental tragedy, and Charles a kind of sentimental hero.[33]

Much of Hume's work in morals is concerned with the nature of true heroism, and the book which stands chronologically closest to the *History*, the *Enquiry Concerning the Principles of Morals*, is both a celebration of the social virtues, and an attempt to define the ideal hero, the 'model of perfect virtue' (*Enquiry*, IX. i: 270). He is a man who combines in his personality qualities useful to others, qualities useful to himself, qualities immediately agreeable to others, and qualities immediately agreeable to himself. The fictional Cleanthes fulfils these requirements: he is 'a man of honour and humanity . . . *fair* and *kind*', industrious, sociable, witty, unaffected; and the tranquillity of soul and 'greatness of mind' to overcome adversity (*Enquiry*, IX. i: 269–70). In common with other eighteenth-century authors in the tradition of benevolist ethics, Hume is here praising the good rather than the great man. Although he ascribes some aesthetic pleasure to the contemplation of what he calls 'sublime' characters, the men he admires most, both in his ethical writings and in the *History*, are those who display 'the merit of benevolence'. Hume is insistent, however, that benevolence is not admired solely on account of its utility. Contemplation of truly benevolent behaviour produces its own kind of aesthetic pleasure, since the 'tenderness of sentiment ... engaging endearments ... fond expressions ... delicate attention ... mutual confidence and regard' which attend benevolence are 'delightful in themselves', and produce a strong effect on the spectator: 'The tear naturally starts in our eye on the apprehension of a warm sentiment of this nature: our breast heaves, our heart is agitated, and every humane tender principle of our frame is set in motion, and gives us the purest and most satisfactory enjoyment.' (*Enquiry*, VII: 257). This sentimental reaction is in fact a *higher* form of aesthetic pleasure – because it is at the same time a moral pleasure – than the ambiguous and cooler response accorded such a character as Charles XII (*Enquiry*, VII: 258).

While Charles I is in no sense presented as ideal in the way that Cleanthes of the *Enquiry* is, the moral/aesthetic redefinition of heroism carries over into the *History*, and to some extent influences Hume's construction of Charles's character. In order that his social virtues may be apparent, Hume shows Charles in private as well as public contexts whenever possible, and his relationships as husband, father and friend are important:[34]

> When we consider Charles as presiding in his court, as associating with his family, it is difficult to imagine a character at once more respectable and more amiable. A kind husband, an indulgent father, a gentle master, a stedfast friend; to all these eulogies his conduct in private life fully entitled him. As a monarch, too, in the exterior qualities, he excelled; in the essential he was not defective.... The moderation and equity which shone forth in his temper *seemed* to secure him against rash and dangerous enterprises: the good sense, which he displayed in his discourse and conversation, *seemed* to warrant his success in every reasonable undertaking. Other endowments likewise he had attained, which, in a private gentleman, would have been highly ornamental, and which, in a great monarch, might have proved extremely useful to his people. He was possessed of an excellent taste in the fine arts; and the love of painting was, in some degree, his favourite passion. Learned beyond what is common in princes, he was a good judge of writing in others, and enjoyed himself no mean talent in composition. In any other age or nation, this monarch had been secure of a prosperous and happy reign.[35]

This is from Hume's first full sketch of Charles's character; and it is not far removed from the picture of 'accomplished merit' in the *Enquiry* (IX. i: 270). Hume goes on to qualify this portrait somewhat by commenting on the king's lack of political 'vigour and foresight', but the emphasis of this section is already on the incongruity between Charles and the age in which, by an accident of history, he found himself. Throughout the first part of the *History*, Hume frequently explains Charles's failure to restore equilibrium to the nation by the fact that the time was out of joint, that a form of madness – 'the spirit of enthusiasm' – had engulfed moderation and civilization and 'disturbed the operation of every motive, which usually influence[s] society' (*History*, ch. LII).

Though Hume is by no means uncritical of Charles's conduct as king, the general explanation of the tragic curve of his career is deterministic. 'Necessity' and 'the situation' are often invoked; and Hume accounts for Charles's handling of constitutional problems by stressing that he was educated to have a high idea of royal prerogative, and that he also suffered from bad counsel. Charles often seems close, indeed, to R. F. Brissenden's description of one kind of sentimental hero:

> The central figure in the sentimental novel . . . tends to be passive rather than active. While the picaroon, or the hero of a renaissance tragedy, attempts to shape the world and other people to his purpose, the sentimental hero is usually depicted as struggling to prevent other people from forcing him to do the things they want.[36]

Charles is, of course, by no means passive throughout the *History*. At first, indeed, he and Parliament are seen by Hume as provoking each other equally (and Hume's language balances violence with violence: liberties are 'ravished' from the people; the Commons 'violate' the law). Gradually however, Charles is forced to adopt a more conciliatory policy, to become more passive; and the struggle shifts to Charles resisting submission to what other people want – that is, the constitutional 'innovations' which the Commons press upon him.

Hume plots Charles's career up to the outbreak of civil war as a series of problems and dilemmas, which are often presented from Charles's point of view. The king is very much the central consciousness of the narrative, in a way that James I never was in the earlier part of the first volume, and Cromwell never becomes in the next volume. Like the sentimental novelist,[37] Hume internalizes his hero's anxieties and uncertainties, and reveals his thought-processes to us on a number of occasions when he is in 'doubt and perplexity', for example when he finds himself in 'an inextricable labyrinth' after the Commons attempt to abolish the levying of tonnage and poundage in 1629 (*History*, ch. LI), or when he has trouble with the Scots Covenanters (ch. LIII). Perhaps the best example of this is Hume's presentation of Charles's reflections on the pressure he is under after Buckingham's impeachment:

> What idea, he asked, must all mankind entertain of his honour, should he sacrifice his innocent friend to pecuniary considerations? What farther authority should he retain in the nation, were he capable, in the beginning of his reign, to give, in so signal an instance, such matter of triumph to his enemies, and discouragement to his adherents? To-day the commons pretend to wrest his minister from him. To-morrow, they will attack some branch of his prerogative.... It was evident, that they desired nothing so much as to see him plunged in inextricable difficulties, of which they intended to take advantage.
>
> (*History*, ch. L)

The cumulative rhetorical force of such passages draws the reader's sympathy towards Charles, despite Hume's more balanced and impartial assessments of his policies.

Unlike the hero of a sentimental novel, however, Charles never becomes obsessed with his own difficulties. If he is a man of feeling, he is a stoical one;[38] and Hume highlights his sensibility and heightens pathos by showing Charles's concern and compassion for his friends. It is interesting to note, in this context, one of Hume's many manipulations of his source material for literary effect. Discussing the king's reaction to the execution of Sir Charles Lucas by order of Fairfax and Ireton, Hume's source, Bulstrode Whitelocke, states simply: 'At the sight of a gentleman in mourning for Sir Charles Lucas, the king wept'.[39] Hume turns this into an eloquent tribute to Charles's feeling heart:

> Soon after, a gentleman appearing in the King's presence clothed in mourning for Sir Charles Lucas, that humane prince, suddenly recollecting the hard fate of his friends, paid them a tribute which none of his own unparalleled misfortunes ever extorted from him – he dissolved into a flood of tears.
>
> (*History*, ch. LIX)

The 'last scene' of Charles's life affords Hume the maximum opportunity to intensify his pathetic effects. As Ian Donaldson has noted, 'Eighteenth-century tragedy is much preoccupied by scenes which depict a man preparing to meet his death',[40] and Hume's historical tragedy is no exception. Charles retains his dignity and tranquillity throughout his trial, sentence and preparations for execution, while Hume piles as much pathos on the reader as possible – even to the extent of tampering with historical fact. On the authority of Clement Walker's *The Compleat History of the Independency* (which Hume recognizes in the same chapter as being both satirical and factually inaccurate) Hume has Charles spend the nights between sentence and execution at Whitehall, where he can hear the sound of his scaffold being built.[41] Charles, however, remains composed and tearless until the archetypally tear-jerking situation, the last interview with his children – and even then he allows himself only 'tears of joy and admiration' (*History*, ch. LIX).[42]

Hume's final verdict on Charles is that he deserves the epithet of a good, rather than of a great man. But as we have seen, in his philosophical works, as well as in the general presentation of Charles in the *History*, goodness is for Hume the only true greatness. In the closing character of Charles, Hume returns to the two dominant themes in his account of 'the King's catastrophe': the unpropitious time into which he was born, and the necessities forced upon him by his situation. Here – as in all of the later revisions of the *History* – Hume intensifies the force of these explanations to evoke even more sympathy for Charles, and to heighten his tragedy: 'Exposed, without revenue, without arms, to the assault of furious, implacable, and bigoted, factions, it was never permitted him, but with the most fatal consequences, to commit the smallest mistake: a condition too rigorous to be imposed on the greatest human capacity.' (*History*, ch. LIX.) The crucial phrase 'without revenue, without arms', which renders Charles helpless, unable to take any defensive action, was not in the first edition.

If Charles is Hume's 'tragic' hero, Cromwell is his antithesis, at once villain and clown: like the picaroon whom Brissenden contrasts with the passive sentimental hero, Cromwell is a manipulator of men and situations, an opportunist, an adept with masks and disguises. Hume states in his final character of Cromwell that he wishes to 'remove... somewhat of the marvellous' (*History*, ch. LXI) from received opinions of the Protector; and in many ways, this is the major theme in Hume's treatment of Cromwell. Concessions to Cromwell's pragmatism are undercut by Hume's emphasis on the accidental circumstances which brought him success, and by his firm rejection of any 'super-natural' abilities. Cromwell's opportunism makes him the man of the moment; but as a corollary to this, Cromwell is defined *by* the times: 'This man, suited to the age in which he lived, *and to that alone*, was equally qualified to gain the affection and confidence of men, by what was mean, vulgar and ridiculous in his character, as to command their obedience by what was great, enterprising, and daring.' (*History*, ch. LX; my italics.) Charles, we remember, was admired by Hume for those universal qualities which would have made him a good king in any age but the one into which he was born, and a good man in any age. Cromwell, on the other hand, could not have been successful, either as man or ruler, in any other era. The word 'great' itself offers Hume a fine opportunity for irony as he describes some of Cromwell's gaucheries:

> The general behaviour and deportment of this man, who had been raised from a very private station, who had passed most of his youth in the

> country, and who was still constrained so much to bad company was such as might befit the greatest monarch.... Among his ancient friends he could relax himself, and by trifling and amusement, jesting and making verses, he feared not exposing himself to their most familiar approaches. With others he sometimes pushed matters to the length of rustic buffoonery; and he would amuse himself by putting burning coals into the boots and hose of the officers who attended him.
>
> (*History*, ch. LXI)

Not only do Hume's ironies here treat us to the spectacle of the 'greatest monarch' indulging in 'rustic buffoonery', but, by another modification of his source, Hume adds brutality to boorishness. The authority for this passage is George Bate,[43] but he notes only that Cromwell encouraged the soldiers to play practical jokes with 'burning coals', not that he himself participated.

The settings in which Cromwell is placed invite further comparison with Charles.[44] In particular, Hume goes out of his way to stress the absence in Cromwell's life of Charles's domestic joy and security. Towards the end of his life, Cromwell finds no relief from his troubles in his family circle: 'The protector might better have supported these fears and apprehensions which the public distempers occasioned, had he enjoyed any domestic satisfaction, or possessed any cordial friend of his own family, in whose bosom he could safely have unloaded his anxious and corroding cares.' (*History*, ch. LXI.) We never see Cromwell with his family, as we do Charles; and even Hume's comment on the Protector's private life in the final character damns him with faint praise: his 'private deportment... is exposed to no considerable censure, if it does not rather merit praise' (*History*, ch. LXI).

Similarly, Cromwell's personal accomplishments compare unfavourably with Charles's. Charles is both a lover of the fine arts and himself an artist: Cromwell patronizes literary men, but is 'himself a barbarian' (*History*, ch. LXII). The king is eloquent; the Protector often inarticulate, usually unintelligible (*History*, ch. LXI). Charles's friendships are deep and sincere: Cromwell's have all the impermanence of expediency. Charles meets his end with dignity and serenity: Cromwell, on the other hand, degenerates into a state of paranoid anxiety towards the end of his life. In a very fine passage, Hume describes the disintegration of Cromwell's private life as he becomes apparently more secure as head of state: he trusts no one, constantly fears assassination, and becomes progressively isolated:

> Each action of his life betrayed the terrors under which he laboured. The aspect of strangers was uneasy to him. With a piercing and anxious eye he surveyed every face to which he was not daily accustomed. He never moved a step without strong guards attending him: he wore

armour under his cloaths, and farther secured himself by offensive weapons . . . which he always carried about with him: he returned from no place by the direct road, or by the same way he went: every journey he performed with hurry and precipitation: seldom he slept above three nights together in the same chamber: and he never let it be known beforehand which chamber he intended to choose, nor intrusted himself in any which was not provided with back-doors, at which sentinels were carefully placed. Society terrified him, while he reflected on his numerous, unknown and implacable enemies: solitude astonished him, by withdrawing the protection which he found so necessary for his security.
(*History*, ch. LXI).

Hume sees Cromwell's mental decline as a direct cause of his physical deterioration. And unlike Charles, whose calm and rational confidence in his God sustains him through his troubles, Cromwell finds no comfort in his religion, which Hume describes as a thing of superstition and oracle, a complete abandonment of reason. With relish, Hume points out that the Protector died on 3 September, 'that day which he had always considered as the most fortunate for him' (*History*, ch. LXI).

In counterpointing the characters of Charles and Cromwell, then, Hume is reinforcing his definition of the heroism of personal merit and goodness by showing it in action. The truly good man transcends the age in which he lives, as Charles does: the superstition and fanaticism of Cromwell's last days are the epitome of the age itself.

[4]

In suggesting that the sentimental tradition in philosophy and literary criticism offers a fruitful context for a reading of the first volumes of the *History*, and that Hume sees Charles's career as approximating sentimental tragedy, I do not wish to imply that Hume's vision of history as a whole, or even of the *History* as a whole, is either sentimental or tragic. Hayden White points out that the eighteenth century 'produced no great Tragic historiography' because enlightenment historians found themselves forced by their philosophical scepticism into the ironic mode of 'emplotment'.[45] The overall shape of Hume's *History* (including the Tudor and mediaeval volumes) is ironic in this sense, as one would expect of a work whose political purpose is demythological: it attacks the teleologies of 'party' historians, and emphatically denies that plots inhere in history.[46] However, it does not follow, as Leo Braudy claims, that Hume's 'dissociation from partisan interpretation becomes a revocation of aesthetic and historical responsibility'.[47] Within the total structural pattern, or non-pattern, of the *History*, one may discern certain localized movements which might be seen, as I have argued here, as the aesthetic *enactment* of the ethics of the *Enquiry*. For Hume, the narrative artist's major concern is with 'the *images* of vice and virtue' (*Enquiry*, V. ii: 225) and their effect on the reader.[48]

One might agree with Braudy that there is a 'tension between the demands of sympathetic character analysis and those of detached narrative' in the early volumes of the *History*;[49] but this tension between sympathy and detachment is deeply rooted in all of Hume's thought (and perhaps in all sentimental philosophies); and Hume is very much aware of it. The correct response of the spectator to the moral situations in the *Enquiry*, and of the reader to the narrative situations of the *History*, is one which combines detachment and sympathy, reason and feeling: in other words, a 'sentimental' response.[50] The rhetoric of the two works confirms this. In the *History*, the narrator characterizes himself and his reader as rational, enlightened observers of the madness and enthusiasm of seventeenth-century history in such phrases as 'to a philosophic mind' (*History*, ch. LVII) or 'among the generality of men educated in regular, civilized societies' (*History*, ch. LIX); but at the same time, as the analysis of the characterization of Charles I above suggests, he expects a sympathetic involvement with its good men. Similarly, in the *Enquiry*, narrator and reader are from the first in league, pledged to moderate, civilized discussion in opposition to the customary acrimonious dogmatics of ethical debate (*Enquiry*, I. i: 169f.). But just as the historian can move from ironic distance to sympathetic, or even pathetic, dramatization of character, so the moralist's coolness breaks down. After offering some examples of benevolence, he stops short to remark that he has caught himself praising rather than analysing 'generosity and benevolence' and 'all the genuine charms of the social virtues'; and he is forced to admit that 'it is difficult to abstain from some sally of panegyric, as often as they occur in discourse or reasoning' (*Enquiry*, II. i: 177). He then goes on to emphasize that his concern is with the 'speculative' rather than the 'practical' part of morals; but his calculated lapse into panegyric is in itself an admission that ultimately, the 'speculative' and the 'practical' *cannot* be dissociated, because reason and feeling are united in the primary, immediate moral/aesthetic response – the '*sentiment* of beauty and deformity, vice and virtue' (*Enquiry*, App. I: 294; my italics).

At least one of Hume's contemporary readers reacted to the *History* in the way that Hume would have wanted. Robert Adam wrote from Rome to his sister Janet, after finishing the first volume, in what surely must be the ideal response to Hume's literary technique:

> I own I suffer'd inwardly, on the miserable state poor Charles was reducd to, & if I coud have help'd him, Humanity I thought woud

call on me to do it. But this Controversy is what will never be agreed about & it is a matter of moon shine whither it is or not. To these disturbances we owe our present happy Constitution.[51]

NOTES

1. Rene Wellek and Austin Warren, *Theory of Literature* (1963), 22.
2. Hayden White, 'The Fictions of Factual Representation', in *The Literature of Fact: Selected Papers from the English Institute*, ed. Angus Fletcher (New York, 1976), 23–4.
3. E.g. Constant Noble Stockton, 'Hume – historian of the English Constitution', *Eighteenth-Century Studies*, IV (1970–1), 277–293; Duncan Forbes, *Hume's Philosophical Politics* (1975). The exception is Leo Braudy's excellent *Narrative Form in History and Fiction: Hume, Fielding & Gibbon* (Princeton, 1970).
4. Duncan Forbes, 'Introduction' to Hume, *The History of Great Britain: The Reigns of James I and Charles I* (1970), 14.
5. E.g. Hugh Trevor-Roper, 'The historical philosophy of the Enlightenment', *Studies on Voltaire and the Eighteenth Century*, XXVII (1963), 1667–87.
6. E.g. J. B. Black, *The Art of History* (1926).
7. Ronald Paulson, in *Satire and the Novel in Eighteenth-Century England* (New Haven and London, 1967), suggests that Hume sees historiography as 'a critical, analytic, and in one sense, satiric undertaking' (153–5). However, Hume would presumably have rejected the satiric mode as essentially partisan: he identifies it as conservative, and, by implication, Tory, in the essay 'Of the Independency of Parliament', *Essays, Moral, Political and Literary* (1904,) (hereafter cited as *Essays*), 41–2.
8. J. W. Johnson, *The Formation of English Neo-Classical Thought* (Princeton, 1967), 195.
9. *Selections from the Family Papers Preserved at Caldwell* (1854), I, 39.
10. Ernest Campbell Mossner, 'Hume's early memoranda, 1729–1740: the complete text', *Journal of the History of Ideas*, II (1941), 225–36.
11. Hume, *Essays*, 562.
12. David Hume, *A Treatise of Human Nature*, ed. E. C. Mossner (1969), III.iii.4: 663; *An Enquiry Concerning the Principles of Morals*, ed. L. A. Selby-Bigge (1966), Appendix I, 290 (hereafter cited as *Treatise* and *Enquiry*).
13. *Philosophical Essays Concerning Human Understanding* (1748) (hereafter cited as *PE*). This is the work we now know as *An Enquiry Concerning Human Understanding*: Hume later excised the section referred to here, and it does not appear in many modern editions, notably Selby-Bigge's, though C. W. Hendel's edition (New York, 1955) includes it.
14. Ernest Campbell Mossner, *The Life of David Hume* (1954), 174–5.
15. National Library of Scotland, MS.732, 'Memoranda for my history of England written in July 1745 or 46'; see also Mossner, *Life*, 175–6.
16. Such comparisons of history and poetry were familiar in neoclassical criticism: in an essay 'Of Historical Composition' in *Essays Read to a Literary Society* (1759), James Moor, also concerned with the question of unity, suggests that historiography should seek its rules in Aristotle's *Poetics*. Hume's procedure clearly marks his divergence from neoclassical versions of the analogy: he examines the classical rules for narrative unity, not to adopt or deny them, but to justify them in terms of the psychology of literary communication.
17. Hume's work deeply influenced these critics, and their views on the art of history may be seen as fleshing out Hume's skeletal remarks. For other eighteenth-century comments on history as literary constructs, see Thomas R.

Preston, 'Historiography as art in eighteenth-century England', *Texas Studies in Literature and Language*, xi (1969), 1197–1208.

18. George H. Nadel, 'Philosophy of history before historicism', *History and Theory*, iii (1964), 291–315.
19. Adam Smith, *Lectures on Rhetoric and Belles Lettres*, ed. John M. Lothian, (1963); 87; Hugh Blair, *Lectures on Rhetoric and Belles Lettres* (1783), II, 267; Henry Home, Lord Kames, *Elements of Criticism* (1807), I, 96.
20. Smith, *op. cit.*, 51.
21. R. E. Hughes, 'Pope's "Imitations of Horace" and the ethical focus', *Modern Language Notes*, lxxii (1956), 569–74.
22. Blair, *op. cit.*, II, 281–2.
23. See R. F. Brissenden, *Virtue in Distress* (1974), ch. 2.
24. See also *Treatise*, III.iii.1: 635.
25. Cf. *Treatise*, III.i.2: 523.
26. *The Letters of David Hume*, ed. J. Y. T. Greig (1932), I, 210 (hereafter cited as *Letters*).
27. Forbes, 'Introduction' to Hume, *History of Great Britain* (see n.4 above), 47.
28. Ernest Campbell Mossner, ed., 'New Hume Letters to Lord Elibank, 1748–1776', *Texas Studies in Literature and Language*, iv (1962), 449.
29. P. 206 above.
30. Samuel Johnson, *A Dictionary of the English Language* (1812).
31. Cf. Hume's response to a reading of John Home's *Douglas*: 'It is interesting, affecting, pathetic' (*Letters*, I, 215). The *Oxford English Dictionary* records the first use of the word 'interest' in this sense as 1748 (Anson's *Voyages*). Susie Tucker's discussion of 'interesting' in *Protean Shape* (1967) misses the meaning I am concerned with here, though some of her examples carry these affective connotations; similarly, Raymond Williams's useful entry on 'interest' in *Keywords* (1976) does not note this sense.
32. See Ralph Cohen, 'The transformation of passion: a study of Hume's theories of tragedy', *Philological Quarterly*, xli (1962), 450–64.
33. Sentimental tragedy, for our purposes, is perhaps best defined by Blair: the end of tragedy, he writes, is 'to affect us with pity for the virtuous in distress, and to afford a probable representation of the state of human life, where calamities often befal the best' (*Lectures*, II, 503).
34. Cf. Ian Donaldson, 'Cato in Tears: Stoical Guises of the Man of Feeling', in *Studies in the Eighteenth Century II*, ed. R. F. Brissenden (Toronto, 1973), 377–95.
35. David Hume, *The History of England* (1805), ch. LII. The many widely varying editions of the *History* renders page references useless: I therefore cite passages within the text by chapter number in the collected editions.
36. Brissenden, *op. cit.*, 129.
37. *Ibid.*, 118.
38. See Donaldson's fine discussion of the relationship between stoicism and sentimentalism in 'Cato in Tears' (n.34 above). In the only early eighteenth-century play about Charles I I have seen, William Havard's *King Charles the First: An Historical Tragedy* (1737), the king is almost the archetype of Donaldson's 'Cato in Tears': on his first entrance, he delivers a stoical soliloquy on the transience of life, then a few lines later, in conversation with the queen, he equates manliness with the display, rather than with the suppression of passion: 'Here, I glory in my weakness./He is no man whom Tenderness not melts,/And Love so soft as thine.' (II.i).
39. Bulstrode Whitelock, *Memorials of the English Affairs* (1682), 22.
40. Ian Donaldson, 'Drama from 1710 to 1780', in *Dryden to Johnson*, ed. Roger Lonsdale (1971), 212.
41. Sir Philip Warwick, *Memoires* (1703), 339. Hume's nineteenth-century critics were fond of citing this as an example of his perversion of truth.

42. In Havard's *King Charles the First*, this scene is also important: the frontispiece illustration shows Charles surrounded by his weeping children, with the motto, 'At this sad SCENE who can from TEARS refrain?'
43. George Bate, *Elenchus Motuum Nuperorum in Anglia* (1685), 195.
44. Formal character-comparisons of Charles and Cromwell were not unknown: see, e.g., John Banks, *A Short Critical Review of the Political Life of Oliver Cromwell* (1742).
45. Hayden White, *Metahistory* (Baltimore and London, 1975), 66; see also Pt I, ch. I *passim*.
46. Braudy, *op. cit.*, 65; Duncan Forbes, *Hume's Philosophical Politics*, ch. 8. See also Hayden White, 'The historical text as literary artefact' *Clio*, III (1974), 294, for a precise description of the 'ironic' mode of Hume's *History*, though White does not specifically apply his model to Hume.
47. Braudy, *op. cit.*, 89.
48. 'Image' and 'picture' are important words throughout the *Enquiry*.
49. Braudy, *op. cit.*, 35.
50. R. F. Brissenden, ' "Sentiment": Some Uses of the Word in the Writings of David Hume'; in *Studies in the Eighteenth Century*, ed. R. F. Brissenden, (Canberra, 1968), 89–108.
51. Rome, 31 January 1756; Scottish Record Office MS.GD 18/4798. Also quoted by John Fleming, *Robert Adam and his Circle* (1962), 201.

14

A Sentimental Journey and the Syntax of Things

MARTIN C. BATTESTIN

Recently I made a case for the fundamental – it might be said, revolutionary – modernity of *Tristram Shandy* (1759–67), in which Sterne, repudiating the Augustan faith in symmetry and rational order, devised a form to mirror and to mitigate the disturbing subjectivist conception of reality he found implicit in Locke's *Essay concerning Human Understanding* – a form that defines the world in terms of the processes of the mind while implying, in its appeal to the senses and the imagination, the means of communication and relationship.[1] Enforced by the mechanism of the mind and the inefficacy of rational discourse to bridge the gulf that separates us, solipsism and frustration are the conditions of life at Shandy Hall, relieved only in those humanizing moments when, by means of the sympathetic or the sexual imagination, we are, in Walter's words, led out 'of our caverns and hiding-places' into communion with another.[2]

In *A Sentimental Journey through France and Italy* (1768) Sterne resumed these themes, but transmuted and softened them by asserting more confidently than before the possibility of relationship, achieved through the sensuous and imaginative apprehension of what I will call the syntax of things. The phrase is convenient because it would have carried for Sterne and his contemporaries a double reference, pointing not only to the logical process of grammatical predication, by which subject is coupled with object or acts upon it, but also to the universal grammar of Nature herself, the system of interrelationships that obtains in what Yorick prefers to call the 'great – great SENSORIUM of the world'.[3] The two senses of *syntax*, linguistic and metaphysical, will help to clarify the ways in which, even at the most elementary and essential level of his narrative, Sterne's form implies his meaning.[4] In carrying his reader along with him on this 'quiet journey of the heart in pursuit of NATURE, and those affections which rise out of her, which make us love each other – and the world, better than we do' (p. 219), Yorick means so to conduct his narrative that we participate in it, that, in the process of reading, we will ourselves become, in terms of the metaphoric classifications of the Preface, 'Sentimental Travellers' capable of responding to life and the vexatious circumstances of our mortality with compassion, and of course with laughter: his reader, he warns, must eventually 'determine his own place and rank in the catalogue' of travellers, whether 'Idle', 'Inquisitive', 'Lying', 'Proud', 'Vain', 'Splenetic', or 'Sentimental' – 'it will be one step towards knowing himself . . .' (pp. 82–3). Both these transactions – the journey of the heart in pursuit of Nature and the narrator's striving to achieve a closer, ameliorative relationship with his reader – may be seen to have a linguistic analogue in the paradigm of the sentence itself, in which the subject (and here especially the subjective *ego* of the first-person narrative) is linked through a copulative or transitive verb to an object beyond itself. Happily, in addition to being helpful in clarifying the interdependence of theme and form in *A Sentimental Journey*, this analogy has the advantage of having occurred to Sterne himself: for Tristram, at least, Yorick, the humorous, philandering parson who is our subject, is 'as heteroclite a creature in all his declensions' as any parsing student of the human comedy could wish for;[5] and, as Yorick himself assures us, his relationships with others are always predicated 'according to the mood I am in, and the case – and I may add the gender too, of the person I am to govern' (p. 124).

If the grammatical paradigm may thus imply the establishment of human relationships, however, the notorious syntactical eccentricities, ambiguities, and interruptions of *A Sentimental Journey* will remind us that, in art as in life, such relationships are seldom so neatly accomplished. Nor, perhaps, is it always desirable that they should be. Sterne's fiction in a sense anticipates E. E. Cummings's observation that 'life is not a paragraph',[6] rounded and coherent, its premisses neatly fulfilled. For Tristram it was rather a fluid, open-ended, whimsical thing that would be conterminous with the narrative he was writing; for Yorick it is, however brief, 'a large volume' of sentimental adventures (p. 114). Like Cummings, too, Sterne understood that in this process Death, from whom Yorick flees toward the pleasant valleys of Italy, is no mere 'parenthesis',[7] but rather the final full stop, whose symbol in *Tristram Shandy* had been blackness filling the pages to the very margins. Understandably, therefore, Yorick inclines to a loose, unconventional punctuation, preferring dashes to periods, and in the narrative of his journey breaks off in mid-sentence as in mid-career, leaving us with the image of himself reaching out toward one kind of syntactical completion he covets, but grasping only the blank vacuity of the unprinted page. On 18 March 1768, with a poignant and appropriately shandean irony, Fortune decreed that Sterne should come to the end of his own volume of adventures, with half his book still to write.

Because Death at last won his race with Sterne, Yorick has remained in that final comical attitude ever since, prevented by impassable mountain roads from reaching his destination, his more immediate objective eluding his grasp. We will never know, then, what Sterne's final intention for his work may have been. Yet to judge from the part of the book he did complete, it would appear that *A Sentimental Journey* represents a modification of one of the conventional thematic motifs of journey literature, that it was in some sense designed, in Gardner Stout's phrase, as 'a comic "Pilgrim's Progress" for the man of feeling'.[8] The stages measuring the spiritual distance Yorick travels in the first two volumes are, on the one hand, the early chapters entitled 'The Monk' and 'The Desobligeant' and, on the other hand, the later episodes concerning Maria and the peasant family whose charity and simple piety are celebrated in 'The Supper' and 'The Grace': seen in this way, Yorick's true progress is from solipsism toward communion, from self-love toward a felt apprehension of the syntax of things. Just how much mental travelling this process will require is suggested upon Yorick's arrival at Calais by his inability to translate his fine-sounding sentiments into deeds. His spirits heightened by a good dinner and a bottle of burgundy, he is in an expansive, altruistic mood. Generalizing from his own generous sentiments, he imagines mankind almost literally as subjects in search of predication, looking round 'for an object to share' their money with; the benign motions of such a soul as his seem proof sufficient against those cynical French materialists who represent man as a mere machine actuated by self-interest (pp. 68–9). Far from oversetting their creed, however, he will instantly seem to confirm it when he refuses alms to the kindly Franciscan who intrudes upon this complacent reverie. The practical demand upon his charity summons up all his selfish impulses and brings reason rushing to their justification: 'The moment I cast my eyes on him, I was predetermined not to give him a single sous; and accordingly I put my purse into my pocket – button'd it up – set myself a little more upon my centre' (p. 70). The doctrine of *L'Homme machine* is thoroughly congenial to Yorick's present mood, who could wish to believe that, since 'the ebbs and flows of our humours' depend upon physical causes beyond our control, there is 'neither sin nor shame' in our actions (p. 70). His purse buttoned up in his pocket, his portmanteau securely locked against all solicitations, Yorick rationalizes his meanness by reminding the monk that he is presuming upon a fund which is the rightful property of the truly unfortunate, 'the lame, the blind, the aged and the infirm' – that charity, as Fielding's Mrs Tow-wouse declared in behalf of the niggardly everywhere, begins at home: 'but of all others, resumed I, the unfortunate of our own country, surely, have the first rights; and I have left thousands in distress upon our own shore' (p. 73).

Critics have found in such episodes evidence for Sterne's persistent mockery of his hero;[9] but it is Yorick, we must remember, who has the honesty to embarrass himself by telling us about them. And he knows better: 'I have behaved very ill; said I within myself; but I have only just set out upon my travels; and shall learn better manners as I get along'

(p. 75). As a traveller requires a vehicle to make his progress, so, in the journey of life (the metaphor again is Yorick's own, p. 114), the vehicle must be our own sensibilities, the quality of which will determine our experience of the world. Reality for Sterne is subjective; we create the world in our own image. The Sentimental Traveller, which Yorick will become, can transform a waste land into a garden, for he goes sympathetically, seeking connexions and relationships that will improve and nourish his heart:

> I pity the man who can travel from *Dan* to *Beersheba*, and cry, 'Tis all barren – and so it is; and so is all the world to him who will not cultivate the fruits it offers. I declare, said I, clapping my hands chearily together that was I in a desart, I would find out wherewith in it to call forth my affections – If I could not do better, I would fasten them upon some sweet myrtle, or seek some melancholy cypress to connect myself to –
>
> (pp. 115–16)

The Splenetic Traveller, for whom Smollett is the archetype, will find at his journey's end that 'heaven itself' is a hell, its happiest mansion only a place to 'do penance . . . to all eternity'; for he has 'brought up no faculties' to appreciate felicity (p. 120).

At this first stage of his journey, however, Yorick's 'vehicle', as we have seen, is cramped and in need of repair. 'Discontented with himself' (p. 76), his spiritual condition after the initial encounter with the monk is symbolized by the ruined *desobligéante*, a single-seat chaise which, having made the tour of Europe and 'not profited much by its adventures' (p. 87), sits mouldering in the farthest corner of the innyard. Finding it 'in tolerable harmony with [his] feelings' (p. 77), Yorick enters this useless and unsociable conveyance, completes his isolation by drawing the curtain to shut out the figure of the monk, an object of charity, and proceeds to write his Preface; it would have been better, as he remarks to the English traveller who interrupts him, 'in a *Vis a Vis*' (p. 85). Later, when the process of his sentimentalizing has opened his heart, he will exclaim, ' – Surely – surely man! it is not good for thee to sit alone – thou wast made for social intercourse' (p. 167); now the *desobligéante* provides the emblem of his self-enclosure.

Yet the symbolism of Yorick's situation here is not entirely negative. It includes two further curious circumstances pointing to a distinctive feature of Sterne's conception of his craft: the notion that an important means of escaping the condition of solipsism is the act of authorship itself. Writing for Tristram, like the Hobby-horses of his uncle and father, is a device for ordering the confusing multiplicity of one's fugitive experience;[10]

unlike most Hobby-horses, however, which tend to confirm us in our isolation, writing about one's private experience is the means of apprehending its latent significance and, therefore, of rendering it intelligible. It is thus the very activity of writing the Preface that sets Yorick's otherwise useless vehicle in motion, beginning, as it were, both the process of his mental travelling out of himself and the process of his developing relationship with us, his readers. By the time he finishes the Preface, Yorick declares, 'I had wrote myself pretty well out of conceit with the *Desobligeant*' (p. 87); his writing seems a kind of therapy, purging his mind of its discontents. What is more, the episode concludes with a dramatization of the fact that only as readers of his narrative may we become participants of the journey it recounts, which is ideally the mutual progress of both author and reader toward self-knowledge and benevolence. Sterne abruptly interjects into the scene a pair of English travellers who have been drawn to the *desobligéante* by the motion Yorick's writing has imparted to it. Though as characters in the narrative they cannot actually have heard the question which concludes his Preface – 'Where then, my dear countrymen, are you going – ' (p. 85) – they are nonetheless made to answer it: 'We are only looking at this chaise, said they.' Responding thus improbably to the written words, these English travellers seem surrogates for us, Sterne's English readers, who, as we will see, by such surprising strategies of his art will be made to answer that same crucial question.

That this curious parable of the *desobligéante* points to an ultimate concern of Sterne's narrative is confirmed by the subject itself of the Preface, the writing of which has set the machine in motion. Springing naturally from Yorick's mood and situation, the Preface sounds the dominant theme of the *Journey*: the difficulties of communication, of leaving our homes (and our selves) behind to seek new relationships abroad. That Sterne means us to regard Yorick's confinement in the *desobligéante* as a symbol of our fundamental solipsism seems clear from the phrasing of the opening sentence, which universalizes his discontent and isolation: 'nature', Yorick observes, 'has set up by her own unquestionable authority certain boundaries and fences to circumscribe the discontent of man... laying him under almost insuperable obligations to work out his ease, and to sustain his sufferings at home':

> 'Tis true we are endued with an imperfect power of spreading our happiness sometimes beyond *her* limits, but 'tis so ordered, that from the want of languages, connections, and dependencies, and from the difference in education, customs and habits, we lie under so many impediments in communicating our sensations out of our own sphere, as often amount to a total impossibility.
>
> (p. 78)

In *A Sentimental Journey* the impediments to breaking 'out of our own sphere' are many, and they cannot be circumvented without much ingenuity and diligence. For one thing, and most essentially, there is the whole intractable mechanism of the self, with all its appetites and vanities – the mechanism described by the likes of Hobbes and the French *philosophes* and which Yorick symbolizes not only by the *desobligéante*, but by the caged starling, crying ' "I can't get out – I can't get out" ' – whose prison is secure and permanent: the door of the cage, Yorick declares, 'was twisted and double twisted so fast with wire, there was no getting it open without pulling the cage to pieces – I took both hands to it' (p. 197). It is the 'poor starling', emblem of the confined and therefore tormented self, that Yorick, and his author, bear as the crest to their arms (p. 205). As Gardner Stout has argued, Sterne, while keeping his place within the Latitudinarian tradition of benevolism, felt in no inconsiderable degree the force of the Augustinian and Hobbesian doctrine that man is a creature of pride and the sport of his appetites. In a fit of selfishness Yorick first refuses the monk charity, and, when he finally offers the snuff-box to make amends, he is motivated as much by vanity and the desire to get on with his philandering as by the impulses of disinterested benevolence (p. 98). He is even disposed, in simile at least, 'to fight a duel' with the innkeeper over the price of a post-chaise: 'Base passion! said I . . . base, ungentle passion! thy hand is against every man, and every man's hand against thee – ' (p. 89). No sooner does he feel the 'impulse' to share his coach with an attractive young woman whom he imagines to be in distress than 'Every dirty passion, and bad propensity in my nature, took the alarm': Avarice, Caution, Cowardice, Discretion, Hypocrisy, Meanness, Pride – all start up, like prudent counsellors, to secure the citadel of the ego (pp. 104–6). Even much later in Paris, Vanity will intrude upon the process of his sentimentalizing, which is then well along: he revels in his lionizing by a coterie of worldly 'children of Art' whose favours he has won by flattery – 'a most vile prostitution of myself to half a dozen different people' (p. 266).

For Sterne, moreover, not only the selfish passions, but reason itself – the faculty that philosophers from Aristotle and the Stoics to Swift's Houyhnhnms had regarded as the primary agent of morality – works to ensure the condition of solipsism and self-delusion. As the example of Walter Shandy perpetually crucifying Truth may suggest, no novelist of the period went as far as Sterne in disparaging what the humanist tradition took to be the noblest faculty of the soul. In passages such as Yorick's summoning up plausible arguments to justify his meanness to the monk, Sterne seems especially close, in fact, to the shocking author of *A Treatise of Human Nature* (1739), for whom reason was 'the slave of the passions, and can never pretend to any other office than to serve and obey them'.[11]

Thus Yorick insists that the purifying of the soul and the calming of the heart's 'commotions' are not to be entrusted 'to reason only', but to the influence of the more benign social affections: 'I can safely say for myself, I was never able to conquer any one single bad sensation in my heart so decisively, as by beating up as fast as I could for some kindly and gentle sensation, to fight it upon its own ground' (p. 226). At other times he would seem to anticipate the Wordsworthian notion that we murder to dissect. As he stands before the remise door holding the hand of an attractive stranger in the first real moment of sentimental communion he has experienced on his journey, Yorick makes the mistake of trying to analyse the circumstances that account for his happiness: 'you thank Fortune', replies the lady, disengaging her hand, '... you had reason – the heart knew it, and was satisfied; and who but an English philosopher would have sent notices of it to the brain to reverse the judgment?' (p. 96). As for the Stoic confidence that philosophy can render us invulnerable to misfortune, Sterne mocks it as a delusion; and, as a man of feeling, he condemns the inhumanity of the doctrine of self-sufficiency it implies. All Yorick's 'systematic reasonings' (p. 198) to persuade himself that there is no more inconvenience in imprisonment in the Bastille than in a confinement for the gout are overthrown in a moment by the cry of the caged starling, awakening his affections and bringing home vividly to his imagination 'the miseries of confinement' (p. 201). As a work of art and morality, Yorick's narrative of his journey, sentimental though it may be, owes everything of course to his author's thoughtful anatomy of the human comedy, and to the sister faculties of the mind, wit and judgment. Yet Yorick insists, 'this is not a work of reasoning' (p. 177), for in Sterne's view the senses and the sympathetic imagination can alone redeem us.

Cooperating with our rationality in the work of self-enclosure are language itself and the prescribed polite forms of social conversation, systems invented by men to facilitate intercourse but which, as they are normally applied, effectively reinforce our privacy. A 'hundred little delicacies' (p. 107) stand in Yorick's way as he tries to know his companions better, and the final chapter comprises a veritable 'Case' of their efficacy in preventing such connections. Our dialogues, furthermore, as those memorable ones between Walter Shandy and his brother attest, are at best only intersecting monologues, each man using words whose meaning eludes the other, hampered not only by the general curse of Babel, but by the impenetrable privacy of our individual experience and the decorums that conceal the heart beneath a fine brocade of formality.

To circumvent such formidable impediments to communication as these, Sterne looked to another, non-verbal kind of language, anticipating what certain twentieth-century psychologists have called 'body language'; and, as a novelist, he attempted to turn the very imprecision of words to his advantage. A useful illustration of both these strategies is the chapter called 'The Translation'. Words being the clumsy things they are, Tristram, we recall, had wished for a Momus's glass that he might see into the soul of man,[12] and Yorick protests that his ambition in pursuing women is 'to spy the *nakedness* of their hearts, and through the different disguises of customs, climates, and religion, find out what is good in them, to fashion my own by – ' (pp. 217–18). The better to achieve this goal of an immediate, intuitive apprehension of another's self, he perfects his skill at rendering an unspoken language with its own rules of syntactical connexion. As Yorick enters the box at the Opera, the old French officer who occupies it puts down his book, removes his spectacles and places them in his pocket. Though no word has been spoken, the sense of this kindly action is instantly translatable, as is the bow Yorick makes in return, because it is expressed in the universal language of looks and gestures and attitudes, a kind of automatic writing of the heart by which the motions of the soul may be read in those of the body. So, earlier in *Tristram Shandy*, Walter's physical attitude as he lies sprawled on his bed grieving over the death of his son is more eloquent testimony of his feelings than any words could supply. The grammar and idioms of this language are immediately intelligible:

> There is not a secret so aiding to the progress of sociality [declares Yorick], as to get master of this *short hand*, and be quick in rendering the several turns of looks and limbs, with all their inflections and delineations, into plain words. For my own part, by long habitude, I do it so mechanically, that when I walk the streets of London, I go translating all the way; and have more than once stood behind in the circle, where not three words have been said, and have brought off twenty different dialogues with me, which I could have fairly wrote down and sworn to.
>
> (pp. 171–2)

For the purpose of communication and relationship, then, words are less useful than the body, reason than the sympathetic imagination. The most satisfactory moments of communion between characters in Sterne's fiction are accordingly those achieved in silence by touch and intuition. Though their spoken discourse fails to bring them together, Toby's hand placed on his brother's shoulder unites them instantly in mutual affection. In *A Sentimental Journey*, indeed, hands are often the means of syntactical connexion, in both senses of the word *syntax*. The holding of hands, the feeling of another's pulse, becomes for Yorick not only (as, say, in *Paradise Lost*) a sign of harmony between man and woman, but the actual means by which their hearts are made intelligible, one to another. The first true moment of relationship he experiences on his journey, Yorick's sentimental intercourse with the lady at the remise door, continues over the course of many pages, while her hand remains in his, their 'communications' – which lead the English travellers to suppose they 'must be *man and wife* at least' (p. 104) – made possible chiefly by the silent rendering of the fingers' subtle pressures: 'The pulsations of the arteries along my fingers pressing across hers', Yorick observes, 'told her what was passing within me' (p. 97). Later, like a true sentimental physician, Yorick will reckon 'the temperature' of the beautiful *grisset* by counting the throbs of her pulse, since, he believes, 'it is the same blood which comes from the heart, which descends to the extremes' (p. 164). At such moments Sterne enacts the cordial part that Fortune played in Yorick's encounter with the lady in Calais, promoting Friendship's cause by taking 'two utter strangers by their hands – of different sexes, and perhaps from different corners of the globe' (p. 96), the physical union enabling a kind of *concordia discors* of the heart.

This, then, is the essential message of the chapter called 'The Translation': that for the Sentimental Traveller who seeks connexions and relationships, the body's 'short hand' may be more revealing than the spoken word, that our intuitions may compensate for the limitations of the intellect. But, as the chapter also makes clear, Sterne goes farther than this in circumventing the obstacles to communication he found so persuasively delineated in *An Essay concerning Human Understanding*. As man of feeling and as author, he continually exploits the very quirks of mind and language of which Locke complained. It is the mechanism of association that brings Yorick closer to the stranger at the Opera by connecting him in Yorick's mind, despite the separation of time and place, with the idea of Captain Tobias Shandy, 'the dearest of my flock and friends, whose philanthropy I never think of at this long distance from his death – but my eyes gush out with tears' (p. 170). Similarly, it is the ambiguity of words that enables Sterne to achieve a simultaneity of thematic, as well as comic, implications – the multiplicity of connotations comprising a sort of linguistic equivalent of the syntax of things in the 'great SENSORIUM of the world'. The word *translation* in the chapter we are considering can also denote the idea of movement from one place to another, specifically from a situation of isolation outside to a situation of communion within: thus Yorick enters the box and takes his place beside the old officer who reminds him of Toby, the type of philanthropy, as later the Marquesina invites him to enter her coach and carries him to her home – 'the connection', Yorick assures us, 'which arose out of that translation, gave me more pleasure than any one I had the honour to make in Italy' (p. 173). Yet another sense of the word seems to lurk here in true shandean fashion, the sense of *translation* as sexual transport – though, of course, Yorick and the Marquesina are ostensibly recalling their awkward encounter in the passage to the concert hall:

> Upon my word, Madame, said I when I had handed her in, I made six different efforts to let you go out – And I made six efforts, replied she, to let you enter – I wish to heaven you would make a seventh, said I – With all my heart, said she, making room –
> (p. 173)[13]

Yorick's philandering and his irrepressible bawdry are not, I think, quite to be dismissed as a case of arrested adolescence. They seem rather to be manifestations of Sterne's belief that, given the inadequacies of those traditional instruments of communication, reason and language, the way out of the self must be through the senses and the imagination, and most especially through the recognition that it is our common sexuality that draws us together in spite of the conventional strictures of morality and the proscriptions of propriety. Though the Sentimental Traveller's ultimate goal is an awareness of the unity and interrelatedness of all beings in the great Sensorium of creation, his first approaches to that condition must be through the frank acceptance of his sexual nature; it is this specifically – source of so much awkwardness and laughter in Shandy Hall – that 'makes us come out of our caverns and hiding-places'. Yorick is nothing less than a 'connoisseur' of women (p. 219) because he believes that *Eros*, the longing of the self for union with another, is the instrument of charity and fellow-feeling. He travels with the picture of Eliza about his neck because, as he assures the innkeeper at Montreuil, he has

> been in love with one princess or another almost all my life, and I hope I shall go on so, till I die, being firmly persuaded, that if ever I do a mean action, it must be in some interval betwixt one passion and another: whilst this interregnum lasts, I always perceive my heart locked up – I can scarce find in it, to give Misery a sixpence; and therefore I always get out of it as fast as I can, and the moment I am rekindled, I am all generosity and good will again; and would do any thing in the world either for, or with any one, if they will but satisfy me there is no sin in it.
> (pp. 128–9)

The 'Fragment' that follows is meant as a kind of parable of this creed. In the reformation of Abdera, 'the vilest and most profligate town in all Thrace', it is the 'pathetic' apostrophe to Eros in Euripides' *Andromeda*, not Democritus's more Augustan applications of 'irony and laughter', that cleanses the city of malice, transforming it at once into an image of the Golden Age: 'Every man almost spoke pure iambics the next day, and talk'd of nothing but Perseus his pathetic address – "O Cupid! prince of God and men" – in every street of Abdera, in every house – "O Cupid! Cupid!" . . . The fire caught – and the whole city, like the heart of one man, open'd itself to Love.' It is worth stressing that this miraculous transformation of a corrupt people is accomplished not through the intellectual appeals of philosophy or satire, but through the 'pathetic' mode of poetry that 'operated more upon their imaginations', the faculty of the mind most nearly allied to the senses, in which the images and motions of desire are vicariously experienced: ''Twas only in the power, says the Fragment, of the God whose empire extendeth from heaven to earth, and even to the depths of the sea, to have done this' (p. 131). As Yorick later explains to the Count, though he is travelling in pursuit of Nature and a universal benevolence, the journey is accomplished only through a process of refining the 'affection' he feels 'for the whole sex' (p. 216). The hearts of women, not the Palais Royal or the Louvre, are the temples he 'would rather enter in' (p. 218).

The pursuit of Nature, then, begins in the frank – which is not to say salacious – acceptance of our sexuality, and Sterne as an author means to involve us in this humanizing enterprise. He does so not only in such sentimental passages as the above, but in those bawdy jokes for which he is equally celebrated. These jokes, moreover, are almost invariably the effect of a distinctive rhetorical strategy calculated, no less than the pathos of Perseus's apostrophe to Eros, to operate upon our imaginations. As in the third sense of the word *translation* discussed above, this strategy is the *double entendre* – some object or action or word which at the level ostensibly intended by the author is perfectly straightforward, but which at another level which the reader's imagination, however reluctantly, is teased into supplying, carries a less 'innocent' meaning.[14] The classic instance of this technique in Sterne's fiction is Tristram's elaborate protestation that the word *nose* in his book always and invariably means a nose and nothing more (or less); as a consequence we never afterward encounter the word without supplying a phallic reference. In *A Sentimental Journey* numerous other examples come to mind, such as the 'proposal' Yorick wishes to make to the young woman at Calais (p. 113), or the gloves which the beautiful *grisset* holds open to receive his hand (p. 168). Better still is the titillating encounter between Yorick and the *fille de chambre* related in the chapters called 'The Temptation' and 'The Conquest'. As they sit side by side on the bed in his room, the essentially sexual nature of their interest in each other is obliquely symbolized by the purse she has made to hold his crown:

> I'll just shew you, said the fair *fille de chambre*, the little purse I have been making to-day to hold your crown . . . it was of green taffeta, lined with a little bit of white quilted sattin, and just big enough to hold the crown – she put it into my hand – it was pretty; and I held it ten minutes with the back of my hand resting upon her lap – looking sometimes at the purse, sometimes on one side of it.
>
> (p. 236)[15]

Having heightened our expectations with further descriptions of 'innocent' intimacies – the *fille de chambre* passing 'her hand in silence across and across [Yorick's] neck' as she mends his stock, Yorick returning the favour by fondling her feet as he fastens the buckle of her shoe – Sterne breaks off the chapter in mid-sentence with the image implanted firmly in the reader's mind of his hero and the temptress tumbling together on the bed: 'and putting in the strap – and lifting up the other foot with it, when I had done, to see both were right – in doing it too suddenly – it unavoidably threw the fair *fille de chambre* off her centre – and then –' (p. 236). In such a predicament even the chastest of Sterne's readers will be inclined to construe the title of the following chapter, 'The Conquest', in a sexual sense. But, as always in Sterne, *honi soit qui mal y pense.* What Yorick has conquered of course is not his companion's virtue, but the temptation she posed. What has ultimately been tested by Sterne's coy presentation of the episode is the quality of his prudish or 'stoical' reader's imagination. By implicating us in the joke, furthermore, he has, for all our vaunted rationality and decorous self-possession, made us face the fact that we are, as nature would have us be, essentially sexual creatures, and that, indeed, the communion of hearts begins in the inclinations of the body:

> YES – and then – Ye whose clay-cold heads and luke-warm hearts can argue down or mask your passions – tell me, what trespass is it that man should have them? or how his spirit stands answerable, to the father of spirits, but for his conduct under them?
>
> If nature has so wove her web of kindness, that some threads of love and desire are entangled with the piece – must the whole web be rent in drawing them out? – Whip me such stoics, great governor of nature! said I to myself – Wherever thy providence shall place me for the trials of my virtue – whatever is my danger – whatever is my situation – let me feel the movements which rise out of it, and which belong to me as a man – and if I govern them as a good one – I will trust the issues to thy justice, for thou hast made us – and not we ourselves.
>
> (pp. 237–8)

But if, not unlike the progress of Plato's philosopher in the *Symposium*, that of the Sentimental Traveller must begin in sexual desire, its goal is something finer and more generous. At Calais, before he 'put [himself] into motion' (p. 114), Yorick's selfishness in the affair of the monk had belied his complacent opinion of his own altruism and served to confirm the cynical materialism of the *philosophes.* By the time he has reached the Bourbonnois, however, the instrument of his sensibilities has been more finely tuned, his sexual epicureanism transmuted into the higher delights of a general and disinterested benevolence. The episode of the *fille de chambre* has a counterpart in Yorick's quite different relationship with Maria of Moulines. Sitting close by her side, his feelings are those of compassion not desire, the purity of his affection, untainted by any baser motive, providing at last the refutation of the materialists he has been seeking:

> I sat down close by her; and Maria let me wipe [her tears] away as they fell with my handkerchief. – I then steep'd it in my own – and then in hers – and then in mine – and then I wip'd hers again – and as I did it, I felt such undescribable emotions within me, as I am sure could not be accounted for from any combinations of matter and motion.
>
> I am positive I have a soul; nor can all the books with which materialists have pester'd the world ever convince me of the contrary.
> (p. 271)

The famous apostrophe to Sensibility which this episode inspires is the culmination of Yorick's sentimental education and of his passage, begun in discontent in the *desobligéante*, from solipsism to a more expansive realm 'beyond' himself: 'all comes from thee, great – great SENSORIUM of the world! which vibrates, if a hair of our heads but falls upon the ground, in the remotest desert of thy creation' (p. 278). This, the apprehension of the syntax of things, is the moment of grace in Sterne's religion of the feeling heart, his own peculiar refinement of the Latitudinarian tradition which, as R. S. Crane has shown,[16] already offered its own peculiarly optimistic reconstruction of Christian assumptions about human nature. The two chapters that follow clearly imply that the sentimental pursuit of Nature in which Yorick, priest and man of feeling, has been engaged is ultimately for Sterne a religious act, having even its own readily improvised sacraments and rituals.[17] 'The Supper', though merely a meal of bread and wine shared with a peasant family, becomes a type of eucharist – 'a feast of love', as Yorick calls it (p. 281). 'The Grace', the dance of thanksgiving in which Yorick beholds '*Religions* mixing' (p. 284), is in a deeper sense an expression of that gift of the Holy Spirit without which there could be no '*Work of Redemption*'[18] – the capacity for love, for feeling those 'generous joys and generous cares beyond [ourselves]' (p. 278).

The trouble with this reading of *A Sentimental Journey* is, of course, that the work – or at least the part of it that Sterne completed – does not end with the celebration of communion, but with another, and the most notorious, of his bawdy jokes. If the book is a 'comic "Pilgrim's Progress" for the man of feeling' as I believe with Gardner Stout it was in some sense meant to be – it is certainly no conventional allegory, any more than it is 'a work of reasoning'. Perhaps the genre to which it is more nearly allied is that of spiritual autobiography, in which, typically, the narrator recounts his unsteady and (since there is always the possibility of a relapse) inconclusive progress from a condition of alienation and despair to a state of grace.[19] But Sterne rejoiced in what he has Yorick call the '*Novelty of my Vehicle*' (p. 82), and he has always been an embarrassment to genericists.

What interests me about the concluding chapter of *A Sentimental Journey* is that, even in its abrupt shift of the tone from one of an exuberant piety to a sort of arch and irreverent verbal pruriency, it comprises a fitting coda and recapitulation of the motifs Sterne has been sounding throughout the work. Serving as prelude to 'The Case of Delicacy' itself is Yorick's description of the terrain over which he passes on his way toward his destination. Between the safe and friendly valleys of France and those of Italy stand those 'mountains impracticable' which impede the passage of 'the way-worn traveller', confronting him with 'the sudden turns and dangers of your roads – your rocks – your precipices – the difficulties of getting up – the horrors of getting down' (p. 285). In this book of obstacles to translations of all kinds – closed doors and drawn curtains, buttoned pockets and locked portmanteaus, the wretch's prison and the starling's cage, not to mention the differences in languages, educations, customs and habits that obstruct us 'in communicating our sensations out of our own spheres' – one of the most noticeable is the great stone that halts Yorick's sentimental journey in mid-career. Greater still than this, however, is the obstacle of mutual embarrassment, thoughts 'too delicate to communicate' (p. 288), that separates Yorick and the attractive Piedmontese whom circumstances oblige to share the only room in the inn: 'There were difficulties every way [Yorick observes] – and the obstacle of the stone in the road, which brought us into the distress, great as it appeared whilst the peasants were removing it, was but a pebble to what lay in our ways now' (pp. 287–8).

In conducting his travellers out of this impasse and leading his readers to the end of the second volume, Sterne presents a sort of comic parable of the theme of estrangement and communion which he has already elaborated. Obliged to sleep side by side in two beds narrowly separated, Yorick and his companion, like two hostile nations, enter into a 'two hours negociation' leading to 'a treaty of peace' between them (p. 288). Dictated by the requirements of decorum, the articles of the treaty are calculated to multiply the 'barriers' separating them and to prevent communication: first, the opening of the lady's bedcurtains, which, besides being of 'a flimsy transparent cotton', are 'too scanty to draw close', is secured by corking pins; second, Yorick must lie all night in his breeches; and third, he is forbidden to 'speak one single word' – except, of course, that he may say his prayers. What the proprieties of social decorum have thus put asunder, however, the irrepressible operations of the sexual imagination – Yorick's, the lady's, and most especially the reader's – will join together. Before allowing the joke to continue, Sterne pauses to make his point inescapably clear: that the real author of his hero's titillating adventures with the opposite sex has been the reader all along. How the lady and the parson contrive to get to bed in such a situation, he will 'leave to the reader to devise; protesting as I do it, that if it is not the most delicate in nature, 'tis the fault of his own imagination – against which this is not my first complaint' (pp. 289–90). Possessing the same lively imagination as the reader, neither Yorick nor the lady can sleep for thinking of each other. 'O my God! said I' – an 'ejaculation' on Yorick's part that instantly elicits the chiding of the lady, so warm that 'she weakened her barrier by it' and the bed curtains part in a shower of corking pins:

> Upon my word and honour, Madame, said I – stretching my arm out of bed, by way of asseveration –
>
> (I was going to have added, that I would not have trespass'd against the remotest idea of decorum for the world) –
>
> – But the Fille de Chambre hearing there were words between us, and fearing that hostilities would ensue in course, had crept silently out of her closet, and it being totally dark, had stolen so close to our beds, that she had got herself into the narrow passage which separated them, and had advanc'd so far up as to be in a line betwixt her mistress and me –
>
> So that when I stretch'd out my hand, I caught hold of the Fille de Chambre's

So Sterne – twice breaking off the syntax of Yorick's narrative (at the beginning and most hilariously at the end of this famous passage) – leaves him frozen forever in a gesture that may serve as the dramatic correlative of the human desire for another sort of syntactical completion, the subjective ego set apart, yet reaching out to close the gap that separates us. That final broken sentence, however, its grammatical predication never closed on the page itself, is nevertheless most certainly completed in the imagination of Sterne's reader. For, as Yorick has been at some pains to make clear in relating his sentimental journey, the imagination is our means of apprehending the syntax of things. At such moments in his fiction Sterne in his relations with his reader almost literally enacts the linguistic metaphor he had playfully applied to his hero: that 'heteroclite . . . creature in all his declensions' whose predications are formed 'according to the mood I am in, and the case – and I may add the gender too, of the person I am to govern.'

NOTES

1. See *The Providence of Wit: Aspects of Form in Augustan Literature and the Arts* (1974), esp. pp. 241–69.
2. *The Life and Opinions of Tristram Shandy, Gentleman*, ed. Ian Watt (Boston, Mass., 1965), 495.

3. *A Sentimental Journey through France and Italy. By Mr. Yorick*, ed. Gardner D. Stout, Jr (Berkeley and Los Angeles, 1967), 278. Subsequent citations of *A Sentimental Journey* will be to this edition. The first meaning of *syntax* given in Johnson's *Dictionary* is 'A system; a number of things joined together', which he illustrates by Glanville's phrase, 'the whole *syntax* of beings'.
4. For an excellent discussion of the relation of style and meaning in Sterne's masterpiece, see Ian Watt's essay, 'The Comic Syntax of *Tristram Shandy*', in H. Anderson and J. S. Shea (eds), *Studies in Criticism and Aesthetics, 1660–1800: Essays in Honor of Samuel Holt Monk* (Minneapolis, 1967), 315–31.
5. *Tristram Shandy*, ed. Watt, p. 20.
6. See Cummings's delightful poem beginning, 'since feeling is first/who pays any attention/to the syntax of things' from *is 5* (1926); in his *Complete Poems, Volume One 1913–1935* (1968), 290.
7. *Loc. cit.*
8. See Stout's excellent article in *English Literary History*, XXX (1963), 395–412, which served as the basis of Section IV of the Introduction to his edition.
9. See, for example, Rufus Putney, 'The evolution of *A Sentimental Journey*', *Philological Quarterly*, XIX (1940), 349–69, and 'Laurence Sterne, Apostle of Laughter', in *The Age of Johnson: Essays Presented to Chauncey Brewster Tinker* (New Haven, 1949), 159–70; and Ernest N. Dilworth, *The Unsentimental Journey of Laurence Sterne* (New York, 1948), ch. V. In a similar vein, though better balanced, is John M. Stedmond's discussion of 'The Faces of Yorick' in *The Comic Art of Laurence Sterne: Convention and Innovation in 'Tristram Shandy' and 'A Sentimental Journey'* (Toronto, 1967), ch. VI.
10. On this aspect of *Tristram Shandy*, see *The Providence of Wit*, esp. pp. 261–2.
11. David Hume, *A Treatise of Human Nature*, II.iii.3 ('Of the influencing motives of the will'); in L. A. Selby-Bigge (ed.) (1888), 413. Though Sterne of course regretted Hume's infidelity, he admired him personally; in *A Sentimental Journey* Yorick praises him as 'a man of an excellent heart' (p. 122 and nn. 28, 31). For an attempt to establish Hume's influence on Sterne, see the article by Francis Doherty, *Essays and Studies, 1969* (1969), pp. 71–87.
12. Watt, ed, 55.
13. At least one of his first readers found a sexual innuendo in Sterne's account of his relationship with the Marquesina. See Stout's edn, 344.
14. For an excellent discussion of this strategy in *Tristram Shandy*, see Robert Alter, '*Tristram Shandy* and the game of love', *American Scholar*, XXXVII (1968), 316–23. Alter, indeed, sees the *double entendre* as 'the basic rhetorical device – almost the narrative method – of *Tristram Shandy*' (p. 317).
15. As Stout's note on this passage makes clear, 'purse' was a common slang term for the female pudendum (p. 236n.). The passage also illustrates one of Sterne's favourite rhetorical methods for assuring that the 'innocent' and sexual references of an object are held together in the reader's mind. Yorick's gaze alternates between the purse and the *fille de chambre*'s lap, suggesting – but of course never explicitly stating – that he is himself aware of the sexual innuendo. Similarly, as Yorick and the *grisset*, whose husband has just left the shop, stand silently facing each other across the narrow counter, with the gloves between them, Sterne uses the same rhetorical alternation of reference to imply what is mutually on their minds:

    > The beautiful Grisset look'd sometimes at the gloves, then sideways to the window, then at the gloves – and then at me. I was not disposed to break silence – I follow'd her example: so I look'd at the gloves, then to the window, then at the gloves, and then at her – and so on alternately (p. 168)

    Again the *locus classicus* of the technique occurs in *Tristram Shandy*, as Maria appears to discern a certain ambivalence about Tristram's interest in her, a perception leading her companion to exclaim, 'What a *Beast* man is' (Watt, ed, 484):

> MARIA look'd wistfully for some time at me, and then at her goat – and then at me – and then at her goat again, and so on, alternately –
> – Well, Maria, said I softly – What resemblance do you find?

16. See 'Suggestions toward a genealogy of the "Man of Feeling"', *ELH: A Journal of Literary History*, I (1934), 205–30.
17. In this context consider how Yorick regards the snuff-box given him by the kindly and forgiving Franciscan: 'I guard this box, as I would the instrumental parts of my religion, to help my mind on to something better; in truth, I seldom go abroad without it; and oft and many a time have I called up by it the courteous spirit of its owner to regulate my own, in the justlings of the world' (p. 101).
18. Sterne's phrase for *A Sentimental Journey*. With Stout I am inclined to see in it something more than Sterne's facetious wish that his final work would redeem his literary and financial fortunes. (See Stout's edn, 18 and 40 n.43.)
19. Critics have recently demonstrated Defoe's affiliation with this tradition: see G. A. Starr, *Defoe and Spiritual Autobiography* (Princeton, 1965), and J. P. Hunter, *The Reluctant Pilgrim: Defoe's Emblematic Method and Quest for Form in 'Robinson Crusoe'* (Baltimore, 1966).

15

'The Dark and Implacable Genius of Superstition': an Aspect of Gibbon's Irony

MARTIN PRICE

[1]

Science with joy saw Superstition fly
Before the lustre of Religion's eye. . . .
The shades of night no more the soul involve,
She sheds her beam, and lo! the shades dissolve;
No jarring monks, to gloomy cell confined,
With mazy rules perplex the weary mind;
No shadowy forms entice the soul aside,
Secure she walks, Philosophy her guide.

These lines were written by a schoolboy of 14 at a time when Edward Gibbon was still completing his history. They were written far from London, and they hardly reveal the new sensibility that was soon to appear in the young Wordsworth's poetry. As the poet remarked of them much later, they were 'but a tame imitation of Pope's versification, and a little in his style.'[1] How tame an imitation they are we can readily see by comparing Pope's lines on Superstition in the third epistle of the *Essay on Man*. Pope has just presented a benign state of nature in which men look up with love to a benevolent patriarch and, through him, learn to see a benevolent God. But suddenly there is an eruption of tyranny, and it is accompanied by the growth of superstition:

Force first made Conquest, and that Conquest, Law;
Till Superstition taught the tyrant awe,
Then shar'd the Tyranny, then lent it aid,
And Gods of Conqu'rors, Slaves of Subjects made. . . .
Gods partial, changeful, passionate, unjust,
Whose attributes were Rage, Revenge, or Lust;
Such as the souls of cowards might conceive,
And, formed like tyrants, tyrants would believe.[2]

Pope draws together those themes that show Superstition to be (in Robert Burton's words) an 'irreligious religion'.[3] Pope makes Superstition the travesty of true religion, one which projects man's passions upon the heavens: 'Fear made her devils, and weak Hope her Gods.' Appropriately the God man creates in his image is one who demands blood sacrifices and can, in turn, be directed as a weapon against one's enemies. Burton remarks of politicians that 'they make religion mere policy, a cloak, a human invention'.[4] And Diderot was to describe the god that superstition creates: 'The God of hosts is a being capricious, cruel, fantastic, vindictive, and ferocious. He tries to lead people into crime in order to have the barbarous pleasure of punishing and exercising his vengeance upon them.'[5]

There is a danger in presenting superstition as the travesty of true religion, as Swift learned from the reception of *A Tale of a Tub*. Both forms of religion seem to arise from the same motives and needs; and those who miss their essential difference may find all religion reduced to passionate fantasy. Pope, as we see, ascribes the power of superstition to both fear and hope; but hope is weak, and the two forces serve only to create an excessively literal and anthropomorphic vision of punishment and reward: 'Here fix'd the dreadful, there the blest abode.' In his famous lines on the 'poor Indian' Pope provides a different, more innocent version of such literalness, in this case the product of an 'untutored mind':

> simple Nature to his hope has giv'n,
> Behind the cloud-topt hill, an humbler heav'n. . . .
> Where slaves once more their native land behold,
> No fiends torment, no Christians thirst for gold! . . .
> [He] thinks, admitted to that equal sky,
> His faithful dog shall bear him company.[6]

We must distinguish between a primitive mind and a corruptly passionate one. The Indian's mind is genuinely primitive and morally superior to those of the Christians who try to enslave him; but it is capable only of a 'corporeal imagination'. Such men as David Hartley and William Warburton stressed the need for man, in his childhood or in the childhood of culture, to think in 'sensible images', through which, at best and only to a degree, he could approach abstract ideas.

In the course of the eighteenth century there was steady growth of interest in comparative religion. It was used at times to humble the classical tradition by dealing, as Pierre Bayle did, with 'paganism as if it were popular superstition', or even by 'unveiling' Plato to reveal a doctrine 'as unpolish'd as the Religion of the most superstitious vulgar.'[7] At the same time there was a growth of new sympathy with the primitive or childlike or superstitious mind (the ideas are often used interchangeably) and with its capacity for imaginative life. It is here that one can see the convergence of primitivism; of the Gothic and the oriental; of folklore, balladry, and comparative myth. A poem like William Collins's ode, 'On the Popular Superstitions of the Highlands of Scotland', exalts this imaginative life but must recognize that it is a kind of awareness to which we can no longer ourselves return.[8] Except through an act of will. James Boswell can say with pride: 'For my own part, I have no difficulty to avow that cast of thinking, which by many modern pretenders to wisdom, is called superstitious.' But when Boswell wrote of Johnson, he was more circumspect: 'He was prone to superstition, but not to credulity. Though his imagination might incline him to a belief of the marvellous and the mysterious, his vigorous reason examined the evidence with jealousy.'[9] There is no more defiant acceptance of superstition than Edmund Burke's, in his rejection of French rationalism:

> We know, and what is better, we feel inwardly, that religion is the basis of civil society, and the source of all good and of all comfort. In England we are so convinced of this, that there is no rust of superstition, with which the accumulated absurdity of the human mind might have crusted it over with in the course of ages, that ninety-nine in a hundred of the people of England would not prefer to impiety.

Burke accepts superstition as the necessary cost of acknowledging and honouring those 'untutored' feelings which underlie and animate our beliefs and our institutions:

> in this enlightened age, I am bold enough to confess, that we are generally men of untaught feelings, that instead of casting away all our old prejudices, we cherish them because they have lasted, and the more generally they have prevailed, the more we cherish them.[10]

Gibbon wrote of Burke's *Reflections* in a letter:

> I admire his eloquence, I approve his politics, I adore his chivalry, and I can even forgive his superstition. The primitive Church, which I have treated with some freedom, was itself, at that time, an innovation, and *I* was attached to the old Pagan establishment.

When he repeated the first sentence in his memoirs, Gibbon altered the final clause to, 'I can almost excuse his reverence for Church establishments.' And then he added: 'I have sometimes thought of writing a dialogue of the dead, in which Lucian, Erasmus, and Voltaire should mutually acknowledge the danger of exposing an *old* superstition to the blind and fanatic multitude.'[11]

For a moment, at least, we see Gibbon and Burke in agreement on the dignifying, if not the sanctifying, power of time. But both men also recognize, in different degree and with different consequences, the arbitrary nature of the 'accumulated absurdity of the human mind'. David Hume plays with this arbitrariness that time builds into our institutions, like the cluster of buildings that grow into a town or the changes of style through which a cathedral testifies to the years of its building. There may be, Hume writes, no adequate reason in the object itself 'for that affection or antipathy, veneration or horror, which have so mighty an influence over a considerable part of mankind.' These feelings grow out of the meanings that an object supports or the structures of meaning into which, in one aspect or another, it is assumed. We live by conventions; we build them in speech acts that make commitments for us, assert our meanings, and provide the ground for those traditions that grow, through accretion or accumulation, upon them. It takes no great effort of detachment to recognize

> that all regards to right and property, seem entirely without foundation, as much as the grossest and most vulgar superstition. Were the interests of society nowise concerned, it is as unintelligible, why another's articulating certain sounds implying consent, should change the nature of my actions . . . as why the reciting of a liturgy by a priest, in a certain habit and posture, should dedicate a heap of brick and timber, and render it, thenceforth and for ever, sacred.[12]

The interests of society (shall we call them 'forms of life'?) generate meanings, and these meanings are applied to sounds and gestures, rather than intrinsic to them. What reason sees as arbitrary and historical (rather than logical and necessary), the imagination gratefully builds into doctrine, tradition, myth. The age was acutely aware of the arbitrariness of historical change, of the lack of 'sufficient reason' in the life of every Candide, of the power of the mind to build vast *carceri* in which we find ourselves lost. Sceptical intelligence used analysis and reduction, a demystifying of terms and institutions, by which the mind might be liberated from its own spectres. The poetic sensibility, in turn, was impressed by the power of our feelings to make sensations coalesce into new unity and vision. It was proud of the intensity which it could attain in seemingly demonic fantasies (cultivated, for example, by William Beckford or the Gothic novelists) or in other forms of what the rational mind might consider pathological. For the poets of sensibility, a power that had been distrusted, repressed, and twisted into perverse forms by reason, now sought the freedom of its own self-generated, organic forms.

We can measure the conflict between scepticism and sensibility by seeing how 'vigorous reason' might, as Boswell put it, examine the evidence 'with jealousy'. Gibbon wrote in a letter to Richard Hurd:

> May I not assume as a principle equally consonant to experience, to reason, and even to true religion, 'that we ought not to admit any thing as the immediate work of God, which can possibly be the work of man; and that whatever is said to deviate from the ordinary course of nature, should be ascribed to accident, to fraud, or to fiction; till we are fully satisfied, that it lies beyond the reach of those causes?' If we cast aside this buckler, the blind fury of superstition, from every age of the world, and from every corner of the globe, will invade us naked and unarmed.[13]

Beside this we can place Hume's account of the self-enslavement of the superstitious man:

> He considers not, that the most genuine way of serving the divinity is by promoting the happiness of his creatures. He still looks out for some more immediate service of the Supreme Being, in order to allay these terrors, with which he is haunted. Any practice . . . which either serves to no purpose in life, or appears the strongest violence to his natural inclinations; that practice he will the more readily embrace on account of those very circumstances, which should make him absolutely reject it. It seems the more purely religious, because it proceeds from no mixture of any other motive or consideration. . . . Hence the greatest crimes have been found, in many instances, compatible with a superstitious piety and devotion

This is not, after all, so very far from a central theme in Dostoevsky, and Hume goes on to describe the kind of God we can create: 'When we abandon ourselves to the natural, undisciplined suggestions of our timid and anxious hearts, every kind of barbarity is ascribed to the Supreme Being, from the terrors with which we are agitated; and every kind of caprice, from the methods we embrace in order to appease him.'[14]

In writers like Swift and Gibbon there survives all of the subtle analysis of enthusiasm and religious perversity that arose from the divisiveness of the Reformation and especially from the behaviour of millenarian sects and other forms of radical Protestantism. What they reveal, too, with some horror and some fascination is the power of imagination and feeling to create a fictitious world that seems at times the only reality we can accept. What troubles the rational sceptic most in all of this is the threat of antinomianism: godliness becomes precisely that which cannot be made congruent with 'mere' goodness. Intensity is of far more value than stability or integrity; its grandeur comes of the very fact that it is absurd, gratuitous, and therefore wholly free. We are coming close now to what Gibbon calls 'the dark and implacable genius of superstition'. But I should like to approach it by what may seem digression and may prove useful indirection.

[2]

Gibbon's history depends upon an acute sense of mixed motives. Men may be actuated at once by ambition and greed, by greed and patriotism, by patriotism and vanity. The combinations are innumerable, and therefore each possible combination contains within itself consequences so various that they are unpredictable. Retrospectively, one may be able, as in Pope's theory of the ruling passion, to detect some deeper force that shows consistency beneath the varied surface in which it is expressed.[15] To uncover or at least to intimate the presence of that deeper structure is a task to which irony is supremely adapted. It can make sharp discriminations in the quality of the various motives at work, and it can suggest the presence of those motives that remain unacknowledged, or even unrecognized, by the actor.

And can we speak of actors with full confidence? We may want to distinguish, as some moral philosophers have, between actions and events.[16] In the language we use for actions, a major element of their explanation is the reasons for which people act. Action then becomes 'intended' behaviour, which is distinctively human and which involves more or less rational decision based upon consciously entertained principles or reasons. An event, in turn, is explained by causes, which require no mediating consciousness; an event may be altogether explained by material forces or 'mechanical operation' (as in Swift's satire) or at most by passions, drives, and response to stimulation. Events may be 'blind' in the absence of estimation of consequences or concern for principle or consistency.

Such a dichotomy of action and event is a separation of two kinds of language that one can apply to the same situation. But we are almost inevitably compelled to think of those cases where behaviour does not clearly belong in one category or the other. How, for example, shall we treat the role of self-deception or rationalization, where conscious deliberation may become the instrument or disguise of a compelling passion? And how shall we classify those instances of 'over-determined' behaviour which mark the confluence of quite distinct forces, forces of both principle and passion? The sense of mixed motives blurs the sharpness of outline and causes us at the very least to waver or even oscillate between two kinds of language and explanation as we do between the colours of an iridescent fabric.

In the following passages Gibbon opposes wealth and liberty, but in ways which resist any nice formulation:

> Money, in a word, is the most universal incitement, iron, the most powerful instrument, of human industry; and it is very difficult to conceive by what means a people, neither actuated by the one nor seconded by the other, could emerge from the grossest barbarism...

> A warlike nation like the Germans, without either cities, letters, arts, or money, found some compensation for this savage state in the enjoyment of liberty. Their poverty secured their freedom, since our desires and our possessions are the strongest fetters of despotism.[17]

In such an opposition, one begins to wonder whether the 'liberty' that was available only at the price of the 'grossest barbarism' can mean what we commonly use 'liberty' to mean. The difficulties become clearer as we consider a passage that comes between the two I have just cited. Here the nature of 'liberty' seems to be the gratification of rather elementary instincts:

> If we contemplate a savage nation in any part of the globe, a supine indolence and carelessness of futurity will be found to constitute their general character. In a civilized state, every faculty of man is expanded and exercised; and the great chain of mutual dependence connects and embraces the several members of society.... And yet, by a wonderful diversity of Nature... the same barbarians are by turns the most indolent and the most restless of mankind. They delight in sloth, they detest tranquillity. The languid soul, oppressed with its own weight, anxiously required some new and powerful sensation; and war and danger were the only amusements adequate to its fierce temper. The sound that summoned the German to arms was grateful to his ear. It roused him from his uncomfortable lethargy, gave him an active pursuit, and, by strong exercise of the body, and violent emotions of the mind, restored him to a more lively sense of his existence.[18]

This passage catches the play of mixed motives. It takes for granted the 'unbounded hopes of plunder and conquest' that attend on war, adding to these motives a fullness of self-realization such as may be achieved in civilized society by less drastic and more subtle practices. If we still suffer a 'restlessness' such as these Germans did, it seems less rudimentary and instinctive in most cases, although ethologists would no doubt see it otherwise. Gibbon's irony can move back and forth, stressing the way in which 'mutual dependence' becomes despotism, the way in which wealth breeds anxiety and poverty lethargy, the way in which a term like 'liberty' can describe actions either bestial or refined.

One can see a typical readiness for irony, clearly hinted but not quite precipitated, in the opening pages of Gibbon's work:

> The gentle but powerful influence of laws and manners had gradually cemented the union of the provinces. Their peaceful inhabitants enjoyed and abused the advantages of wealth and luxury. The image of a free

> constitution was preserved with decent reverence: the Roman senate appeared to possess the sovereign authority, and devolved on the emperor all the executive powers of government.[19]

One could italicize such terms as 'image' or 'appeared', and the bald conjunction of 'enjoyed and abused' is offered without the acknowledgment of incongruity that a 'but' or an 'or' might provide. The word 'advantages' seems about to topple, and 'luxury' tends to draw it further toward the edge. And what shall we say of 'decent reverence', at once so literally apt and yet tellingly bland? Gibbon can, at moments, prepare more openly for such incongruity:

> The various tribes of Britons possessed valour without conduct, and the love of freedom without the spirit of union. They took up arms with savage fierceness; they laid them down, or turned them against each other, with wild inconstancy; and while they fought singly, they were successively subdued.[20]

This passage shows the incongruity brought fully to the surface. There may be a slight surprise at the close, as 'fought singly' suggests, through custom, the heroism of 'single combat', only to give way once more to the virtually mechanical process through which the Britons lost the very freedom they prize. Gibbon usually keeps such ironic possibilities in solution, uninsistent but always ready to crystallize into a sudden clarity that throws much that has preceded into a new pattern. And in doing so he remains true to the idea of mixed motives, to that impurity of intention that history reveals and that fanaticism seeks to remove.

The latent, or ulterior, implications that we find in words are as much present in actions or events themselves. We are familiar enough with that dramatic irony which allows us to look beyond the range of a character's vision and to see consequences of his present conduct that he can scarcely imagine. Gibbon, like all historians, is fascinated by the larger ironies of history; and at times he must protect them from the simplification he finds, for example, in Procopius:

> Ambiguous actions are imputed to the worst motives: error is confounded with guilt, accident with design, and laws with abuses; the partial injustice of a moment is dexterously applied as the general maxim of a reign of thirty-two years.[21]

Again, we find Gibbon warning against the short-sighted passion for reform:

> The experience of an abuse from which our own age and country are not perfectly exempt may sometimes provoke a generous indignation, and extort the hasty wish of exchanging our elaborate jurisprudence for the simple and summary decrees of a Turkish cadhi. Our calmer reflection will suggest that such forms and delays are necessary to guard the person and property of the citizen; that the discretion of the judge is the first engine of tyranny; and that the laws of a free people should foresee and determine every question that may probably arise in the exercise of power and the transactions of industry.

But, having evoked by his cool deliberation the conduct of a free people and raised the possibility (not easily attained) of a clear and free choice, Gibbon closes this chapter on Roman jurisprudence with a mordant sentence that follows immediately upon the last quotation: 'But the government of Justinian united the evils of liberty and servitude, and the Romans were oppressed at the same time by the multiplicity of their laws and the arbitrary will of their master.'[22]

This pattern of reversal, of an outcome altogether different from what is intended or expected, is an essential part of Gibbon's history. One can see the reversal accomplished by either cunning or accident, by a concealed design or a neglect of implicit dangers. The third chapter of Gibbon's history is a magnificent account of the betrayal of republican freedom and independence by the craft of Augustus. And yet Augustus could not have succeeded without the obtuse or fearful complicity of the senate. Gibbon states the issue at the outset: 'unless public liberty is protected by intrepid and vigilant guardians', the power of a monarchy will soon 'degenerate into despotism'. There is only one adequate balance to set against an 'aspiring prince': a 'martial nobility and stubborn commons, possessed of arms, tenacious of property, and collected into constitutional assemblies.'[23] This is the 'mixed state' drawn from Polybius, celebrated by Restoration political writers and by Augustans after them. Pope writes of 'Th'according music of a well-mix'd state', and Swift, having based his first published tract on the doctrine, illustrates it in the polity of Brobdingnag.[24] Gibbon presents the saddening complicity of what might have been countervailing forces: the provinces sigh for a single ruler to control the 'petty tyrants' who govern abroad; the people of Rome take a 'secret pleasure' in the 'humiliation of the aristocracy' and ask only bread and circuses for themselves; and aristocrats, Epicurean in their pursuit of tranquil ease, prefer 'the pleasing dream' to 'the memory of their old tumultuous freedom'.[25] Augustus performs the comedy of preserving names and forms to cover the radical shift of power. 'He solemnly restored the senate and people to all their ancient rights'; but, while he 'restored the dignity, he destroyed the independence, of the senate.' Just as Swift insisted upon the readiness of the Irish to become slaves of English power rather than try to regain their 'old tumultuous freedom', so Gibbon shows the 'propensity of the Romans to servitude'. The oath of loyalty once required only of the soldier is now, voluntarily taken by the magistrates, the senators and the equestrian order, till the homage of flattery was insensibly converted into an annual and solemn protest of fidelity.'[26]

Augustus's method of introducing tyranny is to hollow out old institutions even as their traditional names are preserved and honoured. The people are allowed to engage in elections and to exhibit 'all the inconveniences of a wild democracy', while in fact Augustus creates 'an absolute monarchy disguised by the forms of a commonwealth.' Augustus chose this method of subversion when he was led by danger at the age of 19 to 'assume the mask of hypocrisy, which he never afterwards laid aside.' Cool regard for self-interest made Augustus assume virtues, and even vices, that were 'artificial'. He could, with the same absence of feeling, condemn Cicero or pardon Cinna; and he recognized astutely that the 'senate and people would submit to slavery, provided they were respectfully assured that they still enjoyed their ancient freedom.' Under successors less dexterous, the illusion could not be sustained; but by then 'the dream of liberty was at an end; and the senate awoke to all the horrors of inevitable servitude.'[27]

Gibbon evokes the mild and benevolent despotism of Trajan, Hadrian, and the Antonines, who 'delighted in the image of liberty' and regarded themselves less as having absolute power than as 'the accountable ministers of the law'. They 'deserved the honour of restoring the public,' Gibbon concludes, 'had the Romans of their days been capable of enjoying a rational freedom.' For little of the desire and exercise of freedom has survived the reign of such 'monsters' as Tiberius, Domitian, and Nero. Those rulers seemed to take 'secret pleasure in rendering the senate their accomplice as well as their victim'. The debasement of the senate once attained, 'the last of the Romans were condemned for imaginary crimes and real virtues'. At the close Gibbon presents the splendid range of empire Augustus founded as one vast prison. The 'slave of imperial despotism' had no refuge from imperial power:

> To resist was fatal, and it was impossible to fly. On every side he was encompassed with a vast extent of sea and land, which he could never hope to traverse without being discovered, seized, and restored to his irritated master. Beyond the frontiers, his anxious view could discover nothing, except the ocean, inhospitable deserts, hostile tribes of barbarians, of fierce manners and unknown language, or dependent kings, who would gladly purchase the emperor's protection by the sacrifice of an obnoxious fugitive. 'Wherever you are,' said Cicero to the exiled Marcellus, 'remember that, you are equally within the power of the conqueror.'[28]

[3]

Augustus brought about the transformation of Roman government through craft and deception; he led Rome into becoming great without the inhibiting need to remain good. He was what Bernard Mandeville, in *The Fable of the Bees*, called an 'artful manager' – realistic, not confused or divided in his goal. But one of the teasing questions raised in Mandeville's treatment is whether this change may not come about by chance and drift rather than through management. Gibbon, too, is interested in those radical changes that no one clearly intended to bring about, those changes that may be described as accidental unless one sees beneath the surface of contingency the natural law by which institutions evolve. In chapter XXVIII Gibbon deals with the 'ruin of Paganism', a 'singular event in the history of the human mind', he observes, perhaps the only example of the total extirpation of an 'ancient and popular superstition'. So singular an event that it never quite happens; it is not the 'total extirpation' that Christians mean or believe it to be.[29] By the close of the chapter it is clear that the Christians have 'imitated the profane model which they were impatient to destroy'. Christianity, once it had gained the support of Constantine, conquered the Roman empire in less than a century; but it did so at a cost: 'the victors themselves were insensibly subdued by the arts of their vanquished rivals.'[30]

Gibbon traces this process in a way that catches at once both the intolerance and the self-indulgence of the Christian cause. Its adherents are at once tyrants and slaves, both zealous and credulous; adherents first of all to the 'same uniform original spirit of superstition' they pride themselves in destroying. Gibbon (as in his letter about Burke) offers a benign image of Paganism as a tolerant established church and state religion, whose officers are at once priest and soldier, pontiff and statesman. These priests, capable of winning worldly success, know that it may be won with dignity; they are free of that distrust of the self in its worldly career from which ascetic Christians suffer. It is not the first of the Christian emperors but the first of them to be intolerant who dissolves 'the ancient fabric ... which was supported by the opinions and habits of eleven hundred years.' I have removed the three words, 'of Roman superstition', in order to stress how much this disestablishment, of a faith maintained in ancient ritual and with the tolerance that comes of security, resembles in large measure the plight of the Catholic Church in the world of the Reformation, and particularly in England. Even Gratian spares the desecration of churches that was to mark the English Reformation in its first century and a half. More than 400 temples 'or chapels', Gibbon tells us, 'still remained to satisfy the devotion of the people of Rome' – and then he adds with an ironic glance at a pharisaical nicety like Malvolio's – 'in every quarter of Rome the delicacy of the Christians was offended by the fumes of idolatrous sacrifice.' It is worthwhile in this connection to recall that Johnson in his dictionary defined 'superstition' as 'over-nicety, exactness too scrupulous'.[31]

Gibbon enjoys showing the Christian apologists falling into the arguments that they had lately, out of power, protested and denounced. Paganism found an eloquent champion in Symmachus, a wealthy senator who filled both sacred and secular office. Symmachus deplored the confiscation of church revenues. He feared that the ceremonies of the Pagans would lose 'their force and energy, if they were no longer celebrated at the expense as well as in the name of the republic'. He advanced the claims of a tolerant scepticism (like the fideism that the Catholics of the seventeenth century were to plead). The 'great and incomprehensible secret of the universe' eludes our inquiry. 'Where reason cannot instruct custom may be permitted to guide; and every nation seems to consult the dictates of prudence, by a faithful attachment to those rites and opinions which have received the sanction of ages.' One may be reminded of the appeal of the Catholic Church to oral tradition, and one recalls as well Swift's recognition, in *A Tale of a Tub*, that many religious forms can no longer be removed, whatever their origin, without harm being done to the fabric itself.

There is more: Symmachus has Rome plead her cause with the voice of a venerable matron: 'This religion has reduced the world under my laws. These rites have repelled Hannibal from the city, and the Gauls from the Capitol.' To such appeals Ambrose, the bishop of Milan, replies in the language of a philosopher. Why, he asks 'with some contempt', should it be thought necessary 'to introduce an imaginary and invisible power as the cause of those victories, which were sufficiently explained by the valour and discipline of the legions.' Ambrose is content with secondary causes, just as Gibbon has been in his fifteenth chapter:

> as the wisdom of Providence frequently condescends to use the passions of the heart, and the general circumstances of mankind, as instruments to execute its purpose, we may still be permitted, though with becoming submission, to ask, not indeed what were first, but what were the secondary causes of the rapid growth of the Christian church.

Ambrose, moreover, argues like a Modern in the famous quarrel with the Ancients: 'He justly derides the absurd reverence for antiquity, which could only tend to discourage the improvements of art and to replunge the human race into their original barbarism.'[32]

Finally Gibbon presents the senate's surrender to power as it deliberates on Theodosius's proposal that Christianity become an established religion. The vote is left to the senate only after the emperor has made his own views clear, and the senate's compliance is couched in terms that can remind one of Swift's ironic discussion of a parliamentary abolition of Christianity. 'Jupiter was condemned and degraded by the sense of a very large majority'; he became an 'abdicated deity'. So hasty a conversion of the senate, in which the Christians were a minority, must, Gibbon says, 'be attributed either to supernatural or to sordid motives.' We have returned to the distinction between primary and secondary causes, that is, between two forms of power. And Gibbon allows no doubts to persist. The 'reluctant proselytes' of the senate would wish to 'throw aside the mask of odious dissimulation'; but they are inextricably caught in the service of the new religion once they have yielded 'to the authority of the emperor, to the fashion of the times, and to the entreaties of their wife and children' (the last 'instigated and governed' by the Christian clergy). It is precisely this joyless yielding that Gibbon wants us to recognize through the fulsome words of Prudentius: 'The luminaries of the world, the venerable assembly of Catos ... were impatient to ... cast off the skin of the old serpent – to assume the snowy robes of baptismal innocence'. The 'fancy of a Prudentius', Gibbon observes, 'is warmed and elevated by victory.' In the process, somewhat as the abbeys were to be in Tudor England and church monuments in the Commonwealth, 'the splendour of the Capitol was defaced, and the solitary temples were abandoned to ruin and contempt' – a fate, Gibbon notes, in which St Jerome 'exults'.[33]

The ferocity of the destruction begins to reveal a superstition as great as any that might have been obliterated. When the bishop Marcellus finds tremendous difficulty in levelling a massive temple, he attributes its resistance 'under the allegory of a black daemon, who retarded, though he could not defeat' the Christian engineers. Marcellus becomes a more dangerous Don Quixote as he takes 'the field in person against the powers of darkness' and successively attacks not windmills but 'the villages and country temples of the diocese'. And less like Quixote perhaps than Hudibras, the lame Marcellus places himself prudently 'at a convenient distance', beyond the darts of the enemy, only to be 'surprised and slain by a body of exasperated rustics'.

Throughout the empire one or another 'army of fanatics, without authority and without discipline', leaves behind terrible marks of its presence.[34] The destruction seems almost to arise from a fear of the dark forces which may inhabit old images or sanctuaries. Both the pagan adherent, whose faith hangs on the survival of the image (for example, the gigantic statue of Serapis in Alexandria) and the enemies, whose faith is justified in the conquest of those magical and demonic forces, seem involved in a common superstition, whether of reverence or fear. The reverence for a power that is not altogether invisible, that is thought to be tested as the guardian or the destroyer of a shrine, becomes a danger of Christianity as well as of Paganism so long as it too becomes a form of superstitious worship. And, once the obvious sacrifices or divinations from entrails are denied the pagans, what remains to suffer abolition is not very different from the forms of Christian ritual: 'luminaries, garlands, frankincense, and libations of wine.'[35] It is one thing to win nominal adherence to Christianity, a kind of 'occasional conformity' such as the Church of England exacted from dissenters who wished to hold secular office.[36] It is another to win converts from one form of superstition to another, from the less potent magic to the one that triumphs.

> The ignorant vulgar, whose minds are still agitated by the blind hopes and terrors of superstition, will soon be persuaded by their superiors to direct their vow to the reigning deities of the age; and will insensibly imbibe an ardent zeal for the support and propagation of the new doctrine, which spiritual hunger at first compelled them to accept.[37]

What happens to the worship in which such converts engage? Gibbon cites the horror of a pagan spectator, Eunapius, who described a 'new worship, which, in the place of those deities who are conceived by the understanding, has substituted the meanest and most contemptible slaves'. It collects, 'salted and pickled', the bodies of martyrs and worships them; their tombs are 'consecrated as the objects of veneration of the people.' The corporeal imagination of the superstitious requires tangible relics; by the age of Ambrose and Jerome, 'something was still deemed wanting to the sanctity of a church unless it possessed some relics of the saints and martyrs.' Fictions were devised to give the relics their provenance. Imaginary heroes filled out the ranks of the martyrs. The regard for historical truth and the laws of evidence gave way before the 'temptations of fraud and credulity'. Increasingly, extravagant powers of magic and miracle were attributed to the relics, and Gibbon plays with the dazzling arithmetic of their efficacy. Augustine, selecting only those cases certified by witnesses, counted over 70 miracles (three of them resurrection from the dead) in his own African diocese within two years. The very concept of 'miracle' became threatened: 'a miracle, in that age of superstition and credulity, lost its name and its merit, since it could scarcely be considered as a deviation from the ordinary and established laws of nature.'[38]

Finally, Gibbon explores the pattern of superstition as it adapts its faith to the winning of temporal power. The quality of its imagination becomes apparent in the conception of those saints whose presence was enjoyed by the devout. They went to work at once, wasting none of their immortal existence in 'silent and inglorious sleep'. They devoted their attention to the places where their own mortal lives had been spent or where their relics now rested. They responded warmly to the 'liberality of their votaries' and hurled 'bolts of punishment' against those who violated their shrines or doubted the efficacy of their relics. It is no great task for Gibbon to show the saints engaged in the somewhat shabby role of intercession that might, on earth, be attributed to bribed and flattered courtiers. The point, of course, is that a faith which has claimed earthly power as its right and even as its justification risks all the crass superstitions by which power is appeased:

> The imagination, which had been raised by a painful effort to the contemplation and worship of the universal Cause, eagerly embraced such inferior objects of adoration as were more proportioned to its gross conceptions and imperfect faculties. The sublime and simple theology of the primitive Christians was gradually corrupted . . . by the introduction of a popular mythology which tended to restore the reign of polytheism.[39]

[4]

The full power of superstition emerges in Chapter XXXVII, where Gibbon presents the rise of monasticism. The ascetic Christians 'obeyed and abused the rigid precepts of the Gospel.' They were 'inspired by the savage enthusiasm which represents man as a criminal, and God as a tyrant.' It was in Egypt, 'the fruitful parent of superstition', that monasticism arose, after the examples of Antony and Pachomius. For Gibbon, as for Shaftesbury earlier, the humiliation of the self in the name of Christian devotion is a travesty of true religion. It posits a deity who will be appeased or gratified by exploits of self-torture and of endurance in pain – a tyrant upon whom the slave projects his own self-mistrust or self-hatred.

Like all visible excesses of zeal, the monks' commanded attention: 'at first, horror and contempt, and, at length, applause and zealous imitation.'[40] Gibbon traces a pattern of (perhaps hysterical) contagion:

> Inflamed by the example of Antony, a Syrian youth, whose name was Hilarion, fixed his dreary abode on a sandy beach between the sea and a morass about seven miles from Gaza. The austere penance, in which he persisted forty-eight years, diffused a similar enthusiasm; and the holy man was followed by a train of two or three thousand anchorets, whenever he visited the innumerable monasteries of Palestine.

The growth of monasticism is as rapid and as universal as the rise of Christianity itself – a more intense and rigid doctrine within the larger faith, almost a reformed and more enthusiastic faith within the larger frame of an established church. Gibbon traces its movement to Ethiopia, to Ireland, to the remote Hebridean island of Iona. 'These unhappy exiles from social life were impelled by the dark and implacable genius of superstition.'[41]

The last phrase may call to mind for others besides myself the stern figure of Mrs Clennam in Dickens's *Little Dorrit*:

> she still abided by her old impiety – still reversed the order of Creation, and breathed her own breath into a clay image of her Creator. Verily, verily, travellers have seen many monstrous idols in many countries: but no human eyes have ever seen more daring, gross, and shocking images of the Divine nature than we creatures of the dust make in our own likenesses, of our own bad passions.

As Gibbon observes, no earthly tyrant could impose so miserable a life upon his people as does this 'voluntary martyrdom'. Nor does such suffering necessarily purify or elevate the sufferer; instead it may destroy 'the sensibility both of the mind and body':

> A cruel, unfeeling temper has distinguished the monks of every age and country; their stern indifference, which is seldom mollified by personal friendship, is inflamed by religious hatred, and the merciless zeal has strenuously administered the holy office of the Inquisition.[42]

This is not the place to consider the justness of Gibbon's treatment of monasticism. What matters here is the way in which it seems to extend and intensify Gibbon's idea of superstition. The senate surrendered its burden of freedom with an alacrity that made Augustus's comedy seem less a betrayal than a pretext for self-betrayal. The conquest of Paganism exacted of the Christians a degree of superstition that they seemed all too ready to assume. Gibbon once noted, 'Images opposed whilst the Pagans subsisted, received as soon as they were extinct.' And he generalized this cultivation of images into a universal religious practice: 'Images, ornaments, garlands, lights, odours, music affect the Sense of all Men – are found in the worship of Indians, Chinese, Americans &c.' He also raises the issue for Christianity: 'The Popish worship like the Pagan? Certainly. Huetius's ode will serve for either Mary or Diana.'[43] And he attributes this resemblance to a common need rather than to imitation or historical influence. In the conquest of Paganism, moreover, the Christians saw the struggle as 'the holy war which they had undertaken against the empire of the daemons.' The very zeal which throve on such a conflict became a desire to achieve or retain purity. 'Such was the anxious diligence which was required to guard the chastity of the Gospel from the infectious breath of idolatry.'[44] But, as we have seen, the anxious diligence breeds monsters; the search for purity becomes a collapse into superstition.

In monasticism, man's quarrel with his nature was made the centre of religious devotion. The faculties of mind, which might for a classical philosopher seem man's highest and most distinctive gift, were now distrusted and abused. Even as 'the vanity of spiritual perfection' tempted man, the forms it took might be ludicrously petty efforts to flout his humanity; 'every sensation that is offensive to man', Gibbon writes of the anchorets, 'was thought acceptable to God.' There was the constantly receding goal of purity: if all pleasures were thought guilty, and resisted or punished, there still remained the pleasures of pride, arrogance, and the love of spiritual power over others. 'A blind submission to the commands of the abbot, however absurd, or even criminal, they might seem, was the ruling principle, the first virtue of the Egyptian monks.' A superstitious over-preciseness of ritual is part of the pattern: if the monks deny themselves meats, they may still make a 'singular distinction' and admit fowl, 'as if birds, whether wild or domestic, had been less profane than the grosser animals of the field.' Visits to a monk from kindred might be denied, 'and it was deemed highly meritorious, if he afflicted a tender sister, or an aged parent, by the obstinate refusal of a word or a look.' Some cannot sustain these ostentatious shows of piety, and the failure to attain purity is hardly surprising. 'Their natural descent, from such painful and dangerous virtue, will not, perhaps excite much grief or indignation in the mind of a philosopher.'[45]

Monasticism becomes a supreme instance of the fear and surrender of freedom: 'While they considered each natural impulse as an unpardonable sin, they perpetually trembled on the edge of a flaming and bottomless abyss.' The self-induced terrors foster in turn the superstitious bondage to triviality of observance and the loss of humanity. It is, finally, that humanity by which Gibbon judges superstition:

> These extravagant tales, which display the fiction, without the genius, of poetry, have seriously affected the reason, the faith, and the morals of the Christians. Their credulity debased and vitiated the faculties of the mind: they corrupted the evidence of history; and superstition gradually extinguished the hostile light of philosophy and science.[46]

Christianity is clearly not alone in this tendency. Elsewhere Gibbon speaks of the decline of the independence of thought in the empire: the systems of the Greek philosophers, 'transmitted with blind deference from one generation of disciples to another, precluded every generous attempt to exercise the powers, or enlarge the limits of the human mind.'[47] The faculties of the mind must be exercised to remain strong, and for their exercise they require the stubborn resistance of a world outside. That world may seem intractable to the weak mind and may send it in search of a more comfortable realm of its own making. This retreat into vision, especially with the pressure of anxiety upon it, may lead to the absorbing rituals of superstition.

The alternative Gibbon keeps before us throughout the history is that confident address of the mind to a reality that it cannot wish away and yet may hope, within limits, to change.

NOTES

1. 'Lines Written as a School Exercise at Hawkshead', *The Poetical Works of William Wordsworth*, ed. E. de Selincourt (1940), I, 259, 366.
2. Alexander Pope, *An Essay on Man*, ed. Maynard Mack (1950), Epistle III, ll. 245–8, 257–68.
3. Robert Burton, *The Anatomy of Melancholy*, ed. Holbrook Jackson (1932), III, 353.
4. Burton, *Anatomy*, III, 328.
5. Cited from a letter to Sophie Volland, in Frank Manuel, *The Eighteenth Century Confronts the Gods* (Cambridge, Mass., 1959), 147. I am indebted throughout the first section of the paper to Manuel's excellent book.
6. Pope, *Essay on Man*, Epistle I, ll. 99–112.
7. Manuel, *op. cit.*, 30, citing Matthieu Souverain from an English translation, *Plato Unveiled* (1700).
8. On the theme of the supernatural, see Patricia M. Spacks, *The Insistence of Horror* (Cambridge, Mass., 1962), esp. pp. 73–6, where she discusses Mark Akenside as well as Collins.
9. *Boswell's Life of Johnson*, ed. G. B. Hill and L. F. Powell (1934–64), IV, 276, 426. Boswell speaks of his superstition as 'being not of the gloomy but the grand species' and therefore 'an enjoyment' (in a letter to Temple, 18 March 1775). But David Hume observes that 'men are much more often thrown on their knees by the melancholy than by the agreeable passions' (*The Philosophical Works of David Hume*, ed. T. H. Green and T. H. Grose, 1882, IV, 318–19).
10. Edmund Burke, *Reflections on the Revolution in France*, ed. Conor Cruise O'Brien (1969), 187, 183. Burke turns the Senecan distinction (*religio deum colit, superstitio destruit*) to his own purposes: if a prudent man were obliged to make a choice among 'errors and excesses of enthusiasm', he would think 'the superstition which builds, to be more worth than that which destroys. . . . Such, I think, is very nearly the state of the question between the ancient founders of monkish superstition, and the superstition of the pretended philosophers of the hour' (*Reflections*, 269–70).
11. To Lord Sheffield, 5 February 1791: *The Letters of Edward Gibbon*, ed. J. E. Norton (1956), III, 216; *The Autobiographies of Edward Gibbon*, ed. John Murray (1896), 342n.
12. Hume, *Philosophical Works*, ed. Green and Grose, IV, 191–93.
13. Gibbon, *Letters*, ed. Norton, I, 328–9.
14. Hume, 'The Natural History of Religion', *Philosophical Works*, ed. Green and Grose, IV, 359–60.
15. On Pope's ruling passion, see *The English Essays of Edward Gibbon*, ed. Patricia B. Craddock (1972), 90–1. In his 'Hints' Gibbon considers the ruling passion 'very rare'. Most passions he sees as confined to particular 'times, places, persons, circumstances'. Ambition is 'generally mixed with other passions, often subservient to them – when pure as in Caesar or Richelieu must succeed or perish – Avarice perhaps the only permanent ruling passion.'
16. For a synoptic treatment, with references to recent discussions, see W. D. Hudson, *Modern Moral Philosophy* (1970), 350–65.
17. Edward Gibbon, *The History of the Decline and Fall of the Roman Empire*, ed. J. B. Bury (1909–14), I, 238, 241. (Hereafter cited as Gibbon, *Decline and Fall*.)

18. *Ibid.*, I, 238–9.
19. *Ibid.*, I, 1.
20. *Ibid.*, I, 4.
21. *Ibid.*, I, 252.
22. *Ibid.*, IV, 542.
23. *Ibid.*, I, 65.
24. Zera S. Fink, *The Classical Republicans* (Evanston, Ill., 1945; Jonathan Swift, *A Discourse of the Contests and Dissentions* . . . , ed. Frank H. Ellis (1967); Pope, *Essay on Man*, Epistle III, l. 294; Gibbon, *Decline and Fall*, IV, 172–3.
25. *Ibid.*, I, 66.
26. *Ibid.*, I, 67–8, 71.
27. *Ibid.*, *I*, 78–9.
28. *Ibid.*, I, 86–9, 90.
29. *Ibid.*, III, 198.
30. *Ibid.*, III, 226–7.
31. *Ibid.*, III, 200–1. Cf. 'The Christian, who with pious horror avoided the abomination of the circus or the theatre, found himself encompassed with infernal snares in every convivial entertainment, as often as his friends, invoking the hospitable deities, poured out libations to each other's happiness' (II, 18).
32. Gibbon, *Decline and Fall*, III, 202–3; II, 2.
33. *Ibid.*, III, 204 and n. See John Phillips, *The Reformation of Images: Destruction of Art in England, 1535–1660* (1974).
34. *Ibid.*, III, 207–9.
35. *Ibid.*, III, 215.
36. *Ibid.*, II, 4n.
37. *Ibid.*, III, 218–19.
38. *Ibid.*, III, 223.
39. *Ibid.*, III, 225. At the close of his 'Outlines of the History of the World' Gibbon deals with fifteenth-century Italy: 'By a propensity natural to Man, the Multitude had easily relapsed into the grossest Polytheism. The existence of a Supreme Being was indeed acknowledged; . . . but he was allowed a very small share in the Public worship or the administration of the Universe. The Devotion of the People was directed to the Saints and the Virgin Mary, the Delegates and almost the Partners of his Authority. . . . New legends and new practices of Superstition were daily invented by the interested diligence of the Mendicant Fryars': *English Essays*, ed. Craddock, 197–8.
40. Gibbon, *Decline and Fall*, IV, 62–4.
41. *Ibid.*, IV, 66–7.
42. *Ibid.*, IV, 80.
43. 'Hints', *English Essays*, ed. Craddock, 91.
44. Gibbon, *Decline and Fall*, II, 20.
45. *Ibid.*, IV, 71–6.
46. *Ibid.*, IV, 77, 81.
47. *Ibid.*, I, 63.

16

'Tintern Abbey': from Augustan to Romantic

ISOBEL ARMSTRONG

'Tintern Abbey', we know, transforms a tradition. Behind Wordsworth are Pope, Thomson, Akenside, Young, Thomas Warton and Cowper, and a wonderfully fertile genre of landscape description and the spreading prospect which goes back to Denham.[1] But Wordsworth did more in 'Tintern Abbey' than transform a literary convention: his reshaping of the spaces, visual categories, temporal processes and imaginative conceptions of the familiar topographical poem depends upon an act of transformation from within the poem itself. It expands and revalues the meaning of the language it uses as it proceeds, and this transformation is the shaping impetus of the poem. 'Hear', 'behold', 'view', 'see', the mild words of sensory observation, occur in the opening descriptive lines of 'Tintern Abbey' as they might occur in any eighteenth-century topographical poem, but Wordsworth invests them with a complexity and range of implication which actively explore the nature of perception and its limits. If we 'half create' (words Wordsworth owes to Young) what we perceive, and if sensory experience is fused with the activity of *sensing*, it is likely that a subtle vocabulary will be required to explore the nature of sensing and its limits. The language of associative psychology – 'impress', 'connect', 'sensations' – is enriched and transformed as the poem recapitulates, turns back on its vocabulary and uses its own past to reshape new meanings and qualities of experience, so that 'Tintern Abbey' is in possession of two languages by the time it is completed.[2] Wordsworth never rejected the anchor of the earlier vocabulary, just as he never rejected the 'anchor' (l. 109) of sense and the physical world (indeed, it was vital to him not to), but he made it express a human and psychological and metaphysical awareness, a range of tone, emotion and feeling, and feeling and *thinking*. So, like Coleridge's 'Frost at Midnight,' a poem from which Wordsworth learned much, 'Tintern Abbey' is a self-transforming poem in a way that the earlier landscape poetry is not. My subject is this shift and transformation of meaning and feeling, and how it comes about. At the edge of my discussion is also an interest in the nature of discursive poetry, for 'Tintern Abbey' deliberately uses a language of meditative explication, varying between the excited, the intense, the reflective, and the sober. The tones and possibilities of this language are bound up with the achievement of the poem.

The 'Eye excursive roams', Thomson writes, introducing his bursting prospect in the 'Spring' section of *The Seasons* (ll. 951–69): the Ouse 'conducts the eye along his sinuous course', Cowper writes in Book I of *The Task* (ll. 163–76). Wordsworth would have known both these prospects.[3] The ostensible principle of organization in such passages is the random psychological order of visual and perceptual experience as the eye 'roams', loops, sweeps backwards and forwards over the landscape. But this is a superficial impression: a quite different ordering activity is really going on – the arrangement of items from the phenomenological surface of the landscape into categories and classes, carefully arranged line by line as discrete self-contained groups and made contiguous according to likeness and similitude (Thomson) or according to a principle of contrast (Cowper). If one looks closely at such passages the items might *be* anywhere: it is the itemizing that matters. Thomson pairs Hill, Dale, Wood, Lawn, Field, Heath (Nature), Villages, Towns (Man): Cowper has elms against herdsman's hut, hedge-rows against towers, groves and heaths against 'smoking villages'.

Wordsworth's prospect is quite different in its spatial complexity because its space belongs both to the landscape and the dimensions of the mind. He begins by directing the mind to what is heard and to what is *not seen*, not the power of the eye but the 'soft inland murmur' of the river Wye, the sources of the river and its gently hinted past in 'mountain-springs'. A curious spatial displacement occurs as the mind is drawn away from the as yet undescribed, unitemized prospect and penetrates backwards and inwards to origins. And, because the words 'inland murmur' negatively imply the sea, the mind reaches forwards to comprehend endings, without ever quite reaching them (the sea is out of the poem). So the act of perception is a fusion of imaginative creation, memory, and spatial and temporal projection. There is an alertness of the whole mind implied here, and an alertness, too, to its sense of the vanishing point of perception in the hint of the unreached sea. The sea suggests oceanic fulfilment, but a fulfilment postponed, at the edges of possibility. The reach into hidden sources and possibilities is quite different from the distant sound of Cowper's church bells which 'Just undulates *upon* the list'ning ear'. Magnificent in its way (sound undulates as the river is sinuous), but Cowper is interested in the cause-and-effect relationship of distant spires and faint sound and deals with the rational scientific fact of sound waves.[4]

The syntax of 'Tintern Abbey's' predecessors is *landscaped*. It is laid out for you, seen as pattern from the outside, an external syntax of the surface. The swelling, surging contours of the opening lines of 'Tintern Abbey', on the other hand, flowing with the substantiveness of matter, make you inhabit the motion of the poem with a physical participation which puts the reader inside the syntax, seeing the processes of grammar shaped from within, participating in the connections and relationships that are being made, rather like being inside the processes of living geological change. For all their appearance of psychological verisimilitude, Thomson and Cowper are heirs to the elegant syntactic patterning of such lines as the opening prospect of Pope's *Windsor Forest* with their happy artifice and brilliantly meticulous, gamesome virtuosity. Here the imaginative integration comes from the ordering principles found in the landscape itself (and, indeed, in the universe), and echoed in the arrangement of the syntax – a checquer'd order in variety, where all things differ and all agree.

Here waving Groves a checquer'd Scene display,
And part admit and part exclude the Day;
As some coy Nymph her Lover's warm Address
Nor quite indulges, nor can quite repress.
There, interspers'd in Lawns and opening Glades,
Thin trees arise that shun each others shades.

'Here in full Light . . . There wrapt in clouds': Pope's lines are neatly and fastidiously 'checquer'd' antithetically inside themselves, positive against negative, white against black – 'part admit and part exclude the shade'. And 'checquer'd', too, against one another, so that the simile of the Nymph who 'Nor quite indulges, nor can quite repress' the lover's advances, is described in negatives and so balances the earlier line, black against white. The repetition of difference and agreement, agreement and difference, is infinitely and wittily varied in its symmetry. The 'white' of 'indulges' at the beginning of the line crosses with the black of 'exclude' at the end of the earlier line: the black of 'repress' at the end of the line crosses with the white of 'admit' at the beginning of the earlier line. It is a brilliant way of expressing the complexity and variety of difference and agreement in a universe which manifests order. The dissolution of the conventional syntax of the prospect poem in 'Tintern Abbey', and particularly the insistent asymmetry of Wordsworth's repetition, represents another view of our experience of the world altogether; it is that our response to experience is a process of apprehending and unifying shifting and undetermined relationships. Transition is the governing principle of the syntax, enabling transformations in perception and relationship. 'Transition' is the word Wordsworth used in his 1800 note about the odal qualities of 'Tintern Abbey' (see below, n. 4) and it is as if the turn and return of the classical ode has penetrated to syntax and repetition.

Wordsworth's astonished shock of memory at the beginning of the poem – 'Five years have past' – is sustained by the repeated pressure of 'again'. But this is repetition in motion, never still, because the recapitulated word shifts, never quite centring at the same point on the line, never quite formulated exactly as before, never falling in the same cadences. The repetition impels the poem onwards while moving itself at the same time: 'and again I hear/These waters'. The again + subject + verb pattern is broken up in different ways by line-endings, inverted, reordered in subtly different relationships. The repetition here reminds us that Wordsworth is remembering as powerfully as he is seeing afresh, and its continually restructured asymmetry, hesitant but triumphant, reminds us, too, that the act of memory is itself in motion, breaking up, transforming and reshaping experience. 'Five summers, with the *length*/Of five *long* winters': time is expressed in linear terms, and, by this line's juxtaposition with the 'rolling' waters of the Wye, time becomes imperceptibly assimilated to water, so that past time flows continuously with and into the present, while memory moves with the movement of perception in present time, part of its flow, shaping and being shaped by it.

I dwell on repetition here because Wordsworth uses it to suggest something important about the consciousness that repetition is the mind's way of interpreting itself to itself and its way, not only of constructing experience out of experience but of vitally transforming it. It signifies a double consciousness. For repetition, by one's very consciousness of the act, will never be quite the same as the act of which it is a repetition, nor will the repetition of *that* repetition. The doubling turns out to shift and reorder experience. The reordering going on in the mobile repetition of 'again' is a model of what goes on in larger terms throughout the poem and repetition, shifting, asymmetrical, is the means by which the poem develops and expands.

To return to the poem's opening lines. Because the contours of the sentences are forming as one reads, Wordsworth's geological syntax suggests that the processes of perception, connexion, relationship, are infinitely subtle. Consider the verb 'connect' – 'and connect/The landscape with the quiet of the sky'. That knowledge is about 'connecting' is, of course, one of the assumptions of associative psychology. In a universe of parts an aggregation of discrete experiences moves from simple to complex by being in connexion with one another. Wordsworth's use of the verb does not deny this so much as render the process of connexion as vital, ambiguous, and mysterious. The line-break makes for a slight hesitation about the verb and its object, so that when the new line resolves this with 'The landscape with the quiet of the sky', a very emphatic and vital connexion is made, almost with relief and release. The line-break actually makes one aware of the act of connexion and what it feels like to connect, which is to stretch, hesitate, search, wait. Again, an alertness of the whole mind is necessary, though interestingly, it is strenuous while lacking strain. Wordsworth's gently conflating syntax is so unostentatious that it persuades an acceptance of this as a natural and spontaneous activity.

But there is an even more important effort of connexion to be made: the verb can carry two subjects, and the relationships of the sentence and its meaning shift between one subject and another in what is virtually two different sentences. Either '*I* behold these steep and lofty cliffs, . . . and connect/The landscape with the quiet of the sky', or, 'these steep and lofty cliffs . . . connect/The landscape with the quiet of the sky'. If the cliffs connect landscape and sky they are establishing barriers and limits and a point of demarcation because they are creating the horizon. They draw attention to the solid weight of perceptual objects and to the contrast between the wildness of the landscape and the stillness, weightlessness and noiselessness of the sky. If the beholding, hearing, seeing 'I' connects, something very different happens. The word connect becomes a vital act of forming and creating relationships by the consciousness. It is as if the barrier of cliffs to sky, landscape to air, is perceived and then broken as the eye moves outwards to the space beyond. The cliffs *join* the landscape to the sky, the mind *relates* and fuses one with the other. This way round it is the landscape which partakes of the new qualities of the sky and likeness rather than unlikeness is uppermost, and the lovely word 'quiet' becomes more open and indefinite. It is one of the more overt metaphors in these lines, and one is encouraged to pause on the multiple possibility of 'quiet': how can a sky be noisy or quiet and in what senses and with what senses are we responding to it? Certainly, it takes on a deeper affective colouring here. If the mind connects you know what the sky feels like rather than what it looks like. The content of the sky is not defined as space or form or movement or sound but as *feeling*. With the movement beyond landscape to sky there is a qualitative change, a release and expansion upwards and outwards, as if one is being encouraged to move into new possibilities of feeling and awareness. Here is a living enactment of the 'elevated thoughts' about which Wordsworth writes later in the poem. (Compare the way Thomson and Cowper come up short when they get to their horizons.)

Of course I have exaggerated in analysis the extent to which we tidy our distinction between what the cliffs do and what the mind does. Because he sees the mind and world in vital interaction Wordsworth must blend and conflate the subjects of 'connect'. If 'thinking things' and the 'objects' of thought are alike living and animate it is right that we should be persuaded that both have the power of shaping vital relationships. Nevertheless, the effect of the doubleness of 'connect' at this point in the poem is to cause a vital hesitation between the sense of limit and the sense of release, as the mind adjusts to the possibilities of the syntax and forms and reforms relationships. One is inside the grammar here (or perhaps inside two grammars), making it and seeing it made.

The central metaphor of the poem is penetrative, Clarke notices, writing of Wordsworth's reiteration of the simple word 'deep'.[5] One might modify the idea of penetrativeness by saying that this is only a part of the idea of expansion and extension in the poem. The subtle reach of the mind into space and into new dimensions of experience (the very idea of dimension is questioned) is encouraged everywhere in the opening lines. Barriers and limits are acknowledged or made (perceived and created) but are either broken or pushed back. The 'plots' of cottage ground 'lose themselves' in groves and copses just as the eye loses itself in the quiet of the sky (compare the slicing of dale and heath from village in *The Seasons*). The hedgerows are breaking out of their own order, 'little lines/Of sportive wood run wild'. The 'unripe fruits' hang between seed and maturity in trees – 'orchard-tufts' – whose growth is also incipient, and the mind moves back into the past, forward into the future, to comprehend what they are. And what they are becomes, or at least is inseparably bound up with, this act of reaching.

In 'Thoughts of more deep seclusion', Wordsworth's habitual fondness for curiously hovering comparatives, where what a thing is compared with is either left unexpressed or expressed so indirectly that the mind circles round its 'more than' implications, insists imperceptibly upon the imperceptible openness and possibility in acts of perception. The comparative hangs between two unstated terminal points. It encourages one to search for resting points of departure and limit by leaving these open, and to ask what sort of deepness is being explored here: mental? physical? Such constructions recur at critical points in the poem, and the shape of 'Thoughts of more deep seclusion' is recapitulated, subtly reformed, at one of the poem's climactic points – 'a sense sublime/Of something far more deeply interfused' – and again at the end of the poem – 'Oh! with far deeper zeal/ Of holier love!' Here, at its first occurrence, the comparative initiates that awareness of 'beyondness' which is sensed so richly in the opening lines and which carries with it the dissolution and inter-penetration of categories, of space and time, present and past, substance and spirit.

'Thoughts of more deep seclusion' is Wordsworth's most paradoxical expression of the power of thought to dissolve categories:

> these steep and lofty cliffs,
> That on a wild secluded scene impress
> Thoughts of more deep seclusion;

For, as others have noticed, these might be more and more recessed and inward thoughts (the scene itself might be a mental 'scene') or they might be thoughts about a seclusion beyond the seclusion of the substantive physical scene itself. Moreover, it is the cliffs which directly 'impress' (the sense of physical pressure is powerful) *thoughts* on the solid scene, if we take the syntax at its striking first suggestion. 'Impress' recalls the *tabula rasa* or wax imprint of associative psychology which assumes that the external world is first received by the mind as sensation. But Wordsworth reverses the process, making the cliffs impress thought on the physical world rather than the physical world 'impress' the mind, relieving the word of some, though not all, of the suggestions of hard-edged indentation and restriction. Whether or not this is simply a dramatically elliptical way of expressing associative ideas is unimportant. The syntax enables Wordsworth to express simultaneously the power of thought to push into and penetrate physical barriers and the power of the solid world to generate thought or even to possess the power of thought.

The passionate equanimity of these opening lines – the poem never reaches quite this tone of excited gravity again – anticipates the more discursive writing in the body of 'Tintern Abbey' and gives content to it. What it means to 'see *into* the life of things', to experience 'elevated thoughts', to 'half create' the world, to feel the world of 'eye and ear' as the 'anchor' of 'purest thoughts' is being implicitly suggested by the opening lines as much as it is being corroborated and enriched in the body of the poem. The poem is, as I have said before, interpreting itself to itself through this process. Clarke, arguing against Wimsatt's account of Wordsworth as a transcendental poet, reaching away from the world of things towards the invisible supersensual 'beyond' of mystical experience, beautifully describes what the opening lines are persuading us to accept – 'the way substance and spirit are ambiguously and mysteriously implicated in the simplest act of perception'.[6] When the poem celebrates mystical intuition, these moments are anchored in a world which belongs complexly to mental and substantive physical experience. However, there is more strain and uneasiness than he suggests. 'Tintern Abbey' has its unquietness, and the opening lines do not match the rest of the poem with perfect serenity. (It is interesting to notice that curiously masked word, 'disturb', which occurs twice: the joy of elevated thoughts 'disturbs'; to Dorothy, the world need not 'disturb/Our cheerful faith'. In the 1798 edition of the poem the word appears in the opening lines: the orchard plots do not 'disturb' the 'wild green landscape', and it was not removed until 1845.[7]) The expansion of perception the poem explores carries difficulties within itself. The evolution from '*impress*/ Thoughts of more deep seclusion' (already charged with fresh possibility at the start of the poem) to 'a sense sublime/Of something far more deeply *interfused*',[8] from the language of the *tabula rasa* to a Coleridgean esemplastic language of the imagination which blends, diffuses and dissipates in order to unify, from '*sensations* sweet', to a more mysterious '*sense* sublime/Of something', is not an easy one. The movement from one epistemology to another attempts to include the first within itself, but the delicate resolution of the first section is always in danger of being broken. In the opening lines, substantive physical experience is paradoxically both a barrier or impediment and the means to release beyond it. If there are dimensions beyond immediate sense but opened up by it – 'thoughts of more deep seclusion' – this increases our sense of the richness of perception but hints disturbingly of its limits. However subtly unified and simultaneous the experience of sense and sensing are, the idea of 'to sense' carries with it a reaching out to what is even beyond sensing itself, unreached, and beyond the shape and form of words. It suggests its own defeat. There is something peculiarly threatening about Wordsworth's new Romantic epistemology. It is possible to 'lose' oneself beyond the cliffs, beyond the woods and copses.

Wordsworth's perplexity is hinted in the disturbed, uncontained experience of the last few lines of the first section with the paradoxical description of the 'vagrant *dwellers* in the *houseless* woods', sensed but not seen from the silent wreaths of smoke (think how Wordsworth transforms a phrase such as Thomson's 'rising smoak'). This line gives a wonderfully tentative 'uncertain notice' (as if Wordsworth cannot quite place these displaced people) of other human life besides that implied in the harmonious rural pattern of 'cottage-ground' and 'pastoral farms'. It conjures up an extraordinarily rifted society and makes a sudden transition from memory, personal and psychological, to human and moral experience. It anticipates the 'still, sad music of humanity', subverts 'the power/Of harmony' at work earlier, and, by emphasizing the exile of these vagrant dwellers and hinting at their rejection, looks forward and becomes assimilated to another tragic experience – 'solitude, or fear, or pain, or grief' (l. 143) – the experience which Wordsworth fears might be the 'portion' of his friend and sister. The hermit, another exile, is fired by his solitude (as Harold Bloom points out, the fire suggests an intense inner creativity),[9] but Wordsworth's 'Friend' seems to choose a disintegrative solitude of exile and rejection. It is as if Romantic intensity, 'loses' itself, and makes its possessor in some profound way 'houseless' (*Lear* is behind this word), unanchored, cut off from society and even from the universe of eye and ear as well.

How Wordsworth transforms and re-evaluates his language, exploring as he does so the possibilities of the opening lines, and reaching to their perplexities, is the concern of this part of my essay. The restructuring movement is so complex, one word making possible another, and minute tonal shifts through Wordsworth's peculiar asymmetrical parallelism preparing the way for further transition, that I shall look closely only at the two passages describing supreme moments of mystical experience (ll. 23–49), ll. 93–102) and at the cluster of words and constructions in them which have to do with sensation, feeling, sense. In these passages the movement from one language to another has been accomplished and yet the great tonal difference between them, between consolidated warm serenity and a far-flung rapture which is strangely bound up with intensely elegiac feeling, marks the contradictions of Wordsworth's experience in a way which is remarkable when one considers the great amount of repetition from one passage to the other.

The accumulation of pasts, shifting and interacting with one another and with the present, is one of the achievements of 'Tintern Abbey'. When the narrative of memory and present experience ceases with the opening lines, the first passage – 'These beauteous forms . . . I have owed to them' – asserts itself as a narrative of *that* narrative, a further autobiographical and philosophical gloss on the past of 'five years' ago and the 'past', internal to the poem, of the first section. But the second passage starts out of the poem in a way which makes us ask what the pastness of 'And I have felt' has to do with the other pasts of the poem. We know that it is the experience of maturity, but what temporal relation it has with the past of five years ago, or the intervening time in which Wordsworth 'owed' experience to the beauteous forms of memory, also the experience of maturity, and, indeed, partaking of mystical experience also, is particularly mysterious. 'I have owed to them' is placed: 'And I have felt' exists in its own time. Accordingly, the first mystical experience begins with a wonderfully imaginative description of the grounding of perception in the physical such as Wordsworth might have learned from Cambridge interpretations of Locke:[10] the second has no need of this because by this point in the poem perception and feeling have been redefined as arising *sui generis*. Mystical experience is authorized by sensation in the first passage; in the second the poem has so evolved that mystical intuition is allowed to be the creation of subjective feeling and is authenticated, not merely sanctioned, by it. In the first the poet is acted upon as well as acting: in the second he is the direct agent of his experience and the relation between subject and object is so collapsed that it almost dissolves away and ceases to exist; in the first, sensing subsumes sensation; in the second it is in danger of being severed from sensation, anchored to it only by the residual presence of the first passage in its language and forms. The second passage transforms, virtually reverses the first, but attempts to evolve out of it and to define itself against it. It tries to need the first. Both passages use discursive language in the obvious sense that they explain as well as simultaneously generating the feelings they describe, but the vital tonal being of language exists whether it is metaphorical or not, and the differences of tone come about because one uses a language of consolidation, the other of dissolution. 'Whose dwelling is the light of setting suns': it is as much the falling away of the cadence here as the image, which fuses rapture and loss, triumph and elegy. An affirmation, but it is a strange and 'houseless' experience of 'dwelling', which is generally thought of as a contained and rooted state, to have in the diffusive light of setting suns and, morever, in diffusively fading light.

The setting of the sun is both a consummation and a vanishing point, a death, and the line also dies.

The working of repetition from one passage in the other takes us closer to the movement from serenity to triumphant elegy.

> I have *felt* . . . a *sense*/I have owed to them . . . *sensations* sweet . . . *felt*, *felt* . . . *feeling*, too: that blessed *mood* . . . that serene and blessed *mood*: the *affections*.
>
> the *joy* of elevated thoughts/the deep power of *joy*
>
> of something *far more deeply* interfused/the *deep* power of joy
>
> a sense . . . of *something*: thinking *things*: *objects*: all *things*/we see into the life of *things*.
>
> *living* air/good man's *life*: *living* soul: *life* of things.
>
> *mind* of man: elevated *thoughts*: All *thinking* things, all objects of all *thought*/my purer *mind*
>
> a *motion* and a *spirit*/the *breath* of this corporeal frame: the *motion* of our human blood
>
> And *rolls* through all things/and *passing* even into my purer mind: the affections gently *lead us on*.

The second passage collapses and fuses a series of words and related words, phrases and constructions in its recapitulation of the earlier one, so that the repetition – or new word – carries forward the old words with their qualities complexly interfused one with another. Moreover, the second passage glances back to but transforms the earlier vocabulary because it creates new relationships between the same words or variants of them. The parallelism matches and does not match. So it cannot do what Hopkins (and we tend to follow him) required of repetition, and that is to 'imitate' the pure form of an inscape or pattern or meaning, 'aftering' and 'over-and-overing' an element so that we can isolate a static, irreducible quality, 'and detach it to the mind'.[11] Wordsworth's 'over-and-overing' is unstable and changes with every 'aftering'. 'And I have felt', for instance, borrows the structure of 'I have owed', fuses it with the (significantly) passive participle, 'felt . . . felt', and transforms it into an active verb. For all its seeming immediacy, 'felt . . . felt' is kept at a distance as experience because it has the force of an ablative absolute – having *been* felt. Thus feeling is originative in the second passage, the free controlling determinant of subsequent experience:

it initiates and is innate, neither caused nor passively experienced. 'And I have felt' comes with a shock of assertion because 'felt' is for the first time in a poem about the feelings used in an authoritatively subjective, active and transitive syntax.

Wordsworth's use of 'felt' in the earlier passage is subtle enough, but very different. It registers the happy, almost involuntary, almost unaware receptiveness of the self to 'sensations sweet' and occurs in a sentence which affirms the complexity of the relationships this involves: 'I have owed to them [beauteous forms]... sensations sweet,/Felt in the blood, and felt along the heart'. Wordsworth habitually likes to use indirect objects and prepositions to assert the multiplicity of action and interaction between self and world. They enable him to say here that he has owed experience to experience, sensation to beauteous forms and to sensations, feelings, so that he establishes a triple generative relationship between perceiving self, world, and the experience created by their conjunction; in fact, 'experience' is the union of the three things. It is most likely, as Clarke suggests, that the beauteous forms are ambiguously mental entities, part of memory as well as physical forms, and that the experience which causes sensation is mental as well as physical. This increases the complexity of the relationships between self and world because memory can cause sense responses as well, and so intensifies the powerful idea of interaction which Wordsworth is seeking to affirm. 'Sensations', in spite of its mental applications, however, has strongly physical suggestions, and 'felt', with a lovely union of meaning, is both the physical reaction to sensations felt 'in the blood' and the *consciousness* of having them. The unobtrusive but astonishing inversion of the expected prepositions, 'Felt *in* the blood, and felt *along* the heart', consolidates this doubleness: felt *in* as part of the involuntary substantive physical flow of blood in the body; felt *along* the heart, partly the powerful physiological heart which impels blood through the body, but partly the psychic heart of feelings and conscious emotions which flow and diffuse in the mental life of the self. (We are encouraged to take 'influence' in its root meaning after this, so that feelings flow in and along the moral life.) Prepositions are another powerful way of establishing the multiplicity and ambiguity of relationships, and here they gently shift the meaning or quality of 'felt'. They are the most vital of transitional particles for Wordsworth, releasing metaphysical possibilities by creating multiple relationships. Think how we are made to respond to the multiple possibility of 'in-ness' here with the progression of *in* lonely rooms, *in* hours of weariness, felt *in* the blood, *into* my purer mind, *in*-fluence, that blessed mood,/*In* which ... *in* which ... *In* which ... we are laid asleep *in* body ... and see *into* the life of things. The subsidiary contrapuntal movement of 'to' (to them, to a blind man's eye, into ... into, to them) sometimes pulls away from inwardness, sometimes supports it.

The shift in the quality of 'felt' does not stop here because the word appears in another variant of itself in the redoubled appositional phrase which wells out of the original sentence, 'feelings too/Of unremembered pleasure' (it is strange to find 'unremembered' in a poem about memory: the feelings created by pleasure are knowable, but the pleasure at their source, the causal experience, is unremembered) and releases a fuller psychological possibility in 'felt'. We are dealing with emotion, but 'Sensations' are owed to beauteous forms and so, too, the appositional syntax affirms, are 'feelings'. 'Feelings' might be an expanded equivalent of involuntary sensations or another experience of the emotions altogether, but the parallelism generated by the syntax persuades us to test the words against one another, asking how far feelings partake of sensations or well out of them. 'To them I may have owed . . . another gift . . . that blessed *mood*': the modulation of meaning and qualities of experience goes on through the continuities of the not quite parallelism, making possible further transitions. The syntax mounts on itself, inverting the multiple relationship implicated in 'I have owed to them' with 'To *them* I may have owed', the back to front pattern asserting the equal and opposite pull and reciprocity in the double experience of self and world affirmed in the first statement. It is more tentative, subjunctive, but the matching encourages us to match 'mood' against 'feelings' and to ask how far they partake of one another, and how far 'feelings' partake of 'sensations' and 'mood'. There is a gentle ascent through 'sensations', 'feelings', 'moods', to 'living soul', the state of release in which the motions of the blood are *almost* suspended, and this is supported by the breeding activity of cumulative parallelism and the subtle bonding of relationship throughout the passage.

There is none of this supportiveness behind the emphatic 'And I have felt', which contracts this progression within itself only by allusion to the earlier passage, but the substantive anchor of sense-awareness seems to be left far behind. Its authoritative subjectivity means that we take the word in a newly evolved meaning of pure and passionate awareness and *knowing*. 'Felt' has an emotional force and metaphysical possibilities quite unlike the earlier forms of itself.

The transposition of 'felt' intensifies another re-formation of relationships, the movement from 'sensations sweet' to the cognate 'sense sublime'. Like 'feeling', 'felt', 'sense' both glances back to the primal, direct physical experience of sensation and releases itself from it. 'Sensations sweet' can be mental possessions as well as physical sense-awareness, and by attracting to itself the 'aspect more *sublime*' of the other gift or mood where we are laid asleep in body, and which Wordsworth tentatively distinguishes from that of sensations sweet, 'sense' takes on by the conflation a rarefied mental aspect which asks us to accept it as a wholly new form of awareness. 'Sensation' has been transcendentalized into 'sense' and though this word carries the sediment of the earlier use within itself, the refining and fusing which has gone on means that the sense sublime is used, as Empson says of one of the meanings of 'sense' in *The Prelude*,[12] almost as if it were a separate and special category of sense, a sense *of* or for intuiting the sublime, as well as *being* sublime. (The analogy is the favoured eighteenth-century moral sense.)

'I have felt/A presence . . . ; a sense': the syntax allows us to take it that the poet has directly *felt* a *sense*, and the meanings are so nearly equivalent ('sense' being a noun synonym for the verb 'felt') that they produce an extraordinary refined awareness of awareness; an awareness of awareness 'Of *something*'. It is as if the reach of perception, enacted in the reach of 'sense sublime' over the break of the line to the unresolving indeterminacy of 'Of something' in the following line, is being pushed to its limits and beyond itself.[13]

Wordsworth is able to create this boldly tautological subtlety because this passage is mostly bare of, or sharply contracts, all the elements he uses to establish the sense of relationship earlier. So that rich sense of ambiguous, multiple interchange between inner and outer, between subject and object, of causal and temporal dependence, is gone. Paratactic sentences do without the activating energy of prepositions as far as they can: 'Whose dwelling *is* the light of setting suns', but only (and this is one of the infrequent prepositions) '*in* the mind of man'. The predominant effort of the language is to conflate and 'interfuse' words and experiences without mediation. 'Interfuse' is itself a *merging* of preposition and participle which enacts the principle of fusion in its form and has by this point in the poem become a critical Romantic word, part of a new language. It is true that Wordsworth would have found 'infuse/infused' in the familiar language of eighteenth-century poetic diction, that it looks back to Virgil's 'infusa' and Anchises' use of it as a description of the universal mind, that Wordsworth would have found it in Shaftesbury and Erasmus Darwin, that it conveniently bonds the classical, Augustan and the Romantic by being compatible also with Newtonian theories of motion, just as the passage as a whole is compatible with Burke, who thought of moments of sublimity in terms of the mind being 'hurried on by an irresistible force' (*A Philosophical Enquiry into the Sublime and Beauitful*, Pt II, Section I). Several critics, most recently Schneider and Sheats (see n.8), have pointed this out. But Wordsworth's eclecticism points to differences rather than reconciling world views. 'Interfused' makes a sweepingly inclusive allusion to a whole cultural and linguistic tradition only to transform it. For 'interfused' *is* a new word, suggesting a mutuality of blending which is not present in 'infused', and therefore makes far stronger claims and changes the meaning of the word to which it alludes.

Moreover, 'interfused' appears in a syntax which is not to be found in earlier poetry or even in 'Tintern Abbey' itself. The gentle appositional swell of the earlier passage which established sequence, progression and expansion is contracted into a reflexive circular movement where words turn back upon one another and become unmediated equivalents of one another. 'I have felt/A presence [inside or outside the mind?] that disturbs me with the joy/Of elevated thoughts; a sense sublime': presence, thoughts; sense could be the equivalent of presence or thoughts or both, so that the categories merge into one another. Either 'sense' or 'something' or both could be 'more deeply interfused', and in that case sense dwells in the light of setting suns as well as belonging to Wordsworth's subjective life, and sense is a motion and a spirit, the syntax allows, as well as being the means by which that motion and spirit is perceived. The subject is the object of itself. The verbal adjectives act on themselves, 'setting', 'living', 'thinking', and this is especially so with 'more deeply interfused'. The comparative adverb 'deeply' (the only point at which this form is used) turns to its verb for its definition, but is locked up in an absolute construction which excludes predication and so returns upon itself. 'Deep *seclusion*', 'deep *rivers*', anchor the nature of deepness, but here Wordsworth's hanging comparative is as open as it can be, pointing to an essence of more deepliness. All we can say is, like the absolute construction, that it *is*. Compare these self-acting constructions with the strong alternation of actives and passives at the end of the first passage: 'the breath of this corporeal frame... Almost *suspended* ... we *are laid asleep*/In body, and *become* a living soul ... with an eye *made quiet* ... We *see* into the life of things'. There is a rhythm of interchange here between acting and being acted upon. It establishes an experience which is divisible into perception and the objects of perception – 'We see *into* the life *of* things – whereas the second passage makes them indivisible – either sense or something, but seemingly both, 'rolls *through* all things'.

What is steadying in the earlier passage reappears as unsteadying in the second, or else with its patterns broken up and diffused. When we come to 'see' into the life of things with an eye 'made quiet', the form in which we 'see', 'view', 'behold' the world (the perceptual words of the first lines) has been radically redefined, but 'see', with its double suggestion vision/visionary, still maintains contact with the vision at the source of 'vision'. The quiet eye is made peaceful, and also quietened of or cleared of normal sensory life, but it is not blank like the blind man's eye; it recollects the 'quiet' of the sky, and that liberated awareness achieved through the subtle fusing of sense and sensing. Wordsworth habitually avoids adjectival constructions in favour of an 'of' adjunct: the eye is made quiet by the power *of* harmony, the deep power *of* joy, so that abstract qualities and attributes are given solidity by being given substantiveness with the noun form.[14] Harmony and joy are abstractions of the experiences of the first lines, and bring together its hearing, seeing, connecting, and the feeling which accompanies them. By being expressed as substantive abstractions they keep in touch with the earlier experience (indeed 'harmony' delicately blends sound and vision) while yet preparing us for that clearance of the sensory from the quiet eye. The first passage connects, just as Wordsworth connects in the opening lines, but this hierarchical interdependence is dissolved away in the second mystical experience. The emphasis is on pure mind – 'elevated thoughts', 'the mind of man', 'spirit', 'thinking', 'thought' – unified with its objects, the oneness of mind and universe. Motion, earlier located 'gently' in the blood, heart, 'affections', synthesizes 'all things', and rolls, self-impelled, with almost headlong endlessness through a universe where the topographical items in the classical prospect of the opening lines have been rarefied, diffused, and expanded into a kind of cosmic geography. We are at the limits of the things in the early scene: the unseen, barely intuited sea, 'the round ocean': 'The quiet of the sky', 'the living air/And the blue sky'.

Both passages come to an end with, perhaps are halted by, tautology, the necessary language of mysticism, where the same things have to define one another. Living, we see into life; something permeates all things and *is* all things – 'and become a *living* soul . . . We see into the *life* of things': 'a sense sublime/Of *something* . . . that impels/All thinking *things*, all objects of all thought, And rolls through all *things*'. 'While' [*not* 'and'] with an eye made quiet 'We see into the life of things'. 'While' is one of Wordsworth's habitual adverbs because it denotes different processes, co-extensive with one another but often with a hidden mutual interaction. Simultaneously (not sequentially) as we become a living soul, we see into the life of things. 'While' makes the two things causally and temporally dependent on one another. The activity of being and the perception of being generate an awareness of one another. While we become a living soul we see into the life of things: we see into the life of things while we become a living soul. But 'living' and 'life' are so closely related that the process of definition can go no further. What Wordsworth has defined, and leaves us with, is an awareness of interaction. This *is* life, perhaps, and with that the passage comes to an end, as if it comes to the end of an invisible rope. Synthesis, not interaction, is the principle behind the tautology of the second passage. With 'something', Wordsworth has already used the most inclusive word we have for experience, objects, the *res* of the universe and existence. The movement of the passage is an expansive movement outwards, and yet 'things' constantly includes itself within itself, obliterating the possibility of distinctions or blending them by its generic indefiniteness. Up to this point the vocabulary has allowed past meanings to work in new forms of a word which subsume and develop them. This slow geological shift cannot happen with 'things'. It is as if language has gone as far as it can. The stress emphasizes 'And rólls through áll things', all-ness, one-ness, and renders, of course, in the cumulative push of the sentence, not the content of 'things', but the *vitality* of their being and of being itself. Nevertheless it ends suddenly in the middle of a line with an abrupt blank caesura, as if it has reached a block, but a block of nothing, of emptiness.

Pure knowing, a sense of the intensity of vital being, is strangely bound up with the diffusion of identity and loss of selfhood, the mystic's death. The assured hesitancy and tentative serenity of the first passage – '*may* have owed', '*almost* suspended' – does not mask terror in the way the rapturous gravity of the second only just manages to. The fear is not merely of monism or solipsism but of the engulfing threat of energy, redundant energy, itself. No wonder Wordsworth turns with relief in the extraordinary *non sequitur*, 'Therefore', to assert the continuing power of 'meadows and woods' and consolidates the 'language of the sense' – surely intended in the double meaning of sense and sensing – as an 'anchor'. The 'therefore' relates more properly to the first passage than to the second, and yet there are some reasons for his confidence. The vestigial presence of the first passage remains in the words and structures of the second, reminding us that the earlier passage contains the possibilities for it, allowing that transformation to take place. The contradictions are there, but Romantic experience was too threatening for Wordsworth to want to do without both languages of the sense.

The capacity of the poem's language to transform itself is a living example of the way in which not only the *poet*'s past gives 'life' – self-renewing experience – to 'future years' but also of the way in which the past of the *poem* feeds and nourishes its subsequent life. But this is a reciprocal process, too, as the poem returns upon itself and enriches and explores the meaning of its earlier statements. Wordsworth liked to link the idea of thought with the physical act of taking in food and gives a gently atavistic sense of nourishment to the words which describe contemplation in 'Tintern Abbey', the 'remoter charm' by thought '*supplied*': 'there is life and *food*/For future years': 'so *feed*/With lofty thoughts'. The poem, you might say, contemplates itself as the poet contemplates himself, and the act of contemplation includes the poet's contemplations and is returned to the poem as new experience. This leads us to the nature of discursiveness in 'Tintern Abbey'. It is a reflective poem, meditating on experience and meditating on the experience of meditation, but is it also reflexive in the sense that it turns back on itself and absorbs and constructs out of its past forms, releasing new possibilities. In its structures and the transformation of its language it embodies the mind's ability to interpret itself to itself, mediating experience by releasing generalization from it and reabsorbing these as further experience. Indeed, in the prayer to Dorothy, the poem continues to reorder itself, interfusing the language of the two mystical passages so that all their most integrative possibilities are invoked as a protection against her 'wild' experience – 'beauteous forms' are reabsorbed as 'lovely forms' in the 'mansion' of the mind: 'unremembered pleasure' as 'sober pleasure'. Wordsworth talks of 'mountings of the mind' at the beginning of *The Prelude* (I. 20): not the upward climb of the mind alone, I think, but the mounting of the mind continuously out of itself. It seems right that this generative description should have a muted sexual possibility, granted by the indefiniteness of 'of' – mountings of the mind upon itself.

The form of 'Tintern Abbey' is a mounting of the mind. It fact, in day to day living experience, awareness of experience and introspection upon it, are never actually dissociated from one another in our minds, though we often think of them as entirely separable activities of being. They are actually in a continually dramatic relationship with one another, reabsorbing each other and, in the process, both becoming experiences to one another. The word discursive is often used loosely to express a number of very different attributes – reflective, theoretical, analytic, didactic, abstract, general, and even to cover (used here with a good deal of discomfort) any poem that the poet wants you to *believe.* But the word assumes that we cannot see forms of introspection and analysis as vitally living things in themselves. It assumes that discursive poetry (for sometimes the poem's meditation and the poet's coincide) will be thin, with all living experience rinsed out of its generalizations. We need an account of discursive poetry which expresses the excitement, stress and imaginative intensity of contemplation. Not unexpectedly, George Eliot offers one, not unexpectedly through that rather feckless character, Will Ladislaw:

> To be a poet is to have a soul so quick to discern that no shade of quality escapes it, and so quick to feel, that discernment is but a hand playing with finely-ordered variety on the chords of emotion – a soul in which *knowledge passes instantaneously into feeling, and feeling flashes back as a new organ of knowledge.*
>
> (*Middlemarch*, ch. 22; my italics)

Knowledge passing instantaneously into feeling, feeling flashing back as a new organ of knowledge: this might be an account of the passages in which Wordsworth says that sensations pass into his purer mind, or that he has *felt* a sense. The processes are not merely described, however, but enacted through the form and language of the poem, which becomes a mounting of the mind, constructing itself out of itself, abstracting and reabsorbing its experience. In 'Tintern Abbey' the form of the poem has become a model of the introspecting consciousness itself. It is a seminal Romantic work because it creates the possibility for new ways of shaping a poem.[15] 'But you forget about the poems', Dorothea says to Will, with a characteristic steeliness to her naiveté. Wordsworth did not forget about the poems any more than his Romantic contemporaries or the nineteenth-century poets who followed them. In 'Tintern Abbey' the central form of nineteenth-century poetry emerges.

NOTES

1. M. H. Abrams has given a succinct account of the predecessors of 'the greater Romantic lyric', in *From Sensibility to Romanticism: Essays presented to Frederick A. Pottle*, ed. F. W. Hilles and Harold Bloom (1965), 527–60. See also Mary Jacobus in *Tradition and Experiment in Wordsworth's Lyrical Ballads* (1976).
2. 'Half create', of course, as Wordsworth's note acknowledges, is derived from Young's line in *Night Thoughts*, 'And half create the wondrous world they see' (Night VI, l. 427). That he derived so much from his predecessors even while he transformed what he found should deter us from over-simplifying his relationship both to earlier poetry and thought. Schneider argues that what Wordsworth found, in Young or in Thomson, in Locke and the associationists, carried the possibility of change within itself: 'But though Wordsworth is indebted to Young for the words he is indebted to Locke for the idea, for it was the "materialist" Locke who opened the door to the semi-idealistic concept that the mind partly creates "the mighty world of eye and ear".' – Ben Ross Schneider, Jr, *Wordsworth's Cambridge Education* (1957), 109. C. C. Clarke argues most subtly and convincingly that eighteenth-century poetry and philosophy enabled Wordsworth to develop paradoxical conceptions about the relationship of self and world and to make use of confusions 'which may have been disastrous in philosophy but which Wordsworth turned to good account' (*Romantic Paradox: An Essay on the Poetry of Wordsworth*, 1962, 42). Paul D. Sheats in *The Making of Wordsworth's Poetry, 1785–1798* (Cambridge, Mass., 1973), 213, also asserts that though Wordsworth moved between rival theories of perception, and certainly subverted a mechanistic reading of experience, he would have found the possibilities for his conception of the mind from within eighteenth-century thinking itself. What is more important, as Schneider makes clear, is that the Cambridge of his day interpreted Locke in a materialist-mechanistic way. Wordsworth would have been confronted with a rational dualism which saw the universe as an aggregation of discrete parts.
3. Quoted by Jacobus, *op. cit.*, 74–5.
4. Geoffrey Hartman notices the '*wave effect*' of Wordsworth's rhythms: *Wordsworth's Poetry, 1787–1814* (New Haven and London, 1964), 26. S. M. Parrish, *The Art of the Lyrical Ballads* (Cambridge, Mass., 1973), 207, notices Wordsworth's claim in his 1800 note that 'the transitions, and the impassioned music of the versification' relate 'Tintern Abbey' to the classical ode. The transitions of the classical ode have become virtually transitions of perception.
5. *Ibid.*, 49.
6. *Ibid.*, 44. I can't agree with Sheats (*op. cit.*, 223) that the opening lines represent an epistemological disequilibrium.
7. See l. 14 in the text of 'Tintern Abbey', in *Lyrical Ballads*, ed. R. L. Brett and A. R. Jones (1963).
8. Sheats, echoing Joseph Warren Beach and Schneider, points out that 'Interfused' echoes Anchises' celebrated description of the universal mind, which is to the visible world as the soul is to the body: 'totamque infusa per artus/mens agitat molem' (Sheats, *op. cit.*, 220). The word 'infuse', indeed, is listed by John Arthos in his gloss of the vocabulary of eighteenth-century poetic diction (*The Language of Natural Description in Eighteenth-century*

Poetry, Ann Arbor, 1949). In its context, however, the word must be given 'Coleridgean' as well as 'Virgilian' associations, as I shall argue (see below, p. 273). The *New English Dictionary* quotes Milton's use of interfus'd in *Paradise Lost*, Book VII, l. 89, but the meaning here suggests 'poured' rather than the Wordsworthian sense.

9. Harold Bloom, 'Wordsworth and the Scene of Instruction', *Poetry and Repression* (New Haven and London, 1976), 52–82.
10. See Schneider, *op. cit.*, 106–11, particularly 106–7.
11. Gerard Manley Hopkins, *Journals and Papers*, ed. H. House and G. Storey (1959), 289.
12. William Empson, 'Sense in The Prelude', *The Structure of Complex Words* (1951), 290.
13. I owe much to Christopher Ricks's essay, 'A pure organic pleasure from the lines', *Essays in Criticism*, XXI (1971), 1–20.
14. See Frances O. Austen's discussion of the 'of-adjunct' in Wordsworth's poetry, *Neuphilologische Mitteilungen*, LXX (1969), 124–38.
15. What I have said of Romantic form should not be incompatible with the insight of M. H. Abrams, *Natural Supernaturalism* (New York, 1971), and *idem*, in the essay quoted above (see n.1).

17

Samuel Rogers: the Last Augustan

J. R. WATSON

Samuel Rogers was born in 1763 and died in 1855. He was 20 years old when Johnson died (as a young man he was too timid to knock at the great man's door), and he lived to refuse the laureateship when it went to Tennyson; so not only did he live through the Romantic Period, but had one foot either side of it. From Augustan to Victorian, from Strawberry Hill to the Great Exhibition, from Reynolds (whom he heard lecture) to the Pre-Raphaelites – it is an extraordinary piece of longevity; and Rogers's general manner and appearance, his precise and formal conversation, confirmed the nineteenth-century impression that he was some kind of fossil left over from an earlier age. Ladies were charmed by his antiquated gallantry, and his long life became something of a joke: 'You have seen the love of the Sex for Rogers', wrote Sydney Smith to Lady Grey in 1842; 'Orpheus another poet a contemporary of Rogers was torn to pieces by the Bacchanals.'[1]

Rogers's poetry is curiously related to this longevity, because it contains a remarkable meeting of an Augustan sensibility and a Victorian sentimentality. Although Rogers was in his heyday in the Romantic Period, his work seems to by-pass it: it is polished, urbane, classical in tone and temper, with a certain authoritative restraint and severity; yet it is also intimate, tender and sentimental, with a fondness for a good story. These latter qualities may have had their origins in the age of sensibility: 'Your Muse', wrote his friend Dr Parr, 'holds, and has a right to hold, converse with the spirits of Shenstone and Goldsmith and Gray.'[2] But such converse is turned by Rogers into something more self-indulgent than the distinguished and serious charm of his predecessors; and below the surface of eighteenth-century techniques, his poetry reveals a sentimentality usually associated with a later age.

In his celebrated triangle of poets, Byron placed Rogers at the apex, second only to Scott, though actually suggesting that he liked Rogers better: 'I should place Rogers next in the living list (I value him more as the last of the *best* school)'.[3] *The Pleasures of Memory* (1792) makes clear Rogers's affinity to the old school which Byron admired: the title itself is a bow to Akenside's *The Pleasures of Imagination* (1744) and Thomas Warton's

The Pleasures of Melancholy (1774), while the decorum of the poem and its order of proceeding confirm its adherence to current principles. Its 'Analysis' demonstrates that it moves from effect to cause, and then to a division of causes:

> The Poem begins with the description of an obscure village, and of the pleasing melancholy which it excites on being revisited after a long absence. This mixed sensation is an effect of the Memory. From an effect we naturally ascend to the cause; and the subject proposed is then unfolded with an investigation of the nature and leading principles of this faculty.
>
> It is evident that our ideas flow in continual succession, and introduce each other with a certain degree of regularity. They are sometimes excited by sensible objects, and sometimes by an internal operation of the mind. Of the former species is most probably the memory of brutes; and its many sources of pleasure to them, as well as to us, are considered in the first part. The latter is the most perfect degree of memory, and forms the subject of the second.[4]

Rogers's analysis is Hartleian, and he even uses the terminology of the theory of association:

> When ideas have any relation whatever, they are attractive of each other in the mind; and the perception of any object naturally leads to the idea of another, which was connected with it either in time or place, or which can be compared or contrasted with it. Hence arises our attachment to inanimate objects; hence also, in some degree, the love of our country, and the emotion with which we contemplate the celebrated scenes of antiquity. Hence a picture directs our thoughts to the original: and, as cold and darkness suggest forcibly the ideas of heat and light, he, who feels the infirmities of age, dwells most on whatever reminds him of the vigour and vivacity of his youth.
>
> The associative principle, as here employed, is no less conducive to virtue than to happiness; and, as such, it frequently discovers itself in the most tumultuous scenes of life. It addresses our finer feelings, and gives exercise to every mild and generous propensity.[5]

The poem begins with a deserted village, done in pictorialized gothic with melancholy attached, a blend of Goldsmith and Gray:

> Mark yon old Mansion frowning thro' the trees,
> Whose hollow turret wooes the whistling breeze.
> That casement, arched with ivy's brownest shade,
> First to these eyes the light of heaven conveyed.

The mouldering gateway strews the grass-grown court,
Once the calm scene of many a simple sport;
When nature pleased, for life itself was new,
And the heart promised what the fancy drew.
(p. 8)

The insistent implications of adult unhappiness, inherited from Gray, are found in other poems of the period, notably Wordsworth's *An Evening Walk*, published a year later than *The Pleasures of Memory*. In both poems these is a fiction of distractions (in one case memory, in the other landscape) permitting an escape from the miseries of human existence:

Childhood's loved group revisits every scene;
The tangled wood-walk, and the tufted green!
Indulgent MEMORY wakes, and lo, they live!
Clothed with far softer hues than Light can give.
Thou first, best friend that Heaven assigns below,
To sooth and sweeten all the cares we know;
Whose glad suggestions still each vain alarm,
When nature fades, and life forgets to charm;
Thee would the muse invoke! – to thee belong
The sage's precept, and the poet's song.
(p. 11)

The lines balanced across the caesura, the invocations and rhetorical gestures, all show Rogers's stylistic conservatism; so do his inversions and extended similes:

As when in ocean sinks the orb of day,
Long on the wave reflected lustres play;
Thy tempered gleams of happiness resigned
Glance on the darkened mirror of the mind.
(p. 11)

With its allusions to chains and vibrations, his description of the workings of memory is Hartleian, expressed with a formal and precise elegance:

Lulled in the countless chambers of the brain,
Our thoughts are linked by many a hidden chain.
Awake but one, and lo, what myriads rise!
Each stamps its image as the other flies.
Each, as the various avenues of sense
Delight or sorrow to the soul dispense,
Brightens or fades; yet all, with magic art,

Controul the latent fibres of the heart.
As studious PROSPERO's mysterious spell
Drew every subject-spirit to his cell;
Each, at thy call, advances or retires,
As judgment dictates, or the scene inspires.
Each thrills the seat of sense, that sacred source
Whence the fine nerves direct their mazy course,
And thro' the frame invisibly convey
The subtle, quick vibrations as they play;
Man's little universe at once o'ercast,
At once illumined when the cloud is past.
(p. 15)

The particular effect here is one of a rather beautiful suspension – 'lulled . . . our thoughts'; 'Each . . . Brightens or fades'; 'Each . . . advances or retires' – which suggests the intricate movement of the mental process. This is complemented by the fineness of the nerves, which seem to have a freedom to 'play' with their 'subtle, quick vibrations'. So far, the poem is predictable enough; yet immediately after this there is a vignette of the boy leaving home (beautifully illustrated, in the 1834 edition, by Turner):

The adventurous boy, that asks his little share,
And hies from home with many a gossip's prayer,
Turns on the neighbouring hill, once more to see
The dear abode of peace and privacy;
And as he turns, the thatch among the trees,
The smoke's blue wreaths ascending with the breeze,
The village-common spotted white with sheep,
The church-yard yews round which his fathers sleep;
All rouse Reflection's sadly-pleasing train,
And oft he looks and weeps, and looks again.
(p. 16)

The sentimentality appears in the language, particularly in the adjectives – 'his little share', 'The dear abode' – but also in the whole conventionality (from which Wordsworth is so free in 'Michael') of 'many a gossip's prayer' and of the look back at the old village. The picture which the boy sees is the domestic-rural scene beloved of Victorian painters – see, for instance, Richard Redgrave's 'The Emigrant's Last Sight of Home: Leith Hill, Abinger, Surrey' – the thatched cottage among the trees, the smoke curling from the chimneys, the churchyard and the common, the whole picture suggesting an illusory 'peace and privacy'. As Crabbe knew, the village life was 'a life of pain', but Rogers sees the boy as leaving because he is adventurous, not because life was no longer supportable. Interestingly, however, Rogers also shows that he was dimly aware of something much deeper, a collective awareness of ancestral ties and the love of man for his native place, so that the departure from a native village takes on much more significance. His note to the 'churchyard yews' line shows that he had, like many of his contemporaries, been reading about Indian customs and beliefs:

> Every man, like Gulliver in Lilliput, is fastened to some spot of earth, by the thousand small threads which habit and association are continually stealing over him. Of these, perhaps, one of the strongest is here alluded to.
>
> When the Canadian Indians were once solicited to emigrate, 'What!' they replied, 'shall we say to the bones of our fathers, Arise, and go with us into a foreign land?'[6]

Yet even this deep collective emotion is created by 'habit and association', just as states of mind are created, for Rogers, by the interaction of the senses with the external world:

> Thus kindred objects kindred thoughts inspire,
> As summer-clouds flash forth electric fire.
> And hence this spot gives back the joys of youth,
> Warm as the life, and with the mirror's truth.
> Hence home-felt pleasure prompts the Patriot's sigh;
> This makes him wish to live, and dare to die.
> (p. 17)

He goes on to discuss various examples of strong attachment to a native country. Like Wordsworth in *Descriptive Sketches*, he instances (with a quotation from Rousseau, to whom both poets were probably indebted for the reference) the playing of the Swiss air 'Ranz des Vaches':

> The intrepid Swiss, who guards a foreign shore,
> Condemned to climb his mountain-cliffs no more,
> If chance he hears the song so sweetly wild
> Which on those cliffs his infant hours beguiled,
> Melts at the long-lost scenes that round him rise,
> And sinks a martyr to repentant sighs.
> (p. 19)

Reading Wordsworth's lines on the same subject, one sees why Coleridge described the language of *Descriptive Sketches* as 'not only peculiar and strong, but at times knotty and contorted, as by its own impatient strength;

while the novelty and struggling crowd of images, acting in conjunction with the difficulties of the style, demanded always a greater closeness of attention, than poetry, (at all events, than descriptive poetry) has a right to claim.'[7] Wordsworth's poem, said Coleridge, was sometimes obscure, and certainly Rogers's lines seem clarity itself beside these:

> Lo! by the lazy Seine the exile roves,
> Or where thick sails illume Batavia's groves;
> Soft o'er the waters mournful measures swell,
> Unlocking bleeding Thought's 'memorial cell';
> At once upon his heart Despair has set
> Her seal, the mortal tear his cheek has wet;
> Strong poison not a form of steel can brave
> Bows his young hairs with sorrow to the grave.
> (*Descriptive Sketches*, 1793, ll. 624–31)

Wordsworth's thrusting, allusive style, bursting out of the heroic couplets like an overgrown child, gives promise of the energy to come; Rogers's lines accomplish their task with an unassuming clarity which caused him in his own day to be thought of as 'polished' or 'enamelled', because the images seem so separate and individual.

The second part of *The Pleasures of Memory* is feeble and disappointing. According to its 'Analysis' it deals with 'a higher province' than the first part, the functioning of memory when it is not stimulated by external events; and Rogers anticipates Coleridge in linking memory with the workings of fancy. Memory distinguishes man from animals:

> She preserves, for his use, the treasures of art and science, history and philosophy. She colours all the prospects of life; for we can only anticipate the future, by concluding what is possible from what is past. On her agency depends every effusion of the Fancy, who with the boldest effort can only compound or transpose, augment or diminish the materials which she has collected.[8]

The poem which follows this unimaginative summary is lacking in order and structure; it is an unmethodical series of observations diversified by a fanciful story. In the individual episodes, however, we can recognize Rogers's characteristic blend of clarity and sentimentality, as in the description of the nun taking the veil:

> The beauteous maid, who bids the world adieu,
> Oft of that world will snatch a fond review;
> Oft at the shrine neglect her beads, to trace
> Some social scene, some dear, familiar face:

And ere, with iron-tongue, the vesper-bell
Bursts thro' the cypress-walk, the convent-cell,
Oft will her warm and wayward heart revive,
To love and joy still tremblingly alive;
The whispered vow, the chaste caress prolong,
Weave the light dance and swell the choral song;
With rapt ear drink the enchanting serenade,
And, as it melts along the moonlight-glade,
To each soft note return as soft a sigh,
And bless the youth that bids her slumbers fly.
(pp. 28–9)

Here the emotion is carried at the outset by the adjectives – 'beauteous', 'fond', 'dear', 'familiar' – and then taken up by the verbs as the description gathers speed and strength – 'Bursts', 'revive', 'weave', 'swell', 'drink', 'melts'. The odd thing about this passage, as with all of the second part of *The Pleasures of Memory*, is that Rogers seems quite unaware that such reminders of a past existence might be painful. It is true that his subject is the pleasures, and not the pains of memory; but in order to keep to his subject, he has had to twist some central human facts to his own purpose. The most obvious example of this is the story '(Preserved in Cumbria's rude, romantic clime)' of Florio and Julia, with which the second part of the poem is enlivened. Florio loves Julia, and is loved by her; but she is drowned in a storm on the lake, and her father (who approved the match) dies of grief. The poet requires us to believe that Florio is still, through the power of memory, enjoying their love:

Yes, Florio lived – and, still of each possessed,
The father cherished, and the maid caressed!
For ever would the fond enthusiast rove,
With Julia's spirit, thro' the shadowy grove;
Gaze with delight on every scene she planned,
Kiss every floweret planted by her hand.
Ah! still he traced her steps along the glade,
When hazy hues and glimmering lights betrayed
Half-viewless forms; still listened as the breeze
Heaved its deep sobs among the aged trees;
And at each pause her melting accents caught,
In sweet delirium of romantic thought!
(pp. 41–2)

Rogers is writing of something he knows nothing about; one can only oppose to such blandness the lines from Dante –

Nessun maggior dolore,
che ricordarsi del tempo felice
nella miseria[9]

– and it is tempting to argue that Dante's perception owes something to the turbulent age in which he lived, while Rogers suffered a kind of softening of the brain. Such an argument, though in fond approval rather than disparagement, was made by Sir James Mackintosh in the *Edinburgh Review* when noticing Rogers's *Poems* of 1812:

> During the greater part of the eighteenth century, the connexion of the character of English poetry, with the state of the country, was very easily traced. The period which extended from the English to the French Revolution, was the golden age of authentic history. Governments were secure, nations tranquil, improvements rapid, manners mild beyond the example of any former age. The English nation which possessed the greatest of all human blessings, a wisely constructed popular Government, necessarily enjoyed the largest share of every other benefit. The tranquillity of that fortunate period was not disturbed by any of those calamitous, or even extraordinary events, which excite the imagination and inflame the passions. No age was more exempt from the prevalence of any species of popular enthusiasms. Poetry, in this state of things, partook of that calm, argumentative, moral, and directly useful character into which it naturally subsides, when there are no events which call up the higher passions . . . In such an age, every art becomes rational.[10]

Ignoring Mackintosh's ignorance of the finer details of what he calls 'authentic history' (i.e., as opposed to myths of the golden age), we may see in his complacency the mirror of Rogers's poetic conservatism. It is not surprising, therefore, that in the words of P. W. Clayden, 'Cowper . . . was regarded as the great poet of the evangelical school, while Rogers was the favourite with society.'[11] In his review, Mackintosh goes on to describe the revolution which followed:

> As the agitation of men's minds approached the period of explosion, its effects on literature became more visible. The desire of strong emotion succeeded to the solicitude to avoid disgust. Fictions, both dramatic and narrative, were formed according to the school of Rousseau and Goethe . . . The sublime and energetic feelings of devotion began to be more frequently associated with poetry . . . Poetry became more devout, more contemplative, more mystical, more visionary, – more alien from the taste of those whose poetry is only a polished prosaic verse, – more full of antique superstition, and more prone to daring innovation, –

painting both coarser realities and purer imaginations, than she had before hazarded.[12]

Poetry, said Mackintosh, was also becoming more national, and more unequal and adventurous; and in spite of his remarks about 'a polished prosaic verse' he seems to approve of *The Pleasures of Memory*:

It is not uninteresting, even as a matter of speculation, to observe the fortune of a poem which, like the Pleasures of Memory, appeared at the commencement of this literary revolution, without paying court to the revolutionary tastes, or seeking distinction by resistance to them. It borrowed no aid either from prejudice or innovation. It neither copied the fashion of the age which was passing away, nor offered any homage to the rising novelties. It resembles, only in measure, the poems of the eighteenth century, which were written in heroic rhyme. Neither the brilliant sententiousness of Pope, nor the frequent languor and negligence perhaps inseparable from the exquisite nature of Goldsmith, could be traced in a poem, from which taste and labour equally banished mannerism and inequality.[13]

To modern judgment, this claim for Rogers's independence does not seem justified: his taste and labour, and the absence of mannerism and inequality, suggest a neo-classical temperament and technique. Taste, indeed, is a dubious word in this context: people talk about a taste for poetry, said Wordsworth angrily, 'as if it were a thing as indifferent as a taste for Rope-dancing, or Frontiniac or Sherry.'[14] And if Rogers's poems show the operation of taste, they seem to lack other, more important qualities: the foremost among these is truth to life, for Rogers prefers the sentimental to the serious.

Rogers's individual note is the combination of this sentimentality with an Augustan rationalism and predictability, in which certain objects or places produce specific emotional effects. This is why taste is so important. In the Preface to 'An Epistle to a Friend', he writes:

It is the design of this Epistle to illustrate the virtue of True Taste; and to show how little she requires to secure, not only the comforts, but even the elegancies of life. True Taste is an excellent Economist. She confines her choice to few objects, and delights in producing great effects by small means: while False Taste is for ever sighing after the new and the rare;[15]

This variation on the theme of elegant sufficiency is worked out by contrasting the life of retirement in a villa with the hectic life of London fashion. From the window of the villa, for instance, the poet admires the view, with 'Each fleeting charm that bids the landscape live.' Passers-by are reduced, in this vignette, to elements in a picture, and the reader is inclined to wonder about the social conditions of those who are seen at such a 'pleasing distance':

> Oft o'er the mead, at pleasing distance, pass
> Browsing the hedge by fits the panniered ass;
> The idling shepherd-boy, with rude delight,
> Whistling his dog to mark the pebble's flight;
> And in her kerchief blue the cottage-maid,
> With brimming pitcher from the shadowy glade.
> (p. 120)

The poet's complacency extends to the furnishings of his home, and its scale:

> Here no state-chambers in long line unfold,
> Bright with broad mirrors, rough with fretted gold;
> Yet modest ornament, with use combined,
> Attracts the eye to exercise the mind.
> Small change of scene, small space his home requires,
> Who leads a life of satisfied desires.
> (pp. 121–2)

As might be expected, the eye is the chief source of stimulus, and it exercises the mind in an unstrenuous manner; the pictures on the walls, for instance, lead Rogers into an amiable discourse on engraving:

> What tho' no marble breathes, no canvas glows,
> From every point a ray of genius flows!
> Be mine to bless the more mechanic skill,
> That stamps, renews, and multiplies at will;
> And cheaply circulates, thro' distant climes,
> The fairest relics of the purest times.
> Here from the mould to conscious being start
> Those finer forms, the miracles of art . . .
> And here the faithful graver dares to trace
> A MICHAEL's grandeur, and a RAPHAEL's grace!
> Thy gallery, Florence, gilds my humble walls;
> And my low roof the Vatican recalls!
> (p. 122)

The strategy of this kind of late Augustan poetry is radically different from the practice of the romantic poet. Wallace Jackson, in an interesting article on this subject, sees a theoretical expression of this in Archibald Alison's *Essays on the Nature and Principles of Taste* (1790), especially in Alison's suggestion that 'by means of the Connexion, or Resemblance, which subsists between the qualities of Matter, and qualities capable of producing Emotion, the perception of the one immediately, and very often irresistibly, suggests the idea of the other.' Jackson comments:

> He looked, that is, to the association formed between 'certain sensations and certain qualities,' and his principles led to the idea that a work of art is an arrangement of affective patterns which constitute the structure of the work: structure is an organization of qualities designed to evoke certain sensations... The beautiful, the sublime, and the picturesque were predicated upon psychological principles, and the procedure of descriptive-allegorical poetry in the later period often bears a resemblance to Alison's idea of affective structures.[16]

The procedure involves a separation of emotions which is fundamentally different from the imaginative dissolution and recreation of romantic poetry:

> The normal tendency of eighteenth-century verse is to keep separate states separate; we seldom experience the lingering resonance of one state of mind acting upon another as it forms, seldom experience the dissolution of an emotion and the strangely variegated qualities of mind involved. These observations call attention to what seems distinctive of the lyric as practised by Wordsworth and Coleridge: the interest in the interstices of discrete emotional states, those formative moments that inhabit the interludes between completed sequences.[17]

The point can be illustrated by referring to Rogers's charming poem, 'A Wish'. This is the most delightful of his poems of rural simplicity and retirement, with tripping quatrains and neat, separate pictures that exist, as a physicist might say, 'in series' rather than in parallel. The pattern is cot+hive+brook+mill:

> Mine be a cot beside the hill;
> A bee-hive's hum shall sooth my ear;
> A willowy brook, that turns a mill,
> With many a fall shall linger near.
>
> The swallow, oft, beneath my thatch,
> Shall twitter from her clay-built nest;
> Oft shall the pilgrim lift the latch,
> And share my meal, a welcome guest.
> (pp. 196–7)

This has a childlike quality about the first six lines: the nursery-rhyme qualities of the sound, and the uncluttered images, both suggest this. Stothard, who illustrated this poem, evidently thought so, for his couple, though engaged in adult pursuits – spinning, and smoking a pipe – look very young indeed, like children playing at being grown-up. As in a nursery-rhyme, too, the images are clear and unambiguous, and one only has to think of Wordsworth's 'Lucy' poems to realize the absence in Rogers of anything mysterious or suggestive. When Wordsworth writes 'She dwelt among the untrodden ways' he is beginning a poem which takes some of its subtlety and power from what F. W. Bateson has called the 'unobtrusive contradictions' of the language.[18] The process of the 'Lucy' poems, which reaches its greatest point in 'A slumber did my spirit seal', is the minimal use of language to create the maximum imaginative activity. In Rogers the images are present only to build up the picture of simple and idyllic retirement; which is why the pilgrim, who is a travelling man and dependent upon charity, enters the poem awkwardly.

The 'Lucy' poems come to mind, however unfortunately for Rogers, because of his third verse:

Around my ivy'd porch shall spring
Each fragrant flower that drinks the dew;
And Lucy, at her wheel, shall sing
In russet-gown and apron blue.
(p. 197)

This is delightfully pastoral and pictorial: there is no winter here, and Lucy is set, in blue and brown, beside the porch among the flowers. But Wordsworth, when describing the same thing, introduces a vital and imaginative sense of place, so that Lucy becomes associated with a deep love of the poet's native country:

Among thy mountains did I feel
  The joy of my desire;
And she I cherished turned her wheel
  Beside an English fire.

In Rogers's poem the idyll is completed by the view of the village church, and the sound of bells:

The village-church, among the trees,
Where first our marriage-vows were given,
With merry peals shall swell the breeze,
And point with taper spire to heaven.
(p. 197)

At first sight this is just one more element in the pastoral idyll; in Stothard's illustration the church appears in the distance, peeping between the hollyhocks, the beehives, and the ivy-covered porch. Yet it is more than this, and it serves to deepen the poem significantly. In the first place, the church is the place where 'first our marriage-vows were given': this immediately qualifies the childlike simplicity of the first six lines, and suggests a more mature relationship, one moreover in which love is re-avowed. The simplicity thus becomes childlike and mature, rather than childish make-believe. In the second place, the church points to heaven: it does so pictorially, in the sense that the spire points to the sky, but it also points upward anagogically, to a life after death. Thus momentarily the church becomes a sign of crucial events in human life; there is a Larkin-like glimpse of the church as more than pictorial

> because it held unspilt
> So long and equably what since is found
> Only in separation – marriage, and birth,
> And death, and thoughts of these
> ('Church Going')

and this last verse goes some way to lift Rogers's poem out of the simple images of pastoral make-believe into a sustained vision of a well-spent life. The 'wish' of the poem's title becomes something more than a longing for a pretty cottage and for rural peace and quiet.

The poem is sentimental; it may be classed with those Victorian paintings of happy rural life by Birket Foster, or Thomas Faed, or Thomas Webster. Yet it also glimpses something more serious and substantial, because it is able to imply constancy and faithfulness; and Rogers is sometimes able to surprise the reader with an unexpected insight into more profound areas of human behaviour. In *Italy*, for instance, there is an astonishing passage, which begins the section entitled 'The Alps':

> Who first beholds those everlasting clouds,
> Seed-time and harvest, morning noon and night,
> Still where they were, steadfast, immovable;
> Those mighty hills, so shadowy, so sublime,
> As rather to belong to Heaven than Earth –
> But instantly receives into his soul
> A sense, a feeling that he loses not,
> A something that informs him 'tis an hour
> Whence he may date henceforward and for ever?
> (pp. 29–30)

There are Wordsworthian elements in this description – the hills as clouds, the feeling which can only be defined as a 'something' – but the crucial, lifting word is 'date'. It implies a different ordering of time, one in which the first sight of the Alps is a new beginning of an imaginative time. Wordsworth does the same thing, more explicitly, in 'To my Sister':

> No joyless forms shall regulate
> Our living calendar:
> We from to-day, my Friend, will date
> The opening of the year.

This is his reaction to 'the first mild day of March': ordinary human time, measured from January to December, is made irrelevant by the magnificent morning. The year is beginning now, at this moment, as the spring makes a new, natural beginning to the year. Rogers similarly jettisons the normal date-system: imaginatively, he says, those who see the Alps for the first time feel the need to make that moment the beginning of year I. The rejection of ordinary, mechanical time in favour of this imaginative time is analogous to religious man's need to live in sacred rather than profane time. For religious man, a manifestation of the sacred, or hierophany, marks a new beginning, a return to a time when the world was newly created and man was in close touch with the gods. Wordsworth feels an impulse to date the new year from the first mild day of March, for 'Since the New Year is a reactualization of the cosmogony, it implies *starting time over again at its beginning*, that is, restoration of the primordial time, the 'pure' time, that existed at the moment of Creation.'[19] In Rogers's case, the moment of seeing the Alps suggests to him a new beginning: it is hierophantic in that it inspires him to think in terms of the newly created or re-created world, as a primitive religious man would do in the presence of the gods.

For the most part, though, *Italy* is typical of Rogers: it shows the qualities of his earlier poems almost unchanged, both in subject-matter and technique. 'The Nun', for instance, is an extended version of the passage in *The Pleasures of Memory*, describing a young girl taking the veil. Other narratives diversify the descriptive passages in Italy, sometimes of an affecting kind, such as the story of Ginevra, the young bride playing hide-and-seek who accidentally locked herself in a trunk, or the happier story of 'The Brides of Venice' who were seized by pirates on their wedding-day but later rescued. The descriptive passages themselves are predictable: the places evoke the sensations, and separate states are kept separate. The section entitled 'The Campagna of Rome', for instance, is a series of incidents from Roman history, beginning with the arrival of Aeneas, and the deaths of Nisus and Euryalus at the hands of the Rutulians:

when He from Troy
Went up the Tiber; when refulgent shields,
No strangers to the iron-hail of war,
Streamed far and wide, and dashing oars were heard
Among those woods where Silvia's stag was lying,
His antlers gay with flowers; among those woods
Where, by the Moon, that saw and yet withdrew not,
Two were so soon to wander and be slain,
Two lovely in their lives, nor in their death
Divided.
(p. 154)

Then there comes the building of Rome, followed by a vision of Rome as imperial city, its decline, and finally the arrival of the Vandals and Goths. At its best, the verse of *Italy* has a sweetness of tone and a melancholy restraint that is partly Augustan and partly Tennysonian; the second poem in the Rome section, for instance, is called 'A Funeral', and is intended to sit well next to the description of the Roman Forum, desolate and dreary. It contains these lines on death:

Death, when we meet the Spectre in our walks,
As we did yesterday and shall tomorrow,
Soon grows familiar – like most other things,
Seen, not observed; but in a foreign clime,
Changing his shape to something new and strange,
(And thro' the world he changes as in sport,
Affect he greatness or humility)
Knocks at the heart. His form and fashion here
To me, I do confess, reflect a gloom,
A sadness round; yet one I would not lose;
Being in unison with all things else
In this, this land of shadows, where we live
More in past time than present, where the ground,
League beyond league, like one great cemetery,
Is covered o'er with mouldering monuments;
And, let the living wander where they will,
They cannot leave the footsteps of the dead.
(pp. 146–7)

Here the transition from the first observation about the familiarity of death to the awareness of its appropriateness is beautifully managed. The effect of the passage depends upon the reversal of the process described by Alison, in which objects gives rise to sensations: here the surroundings conform to the mood, external and internal blend in the active operation of the creative mind. From the endearing frankness of death growing 'familiar – like most other things', past the affected and unnecessary parenthesis, Rogers moves to the pivotal verb 'reflect'. Although this is itself neo-classical, the one-to-one mirroring between death and the sadness around quickly gives way to other developing ideas: the syntax allows an organic movement, as one thought succeeds another and gives rise to the next. The last seven lines, particularly, are Wordsworthian in tone and movement, close to *The Excursion* in their generalizing profundity. It is the sensitive transitions of thought through the blank verse that make this comparison possible: from the idea that the sadness is in harmony with everything else, the poet suggests that the past is more real than the present; the whole place, at times, seems like a vast cemetery, and the living walk in the footsteps of the dead. Again and again in this progression, the reader pauses, only to take another step onwards; it is very natural, yet engineered with consummate skill.

From *The Pleasures of Memory* to *Italy*, Rogers shows little development as a poet: *Italy* is more flexible, more occasional, and it makes good use of its informality, but this is only a superficial alteration. Beneath Rogers remains the same – an Augustan poet with a sentimental turn, who is capable of springing an occasional surprise; had he surprised his readers more often, he would have been an individual poet, with a voice alongside his contemporaries. As he is, he has some claim to be seen as the final expression of an earlier age; as the very last Augustan.

NOTES

1. *The Letters of Sydney Smith*, ed. Nowell C. Smith (1953), 770.
2. P. W. Clayden, *The Early Life of Samuel Rogers* (1887), 220.
3. *Byron's Letters and Journals*, ed. Leslie A. Marchand, III ('Alas! the love of Women' (1974), 220.
4. Samuel Rogers, *Poems* (1834), 5. There is no edition of Rogers with line-numbers, and when quoting from the poems I have therefore given page references to this edition of 1834, except in the case of *Italy*, which is quoted from the 1830 edition.
5. *Ibid.*, 5–6.
6. *Ibid.*, 48.
7. *Biographia Literaria*, ed. J. Shawcross (1907), I, 56. Wordsworth borrowed from *The Pleasures of Memory* in *Descriptive Sketches* (l. 56, 1793 text); see Wordsworth, *Poetical Works*, ed. E. de Selincourt (1940–9), I, 326.
8. *Poems*, 25.
9. *Inferno*, v. 121–3.
10. *Edinburgh Review*, October 1813, 32–3.
11. P. W. Clayden, *Rogers and his Contemporaries* (1889), I, 2–3.
12. *Op cit.*, 36–7.
13. *Edinburgh Review*, October 1813, 23–9.
14. Preface to *Lyrical Ballads*; *Poetical Works*, ed. de Selincourt, II, 394.

15. *Poems*, 118.
16. Wallace Jackson, 'Wordsworth and his predecessors: private sensations and public tones', *Criticism*, XVII (1975), 41–58.
17. *Ibid.*, 45.
18. F. W. Bateson, *Wordsworth: a Re-Interpretation*, (2nd edn, 1956), 30–5.
19. Mircea Eliade, *The Sacred and the Profane* (New York, 1959), 78–9.

A. R. Humphreys: a Check-list of his Published Work to 1976

compiled by
J. C. HILSON

The following abbreviations have been used in the checklist:

MLR *Modern Language Review*
NQ *Notes and Queries*
RES *Review of English Studies*

1937 *William Shenstone: An Eighteenth-Century Portrait.* Cambridge: The University Press. 136 pp. Partly reprinted as 'The Quest of the Sharawadgi', in *The Augustan Age*, ed. I. Watt, Connecticut: Fawcett Publications, 1968, pp. 77–96.
'*The Ascent of F6*', *Cambridge Review*, 30 April 1937, 353–5.

1938 Review M. G. Jones, *The Charity School Movement: A Study of Eighteenth-Century Puritanism in Action* (1938). *Times Literary Supplement*, 5 February 1938, 86.

1939 'A classical education and eighteenth-century poetry', *Scrutiny*, VIII, 193–207.
Review *The Letters of William Shenstone*, ed. Marjorie Williams (1939). *Cambridge Review*, 5 May 1939.

1940 Review Dixon Wecter, *Edmund Burke and his Kinsmen* (1939). *MLR*, XXXV, 130.

1943 'Fielding's irony: its methods and effects', *RES*, XVIII, 183–96. Reprinted in *Fielding: A Collection of Critical Essays*, ed. R. Paulson, Englewood Cliffs, N.J.: Prentice-Hall, 1962, pp. 12–24; *Henry Fielding und der Englische Roman des 18. Jahrhunderts*, ed. W. Iser, Darmstadt, 1972, pp. 16–31; (in part) *Henry Fielding: A Critical Anthology*, ed. C. J. Rawson,

Harmondsworth, 1973, pp. 377–84; *Ironie als Literarischen Phänomen*, ed. H.-E. Hass and G.A. Mohrlüder, Köln, 1973, pp. 109–20.

1946 'British Professors in Turkish Universities', *The Asiatic Review*, XLII, 167–9.
'The "rights of woman" in the Age of Reason', *MLR*, XLI, 256–69.
'Presenting Britain Abroad: the British Council and the Future', *Quarterly Review*, CCLXXXIV, 385–93.

1947 'The eternal fitness of things: an aspect of eighteenth-century thought', *MLR*, XLII, 188–98.
Review W. J. Bate, *From Classic to Romantic* (1946). *MLR*, XLII, 509–11.

1948 '"The friend of mankind" (1700–1760) – an aspect of eighteenth-century sensibility', *RES*, XXIV, 203–18.

1949 'Spirits of Hartshorn', *Cambridge Journal*, II, 474–86.
'Lords of Tartary', *Cambridge Journal*, III, 19–31.
Review William Godwin, *An Enquiry Concerning Political Justice and its Influence on Morals and Happiness*, ed. F. E. L. Priestley (1946). *RES*, XXV, 278–80.

1950 *The Study of Literature An Inaugural Lecture Delivered at University College Leicester 5th March 1948*. University College, Leicester.
Review J. R. Sutherland, *A Preface to Eighteenth-Century Poetry* (1948). *RES*, n.s., I, 175–7.
Review A. O. Lovejoy, *Essays in the History of Ideas* (1948). *RES*, n.s., I, 276–8.

1952 'Literature and religion in eighteenth-century England', *Journal of Ecclesiastical History*, III, 159–90.

1953 Review William W. Appleton, *A Cycle of Cathay: The Chinese Vogue in England During the Seventeenth and Eighteenth Centuries* (1951). *RES*, n.s., IV, 92.

1954 *The Augustan World*. London: Methuen. x + 284 pp. Reprinted, New York: Harper & Row, 1963. Revised edition, London: Methuen, 1964.

1955 Review W. C. Brown, *Charles Churchill: Poet, Rake and Rebel* (1953). *RES*, n.s., VI, 89–91.
Review *The Correspondence of John Wilkes and Charles Churchill*, ed. Edward H. Weatherly (1954). *RES*, n.s., VI, 108.

1956 Review W. K. Wimsatt, *The Verbal Icon: Studies in the Meaning of Poetry* (1954). *RES*, n.s., VII, 102–4.

1957 'The Social Setting'; 'The Literary Scene'; 'Fielding and Smollett'; 'Johnson'; 'Architecture and Landscape': in *The Pelican Guide to English Literature, vol. IV: From Dryden to Johnson*. Harmondsworth: Penguin Books, pp. 15–93; 313–32; 399–419; 420–42.
Review Chester F. Chapin, *Personification in Eighteenth-Century English Poetry* (1955). *RES*, n.s., VIII, 310–11.
Review James L. Clifford, *Young Samuel Johnson* (1955). *MLR*, LII, 105–6.
Review Robert W. Rogers, *The Major Satires of Alexander Pope* (1955). *MLR*, LII, 260–1.

1958 Review *The Poetical Works of Charles Churchill*, ed. Douglas Grant (1956). *RES*, n.s., IX, 222–3.
Review R. P. Blackmur, *The Lion and the Honeycomb: Essays in Solicitude and Critique* (1957). *RES*, n.s., IX, 446–8.

1959 *Steele, Addison and their Periodical Essays*. (Writers and their Work, no. 109). London: Longmans, Green & Co. for the British Council and the National Book League. 46 pp.

1960 Ed.: William Shakespeare, *Henry IV, Part I*. London: Methuen. lxxxii + 202 pp. Introduction partly reprinted as 'The unity and background of *Henry IV, Part I*', in *Twentieth Century Interpretations of Henry IV, Part I*, ed. R. J. Dorius, Englewood Cliffs, N.J.: Prentice-Hall, 1970, pp. 18–40; and as 'Falstaff' in *Shakespeare's Histories*, ed. W. A. Armstrong. Harmondsworth: Penguin Books, 1972, pp. 222–36.
Review S. C. Roberts, *Dr. Johnson and Others* (1958). *MLR*, LV, 107–8.

1961 'Herman Melville', *John o' London's*, 6 July 1961, 18–19.
Review Bonamy Dobrée, *English Literature in the Early Eighteenth Century*, (1959). *MLR*, LVI, 105–6.
Review M. C. Battestin, *The Moral Basis of Fielding's Art: A Study of 'Joseph Andrews'* (1959). *RES*, n.s., XII, 211–12.

1962 *Melville*. Edinburgh and London: Oliver & Boyd. vii + 120 pp.
'Dr Johnson: troubled believer', in *Johnsonian Studies*, ed. Magdi Wahba, Cairo: privately printed, pp. 37–49.
'Introduction' to Henry Fielding, *Joseph Andrews*. London: Dent. xv + 280 pp.
'Introduction' to Henry Fielding, *Tom Jones*. London: Dent. xiii + 408 pp.
'Introduction' to Henry Fielding, *Amelia*. London: Dent, xiv + 299 pp.

1963 'George Eliot', *Time & Tide*, 3–9 January 1963, 22–3.
'A Note on *2 Henry IV*', *NQ*, CCVIII, 98.
Review *Richard Steele's The Theatre, 1720*, ed. John Loftis (1962). *MLR*, LVIII, 102.
Review A. L. Owen, *The Famous Druids: A Survey of Three Centuries of English Literature on the Druids* (1962). *NQ*, CCVIII, 235–6.
Review *Studies in English Drama: Presented to Baldwin Maxwell*, edd. C. B. Woods and C. A. Zimansky (1962). *Shakespeare Quarterly*, XIV, 267–8.

1964 'Introduction' to Henry Fielding, *Jonathan Wild* and *The Journal of a Voyage to Lisbon*. London: Dent. xv + 286 pp.
'The idea of an English School: Leicester', *Critical Survey*, II, 60–3.
'Justice Shallow and Gloucestershire', *NQ*, CCIX, 134–5.
'The Poetry of *Hamlet*', *Mysore Literary Half-Yearly*, V, 37–48.
'Two Notes on *2 Henry IV*', *MLR*, LIX, 171–2.
Review William Green, *The Merry Wives of Windsor* (1962). *NQ*, CCIX, 278–9.

1965 with P. A. W. Collins and R. P. Draper: *English Literature from the 16th Century to the Present: a Select List of Editions*. London: Longmans Green & Co. vii + 161 pp.
'Shakespeare's political justice in *Richard II* and *Henry IV*', and 'Shakespeare and the Tudor perception of history', in *Stratford Papers on Shakespeare, Delivered at the 1964 Shakespeare Series*, ed. B. W. Jackson. Toronto: Gage for McMaster University, pp. 30–50 and 51–70. The latter reprinted in *Shakespeare Celebrated: Anniversary Lectures Delivered at the Folger Library*, ed. Louis B. Wright. Published for the Folger Library by Cornell University Press: Ithaca, N.Y., pp. 89–112.
Review Leon Howard, *Herman Melville* (1962); Herman Melville, *Billy Budd, Sailor*, ed. Harrison Hayford and Merton M. Sealts,

Jr. (1962); Warner Berthoff, *The Example of Melville* (1962); H. Bruce Franklin, *The Wake of the Gods: Melville's Mythology* (1963). *MLR*, LX, 263–6.

1966 Ed.: William Shakespeare, *Henry IV, Part II*. London: Methuen. XCI + 242 pp. Introduction partly reprinted as '*Henry IV, Part II*: the style and its functions', in *Twentieth-Century Interpretations of Henry IV, Part II*, ed. D. P. Young, Englewood Cliffs, N.J.: Prentice-Hall, 1968, pp. 107–9; and as 'Falstaff', in *Shakespeare's Histories*, ed. W. A. Armstrong. Harmondsworth: Penguin Books, 1972, pp. 222–36.

Ed.: Herman Melville, *White-Jacket*. London: Oxford University Press. XXX + 433 pp.

'Leicester University here and now', *Transactions of the Leicester Literary and Philosophical Society*, LX, 5–13.

1967 *Shakespeare: Richard II*. London: Edward Arnold. 64 pp.

Review Susie I. Tucker, *Protean Shape: A Study in Eighteenth-Century Vocabulary and Usage* (1967). *Studia Neophilologica*, XXXIX, 339–41.

Review Arthur Johnston, Enchanted Ground: *the Study of Medieval Romance in the Eighteenth Century* (1964). *NQ*, CCXI, 478–9.

1968 Ed. William Shakespeare, *Henry V*. Harmondsworth: Penguin Books. 240 pp.

'Some thoughts on the poetry of Pope', *Litera*, IX, 86–99.

Review *The Complete Poems of Thomas Gray*, ed. H. W. Starr and J. R. Hendrickson (1966), *RES*, n.s., XIX, 209–11.

Review *Studies in Honor of DeWitt T. Starnes*, ed. T. P. Harrison, A. A. Hill, E. C. Mossner and J. Sledd (1967). *Shakespeare Quarterly*, XIX, 395–6.

1969 'Shakespear's Histories and "the emotion of multitude"', *Proceedings of the British Academy*, LIV, 265–87.

1970 Ed.: *Essays and Studies . . . Collected for the English Association*, n.s., XXIII. London: John Murray. 119 pp.

'Richardson's novels: words and the "movements within"', in previous item, pp. 34–50.

with A. Nuttall, *Coriolanus* discussed. Sussex Tapes Recorded Publications.

Review Irvin Ehrenpreis, *Swift: the Man, his Works, the Age*, vol. II (1967). *Hermathena*, CX, 101–2.

1971 Ed.: William Shakespeare, *Henry VIII*. Harmondsworth: Penguin Books. 273 pp.

with R. A. Foakes, *Antony and Cleopatra* discussed. Sussex Tapes Recorded Publications.

Review James Downey, *The Eighteenth-Century Pulpit: A Study of the Sermons of Butler, Berkeley, Sterne, Whitefield and Wesley* (1969). *RES*, n.s. XXII, 85–7.

1972 'Pope, God and Man', in *Writers and their Background: Alexander Pope*, ed. P. Dixon, London: Bell, pp. 60–100.

Review Calhoun Winton, *Sir Richard Steele M.P.: The Later Career* (1970). *Yearbook of English Studies*, II, 277–8.

Review Maynard Mack, *The Garden and the City: Retirement and Politics in the Later Poetry of Alexander Pope, 1741–1743* (1969). *Yearbook of English Studies*, II. 279–81.

1973 *Shakespeare: The Merchant of Venice.* Oxford: Basil Blackwell. viii + 89 pp.

Ed.: Henry Fielding, *Joseph Andrews and Shamela*. London: Dent. xxii + 350 pp.

Ed., with D. Brooks: *Jonathan Wild and The Journal of a Voyage to Lisbon.* London: Dent. xxvi + 305 pp.

'Style and Expression in *Hamlet*', in *Shakespeare's Art: Seven Essays*, ed. M. Crane, Chicago: University of Chicago Press, pp. 29–52.

'The English History Plays', in *Shakespeare: Select Bibliographical Guides*, ed. Stanley Wells, London: Oxford University Press, pp. 239–83.

'Turkey in English Writers', *English Studies Today*, 5th series. Istanbul, pp. 1–21. Reprinted (slightly revised) as 'The genius of the place', *South Atlantic Quarterly*, LXXII, 306–23.

Review Richmond P. Bond, *The Tatler: The Making of a Literary Journal* (1971). *RES*, n.s., XXIV, 217–19.

1974 with G. Lloyd Evans, *1 Henry IV* discussed. Audio-Learning Recorded Publications.

Review Pat Rogers, *The Augustan Vision* (1974). *The Scriblerian*, VII, 38.

Review Henry Fielding, *Miscellanies*, ed. Henry Knight Miller (1972); C. J. Rawson, *Henry Fielding and the Augustan Ideal Under Stress: 'Nature's Dance of Death' and Other Studies* (1972). *RES*, n.s., XXV, 212–14.

1975 'The Long Haul: English '47 to '74', in *Convocation Review, 1975*, Leicester: University of Leicester, pp. 13–20.

Review J. P. Russo, *Alexander Pope: Tradition and Identity* (1972). *NQ*, CCXX, 33–4.

1976 with R. B. Warren: *Macbeth* discussed. Audio-Learning Recorded Publications.

with R. B. Warren: *Richard III* discussed. Audio-Learning Recorded Publications.

Review *Shakespeare: The Critical Heritage, III: 1733–1752*, ed. Brian Vickers (1975). *NQ*, CCXXI, 183–4.

Review W. Gordon Zeeveld, *The Temper of Shakespeare's Thought* (1974). *NQ*, CCXXI, 184–5.

Review Howard Erskine-Hill, *The Social Milieu of Alexander Pope: Lives, Example, and the Poetic Response* (1975). *NQ*, CCXXI, 518–19.

Review *The Poetry and Prose of John Gay*, ed. Vinton A. Dearing and Charles E. Beckwith, 2 vols (1974). *RES*, n.s., XXVII, 352–4.

Index

Note: This index covers only writers mentioned in the text; the works of writers discussed in detail are listed under their author.